JAVA IN TWO SEMESTERS

IN TWO SEMESTERS

Quentin Charatan
University of East London

Aaron Kans
University of East London

THE McGRAW-HILL COMPANIES

London · Burr Ridge IL · New York · St Louis · San Francisco · Auckland
Bogotá · Caracas · Lisbon · Madrid · Mexico · Milan · Montreal · New Delhi
Panama · Paris · San Juan · São Paulo · Singapore · Sydney · Tokyo · Toronto

Published by McGraw-Hill Education
Shoppenhangers Road, Maidenhead, Berkshire, SL6 2QL
Telephone: 44 (0) 1628 502 500
Fax: 44 (0) 1628 770 224
Website: www.mcgraw-hill.co.uk

Acquisitions Editor:	Conor Graham
Editorial Assistant:	Sarah Douglas
Senior Marketing Manager:	Jackie Harbor
Senior Production Manager:	Max Elvey
New Media Developer:	Doug Greenwood

Text design by Steven Gardiner Ltd
Printed and bound in the United Kingdom by Bell and Bain Ltd, Glasgow
Cover design by: Hybert Design

McGraw-Hill

*A Division of The **McGraw·Hill** Companies*

British Library Cataloguing in Publication Data
A catalogue record for this book is available from the British Library

Library of Congress Cataloging in Publication Data
The Library of Congress data for this book has been applied for from the Library of Congress

ISBN 0 07 709804 8

Trademarks
Java®, is a trademark of Sun Microsystems.
Microsoft Windows®, Internet Explorer®, Word for Windows®, Visual Basic®, and J++® are
trademarks of Microsoft Corporation.
Netscape® is a trademark of Netscape Communications Corporation.
All Borland brand and product names are trademarks or registered trademarks of Borland Software
Corporation in the United States and other countries.
UNIX® is a trademark of X/Open Company Ltd.
Macintosh® is a trademark of Apple Computer Inc.

To Gaye (AK)

To my family and friends (QC)

CONTENTS

PREFACE

This book is designed for university students taking a first module in software development or programming, followed by a second, more advanced module. The book uses Java as the vehicle for the teaching of programming concepts; design concepts are explained using the UML notation. The topic is taught from first principles and assumes no prior knowledge of the subject.

The book is organized so as to support two twelve-week, one-semester modules, which might typically comprise a two-hour lecture, a one-hour tutorial and a one- or two-hour laboratory session. The tutorial exercises at the end of each chapter provide the foundation for the practical tasks that follow. In addition to these exercises and questions, a case study is developed in each semester to illustrate the use of the techniques covered in the text to develop a non-trivial application. Lecturers who teach ten-week as opposed to twelve-week modules could treat each of these case studies as a self-directed student learning experience, rather than as a taught topic.

This book includes all the material from the previous publication, Java: the First Semester, with some minor modifications. The approach is ideal for the type of student entering university with no background in the subject matter, often coming from pre-degree courses in other disciplines, or perhaps returning to study after long periods away from formal education. It is the authors' experience that such students have enormous difficulties in grasping the fundamental programming concepts the first time round, and therefore require a simpler and gentler introduction to the subject than is presented in most standard texts.

In the first semester, considerable time is spent concentrating on the fundamental programming concepts such as declarations of variables and basic control structures, prior to introducing students to the concepts of classes and objects, arrays and collection classes, inheritance, software quality, graphics and event-driven programming, applets and programming for the World Wide Web. Prior to students learning how to create graphical interfaces, they use a text console with input being made straightforward by the provision of a simple utility class, EasyIn.java, that can be downloaded from the web, or copied from the accompanying CD-ROM. The book takes an integrated approach to software development by covering such topics as basic design principles and standards, testing methodologies and HCI.

The second semester covers more advanced topics such as packages, the use of exceptions, file-handling techniques and the implementation of multi-threaded programs. The HCI theme is continued and the use of Swing is introduced as an extension of AWT.

In addition to the utility classes needed for the practical work, much supporting material is available on the website. This includes the sample programs used in the text as well as additional questions and answers for tutors, which are password-protected.

We would like to thank our publisher, McGraw-Hill, for the encouragement and guidance that we have received throughout the production of this book. We would also like to thank especially the computing students of the University of East London for their thoughtful comments and feedback. For support and inspiration, special thanks are due once again to our families and friends.

Quentin Charatan (q.h.charatan@uel.ac.uk)
Aaron Kans (a.kans@uel.ac.uk)
London, UK, December 2001

SEMESTER
ONE

THE FIRST STEP

LEARNING OBJECTIVES

By the end of this chapter you should be able to:

➤ explain the meaning of the word **software**;

➤ describe the way in which software is produced in industry;

➤ explain the need for high-level programming languages;

➤ describe the way in which programs are compiled and run;

➤ distinguish between **compilation** and **interpretation**;

➤ explain how Java programs are compiled and run;

➤ write Java programs that display text on the screen.

1.1 Introduction

Like any student starting out on a first programming module, you will be itching to do just one thing – get started on your first program. We can well understand that, and you won't be disappointed, because you will be writing programs in this very first chapter. Designing and writing computer programs can be one of the most enjoyable and satisfying things you can do, although sometimes it can seem a little daunting at first because it is like nothing else you have ever done. But with a bit of perseverance you will not only start to get a real taste for it but you may well find yourself sitting up till two o'clock in the morning trying to solve a problem. And just when you have given up and you are dropping off to sleep the answer pops into your head and you are at the computer again until you notice it is getting light outside! So if this is happening to you, then don't worry – it's normal!

However, before you start writing programs you need some background; so the first part of this chapter is devoted to some fundamental issues that you need to get to grips with before you can understand what programming itself is all about. This chapter therefore starts off with an explanation of some of the terms you will come across, particularly the notion of *software*. It goes on to give a little bit of background as to how software is produced in industry, and the way in which this has changed in recent times. This is followed by a general look at programming languages and the way that programs are written and developed. After this we discuss the Java language and the way in which developing Java programs differs from that of conventional programming languages. Once we have done all this, we will show you how to write and adapt your first program.

1.2   *Software*

A computer is not very useful unless we give it some instructions that tell it what to do. This set of instructions is called a **program**. The word **software** is the name given to a single program or a set of programs.

There are two main kinds of software. **Application software** is the name given to useful programs that a user might need; for example, word-processors, spreadsheets, accounts programs and so on. **System software** is the name given to special programs that help the computer to do its job; for example, operating systems such as UNIX or Windows (which help us to use the computer) and network software (which helps computers to communicate with each other).

1.3   *Developing software*

We will now take a brief look at how software is developed in industry. This has begun to change over the last past decade or so — until quite recently the method was for software developers to go through a number of phases and complete each of these before moving on to the next. It was then necessary to go back one, two or more phases to make corrections. The first phase consisted of **analysis and specification**, the process of determining what the system was required to do (analysis) and writing it down in a clear and unambiguous manner (specification). The next phase was **design**; this phase consisted of making decisions about how the system would be built in order to meet the specification. After this came **implementation**, at which point the design was turned into an actual program. This was followed by the **testing** phase. When testing was complete the system would be **installed** and a period of **operation and maintenance** followed, whereby the system was improved, and if necessary changed to meet changing requirements. This approach to software development (often called the **waterfall model**) is summarized in figure 1.1.

One problem with this approach was that it often meant that customers had to wait a very long time before they actually saw the product. Another problem was that in practice software produced in this way was actually very difficult to adapt to changing needs (consider, for example, the Y2K problem).

Nowadays it is therefore common to use a RAD approach; this stands for **rapid application development**. The RAD approach involves doing the activities described above a "little bit at a time"; in this way we build **prototypes** of the product and the potential user can be actively involved in testing them out and re-building until we eventually end up with the best possible product in the most satisfactory time period. Several programming tools such as *Visual Basic* and *JBuilder* exist to facilitate this process. The RAD process is summarized in figure 1.2.

Crucial to the RAD approach has been the advent of **object-oriented** methods of developing software. This term, *object-oriented*, is going to play a very important role in this book; however, we are not going to explore its meaning just yet as there are a few other concepts that we need to understand first. Nonetheless, we will start to get an idea of its meaning later in this chapter, and we will really start to get to grips with it from chapter 4 onwards. But right now it is time to start exploring the way in which programs are actually written.

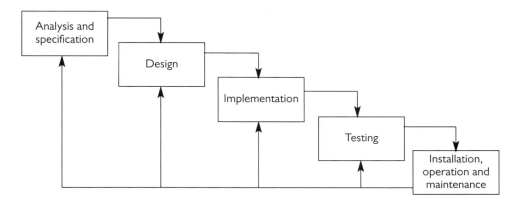

Fig 1.1   The traditional approach to software development (the waterfall model)

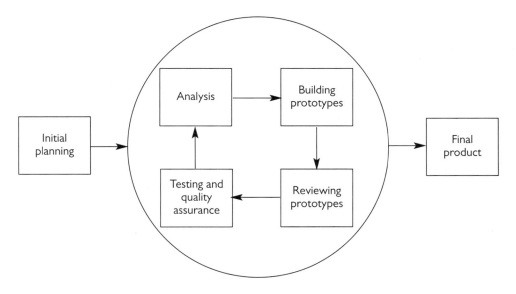

Fig. 1.2   The modern approach to software development (RAD)

1.3.1 Programming languages

A program is written by a developer in a special computer language; these include C++, Java, BASIC, Pascal and many more. It is then translated by a special program (a **compiler**) into something called **machine code**, or, in the case of Java, to **Java byte code**. Machine code and Java byte code consist of binary numbers (0s and 1s) which the computer can understand. For example, 01010011 might mean ADD whereas 01010100 could mean SUBTRACT.

It is of course very difficult to write even the shortest of programs in machine code (although this is what had to be done in the early days of computing) and it is for this reason that programming languages such as Java have been developed. The first, and most basic, of these languages was known as **assembly language**. In assembly language each one of the separate instructions that the computer understands is represented by a word that is a bit like an English word; for example MOV (for "move"), JMP (for "jump"), SUB (for "subtract") and so on. A special piece of software (an **assembler**) is then used to turn what we have written into machine code. Assembly language is called a **low-level language**.

Most programs require fairly sophisticated instructions for control and data-manipulation, and writing such programs in assembly language is a very tedious business. It was for this reason that **high-level** languages – such as C, COBOL, Pascal and Basic – were created. Such languages (also known as **third generation languages** or **3GL**s) combine several basic computer instructions into a single statement or set of statements such as **if . . . else**, or **do . . . while**. So, when you write program instructions in these languages you write lines that are a bit like English. The set of instructions that you write in a programming language is called the **program code** or **source code**. In the case of high-level languages the translation of our source code into machine code is known as **compilation**, and the software that we use to perform this translation is called a **compiler**. The code that is produced by a compiler is often referred to as **object code**.[1]

Java, the language that you will be studying, is an **object-oriented programming language**; object-oriented languages represent the most recent development in the history of programming languages. As we have pointed out earlier, it will not be long before the meaning of this term starts to become clear.

At this stage it is worth mentioning that Java programs are compiled and run in a rather different way to programs written in other programming languages such as C, Pascal or C++ (which is another object-oriented language). In order to appreciate the difference, you need to understand how conventional compilers work, so we will take a brief look at this before exploring the Java development process.

1.4 *Conventional compilers*

The program code that we write must obey the rules of the programming language. These rules are known as the **syntax** (the grammatical structure) of the language. It is very common to

---

[1] Not to be confused with the word *object* that you will come across many times in this book, in connection with object-oriented programming.

make **syntax errors** when we write programs; programs with errors (or **bugs**) in them cannot be compiled. Therefore most compiler programs, when they try to compile what we have written, also tell us about the errors we have made and where they are in the program. So we go through a process of typing the code, trying to compile, correcting the errors (**debugging**) and trying to compile again.

These days, compilers do much more than just compile your programs. They usually provide what is called an **integrated development environment (IDE)**. This means that the one piece of software allows us to write and edit our programs, compile them into object code, and make changes in response to error messages that are generated by the compiler during compilation. In any major project, different bits of the program are developed separately and need to be integrated; this process is called **linking**, and an IDE will also perform this process. This also includes linking any necessary pre-compiled pieces of code which most IDEs provide (collections of pre-written pieces of code are known as **libraries**).

Once the program is compiled and linked it is saved as an **executable** file – that is, a file that can be loaded into the computer's memory (by a special piece of system software called a **loader**) and run. Most IDEs will load and run the program for you without your having to exit from the IDE itself. The process of compiling and running programs in the conventional way is summarized in figure 1.3.

Compiling programs in this way is only one way of doing it – at one time it was more common to use another method of translating and running programs. This method is called **interpretation** and we will take a brief look at this now, because, as we shall see, it plays an important role in the Java development process.

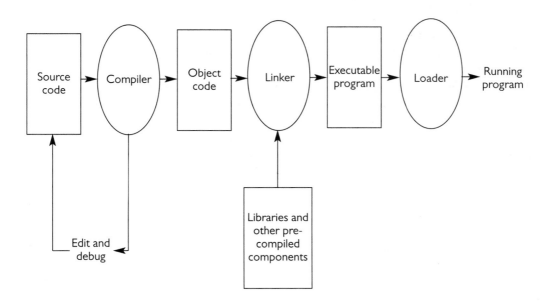

Fig 1.3   Compiling and running conventional programs

1.5   *Interpreters*

At one time it was common to use an **interpreter** rather than a compiler. As we have seen, compilers operate on the entire program, providing a permanent binary file which may be **executed** (or **run**). An interpreter, on the other hand, translates and executes the program one line at a time. This of course is less efficient and execution is slower. It does have the advantage, however, of enabling a program to be changed frequently without going through the whole compilation process again. Until recently, interpreters were not used very much for real-life programs – but with the coming of Java the processes of compilation and interpretation have been cleverly combined to give is us the best of both worlds.

1.6   *The Java development process*

As we have explained above, until recently all programs tended to be compiled and linked so that they formed a separate executable file. At first sight, this sounds like the ideal thing – compile a program so that you can take it away and run it on your computer or some other computer. But there is one major drawback with this process. A compiled program is suitable only for a particular type of computer. For example, a program that is compiled for a PC will not run on an Apple Mac or a UNIX machine. Again, until recently, this was not such a huge problem – but then along came the World Wide Web!

With the advent of the Web it became desirable for us to be able to download a program from a remote site and run it on our machine – and we want it to run in exactly the same way irrespective of whether our machine is a PC, an Apple Mac or any other machine. We need a language that is **platform-independent**.

Java is the language for this! It is designed to work within the World Wide Web of computers through special pieces of software called **browsers**, the most common of which are *Netscape* and *Internet Explorer*. Java programs that run on the Web are called **applets** (meaning little applications).

Inside a modern browser there is a special program, called a **Java Virtual Machine**, or **JVM** for short. This JVM is able to run a Java program for the particular computer on which it is running.

We saw earlier that conventional compilers translate our program code into machine code. This machine code would contain the particular instructions appropriate to the computer it was meant for. Java compilers do not translate the program into machine code – they translate it into special instructions called **Java byte code**. These instructions are then *interpreted* by the JVM for that particular machine. So whereas machine code is specific to a particular type of computer, Java byte code is universal.

So the process consists of typing in the program (source code), compiling it into byte code, correcting errors (debugging) if necessary, and then, if there are no more errors, interpreting the byte code. At this final stage the JVM loads not only your program's byte code but also that contained in any libraries that are required.

Java IDEs such as J++ or *JBuilder* are also able to compile programs that are not just applets, but **applications**; an application is a program designed to run on your machine just like any other program. Rather than being interpreted by the browser's JVM, applications are interpreted by the IDE's built-in interpreter, or by a separate JVM built into the computer's operating system, or by a standalone program (usually called **java**).

Until chapter 12 we will be creating applications only, and not worrying about applets designed for the World Wide Web. However, once you have grasped the programming principles in this book it will be an easy step to move on to writing applets; indeed in chapter 9, the graphical applications that we will write will be constructed in such a way that converting them to applets in the future will be an easy matter.

The process of compiling, interpreting and running Java programs is summarized in figure 1.4.

If you are working in a Windows or Windows-type environment, your compiler program will provide you with an easy-to-use window into which you can type your code; other windows will provide information about the files you are using; and a separate window will be provided to tell you of your errors. Your screen will probably look something like that in figure 1.5.

The source code that you write will be saved in a file with an extension **.java** (for example myProgram.java) and once it is compiled into byte code it will be kept in a file with an extension **.class** (for example myProgram.class).

If you are working in a UNIX or UNIX-type environment you will be working from a command line interface. You will therefore be using a text editor to write your code, and – if

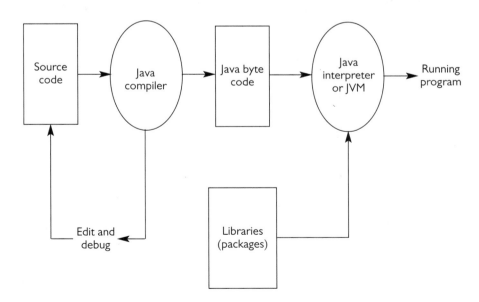

Fig 1.4 Compiling, interpreting and running Java programs

you are writing a program called myProgram, for example – you will probably have to write something like:

vi myProgram.java

You will then need to invoke the compiler with a line like:

javac myProgram.java

And to run your program you will need to invoke the interpreter with a line like:

java myProgram

1.7   *Your first program*

At last it is time to write your first program. Anyone who knows anything about programming will tell you that the first program that you write in a new language has always got to be a program that displays the words "Hello world" on the screen; so we will stick with tradition, and your first program will do exactly that!

When your program runs you will get a black and white black screen with the words "Hello world" displayed; if you are using a Windows-type environment there will probably be some additional stuff displayed before the "Hello world" line. The screen will remain like this until

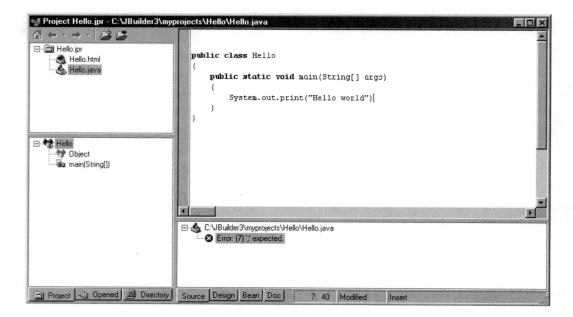

Fig 1.5   A typical Java IDE screen

you press the *Enter* key. Then the program will end and – in a Windows-type environment – the screen will disappear.

It sounds like a rather simple program, and so it is. However, before you type it in and compile and run it there is something we need to tell you about: Java wasn't really designed to write simple text messages on boring black and white screens! It is a language that can produce interesting and attractive graphical applications that run over the Web – but before you can begin to write such programs you need to learn the basics and you are going to be using this simple text screen right up till chapter 9; by that time you will have the fundamentals of programming firmly understood.

Now, because of the potential of the Java language, the people who developed it never really bothered to provide simple methods of getting text from the keyboard and displaying it on the screen, because it is usually done with attractive icons and mouse-clicks and so on. So getting input from the keyboard can involve lots of lines of program code that can look pretty complicated and get in the way of your learning the basic programming principles.

But don't worry! We have made it easy for you! We have created something called `EasyIn`. You will need to download the file called `EasyIn.java` from our website (or copy it from the CD-ROM). You should put this in the folder where your compiler automatically looks for files, so that `EasyIn.java` can be interpreted along with your program.

So now we can get on with our "Hello world" Program, which is written out for you below as program 1.1

PROGRAM 1.1

```
public class Hello
{
  public static void main(String[] args)
  {
    System.out.print("Hello world");
    EasyIn.pause();
  }
}
```

As we have said, when you run the program, you should get a screen with the words "Hello world" written on it. If you are using a Windows-type environment the screen will remain like this until you press the *Enter* key, at which point the program ends and the black screen disappears. In a UNIX-type environment you will simply be returned to your usual prompt when the program terminates.

Let's examine what is really going on here. The program we are writing is really incredibly simple. It displays the words "Hello world" on the screen, then it pauses and waits for you to press the *Enter* key. A simple sequence involving two actions: the program displays the message on the screen and then it pauses until the user presses *Enter*. If we didn't have the pause statement here, then, in a Windows environment, the screen would simply disappear before you had a chance to read what was on it.

1.7.1   Analysis of the "Hello world" program

We will consider the meaning of the program line by line. The first line, which we call the header, looks like this:

```
public class Hello
```

The first, and most important, thing to pay attention to is the word **class**. We noted earlier that Java is referred to as an **object-oriented programming language**. Now the true meaning of this will start to become clear in chapter 4 – but for the time being you just need to know that object-oriented languages require the program to be written in separate units called **classes**. There are two aspects to a class: the information that it holds and the things that it can do. The different bits of information (or **data**) that belong to a class are referred to as the **attributes** of the class; the operations that a class can perform are referred to as the **methods** of the class.

In forthcoming chapters we will be using the notation of the **Unified Modeling Language (UML)**[2] to specify and design our classes; UML is the standard method of specifying and designing object-oriented systems. In UML a class is represented diagrammatically by a rectangle divided into three sections as shown in figure 1.6.

The simple programs that we are starting off with will contain only one class (although they will interact with other classes like EasyIn, and the "built-in" Java libraries) – in this case we have called our class Hello. The first line therefore tells the Java compiler that we are writing a class with the name Hello. You will also have noticed the word public in front of the word class; placing this word here makes our class accessible to the outside world so we should include this word in the header of the main class of an application.

Notice that everything in the class has to be contained between two curly brackets that look like this { }; these tell the compiler where the class begins and ends.

There is one important thing that we should point out here. Java is *case-sensitive* – in other words it interprets upper case and lower case characters as two completely different things – it is very important therefore to type the statements exactly as you see them here, paying attention to the case of the letters.

The next line that we come across (after the opening curly bracket) is this:

```
public static void main(String[] args)
```

This looks rather strange if you are not used to programming – but you will see that every program we write in the first few weeks is going to follow on from this line. Now, we have already noted that the Java language requires that every program consists of at least one class and that a class will contain attributes and methods. Our Hello class in fact contains no attributes and just one method and this line introduces that method. In fact it is a very special

[2] Simon Bennett, Steve McRobb and Ray Farmer, *Object-Oriented Systems Analysis and Design using UML*, McGraw-Hill UK, 1999.

method called a **main** method. Applications in Java (as opposed to applets, which run in a browser) must always contain a class with a method called **main**: this is where the program begins. A program starts with the first instruction of **main**, then obeys each instruction in sequence (unless the instruction itself tells it to jump to some other place in the program). The program terminates when it has finished obeying the final instruction of **main**.

So this line that we see above introduces the **main** method; the program instructions are now written in a second set of curly brackets that show us where this **main** method begins and ends. At the moment we will not worry about the words in front of **main (public static void)** and the bit in the brackets (String[] args) – we will just accept that they always have to be there; you will begin to understand their significance as you learn more about programming concepts.

Now, at last we are in a position to examine the important bits – the two lines of code that represent our instructions, *display "Hello world"* and *pause*.

The line that gets "Hello world" displayed on the screen is this one:

```
System.out.print("Hello world");
```

This is the way we are always going to get stuff printed on the screen; we use System.out.print (or sometimes System.out.println, as explained below) and put whatever we want to be displayed in the brackets. You won't understand at this stage why it has to be in this precise form (with each word separated by a full stop, and the actual phrase in double quotes), but do make sure that you type it exactly as you see it here, with an upper case S at the beginning and all the rest in lower case. Also, you should notice the semi-colon at the end of the statement. This is important; every Java instruction has to end with a semi-colon.

The next line is the *pause* line:

```
EasyIn.pause();
```

| The name of the class goes in this box |
| The attributes of the class are listed in this box |
| The methods of the class are listed in this box |

Fig 1.6 A UML class template

As you can see, we are already starting to make use of the EasyIn class; we will do this every time we want to get input from the keyboard. In this case we are simply waiting for the user to press the Enter key, and to do this we use the pause method of EasyIn. In the next chapter you will see how to use other EasyIn methods to get other types of input.

1.7.2   Some variations to the *Hello world* program

As we mentioned above, there is an alternative form of the System.out.print statement, which uses System.out.println. The println is short for "print line" and the effect of using this statement is to start a new line after displaying whatever is in the brackets. We can see the effect of this from program 1.2 – we have renamed our class Hello2 to avoid confusion; the change to the code is in bold:

PROGRAM 1.2

```java
public class Hello2
{
  public static void main(String[] args)
  {
    System.out.println("Hello world");
    EasyIn.pause();
  }
}
```

At first glance the output from this program might not look very different – but notice that the cursor is now flashing at the start of the line following the "Hello world" line, instead of at the end of the "Hello world" line!

So now you could add extra lines if you wanted, as, for example, in program 1.3:

PROGRAM 1.3

```java
public class Hello3
{
  public static void main(String[] args)
  {
    System.out.println("Hello world");
    System.out.print("This is my third Java Program");
    EasyIn.pause();
  }
}
```

Finally, there is another way in which we can use the pause method of EasyIn. We can get a message printed on the screen by placing text in the brackets. This is demonstrated in program 1.4.

PROGRAM 1.4

```
public class Hello4
{
  public static void main(String[] args)
  {
    System.out.println("Hello world");
    EasyIn.pause("Press <Enter> to quit");
  }
}
```

When you try this out you will see the words "Press <Enter> to quit" displayed beneath "Hello world". In future we are going to end all our text-based programs with a line like this.

Before we finish there is one more thing to tell you. When we write program code, we will often want to include some comments to help remind us what we were doing when we look at our code a few weeks later, or to help other people to understand what we have done.

Of course we want the compiler to ignore these comments when the code is being compiled. There are two ways of doing this. For short comments we place two slashes (//) at the beginning of the line — everything after these slashes, up to the end of the line, is then ignored by the compiler.

For longer comments (that is, ones that run over more than a single line) we usually use another method. The comment is enclosed between two special symbols; the opening symbol is a slash followed by a star (/*) and the closing symbol is a star followed by a slash (*/). Everything between these two symbols is ignored by the compiler. Program 1.5 below shows examples of both types of comment; when you compile and run this program you will see that the comments have no effect on the code, and the output is exactly the same as that of program 1.4.

PROGRAM 1.5

```
// this is a short comment, so we use the first method

public class Hello5
{
  public static void main(String[] args)
  {
    System.out.println("("Hello world");
    EasyIn.pause("Press <Enter> to quit");
  }
  /* this is the second method of including comments - it is more convenient
  to use this method here, because the comment is longer and goes over more
  than one line */
}
```

Tutorial exercises

1. Explain what is meant be by each of the following terms:
   - machine code;
   - assembly language;
   - high-level (third generation) language;
   - source code;
   - Java byte code;
   - library.
2. Explain the difference between *compilation* and *interpretation* of programs.
3. Explain the difference between a Java compiler and a conventional compiler.

Practical work

1. Type, compile and run programs 1.1 to 1.5 from this chapter.
2. Write a program that displays your name, address and telephone number, each on separate lines.
3. Adapt the above program to include a blank line between your address and telephone number.
4. Write a program that displays your initials in big letters made of asterisks. For example:

THE BUILDING BLOCKS

LEARNING OBJECTIVES

By the end of this chapter you should be able to:

➤ distinguish between the eight built-in **scalar types** of Java;

➤ declare **variables**;

➤ **assign** values to variables;

➤ create **constant** values with the keyword **final**;

➤ join messages and values in input commands by using the **concatenation** (+) operator;

➤ use the input methods of the `EasyIn` class to get data from the keyboard;

➤ design the functionality of a method using **pseudocode**.

2.1 Introduction

You will have discovered that writing and running your first program is a very exciting moment. The idea that you can control a computer's actions by giving it a series of instructions is a very powerful one. Machines as tiny as calculators to systems as complex as those that launch space shuttles are controlled in this way – by computer programs.

Of course the first few programs that you wrote do not compare to the examples discussed above – but the programmers of these complex systems all took the same initial steps as you! Now it is time to move on from those first steps and start to look at some of the basic building blocks of a piece of software.

One way in which your first few programs were rather limited is that they had no *data* to work on (see figure 2.1). All interesting programs will have to store data in order to give interesting results; what use would a calculator be without the numbers the user types in to add and multiply? For this reason, one of the first questions you should ask when learning any programming language is "what types of data does this language allow me to store in my programs?"

We begin this chapter by taking a look at the basic types available in the Java language.

2.2   *Simple data types in Java*

The types of value used within a program are referred to as **data types**. If you wish to record the *price* of a cinema ticket in a program, for example, this value would probably need to be kept in the form of a **real number** (a number with a decimal point in it). Whereas if you wished to record *how many* tickets have been sold you would probably need to keep this in the form of an **integer** (whole number). It is necessary to know whether suitable types exist in the programming language to keep these bits of data.

In Java there are a few simple data types that programmers can use. These simple types are often referred to as the **scalar types** of Java as they relate to a single piece of information (a single real number, a single character etc.).

Table 2.1 lists the names of these types in the Java language, the kinds of value they represent, and the exact range of these values. As you can see, some kinds of data, namely integer and real numbers, can be kept as more than one Java type. For example, you can use both the **byte** type and the **short** type to keep integers in Java. However, while each numeric Java type allows for both positive and negative numbers, *the maximum size of numbers that can be stored varies from type to type.*

For example, the type **byte** can represent integers ranging only from −128 to 127, whereas the type **short** can represent integers ranging from −32768 to 32767. Unlike some programming languages, these ranges are *fixed* no matter which Java compiler or operating system you are using.

The character type, **char**, is used to represent characters from a standard set of characters known as the **Unicode** character set. This contains nearly all the characters from most known languages. For the sake of simplicity, you can think of this type as representing any character on your keyboard.

Finally, the **boolean** type is used to keep only one of two possible values: **true** or **false**. This type can be useful when creating tests in programs. For example, the answer to the

A program controlling the space shuttle would not be very useful if it could not record the shuttle's coordinates!

Fig 2.1   An illustration of a program without data

	Table 2.1 The scalar types of Java	
Java type	**Allows for**	**Range of values**
byte	very small integers	−128 to 127
short	small integers	−32768 to 32767
int	big integers	−2147483648 to 2147483647
long	very big integers	−9223372036854775808 to 9223372036854775807
float	real numbers	$+/- 1.4 * 10^{-45}$ to $3.4 * 10^{38}$
double	very big real numbers	$+/- 4.9 * 10^{-324}$ to $1.8 * 10^{308}$
char	characters	Unicode character set
boolean	true or false	not applicable

question "have I passed my exam?" will be either *yes* or *no*. In Java a **boolean** type could be used to keep the answer to this question, with the value **true** being used to represent *yes* and the value **false** to represent *no*.

2.3   *Declaring variables in Java*

The data types listed in table 2.1 are used in programs to create named locations in the computer's memory that will contain values while a program is running. This process is known as **declaring**. These named locations are called **variables** because their values are allowed to *vary* over the life of the program.

For example, a program written to develop a computer game might need a piece of data to record the player's score as secret keys are found in a haunted house. The value held in this piece of data will vary as more keys are found. This piece of data would be referred to as a variable. To create a variable in your program you must:

- give that variable a name (of your choice);
- decide which data type in the language best reflects the kind of values you wish to store in the variable.

What name might you choose to record the score of the player in our computer game?

Although you can choose almost any name, such as *x*, it is best to pick a name that describes the purpose of the item of data; an ideal name would be *score*. You can choose any name for variables as long as:

- the name is not already a word in the Java language (such as **class**, **void**);
- the name has no spaces in it;

- the name does not include mathematical symbols such as + and −;
- the name starts either with a letter, an underscore (_), or a dollar sign ($).

Although the name of a variable can begin with *any* letter, the convention in Java programs is to begin the name of a variable with a *lower case* letter.

Which data type in table 2.1 should you use if you wish to record a player's score? Well, since the score would always be a whole number, an integer type would be appropriate. There are four Java data types that can be used to hold integers (**byte**, **short**, **int** and **long**). As we said before, the only difference among these types is the range of values that they can keep. Unless there is specific reason to do otherwise, however, the **int** type is very often chosen to store integer values in Java programs. We don't don't want to be unconventional so we will stick to the **int** type as well! For a similar reason, when it comes to storing real numbers we will choose the **double** type rather than the **float** type.

Once the name and the type have been decided upon, the variable is declared as follows:

```
dataType variableName;
```

where `dataType` is the chosen scalar type and `variableName` is the chosen name of the variable. So, in the case of a player's score, the variable would be declared as follows:

```
int score;
```

Figure 2.2 illustrates the effect of this instruction on the computer's memory. As you can see, a small part of the computer's memory is set aside for use in your program. You can think of this reserved space in memory as being a small box, big enough to hold an integer. The name of the box will be `score`.

In this way, many variables can be declared in your programs. Let's assume that the player of a game can choose a difficulty level (A, B, or C); another variable could be declared in a similar way.

What name might you give this variable? An obvious choice would be *difficulty level* but remember names can not have spaces in them. You could use an underscore to remove the

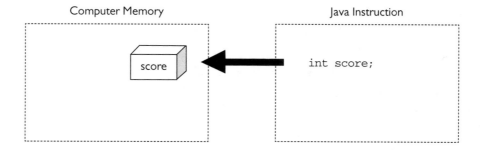

Fig 2.2   The effect of declaring a variable in Java

space (*difficulty_level*) or start the second word with a capital letter to distinguish the two words (*difficultyLevel*). Both are well-established naming conventions in Java. Alternatively you could just shorten the name to, say, *level*. Let us adopt this last approach.

Now, what data type in table 2.1 best represents the difficulty level? Since the levels are given as characters (A, B and C) the **char** type would be the obvious choice. At this point we have two variables declared: one to record the score and one to record the difficulty level:

```
int score;
char level;
```

Finally, several variables can be declared on a *single line* if they are *all of the same type*. For example, let's assume that there are ghosts in the house that hit out at the player; the number of times a player gets hit by a ghost can also be recorded. We can call this variable *hits*. Since the type of this variable is also an integer it can be declared along with score in a single line as follows:

```
int score, hits; // two variables declared at once
char level; // this has to be declared separately
```

Figure 2.3 illustrates the effect of these three declarations on the computer's memory.

Notice that the character box, level, is half the size of the integer boxes score and hits. That is because in Java the **char** type requires half the space of the **int** type. You should also be aware that the **double** type in Java requires twice the space of the **int** type.

You're probably wondering: if declaring a variable is like creating a box in memory, how do I put values into this box? The answer is with assignments.

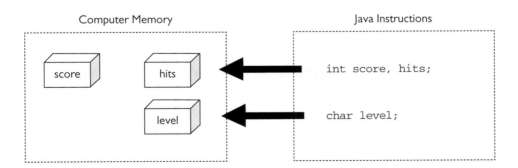

Fig 2.3 The effect of declaring many variables in Java

2.4 *Assignments in Java*

Assignments allow values to be put into variables. They are written in Java with the use of the equality symbol (=). In Java this symbol is known as **the assignment operator**. Simple assignments take the following form:

```
variableName = value;
```

For example, to put the value zero into the variable score, the following assignment statement could be used:

```
score = 0;
```

This is to be read as "*set the value of* score *to zero*". Effectively, this puts the number zero into the box in memory we called score. If you wish, you may combine the assignment statement with a variable declaration to put an initial value into a variable as follows:

```
int score = 0;
```

This is equivalent to the two statements below:

```
int score;
score = 0;
```

Although in some circumstances Java will automatically put initial values into variables when they are declared, this is not always the case and it is better explicitly to initialize variables that require an initial value. Notice that the following declaration will not compile in Java:

```
int score = 2.5;
```

Can you think why?

The reason is that the right hand side of the assignment (2.5) is a *real* number. This value can't be placed into a variable such as score, that is declared to hold only *integers*, without some information loss. In Java, this kind of information loss from real numbers is not permitted.

You may be wondering if it is possible to place a whole number into a variable declared to hold real numbers. The answer is yes. The following is perfectly legal:

```
double someNumber = 1000;
```

Although the value on the right-hand side (1000) appears to be an integer, it can be placed into a variable of type **double** as this would result in no information loss. Once this number is put into the variable of type **double**, it will be treated as the real number 1000.0.

Clearly, you need to think carefully about the best data type to choose for a particular variable. For instance, if a variable is going to be used to hold whole numbers *or* real numbers, use the **double** type as it can cope with both. If the variable is only ever going to be used to hold whole numbers, however, then although the **double** type might be adequate, use the **int** type as it is specifically designed to hold whole numbers.

When assigning a value to a character variable, you must enclose the value in single quotes. For example, to set the initial difficulty level to A, the following assignment statement could be used:

```
char level = 'A';
```

Remember: you need to declare a variable only once. You can then assign to it as many times as you like. For example, later on in the program the difficulty level might be changed to a different value as follows:

```
char level = 'A'; // initial difficulty level
// other Java instructions
level = 'B'; // difficulty level changed
```

2.5   *Creating constants*

There will be occasions where data items in a program have values *that do not change*. The following are examples of such items:

- the maximum score in an exam (100);
- the number of hours in a day (24);
- the mathematical value of π (3.14176).

In these cases the values of the items do not vary. Values that remain constant throughout a program (as opposed to variable) should be named and declared as **constants**.

Constants are declared much like variables in Java except that they are preceded by the keyword **final**, and are always initialized to their fixed value. For example:

```
final int HOURS = 24;
```

Notice that the standard Java convention has been used here of naming constants in UPPER-CASE. Any attempt to change this value later in the program will result in a compiler error. For example:

```
final int HOURS = 24; // create constant
HOURS = 12; // will not compile!
```

2.6   *Arithmetic operators*

Rather than just assign simple values (like such as 24 and 2.5) to variables, it is often useful to carry out some kind of arithmetic in assignment statements. Java has the four familiar arithmetic operators, plus a remainder operator for this purpose. These operators are listed in table 2.2.

You can use these operators in assignment statements, much like you might use a calculator. For example, consider the following instructions:

```
int x;
x = 10 + 25;
```

After these instructions the variable x would contain the value 35: the result of adding 10 to 25. Terms on the right-hand side of assignment operators (like 10 + 25) that have to be *worked out* before they are assigned are referred to as **expressions**. These expressions can involve more than one operator.

Let's consider a calculation to work out the price of a product after a sales tax has been added. If the initial price of the product is 500 and the rate of sales tax is 17.5%, the following calculation could be used to calculate the total cost of the product:

```
double cost;
cost = 500 * (1 + 17.5/100);
```

After this calculation the final cost of the product would be 587.5.

By the way, in case you are wondering, the order in which expressions such as these are evaluated is the same as in most programming languages: with terms in brackets being calculated before division and multiplication, which in turn are calculated before subtraction and addition. This means that the term in the bracket

```
(1 + 17.5/100)
```

Table 2.2 The arithmetic operators of Java	
Operation	**Java operator**
addition	+
subtraction	−
multiplication	*
division	/
remainder	%

evaluates to 1.175, not 0.185, as the division is calculated before the addition. The final operator (%) in table 2.2 returns the remainder after *integer division* (often referred to as the **modulus**). Table 2.3 illustrates some examples of the use of this operator together with the values returned.

As an illustration of the use of both the division operator and the modulus operator, consider the following example:

A large party of 30 people go to visit the roller-coaster rides at a local theme park. When they get to the ultimate ride, "Big Betty", they are told that only groups of four can get on!

To calculate how many groups in the party can get on the ride and how many people in the party will have to miss the ride, the division and modulus operators could be used as follows:

```
int catchRide, missRide;
catchRide = 30/4; // number of groups on ride
missRide = 30%4; // number who missed ride
```

After these instructions the value of catchRide will be 7 (the result of dividing 30 by 4) and the value of missRide will be 2 (the remainder after dividing 30 by 4). You may be wondering why the calculation for catchRide

        30/4

did not yield 7.5 but 7. The reason for this is that there are, in fact, two different in-built division routines in Java, one to calculate an integer answer and another to calculate the answer as a real number.

Rather than having two division operators, however, Java has a single division symbol (/) to represent *both* types of division. The division operator is said to be **overloaded**. This means that the same operator (in this case the division symbol) can behave in different ways. This makes life much easier for programmers as the decision about which routine to call is left to the Java language.

How does the Java compiler know which division routine we mean? Well, it looks at the values that are being divided. If *at least one value* is a real number (as in the product cost example), it assumes we mean the division routine that calculates an answer as a real number,

Table 2.3 Examples of the modulus operator in Java	
Expression	**Value**
29 % 9	2
6 % 8	6
40 % 40	0
10 % 2	0

otherwise it assumes we mean the division routine that calculates an answer as a whole number (as in the roller-coaster example).[1]

2.7   *Expressions in Java*

So far, variable names have appeared only on the left-hand side of assignment statements. However, the expression on the right-hand side of an assignment statement can itself contain variable names. If this is the case then the name does not refer to *the location*, but to *the contents of the location*. For example, the assignment to calculate the cost of the product could have been rewritten as follows:

```
double price, tax, cost; // declare three variables
price = 500; // set price
tax = 17.5; // set tax rate
cost = price * (1 + tax/100); // calculate cost
```

Here, the variables `price` and `tax` that appear in the expression

```
price * (1 + tax/100)
```

are taken to mean *the values contained in* `price` and `tax` respectively. This expression evaluates to 587.5 as before. Notice that although this price happens to be a whole number, it has been declared to be a **double** as generally prices are expressed as real numbers.

There is actually nothing to stop you using the name of the variable you are assigning to in the expression itself. This would just mean that the old value of the variable is being used to calculate its new value. Rather than creating a new variable, `cost`, to store the final cost of the product, the calculation could, for example, have updated *the original price* as follows:

```
price = price * (1 + tax/100);
```

Now, only two variables are required, `price` and `tax`. Let's look at this assignment a bit more closely.

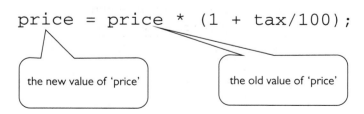

---

[1] To force the use of one division routine over another, a technique known as **type casting** can be used. We will return to this technique later on in the book.

When reading this instruction, the price in the right- hand expression is to be read as the *old value* of price, whereas the price on the left-hand side is to be read as *the new value* of price.

Of course, the code fragments we have been writing so far in this chapter are not complete programs. As you already know, to create a program in Java you must write one or more classes. In program 2.1, we write a class, FindCost, where the main method calculates the price of the product.

PROGRAM 2.1

```java
/* a program to calculate the cost of a product after a sales tax has been
added */

public class FindCost
{
  public static void main(String[] args)
  {
    double price, tax;
    price = 500;
    tax = 17.5;
    price = price * (1 + tax/100);
  }
}
```

What would you see when you run this program? The answer is nothing! There is no instruction to display the result on to the screen. You have already seen how to display messages on to the screen. It is now time to take a closer look at the output command to see how you can also display results on to the screen.

2.8   Output in Java

As you have already seen when writing your first few programs, to output a message on to the screen in Java we use the following command:

```java
System.out.println(message to be printed on screen);
```

which prints the given message on to the screen and then moves the cursor to a new line. For example, we have already seen:

```java
System.out.println("Hello world");
```

This prints the message "Hello world" on to the screen and then moves the cursor to a new line. You have also seen thee print command that displays a message but keeps the cursor on the same line. These messages are in fact what we call **strings** (collections of characters). In Java, literal strings like "Hello world" are always enclosed in speech marks. We shall look at strings in more detail in chapter 4. However, it is necessary to know how several strings can be printed on the screen using a single output command.

In Java, the two strings can be joined together with the plus symbol (+). When using this symbol for this purpose it is known as the **concatenation operator**. For example, instead of printing the single string "Hello world", we could have joined two strings, "Hello" and "world", for output using the following command:

```
System.out.println("Hello " + "world");
```

Note that spaces are printed by including them within the speech marks ("Hello"), not by adding spaces around the concatenation operator (which has no effect at all).

Java also allows any values or expressions of the simple types we showed you in table 2.1, to be printed on the screen using these output commands. It does this by implicitly converting each value/expression to a string before displaying it on the screen. In this way numbers, the value of variables, or the value of expressions can be displayed on the screen. For example, the square of 10 can be displayed on the screen as follows:

```
System.out.println(10*10);
```

This instruction prints the number 100 on the screen. Since these values are converted into strings by Java they can be joined on to literal strings for output.

For example, let's return back to the party of 30 people visiting the roller-coaster ride we discussed in section 2.6. If each person is charged an entrance fee of 7.50, the total cost of tickets could be displayed as follows:

```
System.out.println("cost = " + (30*7.5) );
```

Here the concatenation operator (+), is being used to join the string, "cost = ", onto the value of the expression (30*7.5). Notice that when expressions like 30*7.5 are used in output statements it is best to enclose them in brackets. This would result in the following output:

```
cost = 225.0
```

Bear these ideas in mind and look at program 2.2, where we have rewritten program 2.1 so that the output is visible.

PROGRAM 2.2

```
/* a program to calculate and display the cost of a product after sales tax
has been added */

public class FindCost2
{
  public static void main(String[] args)
  {
    double price, tax;
    price = 500;
    tax = 17.5;
    price = price * (1 + tax/100); // calculate cost
    // display results and pause before closing
    System.out.println("*** Product Price Check ***");
    System.out.println("Cost after tax = " + price);
    EasyIn.pause("Press <Enter> to quit");
  }
}
```

This program produces the following output:

```
*** Product Price Check ***
Cost after tax = 587.5
Press <Enter> to quit
```

When the user presses the *Enter* key the program will terminate.

Although being able to see the result of the calculation is a definite improvement, this program is still very limited. The formatting of the output can certainly be improved, but we shall not deal with such issues until later on in the book. What does concern us now is that this program can only calculate the cost of products when the sales tax rate is 17.5% and the initial price is 500!

What is required is not to fix the rate of sales tax or the price of the product but, instead, to get the *user of your program to input* these values as the program runs.

2.9   *Input in Java:* the **EasyIn** *class*

As we have already mentioned, Java was not really developed for use with simple text screens and to get around this we have provided you with the EasyIn class.

As long as the EasyIn class is accessible, you can use all the input methods that we have defined in this class. The EasyIn class has several input methods: *one for each type of data you may wish to input* (see table 2.4). Notice that the **boolean** type has no EasyIn method as such values are not directly input into programs from the keyboard.

Table 2.4 The input methods of the *EasyIn* class	
Java type	**EasyIn** method
byte	getByte()
short	getShort()
int	getInt()
long	getLong()
float	getFloat()
double	getDouble()
char	getChar()
boolean	n/a

A value can be input from the keyboard by accessing the appropriate method as follows:

```
someVariable = EasyIn.methodName();
```

Let's return to the haunted house game to illustrate this. Rather than *assigning* a difficulty level as follows:

```
char level;
level = 'A';
```

you could take a more flexible approach by asking the user of your program to input a difficulty level while the program runs. Since `level` is declared to be a character variable, you would have to use the specific input method for characters (called `getChar`) as follows:

```
level = EasyIn.getChar();
```

Notice that to access a method of a class you need to join the name of the method (`getChar`) on to the name of the class (`EasyIn`) by using the full-stop symbol '`.`'. Also you must remember the brackets after the name of the method.

In addition to these methods there are the two pause functions you have already met as well as an input method for strings. We shall return to this method when we look at the `String` class in chapter 4.

Each input method of `EasyIn`, has error checking built in so that only values of the appropriate type are entered. If incorrect values are entered, an error message such as the following appears for character input:

Make sure you enter a single character

The user can then re-enter the value. This process continues until a value of the correct type has been entered. All this without any extra programming effort by you!

Let's rewrite program 2.2 so that the price of the product and the rate of sales tax are not fixed in the program, but are input from the keyboard. Since the type used to store the price and the tax is a **double**, the appropriate input method is getDouble.

PROGRAM 2.3

```java
/* a program to input the initial price of a product and then calculate and
display its cost after tax has been added */

public class FindCost3
{
  public static void main(String[] args)
  {
    double price, tax;
    System.out.println("*** Product Price Check ***");
    System.out.print("Enter initial price: "); // prompt for input
    price = EasyIn.getDouble(); // input method called
    System.out.print("Enter tax rate: "); // prompt for input
    tax = EasyIn.getDouble(); // input method called
    price = price * (1 + tax/100);
    System.out.println("Cost after tax = " + price);
    EasyIn.pause("Press <Enter> to quit");
  }
}
```

Note that, by looking at this program code alone, there is no way to determine what the final price of the product will be, as the initial price and the tax rate will be determined *only when the program is run.*

Let's assume that we run the program and the user interacts with it as follows:[2]

```
*** Product Price Check ***
Enter initial price: 1000
Enter tax rate: 12.5%
Make sure you enter a double
12.5
Cost after tax = 1125.0
Press <Enter> to quit
```

When the user presses the *Enter* key, the program terminates. You should notice the following points from this test run:

---

[2] We have used **bold italic** font to represent user input.

- whatever the price of the product and the rate of tax, this program could have evaluated the final price;
- entering numeric values with additional formatting information, such as currency symbols or the percentage symbol, is not permitted;
- EasyIn's input methods allow for re-input with an appropriate error message if values of an incorrect type are entered.

The programs we are looking at now involve input commands, output commands and assignments. Clearly, the order in which you write these instructions affects the results of your programs. For example, if the instructions to calculate the final price and then display the results were reversed as follows:

```
System.out.println("Cost after tax = " + price);
price = price * (1 + tax/100);
```

the price that would be displayed would not be the price *after* tax but the price *before* tax! In order to avoid such mistakes it makes sense to *design your code* by sketching out your instructions before you type them in.

2.10   *Program design*

As we explained in chapter 1, designing a program is the task of considering exactly *how to build* the software, whereas writing the code (the task of *actually building* the software) is referred to as *implementation*. As programs get more complex, it is important to spend time on program design, before launching into program implementation.

As we have already said, Java programs consist of one or more classes, each with one or more methods. In chapter 1 we introduced you to the use of diagrams to help design such classes – your overall program design will be expressed using such diagrams. The programs we have considered so far, however, have only a single class and a single method (main). A class diagram would not be very useful here! So we will return to this design technique as we develop larger programs involving many classes.

At a lower level, it is the instructions *within* a method that determine the *behaviour* of that method. If the behaviour of a method is complex, then it will also be worthwhile spending time on designing the instructions that make up the method. When you sketch out the code for your methods, you don't want to have to worry about the finer details of the Java compiler such as declaring variables, adding semi-colons and using the right brackets. Very often a general purpose "coding language" can be used for this purpose that conveys the meaning of each instruction without worrying too much about a specific language syntax.

Code expressed in this way is often referred to as **pseudocode**. The following is an example of pseudocode that could have been developed for the main method of program 2.3:

```
BEGIN
  DISPLAY program title
  DISPLAY prompt for price
  ENTER price
  DISPLAY prompt for tax
  ENTER tax
  SET price TO price * (1 + tax/100)
  DISPLAY new price
  PAUSE with message
END
```

Note that these pseudocode instructions are not intended to be typed in and compiled as they do not meet the syntax rules of any particular programming language. So, exactly how you write these instructions is up to you: there is no fixed syntax for them. However, each instruction conveys a well-understood programming concept and can easily be translated into a given programming language. Reading these instructions you should be able to see how each line would be coded in Java.

Wouldn't it be much easier to write your main method if you have pseudocode like this to follow! In future, when we present complex methods to you we will do so by presenting their logic using pseudocode.

Tutorial exercises

1. Why are the *scalar types* of Java so called?
2. Consider the following attempt at declaring a variable to store the total number of passengers on a bus:

```
double total number of passengers;
```

   (a) For what reason will this instruction not compile ?
   (b) After amending the instruction so that it will compile, what other changes might you make to this instruction?
3. A warehouse receives orders for goods from one of its 10 outlets (each outlet is identified by a letter). The warehouse needs to know the item number ordered, the price of each item, the number of items required, and the outlet to which the item is to be sent. A covering slip is then prepared as follows:

```
                    ***ORDER SLIP***


     item code                        2145
     item price                       20.5
     quantity in stock                10


     TOTAL COST                       205.0


     send to base                     B
```

Declare variables for each of the five items listed above.

4. Design a program that would print an order slip as given in question 3 above. The program should allow the user to enter the item code and price, the quantity in stock and the base to which the items should be delivered, before printing an appropriate order slip.

5. Explain which, if any, of the following lines would result in a compiler error:

```
int x = 75.5;
double y = 75;
```

6. Which of the following items of data should be declared as a constant?
   - the temperature in a room;
   - the number of months in a year;
   - the distance of the Earth from the Sun;
   - the average distance of the Earth from the Sun;
   - the winning jackpot in a lottery;
   - the population of Asia.

7. A group of students has been told to get into teams of a specific size for their coursework. Use pseudocode to design a program that prompts for the number of students in the group and the size of the teams to be formed, and displays how many teams can be formed and how many students are left without a team.

8. Identify and correct the errors in program 2.4 below, that prompts for the user's age and then attempts to work out the year in which the user was born.

PROGRAM 2.4

```
public class SomeProg
{
  public static void main ()
  {
    final int CURRENT YEAR;
    int age;
    System.out.print("How old are you this year ? ");
    Age = EasyIn.getDouble();
    System.out.println("I think you' were born in " +
                          CURRENT YEAR-age);
    EasyIn.pause("Press <Enter> to quit");
  }
}
```

9. What would be the final output from program 2.5 if the user entered the number 10?

PROGRAM 2.5

```
public class Calculate
{
  public static void main(String[] args)
  {
    int num1, num2;
    num2 = 6;
    System.out.print("Enter value ");
    num1 = EasyIn.getInt();
    num1 = num1 + 2;
    num2 = num1 / num2;
    System.out.println("result = " + num2);
    EasyIn.pause();
  }
}
```

Practical work

1. Implement the program you designed in tutorial question 4.
2. Write and run the corrected version of program 2.4.
3. Implement the program you designed in tutorial question 7.
4. Write and run program 2.5 to check your answer to tutorial question 9.
5. Recently, the European Union has decreed that all traders in the UK sell their goods by the Kilo and not by the Pound (1 Kilo = 2.2 pounds). The following pseudocode has been arrived at in order to carry out this conversion:

```
BEGIN
   DISPLAY prompt for value in pounds
   ENTER value in pounds
   convert value in pounds to value in kilos
   DISPLAY value in kilos
   PAUSE
END
```

Implement this program, remembering to declare any variables that are necessary.

TAKING CONTROL

3.1 Introduction

One of the most rewarding aspects of writing and running a program is knowing that it is *you* who have control over the computer. But looking back at the programs you have already written, just how much control do you actually have? Certainly, it was you who decided upon which instructions to include in your programs but *the order in which these instructions were executed was not* under your control. These instructions were always executed in **sequence**, that is one after the other, from top to bottom.

At first sight this might not seem a problem. After all, why would you need to execute your instructions in any other order? You will soon find that there are numerous instances when this order of execution is too restrictive and you will want to have much more control over the order in which instructions are executed.

3.2   *Selection*

Very often you will want your programs to make *choices among* different courses of action. For example, a program processing requests for airline tickets could have the following choices to make:

- display the price of the seats requested;
- display a list of alternative flights;
- display a message saying that no flights are available to that destination.

A program that can make choices can behave *differently* each time it is run, whereas programs in which instructions are just executed in sequence behave the *same* each time they are run.

As we have already mentioned, unless you indicate otherwise, program instructions are always executed in sequence. **Selection**, however, is a method of program control in which a choice can be made among which instructions to execute. In Java there are three main forms of selection you may use:

- an **if** statement;
- an **if** . . . **else** statement;
- a **switch** statement.

3.2.1   The '**if**' statement

During program execution it is not always appropriate to execute *every* instruction. For example, consider the following simple code fragment that welcomes customers queuing up for a roller-coaster ride:

```
System.out.println("How old are you?");
age = EasyIn.getInt();
System.out.println("Hello Junior!");
System.out.println("Enjoy your ride");
```

As you can see, there are four instructions in this code fragment. Remember that at the moment these instructions will be executed in sequence, from top to bottom. Consider the following interaction with this program:

> *How old are you?*
> **10**
> *Hello Junior!*
> *Enjoy your ride*

This looks fine but the message "*Hello Junior!*" is only meant for children. Now let's assume that someone older comes along and interacts with this program as follows:

How old are you?
45
Hello Junior!
Enjoy your ride

The message "*Hello Junior!*", while flattering, might not be appropriate in this case! In other words, it is not always appropriate to execute the instruction:

```
System.out.println("Hello Junior!");
```

What is required is a way of *deciding* (while the program is running) whether or not to execute this instruction. In effect this instruction needs to be *protected* so that it is *only executed when appropriate*. What would be ideal would be if we could say something like the following:

```
System.out.println("How old are you?");
age = EasyIn.getInt();
IF age is that of a child
BEGIN
   System.out.println("Hello Junior!");
END
System.out.println("Enjoy your ride");
```

In the above, we have emboldened the lines that have been added to protect the "*Hello Junior!*" instruction. Actually these emboldened lines are not quite valid Java syntax; they are therefore to be read as lines of *pseudocode*. We will replace these pseudocode lines with appropriate Java syntax in a while, but for now let's look at the code fragment above in a bit more detail.

It is important to understand that in this code fragment *there are still only the same four instructions*. The emboldened lines that have been added are not to be read as additional *instructions*, they are simply a means *to control the flow of the existing* instructions. The emboldened lines say, in effect, that the instruction to display the message "*Hello Junior!*" should only be executed if the age entered is that of a child.

This then is an example of the form of control known as *selection*. At the moment we have used pseudocode lines to implement this selection. Let's now look at how to code these lines in Java.

This form of selection in Java involves the use of a **boolean condition**. A boolean condition is one that always evaluates to **true** or **false**. Examples of boolean conditions in everyday language are:

- this password is valid;
- there is an empty seat on the plane;
- all students in this group have passed their exams.

When the boolean condition evaluates to **true** the conditional instruction is executed, otherwise the conditional instruction is skipped. This boolean condition is combined with the reserved Java keyword **if** to implement selection as follows:

```
if (/* boolean condition goes here */)
{
  // conditional instruction(s) go here
}
```

Notice that the boolean condition must *always* be enclosed in round brackets. Notice also that more than one conditional instruction can be protected by the **if** and that all these instructions should be enclosed in curly brackets.[1]

One way to think of a boolean condition is as a *test*. In our example we are testing whether or not the age entered is that of a child.

If we assume that a child is someone less than 13 years of age, we can rewrite the initial set of instructions to include an **if** statement around the "*Hello Junior!*" message with the test (**age < 13**) as follows:

```
System.out.println("How old are you?");
age = EasyIn.getInt();
if (age < 13)// test
{
  System.out.print("Hello Junior!");
}
System.out.println("Enjoy your ride");
```

Now the message "*Hello Junior!*" will only be executed if the test is **true**, otherwise it will be skipped (see figure 3.1).

For example, let's assume we run this program again with the same values entered as before. First, the child approaches the ride:

> *How old are you?*
> **10**
> *Hello Junior!*
> *Enjoy your ride*

In this case, the condition has allowed the "*Hello Junior!*" message to be displayed as the age entered is less than 13. Now the adult approaches the ride:

> *How old are you?*
> **45**
> *Enjoy your ride*

[1] Strictly speaking, if there is only a single instruction then it does not need to be surrounded by curly brackets.

In this case the condition has not allowed the given instruction to be executed as the associated test was not **true**. The message is skipped and the program continues with the following instruction to display "*Enjoy your ride*". As we have already mentioned, more than one instruction can be covered by an **if** statement.

For example, program 3.1 not only displays a welcoming message to customers waiting for a ride but also displays the price of a ticket (6.25 for adults, 2.75 for children under the age of 13).

PROGRAM 3.1

```
public class RollerCoaster
{
  public static void main(String[] args)
  {
    int age;
    double price = 6.75; // set standard price of ticket
    System.out.println("How old are you?");
    age = EasyIn.getInt();
    if (age < 13) // condition
    { // conditional instructions
      System.out.print("Hello Junior!");
      price = 2.75; // overwrite standard price with child price
    }
    // remaining instructions
    System.out.println("Ticket price is " + price);
    System.out.println("Enjoy your ride");
    EasyIn.pause();
  }
}
```

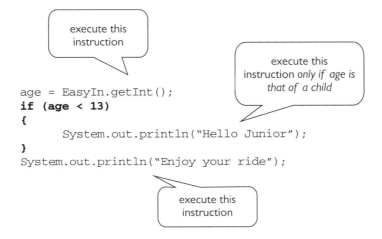

Fig 3.1   The 'if' statement allows a choice to be made in programs

Here is a sample program run when the condition is **true**:

```
How old are you?
12
Hello Junior!
Ticket price is 2.75
Enjoy your ride
```

Here is another sample run when the condition is **false**:

```
How old are you?
25
Ticket price is 6.75
Enjoy your ride
```

3.2.2   The 'if . . . else' statement

Using the **if** statement in the way that we have done so far has allowed us to build the idea of a choice into our programs. In fact, the **if** statement made one of two choices before continuing with the remaining instructions in the program:

- execute the conditional instructions, or
- do not execute the conditional instructions.

The second option amounts to "do nothing". Rather than do nothing if the condition is **false**, an extended version of an **if** statement exists in Java to state an alternative course of action. This extended form of selection is the **if . . . else** statement. As the name implies, the instructions to be executed if the condition is **false** are preceded by the Java keyword **else** as follows:

```
if ( /* test goes here */ )
{
  // instruction(s) if test is true go here
}
else
{
  // instruction(s) if test is false go here
}
```

This is often referred to as a **double-branched** selection as there are strictly two alternative groups of instructions, whereas a single **if** statement is often referred to as a **single-branched** selection. Program 3.2 illustrates the use of a double-branched selection.

PROGRAM 3.2

```
public class DisplayResult
{
  public static void main(String[] args)
  {
    int mark;
    System.out.println("What exam mark did you get?");
    mark = EasyIn.getInt();
    if (mark > 39)
    { // executed when test is true
      System.out.println("Congratulations, you passed");
    }
    else
    { // executed when test is false
      System.out.println("I'm sorry, but you failed");
    }
    System.out.println("Good luck with your other exams");
    EasyIn.pause();
  }
}
```

Program 3.2 checks a student's exam mark and tells the student whether or not he or she has passed (gained a mark over 39), before displaying a good luck message on the screen. Let's examine this program a bit more closely.

Prior to the **if** . . . **else** statement the following lines are executed in sequence:

```
int mark;
System.out.println("What exam mark did you get?");
mark = EasyIn.getInt();
```

Then the following condition is tested as part of the **if** . . . **else** statement:

```
(mark > 39)
```

When this condition is **true** the following line is executed:

```
System.out.println("Congratulations, you passed");
```

When the condition is **false**, however, the following line is executed *instead*:

```
System.out.println("I'm sorry, but you failed");
```

Finally, whichever path was chosen the program continues by executing the remaining lines in sequence:

```
System.out.println("Good luck with your other exams");
EasyIn.pause();
```

The **if** . . . **else** form of control has allowed us to choose from two alternative courses of action. Here is a sample program run:

> *What exam mark did you get?*
> **52**
> *Congratulations, you passed*
> *Good luck with your other exams*

Here is another sample run where a different course of action is chosen.

> *What exam mark did you get?*
> **35**
> *I'm sorry, but you failed*
> *Good luck with your other exams*

Before we move on we should make clear that the instructions within **if** and **if** . . . **else** statements can themselves be *any* legal Java instructions. In particular they could contain other **if** or **if** . . . **else** statements. This form of control is referred to as **nesting**.

As an example, consider program 3.3, which is a variation on program 3.2 that not only determines whether or not a student has passed an exam, but also whether or not that student has earned a distinction by getting a mark of 70 or over.

PROGRAM 3.3

```
public class DisplayResult2
{
  public static void main(String[] args)
  {
    int mark;
    System.out.println("What exam mark did you get?");
    mark = EasyIn.getInt();
    if (mark > 69)   // first test
    {
      System.out.println("Congratulations, you have a distinction");
    }
    else
    {
      if (mark > 39) // second test
      {
        System.out.println("You have passed");
      }
```

```
      else // when both tests are false
      {
          System.out.println("I'm sorry, you failed");
      }
   }
   System.out.println("Good luck with your other exams");
   EasyIn.pause();
  }
}
```

Once again this program uses an **if** . . . **else** statement to control program flow:

```
if (mark > 69)
{
   System.out.println("Congratulations, you have a distinction");
}
else
{
    // second group of instructions go here
}
```

Now when the boolean condition (**mark > 69**) is tested and found to be **true** the message *"Congratulations, you have a distinction"* is displayed. But when this condition is **false** and the mark is not a distinction, the **else** branch is reached. Look closely at the instructions inside this **else** branch.

```
  else
  {
    if (mark > 39)
    {
      System.out.println("You have passed");
    }
    else
    {
      System.out.println("I'm sorry, you failed");
    }
  }
```

The instructions associated with this **else** branch are themselves another **if** . . . **else** selection! This is perfectly legal as we can write any Java instructions here. All we are doing is saying that we would like to make *another* choice in our program at this stage.

Table 3.1 The comparison operators of Java		
Comparison operator	**Meaning**	**Java operator**
=	equal to	==
≠	not equal to	!=
<	less than	<
>	greater than	>
≥	greater than or equal to	>=
≤	less than or equal to	<=

Having already decided that the mark cannot be a distinction we are left to decide whether or not the mark is in fact a pass or a fail. With two choices to make, obviously we would use another **if** . . . **else** statement!

Once the correct choice has been made the program continues with the remaining instructions:

```
System.out.println("Good luck with your other exams");
EasyIn.pause();
```

Here is one sample run:

> *What exam mark did you get?*
> **32**
> *I'm sorry, you failed*
> *Good luck with your other exams*

Can you follow the program instructions to see how these results were arrived at? Run through the program instructions again and assume that the user types in 69. What results would you see on the screen then?

Just before we move on to look at another form of selection in Java, you might be wondering why we used the tests (mark > 39) and (mark > 69) rather than (mark ≥ 40) and (mark ≥ 60). The reason is that the symbol '≥' (greater than or equal to) cannot be used in a Java program as you cannot find it on a keyboard and we haven't yet showed you what the correct Java symbol is!

The alternative symbol in Java to represent this comparison operator is '>='; table 3.1 shows all the Java comparison operator symbols.

Since comparison operators give an answer of **true** or **false** they are often used in tests such as those we have been discussing. Note that a double equals (==) is used to check for equality in Java and not the single equals (=) which as you know is used for assignment.

For example, to check whether or not an angle is a right angle or not the following test could be used:

```
if (angle == 90) // note the use of the double equals
{
   System.out.println("This is a right angle");
}
```

3.2.3 The 'switch' statement

Although nested **if** statements can be used to make several choices, they can begin to make your code look a bit messy. Just look at program 3.3 for example! When they are needed they can be laid out so that the code is a bit more readable. Rather than indent each nested **if** they are often written as follows:

```
if (mark > 69)
{
   System.out.println("Great, you have a distinction");
}
else if (mark > 39) // nested selection on same line
{
   System.out.println("You have passed");
}
else
{
   System.out.println("I'm sorry, you failed");
}
```

As you are no doubt aware, students are always forgetting what time their study sessions are. To help them, consider program 3.4 which asks a student to enter his or her tutorial group (A, B, or C) and then displays on the screen the time of the software lab.

PROGRAM 3.4

```java
public class Timetable
{
  public static void main(String[] args)
  {
    char group; // to store the tutorial group
    System.out.println("***Lab Times***"); // display header
    System.out.println("Enter your group (A,B,C)");
    group = EasyIn.getChar();
    // check tutorial group and display appropriate time
    if (group == 'A')
    {
      System.out.print("10.00 a.m"); // lab time for group A
    }
    else if (group == 'B')
    {
      System.out.print("1.00 p.m"); // lab time for group B
    }
    else if (group == 'C')
    {
      System.out.print("11.00 a.m"); // lab time for group C
    }
    else
    {
      System.out.print("No such group"); //invalid group entered
    }
    EasyIn.pause();
  }
}
```

This program is a little bit different from the ones before because it includes some basic **error checking**. That is, it does not *assume* that the user of this program will always type the *expected* values. If the wrong group (not A, B or C) is entered, an error message is displayed saying "*No such group*".

```java
// valid groups checked here
else // if this 'else' is reached, group entered must be invalid
{
  System.out.print("No such group"); // error message
}
```

Error checking like this is a good habit to get into.

This use of nested selections is okay up to a point, but when the number of options becomes large the program can again look very untidy. Fortunately, this type of selection can also be implemented in Java with another form of control: a **switch** statement. This is demonstrated in program 3.5.

```
public class TimetableWithSwitch
{
  public static void main(String[] args)
  {
    char group;
    System.out.println("***Lab Times***");
    System.out.println("Enter your group (A,B,C)");
    group = EasyIn.getChar();
    switch(group) // beginning of switch
    {
      case 'A': System.out.print("10.00 a.m");break;
      case 'B': System.out.print("1.00 p.m");break;
      case 'C': System.out.print("11.00 a.m");break;
      default: System.out.print("No such group");
    } //end of switch
    EasyIn.pause();
  }
}
```

As you can see, this looks a lot neater. The **switch** statement works in exactly the same way as a set of nested **if** statements, but is more compact and readable. A **switch** statement may be used when

- only one variable is being checked in each condition (in this case every condition involves checking the variable group);
- the check involves specific values of that variable (e.g. 'A', 'B') and not ranges (for example >39).

As can be seen from the example above, the keyword **case** is used to precede a possible value of the variable that is being checked. There may be many **case** statements in a single **switch** statement. The general form of a **switch** statement in Java is given as follows:

```
switch(someVariable)
{
  case value1: // instructions(s) to be executed
               break;
  case value2: // instructions(s) to be executed
               break;
  // more values to be tested can be added
  default: // instruction(s) for default case
}
```

where

- `someVariable` is the name of the variable being tested (this variable is usually of type **int** or **char** but it may also be of type **byte** or **short**);
- `value1`, `value2` . . . etc. are the possible values of that variable;
- **break** is an optional command that forces the program to skip the rest of the **switch** statement;
- **default** is an optional (last) case which allows you to code instructions that deal with the possibility of none of the cases above being **true**.

The **break** statement is important because it means that once a matching case is found, the program can skip the rest of the cases below. If it is not added, not only will the instructions associated with the matching case be executed but, also, all the instructions associated with the all the cases below it. Notice that the last set of instructions does not need a **break** statement as they have no other cases to skip.

3.3   *Iteration*

So far we have considered sequence and selection as forms of program control. One of the advantages of using computers rather than humans to carry out tasks is that they can repeat those tasks over and over again without ever getting tired. With a computer we do not have to worry about mistakes creeping in because of fatigue, whereas humans would need a break to stop their becoming sloppy or careless when carrying out repetitive tasks over a long period of time. Neither sequence nor selection allows us to carry out this kind of control in our programs.

Iteration is the form of program control that allows us to instruct the computer to carry out a task over and over again by repeating a section of code. For this reason this form of control is often also referred to as **repetition**. The programming structure that is used to control this repetition is often called a **loop**. There are three types of loops in Java:

- **for** loop;
- **while** loop;
- **do** . . . **while** loop.

3.3.1   The 'for' loop

Consider a program that needs to display a square of stars (five by five) on the screen as follows:

```
* * * * *
* * * * *
* * * * *
* * * * *
* * * * *
```

This could be achieved with five output statements executed in sequence:

```
System.out.println("*****");
System.out.println("*****");
System.out.println("*****");
System.out.println("*****");
System.out.println("*****");
```

While this would work, all the program is really doing is executing the same instruction five times. Writing out the same line many times is somewhat wasteful of our precious time as programmers. Imagine what would happen if we wanted a square 40 by 40!

Rather than write out this instruction five times we would prefer to write it out once and get the program to *repeat that same line* five times. What we would require is some form of control as follows:

```
REPEAT 5 times // try this?
{
    System.out.println("*****");
}
```

Unfortunately the emboldened expression "REPEAT 5 times" is not a valid command in Java. Instead, if we wish to repeat a section of code a fixed number of times (five in the example above) we would use Java's **for** loop.

The **for** loop is usually used in conjunction with a **counter**. A counter is just another variable (usually integer) that has to be created. We use it to keep track of how many times we have been through the loop so far. We do this by carrying out three tasks:

1. Set the counter to some initial value (usually zero or one).
2. Check the value of the counter before each new repetition of the loop in order to determine when to stop.
3. Change the value of the counter (usually by adding one to the counter) each time it goes around the loop to indicate that another repetition has occurred.

Task number one is usually referred to as setting the **start condition** of the loop.

Task number two sets the **boolean condition** that we met when discussing selections. When used with loops, this condition is often referred to as the **while condition** as the code continues to loop *while* this condition is **true**.

Task number three is referred to as the **action** that takes place at the end of each repetition of the loop.

These items are assembled as follows to construct the **for** loop:

```
for(/* start condition */ ; /* while condition */ ; /* action */)
{
  // instruction(s) to be repeated go here
}
```

Let's assume that a variable called i has been declared for use as a loop counter:

```
int i;
```

We can construct a loop to display a square of stars as follows:

```
for(i = 1; i <= 5; i = i+1)
{
  System.out.println("*****");
}
```

Note that we started our loop counter at one $(i = 1)$. Each time the loop repeats we add one to the counter, and we continue repeating while the counter is less than or equal to five. This is one way of saying "repeat 5 times" in Java. Note that if we had chosen to start the loop counter at zero $(i = 0)$ then our **while condition** would have been $(i < 5)$ and not $(i <= 5)$.

The action associated with this **for** loop is a very common one: add one to the loop counter. It is so common that a short hand exists for this expression in Java:

```
i++;
```

The operator $++$ is known as the **increment operator** of Java and can be used *whenever* you wish to add one to a value. Similarly there exists a **decrement operator** $(--)$ that allows you to reduce the value of a variable by one. Thus

```
i--;
```

is equivalent to the following assignment:

```
i = i - 1;
```

As an example of the use of this operator, program 3.6 prints out the numbers from 10 down to 1.

PROGRAM 3.6

```java
public class Countdown
{
  public static void main(String[] args)
  {
    int i; // declare loop counter
    System.out.println("***Numbers from 10 to 1***");
    for (i=10; i>=1; i--) // counter moving from 10 down to 1
    {
      System.out.println(i);
    }
    EasyIn.pause();
  }
}
```

Note that it is perfectly acceptable to refer to the loop counter inside the loop body as we did in the body of the **for** loop of program 3.6:

```java
System.out.println(i); // counter 'i' used here
```

When you do this, however, be careful not to *change* the loop counter within the loop body as this can throw your loop condition off track!

Finally, before moving on to look at another form of loop in Java, a reminder that the loop body can contain any number of instructions, including another loop. In other words, you may nest loops just as you nested **if**s. As an example of this, consider again the **for** loop we constructed to display a square of stars.

```java
for(i = 1; i <= 5; i = i+1)
{
  System.out.println("*****");
}
```

The body of this loop has an output statement that displays five stars on the screen in a row. We could, if we had wanted, have displayed only a *single* star on the screen as follows:

```java
System.out.print("*");
```

Now, to get the program to display a row of five of these stars we could put this statement in another loop. We will need another loop counter for this new loop. Let's assume we have declared an integer variable 'j' for this purpose. The inner loop would look like this:

```
for (j = 1; j<=5; j++)
{
   System.out.print("*");
}
```

Now to display our square:

```
for(i = 1; i <= 5; i++) // outer loop control
{
   for (j = 1; j<=5; j++) // inner loop control
   {
     System.out.print("*");
   } // inner loop ends here
   System.out.println();
} // outer loop ends here
```

For now let's look at how the control in this program flows.

1. The outer loop has its start condition set (i =1).
2. The while condition (i <= 5) of the outer loop is then checked and found to be **true** so the body of the outer loop is entered.

Now, the body of the outer loop itself contains a loop. We have already told you that when any loop is entered, instructions in the body of that loop are executed. This means that the *entire* inner loop is executed before we finish one cycle of the outer loop. So we effectively print five stars out in a row (moving the inner j counter from one through to five in the process) giving us the following output:

        *****

3. After completing the inner loop the program moves the cursor to a new line, then returns to the action of the outer loop (i++).

Steps two and three are then repeated until the **while condition** of the outer loop is made **false**. Notice that it is also possible to declare the variables i and j within the round brackets of the **for** loop. This would give us the following version:

```
for(int i = 1; i <= 5; i++) // counter 'i' declared in loop control
{
   for (int j = 1; j<=5; j++) // counter 'j' declared in loop control
   {
     System.out.print("*");
   }
   System.out.println();
}
```

Finally, although a **for** loop is used to repeat something a fixed number of times, you don't necessarily need to know this fixed number when you are writing the program. This fixed number could be a value given to you by the user of your program, for example. Program 3.7 asks the user to determine the size of the square of stars.

PROGRAM 3.7

```
public class DisplayStars
{
  public static void main(String[] args)
  {
    int num; // to hold user response
    // prompt and get user response
    System.out.println("Size of square?");
    num = EasyIn.getInt();
    // display square
    for(int i = 1; i <= num; i++) // loop fixed to 'num'
    {
      for (int j = 1; j<=num; j++) // loop fixed to 'num'
      {
        System.out.print("*");
      }
      System.out.println();
    }
    EasyIn.pause();
  }
}
```

In this program you cannot tell from the code exactly how many times the loops will iterate, but you can say that they will iterate num number of times – whatever the user may have entered for 'num''. So in this sense the loop is still fixed. Here is a sample run of program 3.7:

```
Size of square?
8
* * * * * * * *
* * * * * * * *
* * * * * * * *
* * * * * * * *
* * * * * * * *
* * * * * * * *
* * * * * * * *
* * * * * * * *
```

3.3.2 The 'while' loop

As we have already said, much of the power of computers comes from the ability to ask them to carry out repetitive tasks, so iteration is a very important form of program control. The **for** loop is an often used to implement fixed repetitions.

Sometimes, however, a repetition is required that is *not fixed* and a **for** loop is not the best one to use in such a case. Consider the following scenarios, for example:

- a racing game that repeatedly moves a car around a track until the car crashes;
- a ticket issuing program that repeatedly offers tickets for sale until the user chooses to quit the program;
- a password checking program that does not let a user into an application until he or she enters the right password.

Each of the above cases involves repetition; however, the number of repetitions is not fixed but depends upon some condition. The **while** loop offers one type of non-fixed iteration. The syntax for constructing this loop in Java is as follows:

```
while ( /* test goes here */ )
{
   // instruction(s) to be repeated go here
}
```

As you can see, this loop is much simpler to construct than a **for** loop. As this loop is not repeating a fixed number of times, there is no need to create a counter to keep track of the number of repetitions. This means there is no need for a start condition or an end of loop action.

When might this kind of loop be useful? The first example we will explore is the use of the **while** loop to check data that is input by the user. Checking input data for errors is referred to as **input validation**.

For example, look back at program 3.2, which asked the user to enter an exam mark:

```
System.out.println("What exam mark did you get?");
mark = EasyIn.getInt();
if (mark > 39)
// rest of code goes here
```

The mark that is entered should never be greater than 100. At the time we assumed that the user would enter the mark correctly. However, good programmers never make this assumption!

Before accepting the mark that is entered and moving on to the next stage of the program, it is good practice to check that the mark entered is indeed a valid one. If it is not, then the user will be allowed to enter the mark again. This will go on until the user enters a valid mark.

We can express this using pseudocode as follows:

```
DISPLAY prompt for mark
ENTER mark
KEEP REPEATING WHILE mark typed in is > 100
BEGIN
   DISPLAY error message to user
   ENTER mark
END
// REST OF PROGRAM HERE
```

This is an example of an iteration as the user may make many errors. However, the number of iterations is not fixed as it is impossible to say how many, if any, mistakes the user will make.

This sounds like a job for the **while** loop!

```
System.out.println("What exam mark did you get?");
mark = EasyIn.getInt();
while (mark > 100) // check for invalid input
{
   // display error message plus allow for re-input
   System.out.println("invalid mark: Re-enter!");
   mark = EasyIn.getInt();
}
if (mark > 39)
// rest of code goes here
```

Actually, the mark should also never be less than zero. So an invalid input is a mark that's too high or too low. This requires a more complicated test condition; we want our test condition to say (mark > 100 OR mark < 0).

The word 'OR' in the previous sentence is not a valid Java word. We actually have to write the following symbol:

||

Symbols like OR and AND, which are used with boolean conditions, are known as **logical** (or **boolean**) **operators**. Table 3.2 lists the Java counterparts to the three most common of these logical operators. We will see many examples of their use as we progress through the book.

Table 3.2 The logical operators of Java	
Logical operator	**Java counterpart**
AND	&&
OR	||
NOT	!

With this in mind we can re-write the **while** loop as follows:

```
while (mark < 0 || mark > 100)
{
  // instruction(s) to be repeated go here
}
```

Program 3.8 below shows the whole of the previous program re-written out to include the input validation. Notice how this works – we ask the user for the mark; if it is within the acceptable range the **while** loop is not entered and we move past it to the other instructions. But if the mark entered is less than zero or greater than 100 we enter the loop, display an error message and ask the user to input the mark again. This continues until the mark is within the required range.

PROGRAM 3.8

```
public class DisplayResult3
{
  public static void main(String[] args)
  {
    int mark;
    System.out.println("What exam mark did you get?");
    mark = EasyIn.getInt();
    // input validation
    while (mark < 0 || mark > 100) // check if mark is invalid
    {
      // display error message
      System.out.println("Invalid mark: please re-enter");
      // mark must be re-entered
      mark = EasyIn.getInt();
    }
    // by this point loop is finished and mark will be valid
    if (mark > 39)
    {
      // executed when test is true
      System.out.println("Congratulations, you passed");
    }
    else
    {
      // executed when test is false
      System.out.println("I'm sorry, but you failed");
    }
    System.out.println("Good luck with your other exams");
    EasyIn.pause();
  }
}
```

Here is a sample test run:

```
What exam mark did you get?
101
Invalid mark: please re-enter
-10
Invalid mark: please re-enter
10
I'm sorry, but you failed
Good luck with your other exams
```

3.3.3 The do . . . while loop

There is one more loop construct in Java that we need to tell you about: the **do** . . . **while** loop.

The **do** . . . **while** loop is another variable loop construct, but unlike the **while** loop, the **do** . . . **while** loop has its while condition at the *end* of the loop rather than at the *beginning*.

The syntax of a **do** . . . **while** loop is given below:

```
do
{
   // instruction(s) to be repeated go here
}while ( /* test goes here */ ); // note the semi-colon
```

You are probably wondering what difference it makes if the while condition is at the end or the beginning of the loop. Well, there is one subtle difference. If the while condition is at the end of the loop, the loop will iterate *at least once*. If the condition is at the beginning of the loop, however, there is a possibility that the condition will be false to begin with and the loop is never executed. A **while** loop therefore executes *zero or more times* whereas a **do** . . . **while** loop executes *one or more times*.

To make this a little clearer, look back at the **while** loop we just showed you for validating exam marks. If the user entered a valid mark initially (such as 66), the test to trap an invalid mark (mark <0 || mark > 100) would be **false** and the loop would be skipped altogether. A **do** . . . **while** loop would not be appropriate here as the possibility of never getting into the loop should be left open.

When would a **do** . . . **while** loop be suitable? Well, any time you wish to code a non-fixed loop that must execute at least once. Usually, this would be the case when the **while** condition can be tested only *after* the loop has been entered.

Think about all the programs you have written so far. Once the program has done its job it terminates – if you want it to perform the same task again you have to go through the whole procedure of running that program again.

In many cases a better solution would be to put your whole program in a loop that keeps repeating until the user chooses to quit your program. This would involve asking the user each time if he or she would like to continue repeating your program, or to stop.

A **for** loop would not be the best loop to choose here as this is more useful when the number of repetitions can be predicted. A **while** loop would be difficult to use as the test that checks the user's response to a question cannot be made at the beginning of the loop. The answer is to move the test to the end of the loop and use a **do . . . while** loop as follows:

```
char response; // variable to hold user response
do// place code in loop
{ // program instructions go here
  System.out.println("another go (y/n)?");
  response = EasyIn.getChar(); // get user reply
} while (response == 'y'); // test must be at the end
```

A simple program that uses this technique is developed in tutorial question 3. However, another way to allow a program to be run repeatedly using a **do . . . while** loop is to include a menu of options within the loop (this was very common in the days before windows and mice!). One of the options in the menu list would be the option to quit, and this option is checked in the while condition of the loop. Program 3.9 is a reworking of program 3.5 using this technique.

PROGRAM 3.9

```
public class TimetableWithLoop
{
  public static void main(String[] args)
  {
    char group, response;
    System.out.println("***Lab Times***");
    do // put code in loop
    { // offer menu of options
      System.out.println(); // create a blank line
      System.out.println("[1] TIME FOR GROUP A");
      System.out.println("[2] TIME FOR GROUP B");
      System.out.println("[3] TIME FOR GROUP C");
      System.out.println("[4] QUIT PROGRAM");
      System.out.print("enter choice [1,2,3,4]: ");
      response = EasyIn.getChar(); // get response
      System.out.println(); // create a blank line
      switch(response) // process response
      {
        case '1': System.out.println("10.00 a.m");break;
        case '2': System.out.println("1.00 p.m");break;
        case '3': System.out.println("11.00 a.m ");break;
        case '4': System.out.println("Goodbye");break;
        default: System.out.println("Options 1-4 only!");
      }
    } while (response != '4'); // test for Quit option
  }
}
```

Here is a sample test run of this program:

```
***Lab Times***
[1] TIME FOR GROUP A
[2] TIME FOR GROUP B
[3] TIME FOR GROUP C
[4] QUIT PROGRAM
enter choice [1,2,3,4]: 2

1.00 p.m

[1] TIME FOR GROUP A
[2] TIME FOR GROUP B
[3] TIME FOR GROUP C
[4] QUIT PROGRAM
enter choice [1,2,3,4]: 5

Options 1-4 only!

[1] TIME FOR GROUP A
[2] TIME FOR GROUP B
[3] TIME FOR GROUP C
[4] QUIT PROGRAM
enter choice [1,2,3,4]: 1

10.00 a.m.

[1] TIME FOR GROUP A
[2] TIME FOR GROUP B
[3] TIME FOR GROUP C
[4] QUIT PROGRAM
enter choice [1,2,3,4]: 3

11.00 a.m.

[1] TIME FOR GROUP A
[2] TIME FOR GROUP B
[3] TIME FOR GROUP C
[4] QUIT PROGRAM
enter choice [1,2,3,4]: 4

Goodbye
```

Tutorial exercises

1. Consider the following Java program:

PROGRAM 3.10

```java
public class SomeProg
{
  public static void main(String [] args)
  {
    int x, i;
    System.out.print("Please Enter a number: ")
    x = EasyIn.getInt();
    for(i=1;i<=x;i++)
    {
      if (i%2 == 0)
      {
        System.out.println(i);
      }
    }
  }
}
```

What would be the output from this program if the user had entered a value of 10?

2. Which kind of loop would be the most suitable to use for the following purposes:
   (a) to validate a user's password?
   (b) to display the details of all the employees in a company?
   (c) to display the details of employees one by one till the user decides to quit?

3. Program 3.11 asks the user to enter two numbers and displays the sum of these two numbers. It then gives the user the opportunity to have another go or to quit the program; this continues until the user chooses to quit. Study the program, then answer the questions that follow:

PROGRAM 3.11

```java
public class Arithmetic
{
  public static void main(String[] args)
  {
    int num1, num2;
    char choice;
    do
    {
```

```
        System.out.print("Enter a number: ");
        num1 = EasyIn.getInt();
        System.out.print("Enter another number: ");
        num2 = EasyIn.getInt();
        System.out.println("The sum of the two numbers is "
                        + (num1 + num2));
        System.out.print("Do you want another go (y/n): ");
        choice = EasyIn.getChar();
    }while(choice == 'y');
  }
}
```

(a) What happens if the user presses a character other than 'y' or 'n' when asked if he or she wants another go?

(b) What happens if the user presses an upper case 'Y' in response to the question?

(c) How would you adapt the program so that the user would be given another go irrespective of whether or not an upper case or lower case 'y' is entered?

4. What is the purpose of a **default** statement in a **switch** command?

5. Consider a vending machine that offers the following options :

> [1] Get gum
> [2] Get chocolate
> [3] Get popcorn
> [4] Get juice
> [5] Display total sold

Design a program that continually allows users to select from these options. When options 1–4 are selected an appropriate message is to be displayed acknowledging their choice. For example, when option 3 is selected the following message could be displayed:

> Here is your popcorn

The program terminates when option 5 is selected, at which point the total number of each type of item sold is displayed. For example:

> 3 items of gum were sold
> 2 items of chocolate were sold
> 6 items of popcorn were sold
> 9 items of juice were sold

If an option other than 1–5 is entered an appropriate error message should be displayed, such as:

> Error, options 1- 5 only!

Practical work

1. Implement program in tutorial question 1 but give the user the option to either quit or rerun the program.
2. Type, compile and run program 3.11, and then
   (a) make the changes that you considered in tutorial question 3c;
   (b) instead of displaying the sum of the numbers, ask the user to enter the sum. Then, if the user answers correctly, a congratulatory message is displayed; if the user's answer is incorrect then the correct answer is displayed.
3. Implement the program you designed in tutorial question 5.
4. (a) Using a **for** loop, write a program that asks the user to type in three numbers and then displays the total of those numbers;
   (b) rewrite the program (using a **do** . . . **while** loop instead of a **for** loop) so that the user is allowed to type in numbers continually until he or she chooses to finish.
5. (a) Using a **for** loop, write a program that displays a "6 times" multiplication table; the output should look like this:

```
 1 × 6 =  6
 2 × 6 = 12
 3 × 6 = 18
 4 × 6 = 24
 5 × 6 = 30
 6 × 6 = 36
 7 × 6 = 42
 8 × 6 = 48
 9 × 6 = 54
10 × 6 = 60
11 × 6 = 66
12 × 6 = 72
```

   (b) Adapt the program so that instead of a "6 times" table, the user chooses which table is displayed.
   (c) Adapt the program further, so that the user can choose whether to have another go or to quit.

CLASSES AND OBJECTS

4.1 Introduction

Now at last it is time to find out what we really mean by this phrase *object-oriented*. We have been using it already, and hinting at what it is all about; and you have probably heard it being used in all sorts of contexts, since object-oriented development has become very popular over the course of the 1990s.

The object-oriented way of doing things is the most recent development in the building of software systems, and is concerned very much with the production of reusable components; it is arguable that the sophisticated graphical interfaces that are now universal would never have been developed without an object-oriented approach. Object-oriented development also lends itself to the Rapid Application Development approach that you learnt about in the first chapter, because it allows us to move much more smoothly between analysis and design. In addition, because of the technique of **encapsulation** or **information-hiding** that you will learn about soon, object-orientation allows us to build much more secure systems.

4.2 *What is object-orientation?*

First some background. As computers become more and more powerful the software needed to control them becomes more and more complex. Thirty or so years ago the demands on software developers were nothing compared to the demands on today's programmers. As the complexity of software increased it became clear that large, unstructured programs were becoming increasingly difficult to develop and that a **modular** approach was required, whereby programs were broken up into smaller units.

This was referred to as **structured** programming. Structured programming was the first attempt at formally modularizing program code. Now the program was no longer considered one large task, but a collection of smaller tasks (often called **procedures** or **functions** in programming languages). This is illustrated in figure 4.1. The main program is broken down into four tasks; the second task is broken down further into two tasks, and so on.

For some time this approach to modular design dealt adequately with the increased complexity of software. But then, with the rapid microchip advances of the 1980s and the growth of the Internet in the 1990s, the demands on software developers increased again and the structured approach was found to be deficient. The reason for this is that the approach focuses on the actions (functions) but not *the things acted on* − the data. The data becomes spread throughout the system in a very unstructured way (figure 4.2).

However, the *data* is central to the program's existence − so an approach such as that shown in figure 4.2 can lead to the following problems:

- data is subject to change by many functions, and data can therefore become unexpectedly corrupted, leading to unreliable programs that are difficult to debug;
- revising the data requires rewriting every function that interacts with it, leading to programs that are very difficult to maintain;
- functions and the data they act upon are not closely tied together, leading to code that is very difficult to reuse since there is a complex web of links to disentangle.

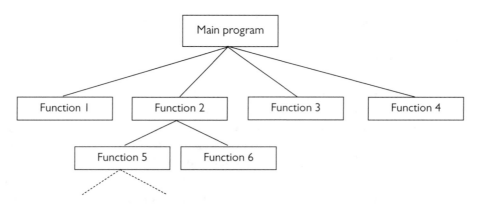

Fig 4.1   A structured approach to modular design

Let us assume, for example, that we wish to write a car-chase game and that we already have a driving game written. We may wish to use the cars from the first game in our new program. The code we are interested in using is not just the functions that control the car (brake, accelerate etc.) but also the data related to the car (speed, colour etc.).

The "old-fashioned" structured approach does not match well with our own view of the world. We do not see the world as a set of functions alone; the data that the functions act upon is equally important (as is the case in the car example above). The structured way of looking at things makes it difficult to conceptualize problems.

From these issues it became clear that functions and the data they act upon should be grouped together. This higher unit of organization was called an **object** (figure 4.3).

Closely related to the idea of an object is a **class**. A class is the blueprint from which objects are generated. In other words, if we have six cars in our car-chase game we do not need to define a car six times. We will define a car once (in a class) and then generate as many **objects** as we want from this class blueprint. In one program we may have many classes as we probably wish to generate many kinds of objects (cars, tracks, players etc.).

Object-oriented programming therefore consists of defining one or more classes that may interact with each other. To exploit the full power of object-orientation requires us to use an

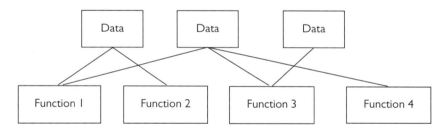

Fig 4.2   A complex web of links between data and functions arises in the structured approach

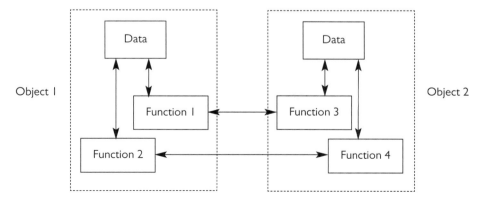

Fig 4.3   An object-oriented approach to modular design

object-oriented programming language. There are many object-oriented languages such as C++, SmallTalk, Eiffel, Object Pascal and of course Java!

4.3   Attributes and methods

We have seen that the term "object-oriented" means that we organize software as a collection of objects that incorporate both data and behaviour (the functions); objects belong to a **class**, which we can think of as the template for all the objects (and potential objects) that can belong to that class.

Let's consider another example, a Student class. The individual objects in that class could be John, Abdul, Ayotunde, Susan, Abiola and other students who will join the university in the future. We often describe the individual objects of the class as **instances** of the class.

Now that you know a little more about classes you are in a better position to understand what you learnt in the first chapter, namely that a class consists of:

- a set of **attributes** (the data);
- a set of **methods** which can access or change those attributes (the functions).

Together the attributes and methods are often referred to as the **members** of a class.

What might be the attributes and methods of a Student class? Let's keep it fairly simple and suggest five attributes, and two methods which we have specified in figure 4.4, using the UML notation that we introduced in the first chapter.

4.4   Encapsulation

As we shall see, when we design our classes we normally arrange things so that the attributes of an object can be manipulated only by methods of that object – in this way we "close off" our classes and protect the attributes from outside interference. This is referred to as **encapsulation**.

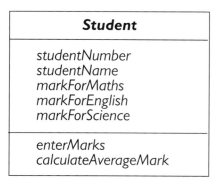

Fig 4.4   A Student class

Any object-oriented programming language w
class and restricting access to the members (th
class). The usual way of doing things is to defir
methods as **public**. By doing this we ensure t'
can be accessed is by the methods of that ob'
in this way encapsulation is achieved.

Let us think about our Student exampl
class for example – needed to know the
class sensibly then the only way that we
one of the methods. In this case the c
needed. An object of the StudentR'
method of a Student object. It could tʰᵉ
one object using another object's methods is a ᴅᵢ
and is therefore often referred to as **message passing**.

This is illustrated in figure 4.5, which shows an object of the ᵤ
a message to an object of the Student class, and getting a message back.

It is not necessary that there is a reply every time a message is sent. For exampₗₑ
class called Admin, which might provide methods for dealing with administrative functiᵤ
the system. An object of the Admin class might send a message to a Student object which calls
the enterMarks method. In this case the Admin object would need to call the enterMarks
method, and will need to *send* information to the method in order for it to be able to do its job.

This is shown in figure 4.6.

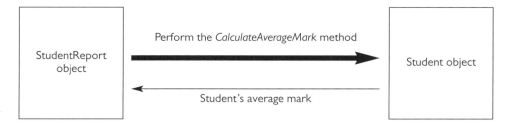

Fig 4.5   An object passing a message and getting a reply

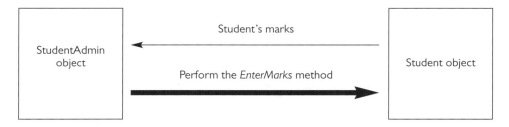

Fig 4.6   An object passing a message with the necessary information

is perfectly possible for a method both to receive information and to
back; or there could be cases where a method needs no information
just has to perform some internal function, which requires no data to be
see that any class method can be set up so that it can receive data or can send
, or neither. It is the methods that provide the means by which we can access
an object (by passing a message) and together they form the **interface** of the
ibing the interface, the crucial information that we have to specify is the type (or
ata that the methods can receive (the **inputs**) and the type of data they can send back
put).

important to understand here that the internal details of the methods of a class are
of any significance to other classes. The StudentReport class had no idea how the
lculateAverageMark method of the Student class did its job – all it cared about was
the result. This is important – it means that we can change the internal details of one part of a
system without affecting another part. This helps us make our systems more secure, and also
encourages us to re-use classes in other systems rather than starting from scratch each time.
These are some of the principal benefits of encapsulation.

4.5   *Classes and objects in Java*

You have already seen that all Java programs must be made up of classes, and now you can see
why. The notion of a class is fundamental to the object-oriented approach, and by declaring a
class in Java we are able to bring into being the classes that we identified when we analysed the
system. We can then declare the **instances** or **objects** that belong to that class; you will see how
to do that in a moment.

In this chapter, in order to help you understand the notion of encapsulation, we are going
to see how to use classes that have already been created; creating our own classes will be left
till the next chapter. You will see that we do not need to know very much about the details of
these classes – all we need to know about is the interface. The classes that you need can be
downloaded from the website or copied from the CD-ROM or chapter 5. In order to run the
programs we are developing in this chapter you don't need look at the detail of these classes,
you just have to download them and use them – that is what encapsulation is all about!

4.5.1   The *Oblong* class

Let's consider a situation in which we wanted a program that created and used oblongs; maybe
it is for the purposes of drawing oblongs on the screen, or for school children to use in order
to practise their understanding of geometry.

Instead of writing a new Oblong class it would be very useful if we could use a ready-made
class. We have prepared such a class (Oblong.java) for you and you can download it from the
website or copy it from the CD-ROM. We have of course made sure that the attributes of the
class are not directly accessible. In order to use the class you do not need to know the specific
names of the attributes, although you do need to know that they exist.

Table 4.1 The methods of the *Oblong* class			
Method	**Description**	**Inputs**	**Output**
setLength	Sets the value of the length attribute	An item of type **double**	None
setHeight	Sets the value of the height attribute	An item of type **double**	None
getLength	Sends back the value of the length attribute	None	An item of type **double**
getHeight	Sends back the value of the height attribute	None	An item of type **double**
calculateArea	Calculates and sends back the area of the oblong	None	An item of type **double**
calculatePerimeter	Calculates and sends back the perimeter of the oblong	None	An item of type **double**
Oblong	A special method called a **constructor** (see below)	Two items of data, both of type **double**, representing the length and height of the oblong respectively	

So, you need to be aware that any Oblong object can hold information about the length and the height of the oblong and that the type **double** is used for this data. An Oblong might also have other attributes that it uses for its own purpose, but anyone using the class doesn't need to know about this.

You also need to know what the class can do – its methods; but of course you do not need to know how these methods work. What you really need to know are the **inputs** and **outputs**. These are listed in table 4.1.

You can see from the table that one of the available methods is a special method called a **constructor**, *which always has the same name as the class*. When you create a new object this special method is always called; its function is to reserve some space in the computer's memory just big enough to hold the required object (in our case an object of the Oblong class). The person developing the class doesn't have to worry about defining the constructor if this is all that he or she wants the constructor to do. However, it is very common to find that you want the constructor to do a bit more than this when a new object is created. In the case of our Oblong class the constructor has been defined so that every time a new Oblong object is created the length and the height are set – and they are set to the values that the user of the class "sends in"; so every time you create an Oblong you have to specify its length and its height at the same time. You will see how to do that in the program below.

4.5.2   Using the *Oblong* class

Program 4.1 shows how the oblong class can be used by another class, in this case a class called OblongTester. You should make sure that your Oblong class is in the same directory as the OblongTester class, in which case your compiler will find it.

PROGRAM 4.1

```
public class OblongTester
{
  public static void main(String [] args)
  {
    /* declare two variables to hold the length and height of the oblong as
    input by the user */
    double oblongLength, oblongHeight;
    // declare a reference to an Oblong object
    Oblong myOblong;
    // now get the values from the user
    System.out.print("Please enter the length of your oblong: ");
    oblongLength = EasyIn.getDouble();
    System.out.print("Please enter the height of your oblong: ");
    oblongHeight = EasyIn.getDouble();
    // create a new Oblong object
    myOblong = new Oblong(oblongLength, oblongHeight);
    /* use the various methods of the Oblong class to display the length,
    height, area and perimeter of the Oblong */
    System.out.println("Oblong length is " + myOblong.getLength());
    System.out.println("Oblong height is " + myOblong.getHeight());
    System.out.println("Oblong area is " + myOblong.calculateArea());
    System.out.println("Oblong perimeter is "
                                    + myOblong.calculatePerimeter());
    EasyIn.pause("Press <Enter> to quit");
  }
}
```

Let's analyse this program line by line. The first line is the declaration of the class, which is followed by the heading for the main method. The first line of the main method declares two variables:

```
double oblongLength, oblongHeight;
```

As you can see, these are of type **double** and they are going to be used to hold the value that the user chooses for the length and height of the oblong.

The next line introduces something new:

```
Oblong myOblong;
```

You can see that this line is similar to a declaration of a variable; however, what we are doing here is not declaring a variable of a scalar type such as **int**, but declaring the name of an *object* (myOblong) of the *class* (Oblong).

You need to be sure that you understand what this line actually does; all it does in fact is to create a variable that can hold something called a **reference**. A reference is simply a *name* for a location in memory. At this stage we have *not* reserved space for our new Oblong object; all we have done is named a memory location myOblong, as shown in figure 4.7.

Now of course you will be asking the question "What is going to be held in the memory location called myOblong?". We will see the answer in a moment.

Let us look at the next few lines first, though.

```
System.out.print("Please enter the length of your oblong: ");
oblongLength = EasyIn.getDouble();
System.out.print("Please enter the height of your oblong: ");
oblongHeight = EasyIn.getDouble();
```

This should be fairly familiar to you by now; we are prompting the user to enter a value for the length of the oblong, then reading the user's chosen value from the keyboard, and then doing the same thing for the height. The values entered are stored in oblongLength and oblongHeight respectively.

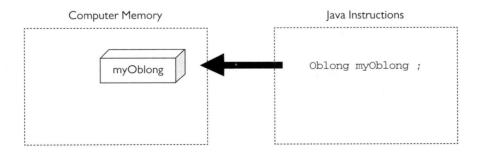

Fig 4.7   Declaring an object reference

Now we can return to the question of what is going to be stored in the memory location myOblong. Look at this line of code:

```
myOblong = new Oblong(oblongLength, oblongHeight);
```

This is the statement that reserves space in memory for a new Oblong object. As you can see, this is done by using the keyword **new**, in conjunction with the name of the class (in this case Oblong) and some stuff in brackets. Remember what we said a while ago about a special method called a *constructor*? Well, using the class name in this way, with the keyword **new**, calls the constructor, and memory is reserved for a new Oblong object. Now, in the case of the Oblong class the people who developed it (okay, that was us!) defined their own constructor method. This method requires that two items of data get sent in, both of type **double**. You can see that they have to be put in the brackets and separated by a comma. The values in brackets are referred to as the **actual parameters** of the method (you will find out more about this in chapter 5). The Oblong constructor was defined so that when the new object is created the length and the height attributes are set − in that order − to the values that are sent in via the brackets. In our program the values that we are sending in are oblongLength and oblongHeight, the values entered by the user of the program.

There are all sorts of ways that we can define constructors (for example, in a BankAccount class we might want to start the balance at zero when the account is created) and we shall see examples of these as we go along.

But wait a minute − how do we know the location in memory where the new object is stored?. Well, now we have the answer to our previous question! The location of the new object is stored in the named reference myOblong. This is illustrated in figure 4.8.

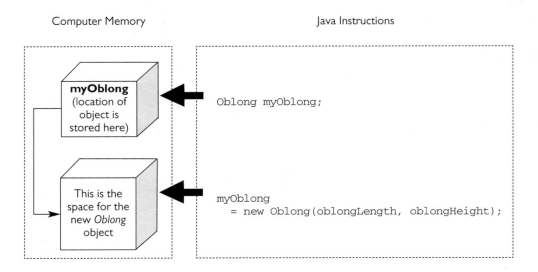

Fig 4.8   Creating a new object

In some programming languages a location like myOblong is often referred to as a pointer, because it "points" to the location of something. Now every time we want to refer to our new Oblong we can use the variable name myOblong. You may have realized that this variable does not have to stay pointing at the Oblong we just created – for example, we could create a different oblong with the **new** keyword, and make myOblong point to that.

Two things are worth noting at this point. First, the process of creating a new object is often referred to as **instantiation**, because we are creating a new *instance* of a class. Second, you should note that, in Java, when a reference is first created it is given a special value of **null**; a **null** value indicates that no storage is allocated. We can assign a **null** value to references and test for it as in the following example:

```
Oblong myOblong;

// more code goes here

myOblong = null;
if(myOblong == null)
{
    System.out.println("No storage is allocated to this object");
}
```

Now let's look at the next line of program 4.1:

```
System.out.println("Oblong Length is " + myOblong.getLength());
```

This line displays the length of the oblong. It uses the method of Oblong called getLength. We say we are **calling** the method. When we call a method of an object we are in fact sending a message to that object as we described in section 4.4. You can see how we do this now – we use the name of the object (in this case myOblong) together with the name of the method (getLength) separated by a full stop. Notice that this time there is nothing in the brackets – we are not sending in any data, as we did when we used the constructor method. As we can see from table 4.1, the getLength method sends back (**return**s) a value (of type **double**); the value sent back from a method is called the **return value**. Because it sends back a value we can use it in the way we have here, simply placing the call to the method – myOblong.getLength() – directly in the output statement, just as if it were a variable or a fixed value. There are other ways we could have used the return value too, such as assigning it to a variable; for example, if we had declared a variable *x* of type **double**, we could assign the return value to *x* with the following statement:

```
x = myOblong.getLength();
```

The next three lines are similar to the first:

```
System.out.println("Oblong height is " + myOblong.getHeight());
System.out.println("Oblong area is " + myOblong.calculateArea());
System.out.println("OblongPerimeter is " + myOblong.calculatePerimeter());
```

We have called the getHeight method, the calculateArea method and the calculatePerimeter method to display the height, area and perimeter of the oblong on the screen. You might have noticed that we haven't used the setLength and setHeight methods – that is because in this program we didn't wish to change the length and height once the oblong had been created – but this is not the last you will see of our Oblong class – and in future programs these methods will come in useful.

Finally, we use one of the pause methods of EasyIn to terminate the program.

Now we can move on to look at using some other classes. The first is not one of our own, but the built-in String class provided with all versions of Java.

4.6   *Using the* **String** *class*

A **string** is a sequence of any characters – letters of the alphabet, numbers, punctuation marks etc. Clearly strings are going to be very important to us in our programming – we are often going to have to store people's names and addresses, a description of a stock item, or countless other things. Ideally we would like to be able to declare variables of type String, just like we can with **int**s or **double**s; however, a string is not a simple scalar value like an integer so it is a bit more complicated than that. But the Java people have come to the rescue with a special String class.

Obviously the most important attribute of a String object will be the string itself, for example "hello", "goodbye", "020 8223 3000", "YP190088A" and so on. But the most interesting thing about the String class is the methods that are provided. We will discuss a few of them here.

First, there are a number of constructors. Remember that a constructor is the method that comes into action every time we create a new object. Remember also that we can define lots of different constructors, which are distinguished from each other by what we place in the brackets.

The first constructor we will look at simply creates an empty string, so there is nothing to put in the brackets when we use it:

```
String str;
str = new String();
```

In fact it is more usual to combine these two statements into one line:

```
String str = new String();
```

Do remember, however, that this one line does two things: it names an object (str) and it creates space in memory for it.

Now why would anyone want to create an empty string? Well, that is a good question, and it can be asked on many occasions about other objects. The answer is that it is best, if possible, to avoid leaving a reference with a null value. Pointing our reference to a location as soon as we declare it will prevent us from doing silly things like creating an uninitialized object and trying to use its methods (although most Java compilers would warn us about this when we tried to compile our code!).

A more useful constructor is the one that allows us to give a value to the string at the time we create it:

```
String str = new String("Hello");
```

Now we have a string with the value "Hello". Actually there is an even quicker way to create this string. As we explained in chapter 2, the assignment operator (=) is *overloaded*. You have seen that it can be used for **double**s, **int**s, **float**s and so on; each of these operations is different because, for example, the way in which **double**s are stored in the computer's memory is different to the way in which **int**s are stored. Now this has also been extended to strings – so we can conveniently use the assignment operator to create a new string as follows:

```
String str = "Hello";
```

The *String* class has a number of interesting and useful methods, and we have listed some of them in table 4.2.

There are many other useful methods of the String class which you can look up. Program 4.2 provides examples of how you can use some of the methods listed in the table; the others are left for you to experiment with in your tutorial and practical sessions.

PROGRAM 4.2

```
public class StringTest
{
  public static void main(String[] args)
  {
    // create a new string
    String str = new String();
    // get the user to enter a string
    System.out.print("Enter a string: ");
    str = EasyIn.getString();
```

Table 4.2 Some *String* methods			
Method	**Description**	**Inputs**	**Output**
length	Returns the length of the string	None	An item of type **int**
charAt	Accepts an integer and returns the character at the position in the string of that integer. Note that indexing starts from zero, not 1!	An item of type **int**	An item of type **char**
substring	Accepts two integers (for example m and n) and returns a chunk of the string. The chunk starts at the m and finishes at the one before n. Remember that indexing starts from zero. (Study program 4.2.)	Two items of type **int**	A String object
concat	Accepts a string and joins this to the end of the original string. The new string is then returned.	A String object	A String object
toUpperCase	Returns the original string, all upper case.	None	A String object
toLowerCase	Returns the original string, all lower case.	None	A String object
compareTo[1]	Accepts a string (say myString) and compares it to the original string. It returns zero if the strings are identical, a negative number if the object's string comes before myString in the alphabet, and a positive number if it comes later.	A String object	An item of type **int**
equals	Accepts an object and compares this to the original string. It returns true if these are identical, otherwise returns false.	An object of any class	A **boolean** value
equalsIgnoreCase	Accepts a String object and compares this to the original string. It returns true if the strings are identical (ignoring case), otherwise returns false.	A String object	A **boolean** value
startsWith	Accepts a string (say str) and returns **true** if the original string starts with str and **false** if it does not (e.g. "hello world" starts with "h" or "he" or "hel" and so on).	A String object	A **boolean** value
endsWith	Accepts a string (say str) and returns **true** if the original string ends with str and **false** if it does not (e.g. "hello world" ends with "d" or "ld" or "rld" and so on).	A String object	A **boolean** value
trim	Returns a String object, having removed any spaces at the beginning or end.	None	A String object

[1] You must never use the equality operator (==) when comparing strings; always use compareTo, equals or equalsIgnoreCase.

```
      // display the length of the user's string
      System.out.println("The length of the string is " + str.length());
      // display the third character of the user's string
      System.out.println("The character at position 3 is " + str.charAt(2));
      // display a selected part of the user's string
      System.out.println("Characters 2 to 4 are " + str.substring(1,4));
      // display the user's string joined with another string
      System.out.println(str.concat(" was the string entered"));
      // display the user's string in upper case
      System.out.println("This is upper case: " + str.toUpperCase());
      // display the user's string in lower case
      System.out.println("This is lower case: " + str.toLowerCase());
      EasyIn.pause("Press <Enter> to quit");
   }
}
```

A sample run from program 4.2:

```
Enter a string: Mary had a little bear
The length of the string is 22
The character at position 3 is r
Characters 2 to 4 are ary
Mary had a little bear was the string entered
This is upper case: MARY HAD A LITTLE BEAR
This is lower case: mary had a little bear
Press <Enter> to quit
```

4.6.1 Comparing strings

A very common mistake that is made by programmers is to use the comparison operator (==) to compare two strings. Doing this will not result in a compilation error, but it won't give you the result you expect! The reason for this is that all you are doing is finding out whether the objects occupy the same space in memory – what you actually want to be doing is comparing the actual value of the string attributes of the objects.

The `String` class has a very useful method called `compareTo`. As you can see from table 4.2 this method accepts a string (called `myString` for example) and compares it to the string value of the object itself. It returns zero if the strings are identical, a negative number if the original string comes before `myString` in the alphabet, and a positive number if it comes later.

Program 4.3 provides an example of how the `compareTo` method is used.

PROGRAM 4.3

```java
public class StringComp
{
  public static void main(String[] args)
  {
    String string1, string2;
    int comparison;
    // get two strings from the user
    System.out.print("Enter a String: ");
    string1 = EasyIn.getString();
    System.out.print("Enter another String: ");
    string2 = EasyIn.getString();
    // compare the strings
    comparison = string1.compareTo(string2);
    if(comparison < 0) // compareTo returned a negative number
    {
      System.out.println(string1 + " comes before "
                                 + string2
                                 + " in the alphabet");
    }
    else if(comparison > 0) // compareTo returned a positive number
    {
      System.out.println(string2 + " comes before "
                                 + string1
                                 + " in the alphabet");
    }
    else // compareTo returned zero
    {
      System.out.println("The strings are identical");
    }
    EasyIn.pause("Press <Enter> to quit");
  }
}
```

Here is a sample run from the program:

```
Enter a String: hello
Enter another String: goodbye
goodbye comes before hello in the alphabet
Press <Enter> to quit
```

You should note that compareTo is case-sensitive – upper case letters will be considered as coming before lower-case letters (their Unicode value is lower). If you are not interested in the case of the letters, you should convert both strings to upper (or lower) case before comparing them.

If all you are interested in is whether the strings are identical, it is easier to use the `equals` method, which returns true if the strings are identical, false otherwise. For example, assuming comparison has been declared as a **boolean**:

```
comparison = string1.equals(string2);
if(comparison == true)
{
   System.out.print("The strings are identical);
}
else
{
   System.out.print("The strings are not identical");
}
```

If the case of the letters is not significant you can use `equalsIgnoreCase`.

4.7   *The BankAccount class*

We have created a class called `BankAccount`, which you can download from the website (`BankAccount.java`), or copy from chapter 5 or from the CD-ROM.

This could be a very useful class in the real world, for example as part of a financial control system. Once again you do not need to look at the details of how this class is coded in order to use it. You do need to know, however, that the class has three attributes, which record the account number, the account name and the account balance. The first two of these will be `String` objects and the final one will a variable of type **double**.

The methods are listed in table 4.3.

A short program which uses the `BankAccount` class is shown in program 4.4. More interesting ways of using this class are left for the tutorial and practical work at the end of the chapter.

PROGRAM 4.4

```
class BankAccountTester
{
   public static void main(String[] args)
   {
      BankAccount account1
             = new BankAccount("99786754", "Martin Luther King");
      account1.deposit(1000);
      System.out.println("Account number " + account1.getAccountNumber());
      System.out.println("Account name: " + account1.getAccountName());
      System.out.println("Current balance: " + account1.getBalance());
      EasyIn.pause("Press <Enter> to quit");
   }
}
```

Table 4.3 The methods of the *BankAccount* class			
Method	**Description**	**Inputs**	**Output**
BankAccount	A constructor. It accepts two strings and assigns them to the account number and account name respectively. It also sets the account balance to zero.	Two String objects	None
getAccountNumber	Returns the value of the accountNumber attribute	None	An item of type **String**
getAccountName	Returns the value of the accountName attribute	None	An item of type **String**
getBalance	Returns the value of the balance attribute	None	An item of type **double**
deposit	Accepts an item of type **double** and adds it to the balance	An item of type **double**	None
withdraw	Accepts an item of type **double** and subtracts it from the balance	An item of type **double**	None

The output from this program is:

```
Account number: 99786754
Account name: Martin Luther King
Current balance: 1000.0
Press <Enter> to quit
```

Now finally, here's one to whet your appetite for the future!

4.8   *The* SmileyFace *class*

This class – SmileyFace.java – is rather different, and we have included it in order to give you your first taste of graphics programming. It has one method only, a special method called paint. This method is associated with graphical applications and is automatically called when the application starts. So you won't see a statement that calls the paint method in our program.

As you can imagine, there is quite a lot to graphical programming, and this is really just a first opportunity to see what might be possible in the future. The paint method of SmileyFace has been defined – as you might expect – to draw a smiley face like the one in figure 4.9.

Program 4.5 below is used to test out the SmileyFace class. You will need to download or copy SmileyFace.java in order to run it.

PROGRAM 4.5

```java
import java.awt.*;

public class RunFace
{
  public static void main(String[] args)
  {
    Frame frame = new Frame();
    SmileyFace face = new SmileyFace();
    frame.setSize(260,200);
    frame.setBackground(Color.yellow);
    frame.add(face);
    frame.setVisible(true);
  }
}
```

Let's take a look at this. First we have something called an **import** statement:

```java
import java.awt.*;
```

This line tells the compiler that we want it to include, along with our own program, the contents of a Java **package**. A package is the name that Java gives to its libraries. Packages keep together a number of different but related files, and you are able to create your own packages if you wish; some of you, depending on what compiler you are using, will have noticed that the compiler puts all your work into a package for you. Using the asterisk at the end means that everything in that package is imported. This particular package, java.awt, is the **Abstract Window Toolkit (AWT)**. It contains lots of stuff that you need for graphics programming

Fig 4.9   The *SmileyFace* class running in a frame

and you will learn much more about it in chapter 9. But we are interested in it now because it contains a class called `Frame`, an instance of which we have created with the following line:

```
Frame frame = new Frame();
```

A `Frame` is a standard graphic component class; whenever we create a graphical application we need to create a frame to run it in (this is not the case with an *applet* because this can run in a browser window).

One problem with the `Frame` class is that it doesn't provide a built-in method to close the window when we click on the little "x" in the top right-hand corner. Now, it is perfectly possible to write our own code for this, but it is not easy to understand unless you have learnt a lot more about Java programming than you have so far; so at this stage so we haven't included it as we are trying to keep things simple for now. Therefore – if you are in a Windows environment – just close the frame by clicking on the black text screen and pressing Ctrl+C (or use equivalent commands if you are not using Windows).[2]

The next line creates a new `SmileyFace` object:

```
SmileyFace face = new SmileyFace();
```

We then set the size for our frame:

```
frame.setSize(260,200);
```

This sends the width and height of the frame (measured in pixels[3]), in that order, into the `setSize` method of `Frame`.

The next line sets the background colour of our frame to yellow.

```
frame.setBackground(Color.yellow);
```

The `SmileyFace` class has been designed in such a way as to allow an object of this class to be added to a frame. We do that with this line which uses the `add` method of `Frame`:

```
frame.add(face);
```

Finally we make our frame visible with the `setVisible` method.

```
frame.setVisible(true);
```

---

[2] Some Java compilers provide an extension of the `Frame` class with a built-in method to close the window.
[3] Pixels are the little coloured dots that make up any video display or graphics screen.

Tutorial exercises

1. Identify two reasons why object-oriented development is rapidly taking the place of structured methods for developing software.
2. With the help of pseudocode, design a program that performs in the following way:
   - when the program starts two bank accounts are created, using names and numbers which are written into the code;
   - the user is then asked to enter an account number, followed by an amount to deposit in that account;
   - the balance of the appropriate account is then updated accordingly – or if an incorrect account number was entered a message to this effect is displayed;
   - the user is then asked if he or she wishes to make more deposits;
   - if the user answers 'yes', then the process continues;
   - if the user answers 'no', then both account details (account number, account name and balance) are displayed;
   - the program then waits for a press of the Enter key before terminating.

Practical work

You will need to have downloaded the following classes (or you can copy them from the CD-ROM or from chapter 5):

- `Oblong.java`
- `BankAccount.java`
- `SmileyFace.java`

1. Type, compile and run the `RunFace` program (program 4.5).
2. Adapt program 4.1 so that the user inputs the length and height of two oblongs, and sees a message on the screen saying which one, if any, has the greater area.
3. Adapt program 4.3 in the following ways:
   (a) re-write the program so that it ignores case;
   (b) re-write the program, using the `equals` method, so that all it does is to test whether the two strings are the same;
   (c) repeat (b) using the `equalsIgnoreCase` method;
   (d) use the `trim` method so that the program ignores leading or trailing spaces.
4. (a) Write a program that asks the user to input a string, followed by a single character, and then tests whether the string starts with that character.
   (b) Make your program work so that the case of the character is irrelevant.
5. Implement the program you designed in question 2 of the tutorial exercises.

IMPLEMENTING CLASSES

LEARNING OBJECTIVES

By the end of this chapter you should be able to:

➤ write the Java code for a specified class;

➤ explain the meaning of the term **polymorphism**;

➤ code simple graphic shapes in Java;

➤ describe the use of the **static** keyword;

➤ explain how **parameters** are passed to class methods in Java;

➤ use the type conversion methods of **wrapper** classes.

5.1   Introduction

This chapter is arguably the most important so far, because it is here that you are going to learn how to develop the classes that you need for your programs. You are already familiar with the concept of a class, and the idea that we can create objects that belong to a class; in the last chapter you saw how to create and use objects; you saw that we could hide or encapsulate information in a class; and you saw how we could use the methods of a class without knowing anything about how they work.

In this chapter you will look inside the classes you have studied to see how they are constructed, and how you can write classes of your own.

5.2   Implementing classes in Java

In the last chapter you saw that a class consists of:

- a set of **attributes** (the data);
- a set of **methods** which can access or change those attributes.

To help you to understand how we actually implement this in Java we are going to look at the code for the classes we used in chapter 4.

5.2.1   The *Oblong* class

We will start with the Oblong class. You should recall the notation for specifying classes that we introduced in the very first chapter.

Let's use this notation to specify our Oblong class, as shown in figure 5.1.

Now we can go on to *design* this class (if you have forgotten the difference between specification and design then look back at the first chapter). This is shown in figure 5.2.

Notice that when we design our classes we tend to enter more detail than we do when we are initially specifying them. So when we drew the class diagram for the Student class discussed in the previous chapter (figure 4.4) we didn't bother to include such methods as getStudentName or getStudentNumber. These "basic" methods that do nothing more than access the attributes are normally not listed until we start to think about the design of our class; the same is true for the constructor.

Oblong
length height
calculateArea calculatePerimeter

Fig 5.1   The specification of the *Oblong* class

Oblong
length height
Oblong setLength setHeight getLength getHeight calculateArea calculatePerimeter

Fig 5.2   The design of the *Oblong* class

So now that we are designing our Oblong class for implementation we can include the following in our class diagram:

- the constructor (Oblong);
- some methods that allow us to assign values (in other words **write**) to the attributes – these are the methods setLength and setHeight;
- some methods to send back (in other words **read**) the values of the attributes – these are the methods getLength and getHeight.

It is not always the case that we choose to supply methods such as setLength or setHeight, which allow us to *change* the attributes. Sometimes we set up our class so that the only way that we can assign values to the attributes is via the constructor. This would mean that the values of the length and height could be set only at the time a new Oblong object was created, and could not be changed after that. Whether or not you want to provide a means of writing to individual attributes depends on the nature of the system you are developing and should be discussed with potential users. However, we believe that it is a good policy to provide write access to only those attributes that clearly require to be changed during the object's life time, and we have taken this approach throughout this book. In this case we have included "set" attributes for length and height because we are going to need them in chapter 9.

Now that we have the basic design of the Oblong class we can go ahead and write the Java code for it:

THE *Oblong* CLASS

```java
class Oblong
{

  // the attributes are declared first
  private double length;
  private double height;

  // then the methods

  // the constructor
  public Oblong(double lengthIn, double heightIn)
  {
    length = lengthIn;
    height = heightIn;
  }

  // the next method allows us to "read" the length attribute
  public double getLength()
  {
    return length;
  }

  // the next method allows us to "read" the height attribute
  public double getHeight()
  {
```

```
      return height;
   }

   // the next method allows us to "write" to the length attribute
   public void setLength(double lengthIn)
   {
      length = lengthIn;
   }

   // the next method allows us to "write" to the height attribute
   public void setHeight(double heightIn)
   {
      height = heightIn;
   }

   // this method returns the area of the oblong
   public double calculateArea()
   {
      return length * height;
   }

   // this method returns the perimeter of the oblong
   public double calculatePerimeter()
   {
      return 2 * (length + height);
   }
}
```

Let's take a closer look at this. The first line declares the Oblong class. Once this is done, we declare the attributes. An Oblong object will need attributes to hold values for the length and the height of the oblong, and these will be of type **double**.

The declaration of the attributes in the Oblong class is as follows:

```
private double length;
private double height;
```

You can now see how, in Java, the keyword **private** is used to restrict access to these attributes. Once they are declared as **private**, the only way to get at them is via the class methods. Take a look back at table 4.1 to remind yourself of the class methods that we are now going to define within our Oblong class.

First comes the constructor. You should recall that it has the same name as the class.

```
public Oblong(double lengthIn, double heightIn)
{
   length = lengthIn;
   height = heightIn;
}
```

The first thing to notice is that this method is declared as **public**. Unlike the attributes, we want our methods to be accessible from outside so that they can be called by methods of other classes.

Do you remember our saying in chapter 4 that this constructor is a *user-defined*[1] constructor? We are defining it so that when a new Oblong object is created (with the keyword **new**) then not only do we get some space reserved in memory, but we also get some other stuff occurring; in this case two assignment statements are executed. The first assigns the value lengthIn to the length attribute, and the second assigns the value heightIn to the height attribute.

But what exactly are these variables lengthIn and heightIn? You can see that the first time they appear is in the brackets. The variables in the brackets are called the **formal parameters** of the method, and they are the variables that *receive* the values that we send into the method when we call it. Cast your mind back to program 4.1, the OblongTester program, when we used the following line to call the constructor:

```
myOblong = new Oblong(oblongLength, oblongHeight);
```

The user of the OblongTester program had been asked to enter values for oblongLength and oblongHeight and with the line above we call the constructor and send in these values by placing them in the brackets. As we told you in chapter 4, the variables oblongLength and oblongHeight are referred to as the **actual parameters** (also known as **arguments**) of the calling method; their values are copied to the formal parameters lengthIn and heightIn in that order.

You should be able to see that the order in which we send values to the parameters of a method is important; they are copied in the order they are sent. You can see that the Oblong constructor has been defined so that it requires the length followed by the height – if we sent them the other way round, then the length would be copied to the height attribute and vice versa.

Notice also that it is possible to send values into a method only by listing the right number of variables of the right type. With the single constructor defined for Oblong, we would get compiler error messages if we tried to call the constructor with any of the following lines:

---

[1] Here the word *user* is referring to the person writing the program, not the person using it!

```
// all these would result in compiler errors:

myOblong = new Oblong(oblongLength);
// one variable too few

myOblong = new Oblong(10.0, 20.0, 30.0);
// one variable too many

myOblong = new Oblong(10.0, 'c');
// second variable of wrong type (char instead of double)
```

One more thing about constructors: in chapter 4 we told you that if you don't define your own constructor then a "default" constructor is provided – this does nothing more than reserve space in memory for the new object. It is called by using the constructor name (which is the same as the class name) with empty brackets. Now once we have defined our own constructors, this default constructor is no longer automatically available. If we want it to be available then we have explicitly to re-define it. In the Oblong case we would define it as:

```
public Oblong()
{
}
```

You may be wondering how the program knows which constructor to call, since we now have two of them. The answer is simple – it knows by matching the actual parameters in the brackets of the calling function to the formal parameters in the constructor.

So this statement would call our original constructor:

```
myOblong = new Oblong(10.0, 20.0);
```

whereas this one would call our newly defined default constructor:

```
myOblong = new Oblong();
```

This idea of having two or even more methods in the same class with the same name is not confined to constructors. We can have as many methods as we like with the same name as long as each one has a different set of parameters. This technique is a very important feature of object-oriented programming languages and is called **polymorphism**, which means *having many forms*. We are not done with polymorphism here – we will come across it again in future chapters.

Now let's take a look at the definition of the next method, getLength. The purpose of this method is simply to send back the value of the length attribute:

```
public double getLength()
{
   return length;
}
```

Once again you can see that the method has been declared as **public**, enabling it to be accessed by methods of other classes.

After the word **public** comes the word **double**, which states the *type* of the method. At first you may wonder why a method should have a type. The answer is that as we have seen, a method can send back or *return* a value, and the *type* of the method (which must be stated before the method name) is the type of the value it returns, in this case **double**. If a method does not return anything, its return type is declared as **void**.

After the word **double** comes the name of the method, getName, followed by a pair of brackets. There is nothing in these brackets (that is, it the method has no parameters) because we do not need to pass any information into this method.

The body of the method is defined between the curly brackets. In this case the code consists of the single line:

```
return length;
```

This line sends the value of the length attribute back to the calling function. Notice also that the word **return** performs another very important function as well as sending back the value; it also ends the method! So whenever a **return** statement is encountered in a method, the method ends and control of the program goes back to the method that called it.

Let's just remind ourselves how we called this method in program 4.1. We did it with the following line:

```
System.out.println("Oblong Length is " + myOblong.getLength());
```

The next method is the getHeight method, which is defined in exactly the same way. This is followed by the setLength method:

```
public void setLength(double lengthIn)
{
   length = lengthIn;
}
```

This method does not return a value, so its return type is **void**. However, it does require a parameter of type **double** that it will assign to the length attribute. We have called this

parameter lengthIn.[2] The body of the method consists of a single line which assigns the value
of lengthIn to the length attribute.

The next method, setHeight, behaves in the same way in respect of the height attribute.
After this comes the calculateArea method:

```
public double calculateArea()
{
   return length * height;
}
```

Once again there are no formal parameters, as this method does not need any data in
order to do its job; it is of type **double** since it returns an item of this type. The actual code
is just one line, namely the statement that returns the area of the oblong, calculated by
multiplying the value of the length attribute by the value of the height attribute.

The calculatePerimeter method is similar.

In a moment we shall take a look at some of the other classes we encountered in chapter 4.
But before we do that we can take a minute to think about the way we design our classes. In
figure 5.2 we added some detail to the specification of an oblong by including in our class
diagram all the methods of the Oblong class that were going to be implemented – even the
"basic" ones.

As our understanding has increased we can now include more information, namely the types
of the attributes, as well as the return types of the method and the types of the parameters
that we pass to the method. Figure 5.3 shows the specification of the Oblong class with this
detail added. As we explained in chapter 1, we are going to make our diagrams conform to
the standard UML notation for specifying and designing classes. Thus for each method, the
parameters are shown in the brackets and the return types appear after the brackets, separated
by a colon.

Notice that when we are specifying the class we do not use Java-specific type names like **int**,
double or **float**, because type names vary from one programming language to the next, and,
although _we_ will be using Java, a good specification should lend itself to being implemented in
more than one programming language.

However, at the design stage we can make the decision that we will be using a specific
language – Java in our case – so it is okay to use Java type names as shown in figure 5.4.

5.2.2   The *BankAccount* class

Cast your mind back to program 4.3, which used our *BankAccount* class. The design is shown in
figure 5.5.

We can now inspect the code for this class, which follows:

---

[2] We are going to adopt the convention of ending all our parameter names with the suffix In.

Oblong
length : real number height : real number
calculateArea() : real number calculatePerimeter() : real number

Fig 5.3   The UML specification of the *Oblong* class

Oblong
length : double height : double
Oblong(double, double) getLength() : double getHeight() : double setLength(double) setHeight(double) calculateArea() : double calculatePerimeter() : double

Fig 5.4   The detailed design of the *Oblong* class

BankAccount
accountNumber : String accountName : String balance : double
BankAccount (String, String) getAccountNumber() : String getAccountName() : String getBalance() : double deposit(double) withdraw(double)

Fig 5.5   The *BankAccount* class

THE *BankAccount* CLASS

```
class BankAccount
{

  // the attributes
  private String accountNumber;
  private String accountName;
  private double balance;

  // the methods

  // the constructor
  public BankAccount(String numberIn, String nameIn)
  {
    accountNumber = numberIn;
    accountName = nameIn;
    balance = 0;
  }

  // methods to read the attributes
  public String getAccountName()
  {
    return accountName;
  }
  public String getAccountNumber()
  {
    return accountNumber;
  }
  public double getBalance()
  {
    return balance;
  }

  // methods to deposit and withdraw money
  public void deposit(double amountIn)
  {
    balance = balance + amountIn;
  }
  public void withdraw(double amountIn)
  {
    balance = balance - amountIn;
  }
}
```

Now that we are getting the idea of how to define a class in Java, we do not need to go into so much detail in our analysis and explanation.

The first three lines declare the attributes of the class, and are as we would expect:

```
private String accountNumber;
private String accountName;
private double balance;
```

One thing to notice, however, is that accountNumber and accountName are declared as Strings; it is perfectly possible for the attributes of one class to be objects of another class.

Now the constructor method, which has an interesting additional feature:

```
public BankAccount(String numberIn, String nameIn)
{
   accountNumber = numberIn;
   accountName = nameIn;
   balance = 0;
}
```

You can see that when a new object of the BankAccount class is created, the accountName and accountNumber will be assigned the values of the parameters passed to the method and also the balance will be assigned the value zero; this makes sense because when someone opens a new account there is a zero balance until a deposit is made.

The next three methods, getAccountNumber, getAccountName and getBalance, are all set up so that we can read the values of the corresponding attributes (which of course have been declared as **private**).

After these we have the deposit method:

```
public void deposit(double amountIn)
{
   balance = balance + amountIn;
}
```

Notice that this method does not return a value; it is therefore declared to be of type **void**. It does however require that a value is sent in (the amount to be deposited), and therefore has one parameter – of type **double** – in the brackets. As you would expect with this method, the action consists of adding the deposit onto the balance attribute of the BankAccount object.

The withdraw method behaves in a similar manner, but the amount is subtracted from the current balance.

5.2.3   The *SmileyFace* class

If you remember, when we ran this class in a frame we got the graphic shown in figure 5.6.

Take a look at the code:

THE *SmileyFace* CLASS

```java
import java.awt.*;

class SmileyFace extends Panel // this will be explained below
{
  public void paint(Graphics g)
  {
    g.setColor(Color.red);
    g.drawOval(85,45,75,75); // the face
    g.setColor(Color.blue);
    g.drawOval(100,65,10,10); // the right eye
    g.drawOval(135,65,10,10); // the left eye
    g.drawArc(102,85,40,25,0,-180); // the mouth
    g.drawString("Smiley Face",90,155);
  }
}
```

There are a number of new concepts here. First, you should remind yourself about the import clause:

```java
import java.awt.*;
```

As we saw in chapter 4, the first of this imports the standard Java **Abstract Window Toolkit** (java.awt), which supplies the graphical components that we need; as we have said, you will find out much more about this in chapter 9.

Now look at the next line:

```java
class SmileyFace extends Panel
```

Fig 5.6   The *SmileyFace* class running in a frame

Our normal class declaration has the words **extends** Panel after it. A Panel is a very useful graphical component that comes with the Abstract Window Toolkit. Unlike a frame we cannot see a panel – but we can add other components to it, or paint things on it, and then add it to a frame, as we did in program 4.4. The word **extends** has a special meaning that you will learn about in chapter 7, but for now it is good enough just to understand that our SmileyFace class is taking the standard Java Panel class and adding more code to it.

Now we come to the paint method:

```
public void paint(Graphics g)
{
  g.setColor(Color.red);
  g.drawOval(85,45,75,75); // the face
  g.setColor(Color.blue);
  g.drawOval(100,65,10,10); // the right eye
  g.drawOval(135,65,10,10); // the left eye
  g.drawArc(102,85,40,25,0,-180); // the mouth
  g.drawString("Smiley Face",90,155);
}
```

This special method is a method of a basic graphics class called Component, of which Panel itself is an extension; you will find out a lot more about this in chapter 9 when we study graphics programming in detail.

When the window that displays the component becomes visible, the paint method is called. When this happens, an object of a core Java class called Graphics (which comes with the AWT package) is automatically sent in to this method. A Graphics object has lots of useful methods.

The first one sets the foreground colour:

```
g.setColor(Color.red);
```

Then we use the drawOval method of the Graphics class to draw our circles. The first of these draws the big circle for the face itself:

```
g.drawOval(85,45,75,75);
```

The drawOval method takes four integer parameters. Referring to these as x, y, l, h, the oval that gets drawn fits into an imaginary rectangle that starts at position (x,y), and is l pixels long and h pixels high. This is illustrated in figure 5.7.

Notice that since we want a circle, we have made the values of l and h equal.

After we have drawn the big circle, we set the colour to blue and draw the right eye and left eye respectively:

```
g.setColor(Color.blue);
g.drawOval(100,65,10,10);
g.drawOval(135,65,10,10);
```

The next line draws the mouth:

```
g.drawArc(102,85,40,25,0,-180);
```

This requires some explanation. As you can see, this method requires six parameters, all integers. We shall call them x, y, l, h, α, θ. The first four define an imaginary rectangle as above. The arc is drawn so that its centre is the centre of this rectangle, as shown in figure 5.8.

The next two parameters, α and θ, represent angles. The first, α, is the start angle – measured from an imaginary horizontal line pointing to the "quarter-past-three" position (representing zero degrees). The next, θ, is the finish angle. If θ is positive then the arc is drawn by rotating from the start position in an anti-clockwise direction; if it is negative we rotate in a clockwise direction. If this is not clear, then you should try some experiments; play about with the SmileyFace class and see what happens.

The final line draws the string "Smiley Face" in the graphics window at the co-ordinates (90,155).

```
g.drawString("Smiley Face",90,155);
```

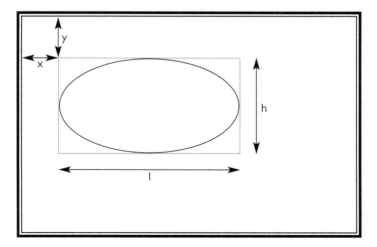

Fig 5.7   The *drawOval* method of the *Graphics* class

Look back at program 4.4 to remind yourself how we show this graphic in a frame.

You now have the basics of how to write the code for a Java class, and you can now move on to learn some important new concepts that will help you to refine your classes.

5.3   *The static keyword*

You might already have noticed the keyword **static** in front of the names of methods or attributes in some Java classes. A word such as this (as well as the words **public** and **private**) is called a **modifier**.

Let's explore what this **static** modifier does. Consider the BankAccount class that we discussed earlier in the chapter. Say we wanted to have an additional method which added interest, at the current rate, to the customer's balance. It would be useful to have an attribute called interestRate to hold the value of the current rate of interest. But of course the interest rate is the same for any customer – and if it changes we want it to change for every customer in the bank; in other words for every object of the class. We can achieve this by declaring the variable as **static**. An attribute declared as **static** is a *class* attribute; any changes that are made to it are made to all the objects in the class.

We have rewritten our BankAccount class as shown below; the new items have been emboldened. Notice that we have included three new methods as well as the new **static** attribute interestRate. The first two of these – setInterestRate and getInterestRate – are the methods that allow us to read and write to our new attribute. The third – addInterestRate – is the method that adds the interest to the customer's balance.

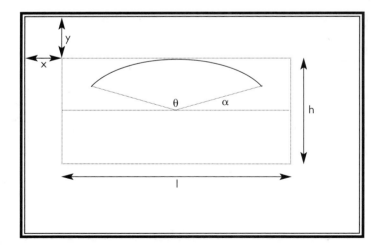

Fig 5.8   The *drawArc* method of the *Graphics* class

THE MODIFIED *BankAccount* CLASS

```
class BankAccount2
{
  private String accountNumber;
  private String accountName;
  private double balance;
  private static double interestRate;

  public BankAccount2(String numberIn, String nameIn)
  {
    accountNumber = numberIn;
    accountName = nameIn;
    balance = 0;
  }
  public String getAccountName()
  {
    return accountName;
  }
  public String getAccountNumber()
  {
    return accountNumber;
  }
  public double getBalance()
  {
    return balance;
  }
  public void deposit(double amountIn)
  {
    balance = balance + amountIn;
  }
  public void withdraw(double amountIn)
  {
    balance = balance - amountIn;
  }
  public void setInterestRate(double rateIn)
  {
    interestRate = rateIn;
  }
  public double getInterestRate()
  {
    return interestRate;
  }
  public void addInterest()
  {
    balance = balance + (balance * interestRate)/100;
  }
}
```

Program 5.1 uses this modified version of the BankAccount class.

PROGRAM 5.1

```java
public class BankAccountTester2
{
  public static void main(String[] args)
  {
    // create a bank account
    BankAccount2 account1 = new BankAccount2("99786754", "Nelson Mandela");
    // create another bank account
    BankAccount2 account2 = new BankAccount2("99887776", "Marie Curie");
    // make a deposit into the first account
    account1.deposit(1000);
    // make a deposit into the second account
    account2.deposit(2000);
    // set the interest rate - we could have chosen account1
    account2.setInterestRate(10);
    // add interest to account 1
    account1.addInterest();
    // display the account details
    System.out.println("Account number: " + account1.getAccountNumber());
    System.out.println("Account name: " + account1.getAccountName());
    System.out.println("Interest Rate: " + account1.getInterestRate());
    System.out.println("Current balance: " + account1.getBalance());
    System.out.println(); // blank line
    System.out.println("Account number: " + account2.getAccountNumber());
    System.out.println("Account name: " + account2.getAccountName());
    System.out.println("Interest Rate: " + account2.getInterestRate());
    System.out.println("Current balance: " + account2.getBalance());
    System.out.println();
    EasyIn.pause("Press <Enter> to quit");
  }
}
```

Take a closer look at the first four lines of the main method of program 5.1. We have created two new bank accounts which we have called account1 and account2, and have assigned account numbers and names to them at the time they were created (via the constructor). We have then deposited amounts of 1000 and 2000 respectively into each of these accounts.

Now look at the next two lines:

```java
account2.setInterestRate(10);
account1.addInterest();
```

The first of these lines sets the interest rate to 10. We have called the setInterestRate method from account2. However, because interestRate has been declared as a **static** variable this change is effective for any object of the class. So we should expect the interest rate to change for account1 as well. Therefore, when we add interest to this account as we do with the next line we should expect it to be calculated with an interest rate of 10, giving us a new balance of 1100.

This is exactly what we get, as can be seen from the output below:

```
Account number: 99786754
Account name: Nelson Mandela
Interest rate: 10.0
Current balance: 1100.0

Account number: 99887776
Account name: Marie Curie
Interest rate: 10.0
Current balance: 2000.0

Press <Enter> to quit
```

The above example shows that it doesn't matter which object's setInterestRate method is called – the same effect is achieved whether it is account1 or account2, because they are changing a **static** attribute. It would make more sense if there were a way to invoke this method without reference to a specific object; and so there is!

All we have to do is to declare our setInterestRate method as **static** as shown below:

```
public static void setInterestRate(double rateIn)
{
   interestRate = rateIn;
}
```

This turns our method into a *class* method; it does not refer to any specific object. We can call a class method by using the class name instead of the object name. So to set the interest rate to 15, for example, for all objects of the BankAccount2 class, we could do the following:

```
BankAccount2.setInterestRate(15);
```

The getInterestRate method could also be declared as static:

```
public static double getInterestRate()
{
   return interestRate;
}
```

Class methods can very useful indeed and we shall see further examples of them in this chapter. You should notice, by the way, that you have already been using **static** methods extensively – all the methods of the EasyIn class are **static** methods – and that is why you have been using the class name – EasyIn – to call them! And of course we have always declared our main method as **static** – because this method obviously belongs to the class and not to a specific object.

Incidentally, it is conventional when producing UML diagrams to underline the names of class attributes and methods; you will see an example of this in our case study in chapter 10.

5.4   *More on parameter passing*

We talked about the notion of passing parameters to methods in section 5.2. There are a couple of very important points that you need to take note of here. First, you should be clear that when a parameter is passed to a method all that is happening is that a copy is made of the value of this parameter somewhere else in the computer's memory, and this value can be used by the method for whatever purpose is required – the original value of the variable is *not* changed.

This is illustrated by the following example, where we have defined a class called ParameterTest that has a single method called treble. This method (which has been declared as static so that we just have to use the class name) accepts an integer i and multiplies it by 3.

THE *ParameterTest* CLASS

```
class ParameterTest
{
  public static void treble(int i)
  {
    i = 3 * i;
  }
}
```

Program 5.2 uses this class. It has a main method in which an integer testInteger is declared and given the value 20; this variable is then sent to the treble method of parameterTest. The value of testInteger is then displayed.

PROGRAM 5.2

```
public class RunParameterTest
{
  public static void main(String[] args)
  {
    int testInteger = 20;
    ParameterTest.treble(testInteger);
    // will the integer now be trebled?
    System.out.println("The value of the integer is " + testInteger);
    EasyIn.pause("Press <Enter> to quit");
  }
}
```

If you run this program you will see that the integer has not been changed, and we get the following output, showing that the value of testInteger is unaltered:

> *The value of the integer is 20*

It is interesting, however, to note that some methods receive objects rather than intrinsic variables. Let's write another method for our ParameterTest class which takes an object of the BankAccount class which we defined earlier, and which we will call objectTest. This method deposits an amount of 1000 into the account.

```
public static void objectTest(BankAccount account)
{
  account.deposit(1000);
}
```

Program 5.3 creates a *BankAccount* object and sends it to this method.

PROGRAM 5.3

```
public class RunParameterTest2
{
  public static void main(String[] args)
  {
    BankAccount testAccount = new BankAccount("1", "Muhammad Ali");
    /* now we send the object to the objectTest method of ParameterTest */
    ParameterTest.objectTest(testAccount);
    System.out.println("Account Number: " + testAccount.getAccountNumber());
    System.out.println("Account Name: " + testAccount.getAccountName());
    System.out.println("Balance: " + testAccount.getBalance());
    EasyIn.pause("Press <Enter> to finish");
  }
}
```

The output from this program is as follows:

```
Account Number: 1
Account Name: Muhammad Ali
Balance: 1000
```

You can see that the deposit has successfully been made. This is because what was sent to the method was, of course, a reference to a BankAccount object. The object in question can be "traced" and its methods invoked in the usual way.

5.5   *Wrapper classes*

The final topic of this chapter has the seemingly strange name of **wrapper** classes. There are times when instead of wanting to use a basic scalar type to represent such things as integers and real numbers you might want to use a class instead. For every intrinsic type, Java provides a corresponding class – the name of the class is similar to the basic type, but begins with a capital letter – for example Integer, Character, Float, Double. They are called *wrappers* because they "wrap" a *class* around the basic *type*. So an object of the **Integer** class, for example, holds an integer value, and also has some useful methods.

You might be wondering why such classes are necessary. One of the main reasons is for their methods. There are a number of methods provided with each wrapper, some of which are class methods, and the most common use of these is to convert from one type to another. You will find that the most often-needed conversion is from strings to numbers and vice versa, particularly when writing graphics programs. This is because when a user enters something in a box on the screen this is always read as a String. If whatever is entered is a number that needs to be used in a calculation, then we first have to convert it to the appropriate type such as **int** or **double**. The methods of the wrapper classes are used for this purpose. Examples of these methods are provided in the programs that follow.

Program 5.4 uses the parseInt method of the Integer class to convert a String to an **int**; to prove that it really is an integer, the program computes its square and displays it!

PROGRAM 5.4

```
public class StringToInteger
{
  public static void main(String[] args)
  {
    String s;
    int i;
    s = "10";
    i = Integer.parseInt(s); // convert the string to an integer
    System.out.print(i * i); // 100 will be displayed
    EasyIn.pause();
  }
}
```

To convert a `String` to a **double** you can use the `parseDouble` method of the `Double` class.

To do this the other way round is even quicker; if for any reason we needed to convert an **integer** or a **double** to a string we can cheat! We can just concatenate the number onto an empty string – because using the "+" operator acting upon a `String` and a scalar type converts the scalar type to a `String`. So we could write:

```
String s = " " + 3;
```

or:

```
String s = " " + 3.12;
```

or even:

```
double d = 10.3;
int i = 20;
String s = " " + i + d;
```

Tutorial exercises

1. Explain how encapsulation is achieved in the Java language.
2. Explain the meaning of the following terms:
   - polymorphism;
   - a **static** attribute;
   - a **static** method;
   - actual parameters;
   - formal parameters;
   - wrapper classes.
3. Imagine that a developer requires a class called `Circle`. An object of this class must hold the value of its radius and its position on the screen – these values, which are all whole numbers, should be set only at the time a circle is created and need not be changed thereafter. A `Circle` object must be capable of reporting its area and its circumference. It should also have a `paint` method which draws the specified circle on a graphics screen, with the area and circumference printed below it as shown:

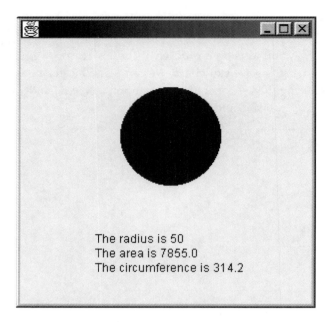

The radius is 50
The area is 7855.0
The circumference is 314.2

Design the class using UML notation.

4. A system is being developed for use in an adult education college. A class called Course is required for this system. A Course object will require the following attributes: an identity number and name (both of which will be strings), and the number of hours the course operates in a week. It will also need an attribute to record the hourly fee – *this will be the same for every object of the class* Course.

The identity number, name and hours per week will need to be set at the time a Course object is created; the first two will not need to be changed after this. However, it will be necessary to provide a method that allows the number of hours per week to be re-set during the object's lifetime. In addition, *class* methods are required for the purposes of setting and getting the hourly fee.

Finally, methods are required to read the values of the remaining attributes, as well as a method that calculates and returns the total weekly cost of the course.

(a) Write the code for the Course class.

(b) (i) Assume the following variables have been declared within a program:

```
String id;
String name;
int hoursPerWeek;
```

Now write a fragment of code (not a whole program) that uses the Course class and obtains the identity number, name and number of hours per week from a user and creates a new Course object.

(ii) Write a line of code that will output (on a text screen) the total weekly cost of the course for this Course object.

(c) Write a line of code that does not refer to any particular Course object, and that will set the fees for the course to 25.

Practical work

1. The diagram below represents the design for the Student class that we discussed in chapter 4.

Student
studentNumber : String studentName : String markForMaths : int markForEnglish : int markForScience : int
Student(String, String) getNumber() : String getName() : String enterMarks(int, int, int) getMathsMark() : int getEnglishMark() : int getScienceMark() : int calculateAverageMark() : double

(a) Write the code for the Student class. You should note that in order to ensure that a **double** is returned from the calculateAverageMark method you should specifically divide the total of the three marks by 3.0 and not simply by 3 (look back at chapter 2 to remind yourself why this is the case).

(b) Write a tester class to test out your student class; it should create two or three students, and use the methods of the student class to test whether they work according to the specification.

2. Implement the Circle class that you designed in tutorial question 3. To draw the circle you should use the fillOval method which works in the same way as drawOval. You can run the class in a frame with the code shown below. We suggest that you display your first string at (75, 210) – after you have your program working you can try changing some of the settings.

```java
import java.awt.*;
public class RunCircle
{
  public static void main(String[] args)
  {
    Frame frame = new Frame();
    Circle myCircle = new Circle(100,50,50);
    frame.setSize(300,300);
    frame.setBackground(Color.yellow);
    frame.add(myCircle);
    frame.setVisible(true);
  }
}
```

6 ARRAYS AND COLLECTION CLASSES

LEARNING OBJECTIVES

By the end of this chapter you should be able to:

➤ create arrays of scalar types;

➤ create arrays of objects;

➤ use the `length` attribute of arrays;

➤ use arrays as parameters to methods;

➤ develop collection classes using arrays of scalar types and arrays of objects.

6.1   Introduction

In the previous chapters we have shown you how to create simple variables from the basic scalar types (such as **int** and **char**), and objects from classes (such as String and Student). In each case we created as many variables or objects as we needed. How, though, would you deal with the situation in which you had to create and handle a very large number of variables or objects?

An obvious approach would be just to declare as many variables or objects as you need. This sounds reasonable – but it is not as straightforward as it might seem. Let's assume that these items are closely related to each other, like the maximum daily temperature readings in a week or details of all students in a group. You'd probably wish to process these items together. For example entering all the temperature readings, or displaying details of all students.

Declaring a larger number of variables or objects is a nuisance but simple enough. For example, let's start to consider a very simple application that records seven temperature readings (one for each day of the week). As this application is quite small we will just develop it within a main method for now.

```
public class TemperatureReadings
{
  public static void main(String[] args)
  { // declare 7 variables to hold readings
       double temperature1, temperature2, temperature3, temperature4,
                            temperature5, temperature6, temperature7;
    // more code will go here
  }
}
```

Here we have declared seven variables each of type **double** (as temperatures will be recorded as real numbers). So far so good. Now to write some code that allows the user to enter these temperatures. Getting one temperature is easy:

```
System.out.println("max temperature for day 1 ?");
temperature1 = EasyIn.getDouble( );
```

But how would you write the code to get the second temperature, the third temperature and all the remaining temperatures? Well, you could repeat the above pair of lines for each temperature entered, but surely you've got better things to do with your time!

Essentially you want to repeat the same pair of lines seven times. You already know that a **for** loop is useful when repeating lines of code a fixed number of times. Maybe you could try using a **for** loop here?

```
for (int i=1; i<=7; i++) // try this?
{
  System.out.println("max temperature for day " +i);
  temperature1 = EasyIn.getDouble( );
}
```

This looks like a neat solution. Unfortunately it won't do what you want it to do. Can you see what the problem is?

The problem is that each time a temperature is entered, it is placed in the same variable, temperature1.

```
temperature1 = EasyIn.getDouble( );
```

When the loop finishes, this variable will contain only the last temperature entered, and all the other variables will not have a temperature stored in them at all! As things stand there is no way around this, as each variable has a *distinct* name.

Ideally we would like each variable to be given the *same* name (`temperature`, say) so that we could use a loop here, but we would like some way of being able to distinguish between each variable, say by means of an index (`temperature[1]`, `temperature[2]` and so on). In fact, this is exactly what an **array** allows us to do.

6.2   *Creating an array*

An **array** is a special kind of object in Java and is used to hold a *collection of items all of the same type*. For example, an array object could hold a collection of temperatures, or a collection of students. It couldn't hold a few students and a few temperatures as this is a collection involving two types.

Actually, an array doesn't quite fit perfectly with the idea of an object that we have met already. For example, there is no obvious class from which it is generated, and the syntax for method calls is peculiar to arrays. For this reason an array is often thought of as a type all of its own – not a scalar type and not quite an object.

However, we aren't going to worry too much about how arrays are categorized – we are far more interested in showing you how to use them in your programs. First, you need to know how to create an array. Just as with the creation of objects, array creation is a two-stage process:

1. Declare an array.
2. Create memory to store the array.

For convenience, let's say every element in the array is of type `ArrayType` (where `ArrayType` may be any type such as **int**, **char**, `String`, `Student`); then an array is declared as follows:

```
ArrayType [] arrayName;
```

Note that this declaration is just like the declaration of a simple variable or an object except that square brackets '[ ]' are included after the type name. These brackets indicate that the data item called `arrayName` is in fact an array.

So, to declare an array `temperature` of **double** values you would write the following:

```
double [] temperature;
```

At the moment this simply defines `temperature` to be a variable that will hold a *reference* to an array object. The memory that will eventually hold the array has not been allocated. This is done as before with the **new** operator. This time, however, as well as using the **new** operator, you must state how big your array will be – that is, how many elements you want your array to hold.

```
arrayName = new ArrayType [sizeOfArray];
```

The variable `sizeOfArray` is some integer value. So, for the temperature example above, if you wanted the array to hold seven temperatures you would allocate memory as follows:

```
temperature = new double [7];
```

Just like the creation of objects, we could have combined the two procedures of declaring and creating an array in one step as follows:

```
double [] temperature = new double [7];
```

We have already said that arrays can be used to hold *any* collection of items as long as they are of the same type. This type can be a simple scalar type such as **int** or **char** or a class such as String or Student. In other words, you can create an array of simple scalar items or an array of objects. The effect of the **new** operator differs slightly depending upon whether you are creating an array of simple scalar items (as in this case) or an array of objects. We will return to look at an array of objects later. For now, let's see what effect the **new** operator has when creating this array temperature in figure 6.1.

As can be seen from figure 6.1, the array creation creates an array object of seven elements and assigns the reference of it to the temperature variable. As this array was declared to hold values of type **double**, each of the seven memory locations is big enough to hold a value of type **double**. In effect the array reference, temperature, points to seven *new variables*. These variables are often referred to as the **elements** of the array.

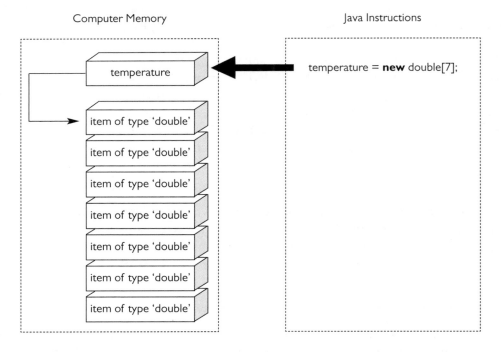

Fig 6.1   The effect on computer memory of declaring an array of values of type 'double'

You may be wondering: what names have each of these elements been given? Well, each element in an array shares *the same name as the array*, so in this case each element is called temperature. The individual elements are then *uniquely identified* by an additional **index value**. An index value acts rather like a street number to identify houses on the same street. Like a street number, these index values are always continuous integers. Note carefully that, in Java, *array indices start from 0 and not from 1*. This index value is always enclosed in square brackets, so the first temperature in the list is identified as temperature[0], the second temperature by temperature[1] and so on.

This means that the size of the array and the last index value are not the same thing. In this case the size is 7 and the last index is 6. There is no such value as temperature[7], for example. Remember this, as it is a common cause of error in programs!

Usually, when an array is created, values will be added into it as the program runs. If, however, all the values of the array elements are known beforehand, then an array can be created without use of the **new** operator by initialization as follows:

```
double [] temperature = {9, 11.5, 11, 8.5, 7, 9, 8.5} ;
```

Here each initial value is placed in braces and separated by commas. The compiler determines the length of the array by the number of initial values (in this case 7). Each value is placed into the array in order, so temperature[0] is set to 9, temperature[1] to 11.5 and so on. This is the only instance in which *all the elements* of an array can be assigned explicitly by listing out the elements in a single assignment statement. Once an array has been created, elements must be accessed *individually*.

6.3   *Accessing array elements*

Once an array has been created, its elements can be used like any other variable of the given type in Java. If you look back at the temperature example, initializing the values of each temperature when the array is created is actually quite unrealistic. It is much more likely that temperatures would be entered into the program as it runs. Let's look at how to achieve this.

Whether an array is initialized or not, values can be placed into the individual array elements. We know that each element in this array is a variable of type **double**. As with any variable of a scalar type, the assignment operator can be used to enter a value.

The only thing you have to remember when using the assignment operator with an array element is to specify *which* element to place the value in. For example, to allow the user of the program to enter the value of the first temperature, the following assignment could be used:

```
temperature[0] = EasyIn.getDouble();
```

We know we have to use the getDouble method of the EasyIn class here as every element of the temperature array is of type **double**. Note again that, since array indices begin at 0, the first temperature is not at index 1 but index 0.

Array elements can also be printed on the screen; for example, the following command prints out the value of the *sixth* array element:

```
System.out.println(temperature[5]); // index 5 is the sixth element!
```

Note that an array index (such as 5) is just used to *locate* a position in the array; it is *not* the item at that position.

For example, let's assume that the user enters a value of 69.5 for the first temperature in the array; the following statement:

```
System.out.println ("temperature for day 1 is "+ temperature[0]);
```

would then print out the message:

> *temperature for day 1 is 69.5*

Statements like the println command above might seem a bit confusing at first. The message refers to "temperature for day **1**" but the temperature that is displayed is temperature[**0**]. Remember though that the temperature at index position 0 *is* the first temperature!

After a while you will get used to this rather unfortunate indexing system of Java. Later on in this chapter we will look at ways to overcome this difference between the natural way of indexing lists (1,2,3 etc.) and array indices (0,1,2 etc.).

As you can see from the examples above, you can use array elements in exactly the same way you can use any other kind of variable of the given type. Here are a few more examples:

```
temperature[4] = temperature[4] * 2; //doubles the fifth temperature
if (temperature[2]>=18) // checks if day 3 was a hot day
{
   System.out.println("it was hot today");
}
```

So far so good, but if you are just going to use array elements in the way you used regular variables, why bother with arrays at all?

The reason is that the indexing system of arrays is in fact a very powerful programming tool. The index value does not need to be a literal number such as 5 or 2 as in the examples we have just shown you; it can be *any expression that returns an integer value*.

More often than not an integer *variable* is used, in place of a fixed index value, to access an array element. For example, if we assume that i is some integer variable, then the following is a perfectly legal way of accessing an array element:

```
System.out.println(temperature[i]); // index is a variable
```

Here the array index is not a literal number (like 2 or 5) but the variable i. The *value* of i will determine the array index. If the value of i is 4 then this will display temperature[4], if the value of i is 6 then this will display temperature[6], and so on.[1]

The advantage of using a variable in place of a fixed number as an array index is that the name of each array element can be *computed*. One useful application of this is to place the array instructions within a loop (usually a **for** loop), with the loop counter being used as the array index.

In this way *entire* arrays can be processed by writing the code to process a *single* array element and placing that code within a loop. For example, returning to the original problem in section 6.1 of entering all seven temperature readings, the following loop could now be used:

```
for(int i = 0; i<7; i++) // note, loop counter runs from 0 to 6
{
   System.out.println("max temperature for day "+(i+1));
   temperature[i] = EasyIn.getDouble(); // use loop counter
}
```

Note carefully the following points from this loop:

- Unlike the previous examples of **for** loop counters that started at 1, this counter starts at 0. Since the counter is meant to track the array indices, 0 is the natural number to start from.
- The counter goes up to, but does not include, the number of items in the array. In this case this means the counter goes up to 6 and not 7. Again this is because the array index for an array of size seven stops at six.
- The println command uses the loop counter to display the number of the given day being entered. The loop counter starts from 0, however. We would not think of the first day of the week as being day 0! In order for the message to be more meaningful for the user, therefore, we have displayed (i+1) rather than i.

Effectively this loop implies that the following statements are executed:

---

[1] Note that the array index value must always be a *valid* value. In this case it must be a number from zero to six. If it is not, for example if i is 7, then your program will terminate when this line is executed with a message ArrayIndexOutOfBounds. We will look at approaches to guard against this kind of error in chapter 8.

```
System.out.println("max temperature for day 1 ");     }   1st time round
temperature[0] = EasyIn.getDouble();                      loop

System.out.println("max temperature for day 2 ");     }   2nd time round
temperature [1] = EasyIn.getDouble();                     loop

//as above but with indices 2-5                       }   3rd-6th time
                                                          round loop

System.out.println("max temperature for day 7 ");     }   7th time round
temperature [6] = EasyIn.getDouble();                     loop
```

You should now be able to see the value of an array. This loop can be made more readable if we make use of a built-in feature of all arrays. That is the **public attribute** length. This attribute of an array holds the **number of elements** that can be placed in the array.

As with any public component of an object, you access it with the dot operator. For example:

```
System.out.print("number of temperatures = ");
System.out.println(temperature.length);
```

which displays the following on to the screen:

```
number of temperatures = 7
```

Note that length is an *attribute* of an array, not a *method*, so it is not accessed with round brackets as temperature.length(). This attribute can be used in place of a fixed number in the **for** loop as follows:

```
for (int i = 0; i < temperature.length, i++)
{
   // code for loop goes here
}
```

To see this technique being exploited, look at program 6.1 to see the completed TemperatureReadings class, which stores and displays the maximum daily temperatures in a week.

PROGRAM 6.1

```java
public class TemperatureReadings
{
  public static void main(String[] args)
  { // create array
    double [] temperature = new double[7];
    // enter temperatures
    for (int i = 0; i < temperature.length; i++)
    {
      System.out.println("max temperature for day " + (i+1));
      temperature[i] = EasyIn.getDouble();
    }
    // display temperatures
    System.out.println(); // blank line
    System.out.println("***TEMPERATURES ENTERED***");
    for (int i = 0; i < temperature.length; i++)
    {
      System.out.println("day "+(i+1)+" "+ temperature[i]);
    }
    EasyIn.pause("Press <Enter> to quit");
  }
}
```

Note how the `length` attribute was used to control the two **for** loops. Here is a sample test run.

```
max temperature for day 1 12.2
max temperature for day 2 10.5
max temperature for day 3 13
max temperature for day 4 15
max temperature for day 5 13
max temperature for day 6 12.5
max temperature for day 7 12

***TEMPERATURES ENTERED***
day 1 12.2
day 2 10.5
day 3 13.0
day 4 15.0
day 5 13.0
day 6 12.5
day 7 12.0
Press <Enter> to quit
```

Note that as each temperature is stored as a **double** value, this value will be displayed with a decimal point. This means, for example, that a temperature of 12 will be displayed as 12.0.

6.4   *Passing arrays as parameters*

We have said that an array is a kind of object in Java. Apart from a few discrepancies that we told you about, you can pretty much treat an array as you would any other object. In particular you can use an array as a parameter to a method just as you would use an object as a parameter to a method.

As an example of passing an array to a method, consider once again program 6.1 which processes temperature readings. That program contains all the processing within the main method. As a result, the code for this method is becoming a little difficult to read. Let's do something about that.

Up until now we have always declared attributes of classes as **private** and methods of classes as **public**. Most of the time that is exactly what you need to do – keep your data hidden and make your methods accessible. Sometimes, however, you may not wish to keep an attribute **private**, or a method **public**. For instance, arrays (as you have already seen) have an attribute, length, that is **public**.

When might you choose to declare a method as **private**? One answer is when this method is just being used by *other methods within the class*. For this reason, these methods are sometimes called **worker methods**; they simply carry out some work for other methods within the class – they themselves are not publicly accessible.

We will use this idea to relieve the main method of all the hard work it is being asked to carry out. We will create two worker methods, enterTemps and displayTemps, to enter and display temperatures respectively. As a first attempt you might consider the following code for enterTemps:

```
private void enterTemps( ) // try this ?
{
  for (int i = 0; i < temperature.length; i++)
  {
    System.out.println("max temperature for day " +(i+1));
    temperature[i] = EasyIn.getDouble();
  }
}
```

Here, we have taken the code for entering temperature readings from the main method and placed it in this worker method. This is fine, but there are a few problems with the method header.

```
private void enterTemps( ) // what is wrong ?
```

The first problem is that this worker method is going to be called by the main method. The main method, however, is an example of a *class* method that we discussed in the last chapter. You can see that because it is declared as **static**. Class methods can call only *other* class methods from that class. This means that any worker method that main calls upon *must* be declared as **static**.

```
private static void enterTemps( )  // a bit better
```

There is still something wrong with this method header. Look back at the code within this method. There are two items of data being accessed, the loop counter i and the array temperature.

```
for (int i = 0; i < temperature.length; i++)
{
    System.out.println("max temperature for day " + (i+1)):
    temperature[i] = EasyIn.getDouble();
}
```

There is no problem with the loop counter as it is declared within the loop and so is local to the worker method. The problem is the array, temperature, as it was declared within the main method. When an item of data is declared within one method, it is not (by default) visible *outside of this method.*[2] Therefore, this worker method *does not have access to the array* and so cannot refer to it. To give this worker method access to the array it must receive it as a parameter as follows:

```
private static void enterTemps( double[] temperatureIn )
```

Notice that when a parameter is declared as an array type, the size of the array is not required. This array can now be accessed by the body of the method. The name of this parameter is entirely up to you. In this case we have called it temperatureIn. Remember that, like any other object, an array is a reference type, so the parameter temperatureIn is a copy of that reference. Any changes you make to the contents of the array temperatureIn you make to the original array. In other words, when this method is called from within main, temperatureIn is just another name for the array that is sent from main.

Having created this worker method, main can now call upon this method to carry out its work. Since worker methods live in the same class as the methods that call upon them, a dot operator is not necessary to associate the method with a particular object or class. This is how main would call the method enterTemps:

---

[2] The visibility of a variable is often referred to as the **scope** of a variable.

```
public static void main(String[] args)
{
  double [] temperature = new double [7]; // create array
  enterTemps (temperature); // call worker with array temperature
  // more code goes here
}
```

Notice that (just as with any other parameter) when you call a method that is expecting an array, you plug in only the array *name*, in this case temperature; you do not include the array *type*. Program 6.2 rewrites program 6.1 by giving the main method two worker methods.

PROGRAM 6.2

```
public class TemperatureReadings2
{
  public static void main(String[] args)
  {
    double [ ] temperature = new double[7];
    enterTemps(temperature); // call static enter method
    displayTemps(temperature); // call static display method
    EasyIn.pause("press <Enter> to Quit");
  }

  // worker method to enter temperatures
  private static void enterTemps(double [] temperatureIn)
  {
    for (int i = 0; i < temperatureIn.length; i++)
    {
      System.out.println("max temperature for day " + (i+1));
      temperatureIn[i] = EasyIn.getDouble();
    }
  }

  // worker method to display temperatures
  private static void displayTemps(double[] temperatureIn)
  {
    System.out.println(); // blank line
    System.out.println("***TEMPERATURES ENTERED***");
    for (int i = 0; i < temperatureIn.length; i++)
    {
      System.out.println("day "+(i+1)+" "+ temperatureIn[i]);
    }
  }
}
```

Notice how the main method now becomes much more readable. Although we have written this program differently, it produces exactly the same results as program 6.1.

6.5   *Collection classes*

So far we have used an array only as a variable within a method. However, an array can also be used as an *attribute* of a class. In this way we can hide some of the inconveniences of the array type (such as remembering to start array indices at zero) by providing our own methods to control array access. A class that contains many items of the same type is said to be a **collection class**. In our everyday lives we can see many examples of collections:

- a train contains a collection of passengers;
- a post bag contains a collection of letters;
- a letter contains a collection of words.

As can be seen from the examples above, some collections can themselves contain other collections.

6.5.1   **Types of collections**

Collections must have some *internal structure*, which determines the relationship between the members of the collection, and some access rules. For example:

- **a set** is an *unordered* collection of elements, from which any item may be removed;
- **a list** (figure 6.2) is an *ordered* collection of elements, from which any item may be removed;
- **a stack** (figure 6.3) is a restrictive form of list that obeys a last-in-first-out (LIFO) rule, like a stack of plates that are stored after being washed, then used again – the last one to join the stack is the first one to leave;
- **a queue** (figure 6.4) is also a restrictive form of list that obeys a first-in-first-out (FIFO) rule, like the queue at a bus-stop – the first one to join the queue is the first one to leave (imagine the arguments at the post office if a queue obeyed a LIFO rule!).

In practice we can implement collection classes in a number of ways.[3] For the purpose of this chapter we will show you how to use an array to implement a collection class. We will begin with a stack of integers.

6.5.2   **The *IntegerStack* class**

As we have already said, a stack is defined as a LIFO collection. Computer texts refer to the operation that places an item on the stack as a **push** operation, and the operation to remove an item as a **pop** operation. We will use the same convention here.

Unlike the array we used in programs 6.1 and 6.2, the number of elements in a stack shrinks and grows over time. One of the limitations of an array is that, once it is created, its maximum size is fixed. This means that most of the time the array will have many positions empty.

---

[3] In some texts the term *container* class is used in place of *collection* class.

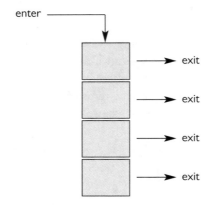

Fig 6.2   Items may leave from any point in a list

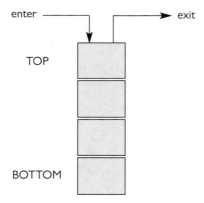

Fig 6.3   Items leave from the top of a stack

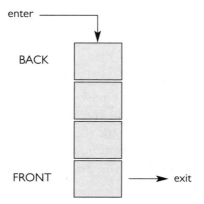

Fig 6.4   Items leave from the front of a queue

We have already shown you that loops are useful when processing arrays and that the length attribute can be used to help track array indices. Let's assume that a stack is fixed at size five. If the array is partially filled with only two elements, the length attribute is no longer of any use when checking these elements as it just returns the *maximum* capacity (see figure 6.5).

Note that we are viewing the first element of the array, stack[0], as being the *bottom* of the stack. To be able to process a partially filled array we will need to keep track of the actual number of elements entered by introducing a new attribute. If we call this attribute total, we will also need to provide a method to read this value, getTotal say.

Now, before we show you the UML diagram for the IntegerStack class, let's go back to the problem of arrays needing to be of a fixed size. While there is nothing we can do about that, we can at least allow the user of our class to decide what this size should be, rather than size the array ourselves.

How will we go about doing this? Well, remember that we told you that creating an array is a two-stage process:, first, you declare and then you allocate memory. You have to fix a size for the array only *when you allocate memory for it*. If we put off the array creation in the IntegerStack constructor, then we can allow the size of the array to be set to the value of some parameter.

Now, let's have a look at the UML diagram for the design of the IntegerStack class in figure 6.6.

The *push* operation will require one parameter (a value of type **int**), which is the value to be pushed onto the stack; the *pop* operation will not require any parameters, as the item removed will always be the last one that was pushed onto the stack. Both of these operations return a **boolean** value to indicate whether or not the operation was processed successfully. A *push* operation will not be successful if the stack is already full and a *pop* will be unsuccessful if the stack is empty. Notice that we have also included three additional methods:

- IsEmpty, which reports on whether or not the stack is empty;
- IsFull, which reports on whether or not the stack is full;
- getItem, which returns the value of the item at a given position in the stack.

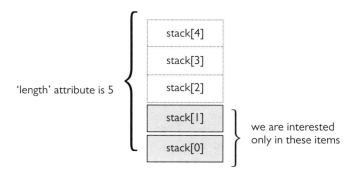

Fig 6.5   The *length* attribute is not as useful with a partially filled array

IntegerStack
stack: int [ ] *total : int*
IntegerStack(int) *push (int): boolean* *pop( ): boolean* *isEmpty(): boolean* *isFull(): boolean* *getItem(int): int* *getTotal(): int*

Fig 6.6　**The *IntegerStack* class**

The code for this class is given in the box below. Have a look at the code and read the comments carefully.

THE *IntegerStack* CLASS

```
class IntegerStack
{
  private int[] stack; // to hold the stack of integers
  private int total; // to track number of items

  public IntegerStack(int sizeIn)
  { // size array with parameter
    stack = new int[sizeIn];
    // set number of items to zero
    total = 0;
  }

  // add an item to the array
  public boolean push(int j)
  {
    if( isFull() == false ) // checks if space in stack
    {
      stack[total] = j; // add item
      total++; // increment item counter
      return true; // to indicate success
    }
    else
    {
      return false; // to indicate failure
    }
  }

  // remove an item by obeying LIFO rule
  public boolean pop()
  {
```

```java
    if( isEmpty() == false) // makes sure stack is not empty
    {
      total--; // reduce counter by one
      return true; // to indicate success
    }
    else
    {
      return false; // to indicate failure
    }
  }

  // checks if array is empty
  public boolean isEmpty()
  {
    if(total==0)
    {
      return true;
    }
    else
    {
      return false;
    }
  }

  // checks if array is full
  public boolean isFull()
  {
    if(total==stack.length)
    {
      return true;
    }
    else
    {
      return false;
    }
  }

  // returns the ith item
  public int getItem(int i)
  {
    return stack[i-1]; // ith item at position i-1
  }

  // return the number of items in the array
  public int getTotal()
  {
    return total;
  }
}
```

All these methods should be easy to follow. Look again at the getItem method. Do you see what we've done? We said earlier that arrays have an unfortunate indexing system where the fourth element, for example, is at index number 3. Here, we have allowed the getItem method to take a natural index, 4 for the fourth element, 3 for the third and so on, and we have taken one off this index within the method.

Below is program 6.3 that which tests the IntegerStack class.

PROGRAM 6.3

```java
public class IntegerStackTester
{
  public static void main(String[] args)
  {
    char choice;
    int size;
    // ask user to fix maximum size of stack
    System.out.print("Maximum number of items on stack?");
    size = EasyIn.getInt();
    // create new stack
    IntegerStack stack = new IntegerStack(size);
    // offer menu
    do
    {
      System.out.println();
      System.out.println("1. Push number onto stack");
      System.out.println("2. Pop number from stack");
      System.out.println("3. Check if stack is empty");
      System.out.println("4. Check if stack is full");
      System.out.println("5. Display numbers in stack");
      System.out.println("6. Quit");
      System.out.println();
      System.out.print("Enter choice [1-6]: ");
      choice = EasyIn.getChar();
      System.out.println();
      // process choice
      switch(choice)
      { // call static methods
        case '1': option1(stack); break;
        case '2': option2(stack); break;
        case '3': option3(stack); break;
        case '4': option4(stack); break;
        case '5': option5(stack); break;
        case '6': break;
        default : System.out.println("Invalid entry");
      }
    }while(choice!="6");
  }
```

```java
// static method to push item onto stack
private static void option1(IntegerStack stackIn)
{
  System.out.print("Enter number: ");
  int num = EasyIn.getInt();
  boolean ok = stackIn.push(num); // attempt to push
  if(!ok) // check if push was unsuccessful
  {
    System.out.println("Push unsuccessful");
  }
}

// static method to pop item onto stack
private static void option2(IntegerStack stackIn)
{
  boolean ok = stackIn.pop(); // attempt to pop
  if(!ok) // check if pop was unsuccessful
  {
    System.out.println("Pop unsuccessful");
  }
}

// static method to check if stack is empty
private static void option3(IntegerStack stackIn)
{
  if(stackIn.isEmpty())
  {
    System.out.println("Stack empty");
  }
  else
  {
    System.out.println("Stack not empty");
  }
}

// static method to check if stack is full
private static void option4(IntegerStack stackIn)
{
  if(stackIn.isFull())
  {
    System.out.println("Stack full");
  }
  else
  {
    System.out.println("Stack not full");
  }
}
```

```
  // static method to display stack
  private static void option5(IntegerStack stackIn)
  {
    if(stackIn.isEmpty())
    {
      System.out.println("Stack empty");
    }
    else
    {
      System.out.println("Numbers in stack are: ");
      System.out.println();
      for(int i = 1; i<=stackIn.getTotal(); i++)
      {
        System.out.println(stackIn.getItem(i));
      }
      System.out.println();
    }
  }
}
```

Again, most of the techniques used in this program you have met before. We will just point out one or two things that you should note.

Both the **static** option1 method (to *push* an item) and the **static** option2 method (to *pop* an item) involve checking whether the associated IntegerStack methods completed their task successfully. Recall that both push and pop in the IntegerStack class return a **boolean** value. This value is set to **true** to indicate that the operation was successful and **false** otherwise. Now, take a look at the call to the pop method:

```
boolean ok = stackIn.pop();
```

The **boolean** value is returned and placed into a variable that we have called ok. The **if** statement that follows then checks the value of this variable:

```
if(!ok) // check if pop was unsuccessful
{
  System.out.println("Pop unsuccessful");
}
```

If you look at the test associated with this selection, it is expressed in a very intuitive way:

```
if(!ok)
```

This is equivalent to the following longer, and not so intuitive test :

```
if (ok == false)
```

Second, notice how the loop used in the `option5` method is also more intuitive than the **for** loops we used earlier to process arrays.

```
for(int i = 1; i<=stackIn.getTotal(); i++)
{
   System.out.println(stackIn.getItem(i));
}
```

Here the loop can start from 1 and go up to the number of items in the stack. That is because the `getItem` method takes one off this index for us to translate back into true array indices. Now, here is a test run of this program; study it carefully.

Maximum number of items on stack? **5**

1. Push number onto stack
2. Pop number from stack
3. Check if stack is empty
4. Check if stack is full
5. Display numbers in stack
6. Quit
*Enter choice [1-6]:***2**

Pop unsuccessful

1. Push number onto stack
2. Pop number from stack
3. Check if stack is empty
4. Check if stack is full
5. Display numbers in stack
6. Quit
*Enter choice [1-6]:***3**

Stack is empty

1. Push number onto stack
2. Pop number from stack
3. Check if stack is empty
4. Check if stack is full
5. Display numbers in stack
6. Quit

Enter choice [1-6]:**4**

Stack not full

1. Push number onto stack
2. Pop number from stack
3. Check if stack is empty
4. Check if stack is full
5. Display numbers in stack
6. Quit

Enter choice [1-6]:**1**

enter number: **22**

1. Push number onto stack
2. Pop number from stack
3. Check if stack is empty
4. Check if stack is full
5. Display numbers in stack
6. Quit

Enter choice [1-6]:**1**

enter number: **9**

1. Push number onto stack
2. Pop number from stack
3. Check if stack is empty
4. Check if stack is full
5. Display numbers in stack
6. Quit

Enter choice [1-6]:**1**

enter number: **15**

1. Push number onto stack
2. Pop number from stack
3. Check if stack is empty
4. Check if stack is full
5. Display numbers in stack
6. Quit

Enter choice [1-6]:**5**
22
9
15

```
1. Push number onto stack
2. Pop number from stack
3. Check if stack is empty
4. Check if stack is full
5. Display numbers in stack
6. Quit

Enter choice [1-6]:2

1. Push number onto stack
2. Pop number from stack
3. Check if stack is empty
4. Check if stack is full
5. Display numbers in stack
6. Quit

Enter choice [1-6]:5
22
9

1. Push number onto stack
2. Pop number from stack
3. Check if stack is empty
4. Check if stack is full
5. Display numbers in stack
6. Quit

Enter choice [1-6]:6
```

This `IntegerStack` class is an example of the use of an array to model a collection of scalar types. Collection classes are, however, most commonly required to hold objects.

6.5.3   The *StringList* class

Consider an object that contains a simple collection of fruit names, where each fruit name is implemented as a `String`. These names will be added to and deleted from the collection freely. A stack is too restrictive a collection here as only the *last* name added could be deleted. A much more suitable type of collection would be a *list*. We will develop a collection class, `StringList`, to be a list of `String` objects.

When one object itself consists of other objects, this relationship is called **aggregation**. This association is often referred to as a *part-of* relationship. For example, the association between a car object and wheel objects is one of *aggregation*: wheels are *part-of* a car. **Containment** is a special form of aggregation where the one object exists in its own right, regardless of the number of objects it contains. For instance, the association between a car object and passenger objects is one of *containment* as a car exists whether or not it contains any passengers. A collection class is an implementation of this containment relationship.

The association between the container object, StringList, and the contained object, String, is shown in the UML diagram of figure 6.7.

The diamond indicates aggregation. The asterisk at the other end of the joining line indicates that the StringList object contains *zero or more* String objects. The design for the StringList class is now given in figure 6.8.

As you can see, the design for this class looks very like the IntegerStack class that we have already developed. One important difference is that our array will contain objects (of type String) as opposed to scalar types. You create an array of simple scalar types or objects in the same way. If the array is to contain objects, then the type of the array elements will be the class to which the objects belong. So, to declare an array of four String objects, for example, you could do the following:

```
String [] list;
list = new String [4];
```

Fig 6.7   The *StringList* object can contain many *String* objects

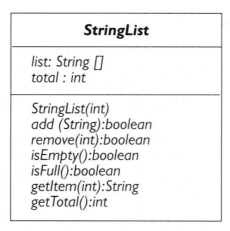

Fig 6.8   The *StringList* class

We have already illustrated the effect of the **new** operator on arrays in figure 6.1. Then, the **new** operator created enough memory for the given array. As we indicated earlier though, the **new** operator behaves slightly differently when creating an array of objects. Instead of setting up an array of the given objects, it sets up an array of *references* to such objects (see figure 6.9).

At the moment, space has been reserved for the four String references only, *not* the four String objects. As we told you in chapter 4, when a reference is initially created it points to the constant **null**, so at this point each reference in the array points to **null**.

This means that memory would still need to be reserved for individual String objects each time we wish to link a String object to the array. For example, if we wanted to associate a String object with the first element in the array, the following instructions could be used:

```
String [ ] list; // sets up a single array reference
list = new String [4]; // sets up space for four String references
list[0] = new String("Strawberry"); // creates space for the string
```

Here, in the last line, a String object has been created with value of "Strawberry" and the reference at list[0] is set to point to it (see figure 6.10).

Apart from the fact that the StringList class is a collection of objects whereas the IntegerStack class was a collection of integers, the only other real difference between the two classes is that the pop method of the IntegerStack class is replaced by a remove method in the StringList class.

Removing an item from any point in a list is a bit more complicated than just taking something off the top of a stack. For this reason we will present the code for the StringList class, but leave the remove method incomplete for now. Examine the code for this class closely and then we'll pick up the discussion of the remove method.

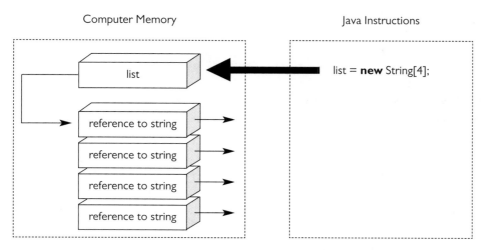

Fig 6.9   The effect on computer memory of creating an array of objects

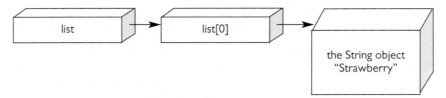

Fig 6.10   Objects are linked to arrays by reference

THE *StringList* CLASS WITH *Remove* METHOD LEFT INCOMPLETE

```
class StringList
{
  // attributes
  private String[] list;
  private int total;

  // methods
  public StringList(int sizeIn)
  { // equivalent to the constructor of IntegerStack
    list = new String[sizeIn];
    total = 0;
  }

  public boolean add(String s)
  { // equivalent to the push method of IntegerStack
    if(!isFull())
    {
      list[total] = s;
      total++;
      return true;
    }
    else
    {
      return false;
    }
  }

  public boolean isEmpty()
  { // equivalent to the isEmpty method of IntegerStack
    if(total==0)
    {
      return true;
    }
    else
    {
      return false;
    }
  }
}
```

```
  public boolean isFull()
  { // equivalent to the isFull method of IntegerStack
    if(total==list.length)
    {
      return true;
    }
    else
    {
      return false;
    }
  }

  public String getItem(int i)
  { // equivalent to the getItem method of IntegerStack
    return list[i-1];
  }

  public int getTotal()
  { // same as the getTotal method of IntegerStack
    return total;
  }

  public boolean remove(int numberIn)
  {
    //to be completed!!!
  }
}
```

As you can see, the interface for the remove method is given as follows:

```
public boolean remove (int numberIn)
```

This method accepts an integer value, numberIn, which represents *the position of the item to be removed*, and it returns a **boolean** value to indicate whether or not that item was removed successfully. One reason why an item might not be removed from a given list would be that there was no item at the given position.

Effectively this means that the position of the item to be removed, numberIn, must lie between the range of 1 and the value of total. We can check whether or not this is the case and return a value of **true** or **false** to indicate whether or not an attempt to remove an item has been successful. This can easily be coded into an **if-else** statement as follows:

```
if (numberIn >= 1 && numberIn <= total())
{
   // code to remove item from list here goes here
   return true; // remove successful
}
else
{
   return false; // remove unsuccessful
}
```

Now let's look at a strategy to remove the given item from a list. One very common approach is to shuffle the previous items in the list along so that the given item is *overwritten* (see figure 6.11).

In the case of figure 6.11, the item to be removed ('orange') was the second item in the list. The items to be shuffled ('pear' and 'apple') were the third and fourth items in the list respectively. Remembering that this list is implemented as an array and that array indices begin at zero, the following assignments could be used to achieve this shuffling:

```
list[1] = list[2]; // overwrite 'orange' with 'pear'
list[2] = list[3]; // overwrite 'pear' with 'apple'
```

This is fine for the small list given in figure 6.11 but what if we had to shuffle 50 items rather than just two? Writing 50 assignment statements is going to be an awful waste of effort. Can you see an easier way to deal with the general case?

As each assignment statement is basically the same apart from the value of the array indices, a much more concise approach would be to use a loop rather than a long series of assignments, and then to use the loop counter in place of the array indices.

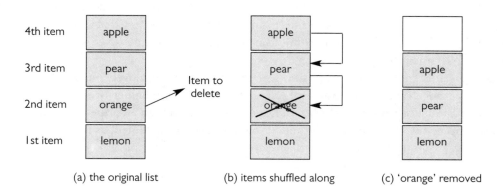

Fig 6.11   An item can be deleted from a list by shuffling adjacent items along

We can express this using pseudocode as follows:

```
LOOP FROM index of item to delete TO index of last but one item
BEGIN
   SET current item TO next item
END
```

We already know that the *position* of the item to delete is given by the parameter `numberIn`. Since array indices begin at zero we must take one off this attribute to get the array index of the item to delete. This gives us so far:

```
LOOP FROM numberIn-1 TO index of last but one item
BEGIN
   SET current item TO next item
END
```

Now, the *position* of the *last* item in the list is the same as the total number of items in the list (stored in the `total` attribute). Therefore the position of the *last but one* item is given as `total−1`. Again, since array indices start at zero, we must remember to take one off this value to arrive at the array index, giving us:

```
LOOP FROM numberIn-1 TO total-2
BEGIN
   SET current item TO next item
END
```

Having thought that through carefully using pseudocode, it is relatively easy to code this into a **for** loop in Java as follows:

```
// loops from item to delete to last but one item
for (int i=numberIn-1; i<= total-2; i++)
{ // overwrite current item with next item
   list[i]= list[i+1];
}
```

This isn't quite the whole story! If we used this loop on the initial list of fruit, to delete 'orange', the array would be left as depicted in figure 6.12.

As you can see, 'apple' is in two positions in the array. There is still an 'apple' in the last position of the list as it hasn't been overwritten with anything. We don't really want that 'apple' in the last position. One way to achieve this is simply to ignore it!

If we wish to ignore it we must remember to reduce the total number of elements in the list, as stored in the `total` attribute, by one. We can achieve this simply as follows:

```
total--;
```

Now the extra 'apple' is effectively hidden from the list.[4] Putting all this back together gives us the following code for the `remove` method:

```
public boolean remove(int numberIn)
{ // check if index is valid before removing
  if(numberIn >= 1 && numberIn <= total())
  { // overwrite items by shifting other items along
    for(int i = numberIn-1; i<= total-2; i++)
    {
      list[i] = list[i+1];
    }
    total--; // decrement total number of objects
    return true; // remove successful
  }
  else
  {
    return false; // remove unsuccessful
  }
}
```

Program 6.4 is a tester class for the `StringList` collection. As you would expect, it is also very similar to the tester class for `IntegerStack`.

list[3]   apple

list[2]   apple

list[1]   pear

list[0]   lemon

Fig 6.12   The 'list' array after 'orange' has been deleted

---

[4] In fact when a new item is added into the list it will overwrite this extra 'apple' item.

PROGRAM 6.4

```java
public class StringListTester
{
  public static void main(String[] args)
  {
    char choice;
    int size;
    System.out.print("Maximum number of items in list? ");
    size = EasyIn.getInt();
    // create StringList object to test
    StringList fruit = new StringList(size);

    // offer menu
    do
    {
      System.out.println();
      System.out.println("1. Add fruit to list");
      System.out.println("2. Remove fruit from list");
      System.out.println("3. Check if list is empty");
      System.out.println("4. Check if list is full");
      System.out.println("5. Display list of fruit");
      System.out.println("6. Quit");
      System.out.println();
      System.out.print("Enter choice [1-6]: ");
      // get choice
      choice = EasyIn.getChar();
      System.out.println();
      // process menu options
      switch(choice)
      {
        case '1': option1(fruit); break;
        case '2': option2(fruit); break;
        case '3': option3(fruit); break;
        case '4': option4(fruit); break;
        case '5': option5(fruit);break;
        case '6': break;
        default : System.out.println("Invalid entry");
      }
    }while(choice!='6');
  }

  // add fruit
  private static void option1 (StringList fruitIn)
  {
```

```java
        System.out.print("Enter name of fruit: ");
        // create String object to add to list
        String name = EasyIn.getString();
        // add string to list
        boolean ok = fruitIn.add(name);
        if(!ok)
        {
          System.out.println("Can't add to a full list");
        }
    }

    // remove fruit
    private static void option2 (StringList fruitIn)
    {
        // get position of item
        System.out.print("Enter position to remove ");
        int position = EasyIn.getInt();
        // delete item if it exists
        boolean ok = fruitIn.remove(position);
        if(!ok)
        {
          System.out.println("No such position");
        }
    }

    // check if empty
    private static void option3 (StringList fruitIn)
    {
        if(fruitIn.isEmpty())
        {
          System.out.println("list is empty");
        }
        else
        {
          System.out.println("list is not empty");
        }
    }

    // check if full
    private static void option4 (StringList fruitIn)
    {
        if(fruitIn.isFull())
        {
          System.out.println("list is full");
        }
        else
        {
```

```
          System.out.println("list is not full");
      }
  }

  // display list
  private static void option5 (StringList fruitIn)
  {
    if(fruitIn.isEmpty()) // no need to display if list is empty
    {
      System.out.println("list is empty");
    }
    else
    {
      System.out.println("Fruits in list are: "); // header
      System.out.println();
      // loop through list
      for(int i = 1; i<= fruitIn.getTotal(); i++)
      {
        System.out.println("item " + i +": " +fruitIn.getItem(i));
      }
    }
  }
}
```

Here is a sample test run; examine it closely and make sure you understand how the underlying StringList class is working.

Maximum number of items in list? **5**

> *1. Add fruit to list*
> *2. Remove fruit from list*
> *3. Check if list is empty*
> *4. Check if list is full*
> *5. Display list of fruit*
> *6. Quit*
>
> *Enter choice [1-6]:* **3**
>
> *list is empty*
>
> *1. Add fruit to list*
> *2. Remove fruit from list*
> *3. Check if list is empty*
> *4. Check if list is full*
> *5. Display list of fruit*
> *6. Quit*

Enter choice [1-6]: **4**

list is not full

1. Add fruit to list
2. Remove fruit from list
3. Check if list is empty
4. Check if list is full
5. Display list of fruit
6. Quit

Enter choice [1-6]: **1**

Enter name of fruit: **Apple**

1. Add fruit to list
2. Remove fruit from list
3. Check if list is empty
4. Check if list is full
5. Display list of fruit
6. Quit

Enter choice [1-6]: **1**

Enter name of fruit: **Orange**

1. Add fruit to list
2. Remove fruit from list
3. Check if list is empty
4. Check if list is full
5. Display list of fruit
6. Quit

Enter choice [1-6]: **1**

Enter name of fruit: **Pear**

1. Add fruit to list
2. Remove fruit from list
3. Check if list is empty
4. Check if list is full
5. Display list of fruit
6. Quit

Enter choice [1-6]: **5**

Fruits in list are:

item 1: Apple
item 2: Orange
item 3: Pear

1. Add fruit to list
2. Remove fruit from list
3. Check if list is empty
4. Check if list is full
5. Display list of fruit
6. Quit

Enter choice [1-6]: **2**

Enter position to remove: **4**
No such position

1. Add fruit to list
2. Remove fruit from list
3. Check if list is empty
4. Check if list is full
5. Display list of fruit
6. Quit

Enter choice [1-6]: **2**

Enter position to remove: **2**

1. Add fruit to list
2. Remove fruit from list
3. Check if list is empty
4. Check if list is full
5. Display list of fruit
6. Quit

Enter choice [1-6]: **5**

Fruits in list are:
item 1: Apple
item 2: Pear

1. Add fruit to list
2. Remove fruit from list
3. Check if list is empty
4. Check if list is full
5. Display list of fruit
6. Quit

Enter choice [1-6]: **6**

Tutorial exercises

1. Consider the following explicit creation of an array:

```
int [] someArray = {8,2,19,0,3,-12,6};
```

    (a) What would be the value of someArray.length?
    (b) What is the value of someArray[3]?
    (c) Create the equivalent array by using the **new** operator and then assigning the value of each element individually.
    (d) Write a loop that will triple the value of every item in someArray.
    (e) Write a loop that will display all those items in the array less than or equal to 6.
2. How do the creation of an array of scalar values and an array of objects differ?
3. How does a **stack** collection differ from a **queue** collection?
4. Look back at program 6.2 which read in and displayed a series of temperature readings. Now define another **static** method, wasCold, which displays all days that recorded temperatures of 8 degrees or less.
5. Consider the class Course that you developed in tutorial question 4 of chapter 5. Now, write the code to
    (a) create an array, computingDepartment, to hold 5 courses;
    (b) add into the 3rd element in the array the course C003, Programming, which runs for six hours per week;
    (c) display the names of all courses that have a total cost of less than 60.

Practical work

1. Implement program 6.2 and add the wasCold method you developed in tutorial question 4 (remember to include a call to this method in your main method).
2. The StringList class was an example of the use of an array to hold a collection of objects. An array can be used to hold not only objects created from built-in predefined classes, like String, but also objects created from your own user-defined classes. For example, look back at the first practical task we gave you at the end of chapter 5. There we defined a Student class for you to implement. Take this implementation of the Student class and use an array to develop a StudentList class. The UML diagram depicting the association between a StudentList object and a Student object is given in the figure opposite:

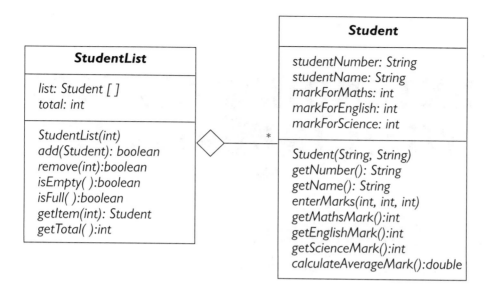

3. Develop a `StudentListTester` class to test the `StudentList` class you defined in practical task 2 above.

4. Look back at figure 6.4 depicting a *queue*. Use an array to help you implement an `IntegerQueue` class to store a queue of integers. This class should have the same methods as the `IntegerStack` class except that the `push` and `pop` methods should be renamed `addToQueue` and `removeFromQueue` respectively.

5. Develop a program to test your `IntegerQueue` class.

6. Develop a `StringQueue` class to hold a queue of `String` objects.

7. Develop a program to test your `StringQueue` class.

7 EXTENDING CLASSES WITH INHERITANCE

LEARNING OBJECTIVES

By the end of this chapter you should be able to:

➤ explain the term **inheritance**;

➤ specify and design inheritance structures using UML notation;

➤ implement inheritance relationships in Java;

➤ explain the term **method overriding**;

➤ explain the term **type cast** and implement this in Java;

➤ create and use a generic collection class.

7.1 Introduction

One of the greatest benefits of the object-oriented approach to software development is that it offers the opportunity for us to *reuse* classes that have already been written – either by ourselves or by someone else. Let's look at a possible scenario. Say you wanted to develop a software system and you have, during your analysis, identified the need for a class called Employee. You might be aware that a colleague in your organization has already written an Employee class; rather than having to write your own class, it would be easier to approach your colleague and ask him/her to let you use his/her Employee class.

So far so good, but what if the Employee class that you are given doesn't quite do everything that you had hoped? Maybe it was written to deal with full-time employees whereas you want a class that can also handle the sort of attributes and methods that are relevant to part-time employees. For example, you might want your class to have an attribute like hourlyPay, or methods like calculateWeeklyPay and setHourlyPay; and these attributes and methods do not exist because they are not applicable to full-time employees.

You may think it would be necessary to go into the old class and start messing about with the code. But there is no need, because object-oriented programming languages provide the ability to extend existing classes by adding attributes and methods to them. This is called **inheritance**.

7.2   *Defining inheritance*

Inheritance is the sharing of attributes and methods among classes. We take a class, and then define other classes based on the first one. The new classes *inherit* all the attributes and methods of the first one, but also have attributes and methods of their own. Let's try to understand this by thinking about the Employee class.

Say our Employee class has three attributes, number, name and annualSalary, and one method, calculateMonthlyPay. We now define our PartTimeEmployee class; this class will *inherit* these attributes and methods, but can also have attributes and methods of its own. We will give it one additional attribute, hourlyPay, and one new method, calculateWeeklyPay.

This is illustrated in figure 7.1 which uses the UML notation for inheritance, namely a triangle.

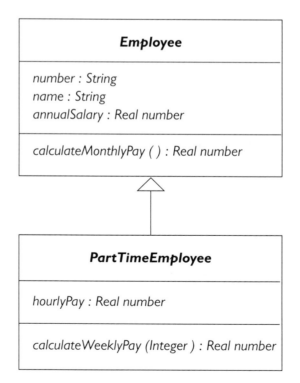

Fig 7.1   An inheritance relationship

You can see from this diagram that an inheritance relationship is a *hierarchical* relationship. The class at the top of the hierarchy – in this case the `Employee` class – is referred to as the **superclass** (or **base class**) and the `PartTimeEmployee` as the **subclass** (or **derived class**).

The inheritance relationship is also often referred to as an *is-a-kind-of* relationship; in this case a `PartTimeEmployee` *is a* kind of `Employee`.

7.3   *Implementing inheritance in Java*

Let's think about the design of our classes by filling in some more detail.

First, the `Employee` class. In addition to the `calculateMonthlyPay` method, we need to think about how we are going to access the attributes. We will certainly need to be able to read all three attributes – but what about writing to them? It would seem like a good idea to set the employee's name and number at the time an `Employee` is created (that is, via a constructor), but not to allow the number to be changed thereafter. We should, however, allow the user to change the employee's name or set the salary.

The complete design of the `Employee` class is shown in figure 7.2; the program code then follows.

<table>
<tr><td align="center">***Employee***</td></tr>
<tr><td>

number : String
name : String
annualSalary : double
</td></tr>
<tr><td>

Employee(String, String)
setName(String)
setAnnualSalary(double)
getNumber() : String
getName() : String
getAnnualSalary() : double
calculateMonthlyPay () : double
</td></tr>
</table>

Fig 7.2   The design of the *Employee* class

THE *Employee* CLASS

```
class Employee
{
  private String number;
  private String name;
  private double annualSalary;

  public Employee(String numberIn, String nameIn)
  {
    number = numberIn;
    name = nameIn;
  }

  public void setName(String nameIn)
  {
    name = nameIn;
  }

  public void setAnnualSalary(double salaryIn)
  {
    annualSalary = salaryIn;
  }

  public String getNumber()
  {
    return number;
  }

  public String getName()
  {
    return name;
  }

  public double getAnnualSalary()
  {
    return annualSalary;
  }

  public double calculateMonthlyPay()
  {
    return annualSalary/12;
  }
}
```

There is nothing new here, so let's get on and design our `PartTimeEmployee` class. We will do the same thing as before with the constructor – send in the number and name when a new `PartTimeEmployee` object is created. We'll also need "set" and "get" methods for the `hourlyPay` attribute as well as the `calculateMonthlyPay` method that we identified earlier. The design is shown in figure 7.3.

Now we can code our PartTimeEmployee class. We will present the code first and analyse it afterwards.

THE *PartTimeEmployee* CLASS

```java
class PartTimeEmployee extends Employee
{
   private double hourlyPay;
   public PartTimeEmployee(String numberIn, String nameIn)
   {
      super(numberIn, nameIn);
   }

   public double getHourlyPay()
   {
      return hourlyPay;
   }

   public void setHourlyPay(double hourlyPayIn)
   {
      hourlyPay = hourlyPayIn;
   }
   public double calculateWeeklyPay(int noOfHoursIn)
   {
      return noOfHoursIn * hourlyPay;
   }
}
```

The first line of interest is the class header itself:

```java
class PartTimeEmployee extends Employee
```

PartTimeEmployee
hourlyPay : double
PartTimeEmployee(String, String) *setHourlyPay(double)* *getHourlyPay() :double* *calculateWeeklyPay(int) :double*

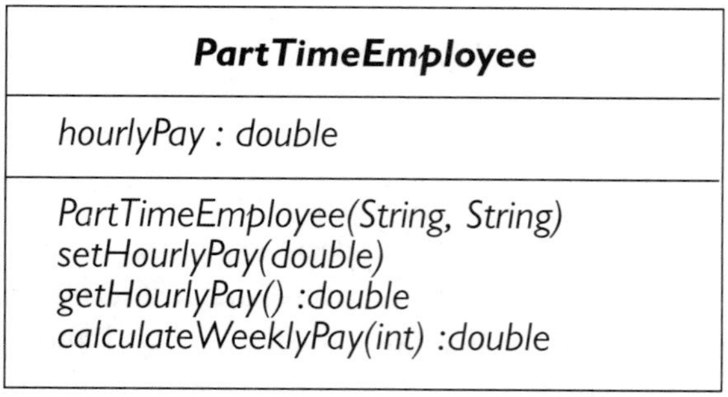

Fig 7.3   The design of the *PartTimeEmployee* class

Here we see the use of the keyword **extends**. Using this word in this way means that the PartTimeEmployee class (the *subclass*) inherits all the attributes of the Employee class (the *superclass*). So although we haven't coded them, any object of the PartTimeEmployee class will have, for example, an attribute called name and a method called getNumber.

But can you see a problem here? The attributes have been declared as private in the superclass so although they are now part of our PartTimeEmployee class, none of the PartTimeEmployee class methods can directly access them – the subclass has only the same access rights as any other class!

There are a number of possible ways around this:

1. We could declare the attributes as **public** – but this would take away the whole point of encapsulation!
2. We could use the special keyword **protected** instead of **private**. The effect of this is that anything declared as **protected** is accessible to the methods of any subclasses. There are, however, two problems with this. The first problem is that you have to anticipate in advance when you want your class to be able to be inherited. The second problem is that it weakens your efforts to encapsulate information within the class, since, in Java, **protected** attributes are also accessible to any other class in the same package.
3. The other solution is the one that we like best – and this is the one that we will be using in this book. This is to leave the attributes as **private**, but to plan in advance how we code the methods that provide access to these attributes. You will see examples of this as we proceed.

After the class header we have the following declaration:

```
private double hourlyPay;
```

This declares an attribute, hourlyPay, which is unique to our subclass – but remember that the attributes of the superclass, Employee, will be inherited, so in fact any PartTimeEmployee object will have four attributes.

Next comes the constructor. As we said before, we want to be able to assign values to the number and name at the time that the object is created, just as we do with an Employee object; so our constructor will need two parameters, which will be assigned to the number and name attributes.

But wait a minute! How are we going to do this? The number and name attributes have been declared as private in the superclass – so they aren't accessible to objects of the subclass. Luckily there is a way around this problem. We can call the constructor of the super class by using the keyword **super**. Look how this is done:

```
public PartTimeEmployee(String numberIn, String nameIn)
{
  // call the constructor of the superclass
  super(numberIn, nameIn);
}
```

The remaining methods are new methods specific to the derived class:

```
public double getHourlyPay()
{
  return hourlyPay;
}

public void setHourlyPay(double hourlyPayIn)
{
  hourlyPay = hourlyPayIn;
}

public double calculateWeeklyPay(int noOfHoursIn)
{
  return noOfHoursIn * hourlyPay;
}
```

The first two provide read and write access respectively to the hourlyPay attribute. The third one receives the number of hours worked and calculates the pay by multiplying this by the hourly rate. Program 7.1 demonstrates the use of the PartTimeEmployee class.

PROGRAM 7.1

```
public class PartTimeEmpTester
{
  public static void main(String[] args)
  {
    String number, name;
    double pay;
    int hours;
    PartTimeEmployee emp;
    // get the details from the user
    System.out.print("Employee Number? ");
    number = EasyIn.getString();
```

```
        System.out.print("Employee's Name? ");
        name = EasyIn.getString();
        System.out.print("Hourly Pay? ");
        pay = EasyIn.getDouble();
        System.out.print("Hours worked this week? ");
        hours = EasyIn.getInt();
        // create a new part-time employee
        emp = new PartTimeEmployee(number, name);
        // set the employee's hourly pay
        emp.setHourlyPay(pay);
        // display employee's details, including the weekly pay
        System.out.println();
        System.out.println(emp.getName());
        System.out.println(emp.getNumber());
        System.out.println(emp.calculateWeeklyPay(hours));
        EasyIn.pause();
    }
}
```

Here is a sample test run:

```
Employee Number? A103456
Employee's Name? Walter Wallcarpeting
Hourly Pay? 15.50
Hours worked this week? 20

Walter Wallcarpeting
A103456
310.0
```

We can now move on to look at another inheritance example; let's choose the Oblong class from chapter 5.

7.3.1   Extending the *Oblong* class

We are going to define a new class called ExtendedOblong, which extends the Oblong class. First, let's remind ourselves of the Oblong class itself.

THE *Oblong* CLASS

```java
class Oblong
{
    // the attributes are declared first
    private double length;
    private double height;

    // then the methods

    // the constructor
    public Oblong(double l, double h)
    {
        length = l;
        height = h;
    }

    // the next method allows us to "read" the length attribute
    public double getLength()
    {
        return length;
    }

    // the next method allows us to "read" the height attribute
    public double getHeight()
    {
        return height;
    }

    // the next method allows us to "write" to the length attribute
    public void setLength(double lengthIn)
    {
        length = lengthIn;
    }

    // the next method allows us to "write" to the height attribute
    public void setHeight(double heightIn)
    {
        height = heightIn;
    }

    // this method returns the area of the oblong
    public double calculateArea()
    {
        return length * height;
    }

    // this method returns the perimeter of the oblong
    public double calculatePerimeter()
    {
        return 2 * (length + height);
    }
}
```

The original `Oblong` class had the capability of reporting on the perimeter and area of the oblong. Our extended class will have the additional capability of drawing a text oblong on the screen by repeatedly displaying a symbol such as an asterisk.

So we will need an additional attribute, which we will call `symbol`, to hold the character that is to be used to draw the oblong. We will also provide a `setSymbol` method, and of course we will need a `draw` method. The new constructor will accept values for the length and height as before, but will also receive the character to be used for drawing the oblong.

The design is shown in figure 7.4.

Now for the implementation. As well as those aspects of the code that relate to inheritance, there is an additional new technique used in this class – this is the technique known as **type casting**. Take a look at the complete code first – then we can discuss this new concept along with some other important features of the class.

THE *ExtendedOblong* CLASS

```
class ExtendedOblong extends Oblong
{
   private char symbol;

   // the constructor
   public ExtendedOblong(double lengthIn, double heightIn, char symbolIn)
   {
      /* the 'super' method must be called before any other methods in the
      constructor */
      super(lengthIn, heightIn);
      symbol = symbolIn;
   }

   public void setSymbol(char symbolIn)
   {
      symbol = symbolIn;
   }
}
```

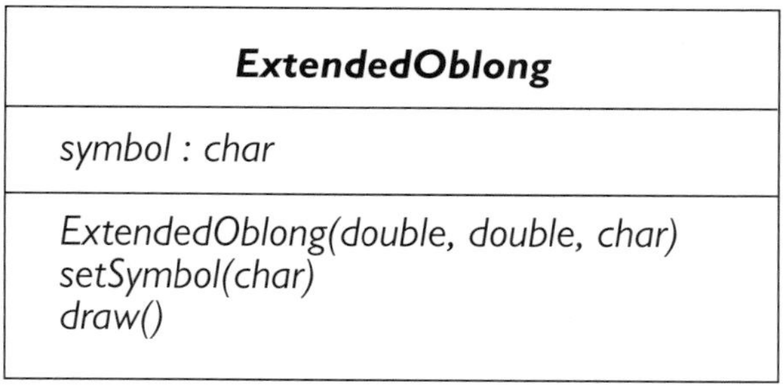

ExtendedOblong
symbol : char
ExtendedOblong(double, double, char) setSymbol(char) draw()

Fig 7.4 **The design of the *ExtendedOblong* class**

```
public void draw()
{
  int l, h, i, j;
  /* in the next two lines we type cast from double to integer so that we
  are able to count how many times we print the symbol */
  l = (int) getLength();
  h = (int) getHeight();
  for(i = 1; i <= h; i++)
  {
    for(j = 1; j <=l; j++)
    {
      System.out.print(symbol);
    }
    System.out.println();
  }
}
```

So let's take a closer look at all this. After the class header – which **extend**s the Oblong class – we declare the additional attribute, symbol, and then define our constructor:

```
public ExtendedOblong(double lengthIn, double heightIn, char symbolIn)
{
  super(lengthIn, heightIn);
  symbol = symbolIn;
}
```

Once again we call the constructor of the superclass with the keyword **super**, but this time we need to perform one more task – namely to assign the third parameter, symbolIn, to the symbol attribute. Notice, however, that the line that calls **super** has to be the first one!

After the constructor comes the setSymbol method – which allows the symbol to be changed during the oblong's lifetime – and then we have the draw method, which introduces the new concept of **type casting**.

```
public void draw()
{
   int i, j, l, h;
   // in the next two lines we type cast from double to integer
   l = (int) getLength();
   h = (int) getHeight();
   for(i = 1; i <= h; i++)
   {
      for(j = 1; j <=l; j++)
      {
         System.out.print(symbol);
      }
      System.out.println();
   }
}
```

Inspect the code carefully – notice that we have declared four local variables of type int. The first two, i and j, are simply to be used as loop counters. But to understand the purpose of the last two, l and h, we need to explore this business of type casting, which means forcing an item to change from one type to another.

The draw method is going to draw the oblong by displaying one or more rows of stars or crosses or whatever symbol is chosen. Now, the dimensions of the oblong are defined as **double**s. Clearly our draw method needs to be dealing with whole numbers of rows and columns – so we must convert the length and height of the oblong from doubles to ints. There will obviously be some loss of precision here, but that won't matter in this particular case.

As you can see from the above code, type casting is achieved by placing the new type name in brackets before the item you wish to change. A further example appears in section 7.7.

Program 7.2 uses the ExtendedOblong class. It creates an oblong of length 10 and height 5, with an asterisk as the symbol; it then draws the oblong, changes the symbol to a cross, and draws it again.

PROGRAM 7.2

```
public class ExtendedOblongTester
{
   public static void main(String[] args)
   {
      ExtendedOblong extOblong = new ExtendedOblong(10,5,'*');
      extOblong.draw();
      System.out.println();
      extOblong.setSymbol('+');
      extOblong.draw();
      EasyIn.pause();
   }
}
```

The output from program 7.2 is shown below:

```
* * * * * * * * *
* * * * * * * * *
* * * * * * * * *
* * * * * * * * *
* * * * * * * * *

++++++++++
++++++++++
++++++++++
++++++++++
++++++++++
```

7.4   *Overriding class methods*

Let's write another class that is derived from Oblong. This time we will develop a class that represents a three-dimensional oblong (a cuboid) as shown in figure 7.5. We will call this class ThreeDOblong.

Clearly we are going to need another attribute, depth, to represent the additional dimension. We will also include a calculateVolume method. So far so good. But wait a second – the ThreeDOblong is going to inherit *all* the attributes and methods from the Oblong class. This includes the calculateArea method. And if we were to invoke this method for a ThreeDOblong object we would get the value of the length times the height – in other words, the area of one face of the oblong. In actual fact, finding the surface area of a three-dimensional oblong involves adding up the areas of all six faces. So the means of calculating the area differs according to whether the object is an Oblong object or a ThreeDOblong object.

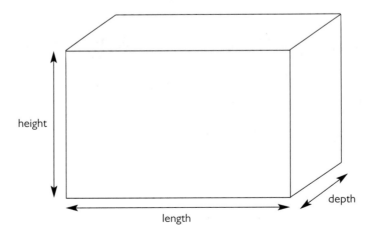

Fig 7.5   A cuboid

Do you remember the term *polymorphism*? If not, then look back at chapter 5 and remind yourself. It means we can use the same name for two different methods. In chapter 5 the program knew which method to call because the parameter list was different for each method. We are going to use a different form of polymorphism here. In our ThreeDOblong class we are going to re-define the calculateArea method. This is called **overriding** the method of the superclass. Look at the code for the ThreeDOblong class below. Notice how we have declared and defined a calculateArea method for that class.

THE *ThreeDOblong* CLASS

```
class ThreeDOblong extends Oblong
{
  private double depth;

  public ThreeDOblong(double l, double h, double d)
  {
    super(l,h);
    depth = d;
  }

  public void setDepth(double depthIn)
  {
    depth = depthIn;
  }

  public double getDepth()
  {
    return depth;
  }

  public double calculateVolume()
  {
    return getLength() * getHeight() * depth;
  }

  public double calculateArea()
  {
    /* Notice that we cannot access the length and height attributes
    directly as they are declared as private in the superclass, so we must
    use the getLength and getHeight methods. The depth attribute is
    accessible as it is declared in the subclass */
    return 2 *(getLength() * getHeight()
              + getLength() * depth
              + getHeight() * depth);
  }
}
```

So how does the program know which method we mean when we call calculateArea? Well, it knows because the call to the method will always be a associated with a particular object – and the `calculateArea` method of the corresponding object will be called. This is illustrated in program 7.3, the output of which is displayed after the program. The two calls to the `calculateArea` method have been emboldened to help you understand it.

PROGRAM 7.3

```
public class ThreeDOblongTester
{
  public static void main(String[] args)
  {
    Oblong oblong = new Oblong(5,10);
    ThreeDOblong threeDOblong = new ThreeDOblong(5,10,20);
    System.out.println("Area of the oblong is: "
                                    + oblong.calculateArea());
    System.out.println("Surface area of the 3D oblong is: "
                                    + threeDOblong.calculateArea());
    EasyIn.pause();
  }
}
```

The output from this program is:

```
Area of the oblong is: 50.0
Surface area of the 3D oblong is: 700.0
```

One final thing to point our here: the keyword **super** can be used with the dot operator to call *any* method of the superclass. So an alternative way of coding the calulateArea method of `ThreeDOblong` could have been like this:

```
return 2 *(super.calculateArea()
                    + getLength() * depth
                    + getHeight() * depth );
```

7.5   Abstract classes

Let's think again about our `Employee` class. Imagine that we had been developing our system from scratch – it might well have occurred to us at that time that there could be two types of employee, full-time and part-time. We might also have thought about the fact that in the future, as our business expands, there could be other types of employee (maybe "casual" or "fractional"). It would make sense to create a generalized `Employee` class, so that we can easily create other kinds of `Employees` later.

Figure 7.6 shows the structure of an employee **hierarchy** with the two types of employee that we already know about, the full-time and the part-time employee. We have gone straight into the design and have included all the basic access methods here – including a new method in the Employee class, called getStatus – which also appears in both subclasses! We will discuss this method later.

Notice how the two subclasses now both contain the appropriate attributes and methods. If you think about this a bit more, it will occur to you that *any* employee will always be either a full-time employee or a part-time employee. There is never going to be a situation in which an individual is just a plain old employee! So users of a program that included all these classes would never find themselves creating objects of the Employee class. In fact it would be a good

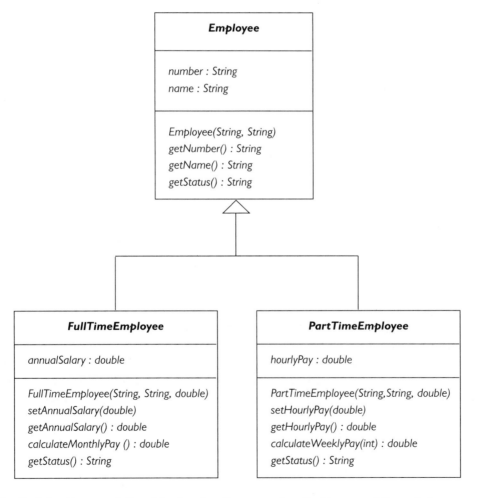

Fig 7.6   **An inheritance relationship showing the superclass *Employee* and the subclasses *FullTimeEmployee* and *PartTimeEmployee***

idea to prevent people from doing this – and, as you might have guessed, there is a way to do so, and that is to declare the class as **abstract**. Once a class has been declared in this way it means that you are not allowed to create objects of that class. The Employee simply acts a basis on which to build other classes.

The code for the Employee appears below. If you inspect it you will notice something else interesting. Do you see that the getStatus method has also been declared **abstract**? Not only that, it also has a header but no body! Study the class for a moment and then we will tell you what this is all about.

THE *Employee* CLASS

```
abstract class Employee // the class is declared abstract
{
  private String number;
  private String name;

  public Employee(String numberIn, String nameIn)
  {
    number = numberIn;
    name = nameIn;
  }

  public String getNumber()
  {
    return number;
  }

  public String getName()
  {
    return name;
  }

  abstract public String getStatus(); // an abstract method
}
```

The purpose of declaring a *method* as **abstract** is to force all subclasses of our class to implement this method. In this case, a FullTimeEmployee and a PartTimeEmployee – and any future subclasses of Employee – will have to have a method called getStatus. The purpose of the getStatus method is to enable an object to report on what kind of employee it is – it will send back a String saying either "Full-time" or "Part-time" accordingly. Each subclass will *override* the getStatus method in a slightly different way.

We shall now implement the two derived classes. First the FullTimeEmployee:

THE *FullTimeEmployee* CLASS

```java
class FullTimeEmployee extends Employee
{
  private double annualSalary;

  public FullTimeEmployee(String numberIn,
                                    String nameIn, double salaryIn)
  {
    super(numberIn,nameIn);
    annualSalary = salaryIn;
  }

  public void setAnnualSalary(double salaryIn)
  {
    annualSalary = salaryIn;
  }

  public double getAnnualSalary()
  {
    return annualSalary;
  }

  public double calculateMonthlyPay()
  {
    return annualSalary/12;
  }

  public String getStatus()
  {
    return "Full-Time";
  }
}
```

And now the PartTimeEmployee:

THE *PartTimeEmployee* CLASS

```
class PartTimeEmployee extends Employee
{
  private double hourlyPay;
  public PartTimeEmployee(String numberIn,
                                  String nameIn, double hourlyPayIn)
  {
    super(numberIn, nameIn);
    hourlyPay = hourlyPayIn;
  }
  public void setHourlyPay(double hourlyPayIn)
  {
    hourlyPay = hourlyPayIn;
  }
  public double getHourlyPay()
  {
    return hourlyPay;
  }
  public double calculateWeeklyPay(int noOfHoursIn)
  {
    return hourlyPay * noOfHoursIn;
  }
  public String getStatus()
  {
    return "Part-Time";
  }
}
```

You may be thinking that abstract classes and abstract methods are quite interesting, but is it worth all the bother? Well, there is another really useful thing we can do with abstract classes and methods.

Say a method of some class somewhere expects to receive as a parameter a particular class – an Employee class for example; and inside this method there is some code that calls a particular method of Employee – for example a method called getStatus. The marvellous thing about inheritance is that an object of any subclass of Employee is *a kind of* Employee and can therefore be passed as a parameter into a method that expects an Employee object. However, this subclass *must* have a getStatus method for it to be able to be passed as a parameter into a method that calls getStatus. By declaring the abstract method getStatus in the superclass we can *insist* that every subclass must have a getStatus method. We can tell anyone who is going to use a derivative of Employee to go right ahead and call a getStatus method because it will definitely be there – and what is more, it will behave differently for each object that it applies to.

If you think this sounds a bit complicated then an example will help. We have written a very simple class called `StatusTester`, whose sole purpose is to test out this abstract method stuff:

THE *StatusTester* CLASS

```
class StatusTester
{
  public static void tester(Employee employeeIn)
  {
    System.out.println(employeeIn.getStatus());
  }
}
```

You can see that this class has a single method, `tester`, which receives an `Employee` object, `employeeIn`, as a parameter. It then calls the `getStatus` method of `employeeIn`. Now, because objects of the class `FullTimeEmployee` and objects of the class `PartTimeEmployee` are both kinds of `Employee`, we can pass either of them to this `tester` method. We have made this a **static** method, so it can be called by using the class name.

In program 7.4 objects of both of these types are sent to the `tester` method.

PROGRAM 7.4

```
public class RunStatusTester
{
  public static void main(String[] args)
  {
    // create a FullTimeEmployee object
    FullTimeEmployee fte = new FullTimeEmployee ("100", "Patel", 30000);
    // create a PartTimeEmployee object
    PartTimeEmployee pte = new PartTimeEmployee ("101", "Jones", 12);
    // call tester with the full-time employee
    StatusTester.tester(fte);
    // now call tester with the part-time employee
    StatusTester.tester(pte);
    EasyIn.pause("Press <enter> to quit");
  }
}
```

The `tester` method will call the appropriate `getStatus` method according to the type of object it receives. Thus the output from this program will be:

```
Full-Time
Part-Time
```

7.6   *The final modifier*

You have already seen the use of the keyword **final** in chapter 2, where it was used to modify a variable and turn it into a constant. It can also be used to modify a class and a method. In the case of a class it is placed before the class declaration, like this:

```
final class SomeClass
{
    // code goes here
}
```

This means that the class cannot be subclassed. In the case of a method it is used like this:

```
public final someMethod
{
    // code goes here
}
```

This means that the method cannot be overridden.

7.7   *Generic collection classes*

In the last chapter we constructed collection classes to hold specific items (for example integers or students). Sometimes it is desirable to have a collection class that can hold *any* item, and inheritance can help us to achieve this.

Remember the StudentList class you developed in your second practical task at the end of chapter 6. Apart from the type of the array elements, the code you wrote should have been exactly the same as the code for the StringList class that we developed in that chapter. Rather than write many lists, each to hold a different type, it would be much more productive to develop a list that could contain *any* type.

A collection that can contain items of any type is called a **generic collection class**. We will re-write the StringList collection class from chapter 6 so that it can be used to contain items of *any* class, not just a String class. In some programming languages this is difficult; but in Java it is relatively easy because every object is in fact a subclass of a basic class called an **Object** class. In other words, any object in Java *is a kind of* **Object**! So all we have to do to make our list class generic is to use the type **Object** rather than a specific type like Student.

Below is the code for this generic class, which we have called ObjectList.

THE *ObjectList* CLASS

```
class ObjectList
{
  private Object[] object ;
  private int total ;

  public ObjectList(int sizeIn)
  {
    object = new Object[sizeIn];
    total = 0;
  }

  public boolean add(Object objectIn)
  {
    if(!isFull())
    {
      object[total] = objectIn;
      total++;
      return true;
    }
    else
    {
      return false;
    }
  }

  public boolean isEmpty()
  {
    if(total==0)
    {
      return true;
    }
    else
    {
      return false;
    }
  }

  public boolean isFull()
  {
    if(total==object.length)
    {
      return true;
    }
    else
    {
      return false;
    }
```

```
   }
   public Object getObject(int i)
   {
     return object[i-1];
   }
   public int getTotal()
   {
     return total;
   }
   public boolean remove(int numberIn)
   {
     // check that a valid index has been supplied
     if(numberIn >= 1 && numberIn <= total)
     { // overwrite object by shifting following objects along
       for(int i = numberIn-1; i <= total-2; i++)
       {
         object[i] = object[i+1];
       }
       total--; // Decrement total number of objects
       return true;
     }
     else // remove was unsuccessful
     {
       return false;
     }
   }
 }
```

As you can see, apart from changing the type of the array elements from String to Object, this code is identical to the StringList class that we developed in chapter 6. The advantage it has, however, is that this class can be used to hold objects of *any* type.

For example, you could use it to hold a list of BankAccount objects or a list of Student objects. You just have to be careful of one thing. That is, when an object is returned from a method in a generic collection class such as this, the type of that object will be Object. This collection class has one such method, getObject.

```
public Object getObject(int i) // returns Object type
{
  return object[i-1];
}
```

This item of type Object must be converted back into the actual type used within the list. That is, back to a BankAccount if the list was used to hold BankAccount objects, back to String if the list was used to hold String objects and so on. This is easily done by – by **type casting**.

For example, assume an object of type ObjectList has been created and named list. If the list was used to hold Student objects, the second student in the list could be accessed as follows:

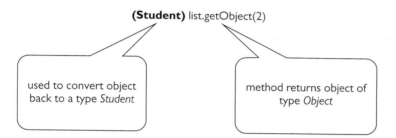

Program 7.5 is an ObjectListTester class, which illustrates the generic list being used to hold items of type String. Since the code is almost identical to the StringListTester in chapter 6, most lines have been replaced by comments, with only the changes highlighted.

PROGRAM 7.5

```java
public class ObjectListTester
{
  public static void main(String[] args)
  {
    char choice;
    int size;
    System.out.println("Maximum number of items in list?");
    size = EasyIn.getInt();
    // create generic list
    ObjectList list = new ObjectList(size);
    // menu control goes here as before
  }
  public static void option1 (ObjectList list)
  {
    // code for adding object, as before
  }
  public static void option2 (ObjectList list)
  {
    // code for removing item, as before
  }
  public static void option3 (ObjectList list)
  {
    // code for checking if list is empty, as before
  }
```

```
  public static void option4 (ObjectList list)
  {
    // code for checking if list is full, as before
  }
  public static void option5 (ObjectList list) // displays items
  {
    // as before up to loop
    for(int i = 1; i<= list.getTotal(); i++)
    {
      // remember to type cast back
      System.out.println((String)list.getObject(i));
    }
    System.out.println();
  }
}
```

Of course, if you were to run this program it would behave exactly the same as program 6.4. The advantage with the `ObjectList` class is that you could reuse it to hold objects of other types simply by replacing `String` in the tester above with another class!

This all sounds great, but what are you going to do if you wanted a generic collection class to hold values of the simple scalar types? Unfortunately, you can't just write a tester class and replace the `String` class in program 7.5 with the type **int**.

Can you see why you can't do this?

The reason you can't use the generic list to hold items of type **int** is that the generic class can hold values of any type, *as long as they are objects* and not simple intrinsic types like **double**s.

All is not lost, however. At the end of chapter 5 we told you about a special group of classes that would be ideal for our purposes right now – **wrapper classes**.

If you remember, wrapper classes provide a class wrapper for simple scalar types. Each scalar type has a class wrapper. Once we put a scalar value into its wrapper class we can pass it into the `ObjectList` for storage.

The wrapper class for integers is `Integer`. Look at the following example to see how to place a value of type **int** into an **Integer** wrapper.

```
// create a simple variable
int x = 10;
// create wrapper object from the value of x
Integer value = new Integer (x);
System.out.println("object has an integer value of " + value.intValue());
```

In this example x is a simple variable of type **int**. The value of x is initialized to 10. A new object, value, of type `Integer` (a wrapper class) is then created to contain the value of x by using the **new** operator. The final output then displays the value of the Integer object as follows:

> object has value of 10

We have used the intValue method of Integer to extract the **int** value that the object holds.[1]

Program 7.6 illustrates another tester program that uses the ObjectList as a list of integers. Once again, only those parts of the class that have changed from program 7.5 have been highlighted.

PROGRAM 7.6

```java
public class ObjectListTester2
{
  public static void main(String[] args)
  {
    char choice;
    boolean ok;
    int size;
    System.out.println("Maximum number of items in list? ");
    size = EasyIn.getInt();
    // create generic list
    ObjectList list = new ObjectList(size);
    // offer menu for an integer list
    do
    {
      System.out.println();
      System.out.println("1. Add integer to list");
      System.out.println("2. Remove integer from list");
      System.out.println("3. Check if list is empty");
      System.out.println("4. Check if list is full");
      System.out.println("5. Display integers in list");
      System.out.println("6. Quit");
      System.out.println();
      System.out.print("Enter choice [1-6]: ");
      choice = EasyIn.getChar();
      System.out.println();
      // process choice
      switch(choice)
      {
        case '1': option1(list); break;
        case '2': option2(list); break;
        case '3': option3(list); break;
        case '4': option4(list);break;
```

---

[1] Actually, the concatenation operator allows you to join an Integer object with a string, so we could have got away with just using value instead of value.intValue().

```java
         case '5': option5(list);break;
         case '6' : break;
         default : System.out.println("Invalid entry");
      }
   }while(choice!='6');
}

private static void addInteger (ObjectList listIn)
{
   System.out.print("Enter an integer number: ");
   int number = EasyIn.getInt(); // enter value
   Integer item = new Integer (number); // place in wrapper
   boolean ok = listIn.add(item); // add object
   // other code same as before
}

private static void removeInteger (ObjectList listIn)
{
   // as before
}

private static void checkEmpty (ObjectList listIn)
{
   // as before
}

private static void checkFull (ObjectList listIn)
{
   // as before
}

private static void displayIntegers (ObjectList listIn)
{
   if(listIn.isEmpty())
   {
      // as before
   }
   else
   {
      System.out.println("Integers in list are: ");
      System.out.println();
      for(int i=1; i<= listIn.getTotal(); i++)
      { // type cast back to Integer
         System.out.println((Integer)listIn.getObject(i));
      }
      System.out.println();
   }
}
}
```

7.8　*Pros and cons of generic collections*

The idea of a generic collection class sounds good – and so it is; however, as with most things in life there are drawbacks as well as advantages. One obvious drawback is that we have to remember to type cast every time we retrieve an item from the collection. Another disadvantage is that we are limited as to what we can do with the methods of a generic collection class, since we cannot anticipate in advance the sort of objects it is going to contain.

The choice of whether to use a generic collection class (which might well mean we can reuse an existing class) or to use a specialized class is one of the many decisions that we have to make at the design stage, and will depend on the application we are building and the way we want it to work. In chapter 10, when we develop our case study, you will be able to see how we take our generic `ObjectList` class from this chapter and develop it using inheritance.

Tutorial exercises

1. Explain the meaning of the following terms:
   - inheritance;
   - method overriding;
   - type casting;
   - generic collection.
2. A class called `Vehicle` is required by a programmer who is writing software for a car dealer. An object of the class `Vehicle` will consist of a registration number, the make of the vehicle, the year of manufacture and the current value of the vehicle. The first three of these will need to be set only at the time an object is created. The current value will also be set at the time of creation, but may need to be changed during the vehicle's lifetime.

   It will be necessary to have a means of reading the values of all the above data items. A method should also be provided which accepts a year as input, and returns the age of the vehicle.

   (a) Design the `Vehicle` class using UML notation and then write the code for this class.

   (b) Design and code a subclass of `Vehicle` called `SecondHandVehicle`. The subclass will have an additional attribute, `numberOfOwners`, which will need to be set at the time a new `vehicle` is created, and will also need to have read access. An additional method is also required which will report on whether or not the vehicle has had more than one previous owner.
3. Explain why it is not possible to use a generic collection class to store items of type `char`, and describe what you would need to do in order to use a generic class to store characters.

4. The following UML diagram shows an inheritance relationship between three classes:

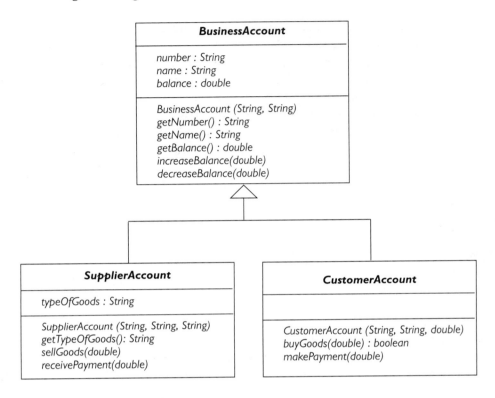

Make a note of the following points, then answer the questions:
- In the case of the `BusinessAccount` class, the constructor sets the first two attributes to the values of the incoming parameters and sets the balance to zero.
- In the case of the `SupplierAccount` class, the constructor behaves similarly to that of the `BusinessAccount` class, but also sets the `typeOfGoods` attribute to the value of the third parameter.
- In the case of the `CustomerAccount` class, the constructor behaves similarly to that of the `Account` class, but sets the initial balance to the value of the third parameter.
- The `sellGoods` method of `SupplierAccount` receives the value of the goods sold as a parameter and adds this to the supplier's balance.
- The `receivePayment` method of `SupplierAccount` receives the amount of the payment as a parameter and subtracts this amount from the supplier's balance.
- The `buyGoods` method of `CustomerAccount` receives the value of the goods purchased as a parameter and subtracts this from the customer's balance. However, this operation must not go ahead if the transaction were to leave the customer with a negative balance. The method therefore returns a **boolean** value indicating whether or not the transaction was successful.
- The `makePayment` method of `CustomerAccount` receives the amount of the payment as a parameter and adds this amount to the customer's balance.

(a) Assuming the code for the BusinessAccount class already exists, write the code for the SupplierAccount and the CustomerAccount.

(b) Consider the following code fragment taken from a program that uses the above classes:

```
BusinessAccount account1 = new Account("A001", "Oladapo");
SupplierAccount account2 = new SupplierAccount("S001", "Jones", "Food");
CustomerAccount account3 = new CustomerAccount("C001", "Shah", 1000);
account2.sellGoods(2000);
account3.buyGoods(2000);
System.out.println(account1.getBalance());
System.out.println(account2.getBalance());
System.out.println(account3.getBalance());
```

What would be the output from this code?

(c) Explain why this fragment of code would not compile if the BusinessAccount class had been declared as **abstract**.

Practical work

1. Implement the Vehicle and the SecondHandVehicle classes from tutorial question 2 above.

2. Write a tester class to test out all the methods of the SecondHandVehicle class.

3. Write a menu-driven program that uses a generic collection class to hold Vehicles. The menu should offer the following options:

```
1. Add a vehicle
2. Display a list of vehicle details
3. Delete a vehicle
4. Quit
```

4. (a) Implement a generic ObjectQueue class. Test this out by using it to hold first characters and then integers (refer back to tutorial question 3 before you do this).

(b) Repeat the above with a generic ObjectStack class.

SOFTWARE QUALITY

LEARNING OBJECTIVES

By the end of this chapter you should be able to:

➤ document your code so that it is easy to **maintain**;

➤ distinguish between **compile-time errors** and **run-time errors**;

➤ test a program using the strategies of **unit testing** and **integration testing**;

➤ generate test data using the strategies of **black box testing**, **white box testing** and **stress testing**;

➤ document your test results professionally using a test log;

➤ explain the meaning of a Java program **throwing an exception**;

➤ format your output to improve the **usability** of your programs.

8.1 *Introduction*

If you buy a new computer, you will probably want that computer to be of a **high quality**. The features you would expect to find in a computer of high quality would be that it is fast, it has a large storage capacity, it supports the latest graphic and sound features – you may be able to think of others. Similarly, if you buy a piece of software you would want that software to be produced to a high quality. But what does it mean for software to be of a high quality? How can you measure software quality?

There are many desirable features of a piece of software. In this chapter we will concentrate on the following:

- maintainability;
- reliability;
- robustness;
- usability.

The more the software exhibits these features, the greater is the **quality** of the software. Let's look at each of these features in turn.

8.2 *Maintainability*

The requirements of an application often change over time. **Maintaining** a system refers to the need to *update* an existing system to reflect these changing requirements. Code should be designed in such a way as to make these changes easier rather than harder.

8.2.1 The importance of encapsulation

One of the problems associated with maintaining software systems has been the so-called **ripple effect**. That is, changes to one part of the system having undesirable knock-on effects on the rest of the system, resulting in system errors.

Such effects can often be hard to detect and to trace. As we discussed in chapter 4, programs written in the old structured way can often lead to such ripple effects. The object-oriented principle of *encapsulation*, however, helps ensure that object-oriented code is easier to maintain by reducing such effects: each object should contain within it all the details it needs to operate, and this data should be hidden inside the object so that changes made to it do not affect the rest of the system.

Java is a pure object-oriented language so programs written in Java should be easier to maintain than their structured counterparts. However, the language does not *insist* that you follow the principles of encapsulation when developing your code – that is your responsibility!

In particular, a class could be defined so that its data members are accessible to any other class – thus breaking the principles of encapsulation. Any future changes to such data would require changes to each method that accessed this data directly, resulting once again in the ripple effects you should aim to avoid. The lesson is a simple one – to ensure that your applications are easy to maintain, keep the data attributes of your classes **private**.

8.2.2 Documentation

A complete software system consists of more than just the final program. For example, most applications that you buy will come with some kind of user manual. Additional supporting materials such as these are referred to as the system's **documentation**. A comprehensive system should have documentation supporting *every* stage of software development. The user manual is an example of a piece of documentation that supports software installation and operation.

For a software system to be easy to maintain, the software *design* also needs to be clearly documented. Often, the people responsible for maintaining a software system are not the same people who initially developed the system. Think of the infamous Y2K bug that worried many companies a few years ago. Many of the systems affected were decades old and the identity of the original developers was no longer known. Design documentation helps new developers understand the working of systems that they themselves may not have produced. When developing object-oriented programs, this design documentation should include:

- complete class diagrams;
- clear method definitions (parameter and return types, plus pseudocode when appropriate).

The UML notation that we have been using throughout this book is becoming a common way of expressing these design decisions. The layout of the code itself can help clarify design decisions and make code maintenance easier.

To understand how important in-code documentation like this can be, consider the two classes below: BadReactor and Reactor. Both classes keep track of the temperature within a reactor in exactly the same way except that one has been documented with care, while the other has been documented poorly. If you were asked to maintain this system so that the maximum safe temperature was to be reduced by two degrees, which class would you find easier to understand and modify?

THE *BadReactor* CLASS IS VERY POORLY DOCUMENTED

```
class BadReactor
{
private int t;
public BadReactor()
{
t = 0;
}
public int getValue (){
return t;
}
public boolean increase(){
boolean b;
if (t < 10)
{t++;
b = false;
}
else
{
t = 0;
b = true;
}
return b;
}
}
```

THE *Reactor* CLASS HAS BEEN DOCUMENTED WITH CARE

```
// controls reactor temperature ensuring it does not go over some maximum
class Reactor
{
  private static final int MAX=10; // set maximum temperature
  private int temperature;

  public Reactor()
  {
    temperature = 0; // set initial level
  }

  public int getTemperature ()
  { // return current level
    return temperature;
  }

  public boolean increaseTemp()
  { /* increase temperature if safe,
    drop to zero and raise alarm if not */
    boolean alarm;
    if (temperature < MAX)
    {
      temperature ++;
      alarm = false;
    }
    else
    {
      temperature = 0;
      alarm = true;
    }
    return alarm;
  }
}
```

When including in-code documentation consider the following:

- comments to make the meaning of your code clear;
- meaningful data names;
- constants in place of fixed literal numbers;
- consistent and clear indentation.

Look at the example programs that we have presented to you and notice how we have tried to stick to these principles throughout this book. In particular, notice the care we have taken with our indentation. We are following two simple rules all the time:

- keep braces lined up under the structure to which they belong;
- indent, by one level, all code that belongs within those braces.

For example, look back at the increaseTemp method of the Reactor class.

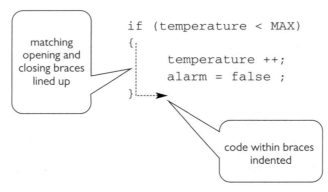

```
public boolean increaseTemp()
{   /*increase temperature if safe
    drop to zero and raise alarm if not */
    boolean alarm;
    if (temperature < MAX)
    {
        temperature ++;
        alarm = false ;
    }
    else
    {
        temperature = 0;
        alarm = true;
    }
    return alarm;
}
```

matching opening and closing braces lined up

code within braces indented

Notice how these rules are applied again with the braces of the inner **if** and **else** statements:

```
if (temperature < MAX)
{
    temperature ++;
    alarm = false ;
}
```

matching opening and closing braces lined up

code within braces indented

Also, if you look back at the Reactor class you can see that the careful choice of variable names greatly reduces the need for comments. Always attempt to make the code as self-documenting as possible by choosing meaningful names.

8.3 *Reliability*

A **reliable** program is one that does what it is supposed to do, in other words what it is *specified* to do. When attempting to build a program, two kinds of errors could occur:

- compile-time errors;
- run-time errors.

As the name implies, **compile-time errors** occur during the process of compilation. Such errors would mean you could not run your program at all as you have not followed the rules of the language to construct a valid program. Examples of these kinds of mistakes include:

- missing semi-colons;
- forgetting to close a bracket;
- being inconsistent with names and/or types;
- attempting to access a variable/object without having first initialized it.

Most Java compilers work very hard in this respect as they trap many errors that many other language compilers do not check for: ensuring that you haven't attempted to access an uninitialized variable being one example. You should become familiar with messages associated with certain kinds of errors, in order to find and fix them quickly. Often, a single mistake can cause the compiler to get confused and produce a long list of errors. Rather than attempting to fix them all, fix the first and then recompile. Look at the program and associated error list in figure 8.1. Although there appear to be many errors, there is in fact just one. Can you spot it?

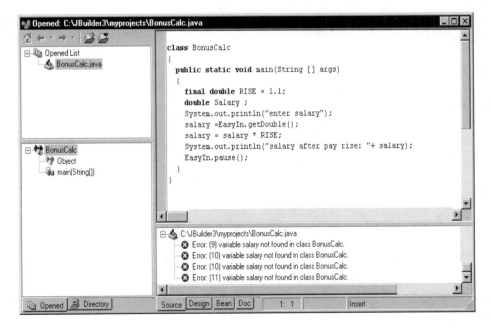

Fig 8.1 A simple mistake may result in many error messages

The only error in the code of figure 8.1 is that the variable `salary`, referenced at many points in the code, was named `Salary` (note a capital 'S') when declared.

```
double Salary; // notice capital letter
salary = EasyIn.getDouble; // will result in compiler error
// more references to 'salary' here causing further compiler errors
```

All these errors can be removed by re-declaring this variable as follows:

```
double salary;
```

If you have no compilation errors then you can begin to think about running your program in order to ensure that it does what it is supposed to do. This process is known as **testing**.

Testing can never show the *absence* of errors, only the *presence* of them. The aim therefore of any testing strategy is to uncover these errors. A program may not do what it is supposed to do because the original requirements were not precise enough and/or because the programmer has made logical errors in the program. Either way the final program will contain defects. This leads to two areas of testing:

- **validation** (making sure you are building the right product);
- **verification** (making sure you are building the product right).

Validation is a process of ensuring that your final system meets *the user's* requirements. This is an important process as developers often misjudge the original requirements given to them by clients. This may be because the requirements were not expressed clearly to begin with, or the clients were not sure themselves of the exact needs of the final system. Either way, validation will obviously require the interaction of the client. The RAD approach to software development, which we told you about in chapter 1, allows systems to be developed incrementally by means of regular validation.

Verification is a process of ensuring that the code you develop meets *your own* understanding of the user requirements. This will involve running your application in order to trap errors you may have made in program logic. A Java application typically consists of many classes working together. Testing for such errors will start with a process of **unit testing** (testing individual classes) followed by **integration testing** (testing classes that together make up an application).

8.3.1   Unit testing

Let's look at the `Reactor` class as our first example. Before incorporating this class into a larger program you would want to run it in order to test it was working reliably. This class as it stands, however, cannot be run as it has no `main` method in it.

All applications require a class with a `main` method before they can be run. Eventually, when this class is incorporated into a larger program a suitable class with a `main` method will exist, but you'll want to test this class before an entire suite of classes have been developed. One possibility would be to add a `main` method into *this* class.

```
public class Reactor
{
  private static final int MAX=10;
  private int temperature;
  // add main method
  public static void main(String[] args)
  {
    // generate Reactor object to test
    Reactor b = new Reactor();
    // testing methods of Reactor object here
  }
  // original methods still here
}
```

Here an object of type `Reactor` is instantiated within the `Reactor` class:

```
class Reactor
{
  // some code here
  Reactor b = new Reactor();
  // some more code here
}
```

This object can then be used for testing purposes. While some people do take this approach, we feel it clutters up the original class and mistakes could inadvertently be typed into the original class. For this reason we prefer to take the alternative approach of writing a separate class especially to contain the `main` method. This new class then acts as the **driver** for the original class. A driver is a special program designed to do nothing except exercise a particular class. If you look back at all our previous examples, this is exactly how we tested individual classes. When testing classes in this way, *every method* of the class should be tested. Program 8.1 is an example of a driver for the `Reactor` class.

PROGRAM 8.1

```java
public class ReactorTester
{
  // define main method
  public static void main(String[] args)
  {
    char reply;
    Reactor b = new Reactor(); // generate object to test
    do
    { // test all methods
      System.out.print("current temperature is ");
      System.out.println(b.getTemperature());
      boolean error = b.increaseTemp();
      if (error) // check if increase raised an error
      {
        System.out.print("warning: alarm raised");
      }
      System.out.print("temperature after increase is ");
      System.out.println(b.getTemperature());
      System.out.print("test some more (y/n)? ");
      reply = EasyIn.getChar();
    } while (reply != 'n'); // loop until user quits
  }
}
```

At the moment the methods are tested in strict sequence. The usability of this driver can be improved by, for example, including a menu system to test each method. We shall return to issues that affect the usability of programs later on in this chapter.

Let's continue our look at unit testing by turning our attention to the StudentList class that we asked you to develop in the second practical task of chapter 6. The procedure for testing an individual class requires a bit more thought if that class *relies upon another class* that is yet to be developed. In this case the StudentList class requires the Student class to be available.

```java
class StudentList
{
  private Student [] list; // requires access to Student class
  // more attributes and methods of StudentList written here
}
```

If you were developing the StudentList class, you may not have the Student class available to you, either because you had not yet developed it or it was not your responsibility to develop it. It would be impossible, however, to proceed with your class development if you did not know what to expect of the classes you were relying on. The following information on the class you are relying upon is essential before you can start constructing your own class:

- the name of the class;
- the name of the methods;
- the interface (return type and parameter list) of each method.

All this information should already have been recorded in the detailed design documentation for the application you are developing (see figure 8.2).

If you need to unit test a given class that relies upon the development of another class to which you do not have access, you can develop your own **dummy** class in place of the missing class. A dummy class is one that mimics an actual class in order for testing to proceed.

Such a class is often much simpler than the class it is mimicking as it only needs to include enough information to allow the given class you are testing to compile and run effectively.

In order to allow this `StudentList` class to compile, an appropriate dummy `Student` class can be developed as follows:

A DUMMY *Student* **CLASS**

```
class Student
{
    // no code in class
}
```

If you look carefully at the `StudentList` class you will see that the methods of a `Student` object are never accessed. For this reason, this dummy `Student` class contains no attributes

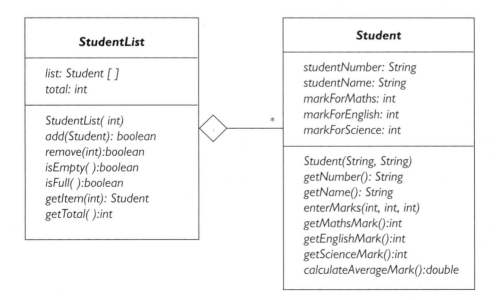

Fig 8.2   Detailed design documentation for the *StudentList* system

or methods. If the `StudentList` class accessed any of the methods of the `Student` class, associated dummy methods would have to be added into the dummy `Student` class in order to allow the `StudentList` class to compile.

For example, consider the situation where there was a findStudentAverage method in the `StudentList` class as follows:

```
public double findStudentAverage (int i)
{
   return student[i-1].calculateAverageMark( );
}
```

Here, the findStudentAverage method of the `Studentlist` class is calling a method, calculateAverageMark, of the `Student` class. But our dummy `Student` class contains no methods! To get around this problem, the dummy `Student` class would need to be amended so that an implementation existed for the calculateAverageMark method. This implementation should have an interface that is consistent with that outlined in the design documentation of figure 8.2:

```
calculateAverageMark():double
```

So the new dummy `Student` class could, for example, be implemented as follows:

THE AMENDED DUMMY *Student* CLASS

```
class Student
{
   // additional dummy method
   public double calculateAverageMark()
   {
      return 50.5;
   }
}
```

The additional dummy method in this case just returns a set mark of 50.5. In the real `Student` class this may have involved a complicated calculation amongst many individual unit marks.

Note that with this dummy class in place, a driver class with a main function still needs to be written in order to run this application. Any additional `Student` methods that this tester class requires (such as a constructor) will have to be added into this dummy class in the form of additional dummy methods.[1] This is left as a practical exercise at the end of this chapter.

---

[1] A particularly useful method to add into a dummy class is a toString method. Objects generated from classes that define such a method can be displayed on the screen in println commands. The toString method returns a String representation of the object attributes.

8.3.2 Integration testing

When the individual classes in a program have been tested they can be integrated and tested together in order to ensure that the interface between classes is working correctly.

In order to test this interface the whole suite of classes needs to be recompiled together. The reason for this is that the interfaces between classes may be inconsistent. If compiler errors occur during integration then check the following:

- all methods that are called have an implementation in the receiving class;

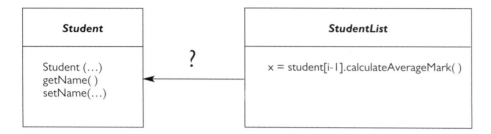

- the names of method calls match **exactly** the names of these methods in the receiving class;

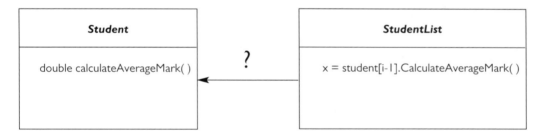

- the parameter list of a method call matches **exactly** the parameter list of these methods in the receiving class;

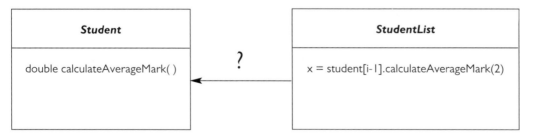

- the expected types of values returned from the method calls match the return types of these methods in the receiving class.

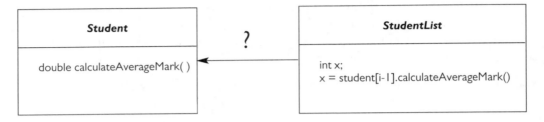

Whether you are carrying out unit testing or integration testing, the choice of test data is crucial in locating defects that may be present in the component. Two common approaches are **black box** and **white box** testing.

8.3.3   Black box testing

Black box testing is an approach to test data generation that treats the component being tested as an opaque box; that is, the details of the code are ignored (see figure 8.3). The specification is used to determine different groups of input values. A group of inputs that all produce the *same output* are regarded as equivalent. In this way inputs can be categorized into **equivalent groups**.

For example, consider a method getGrade, which accepts a student mark and returns a student grade ('A', 'B', 'C', 'D', 'E' or 'F'). Table 8.1 illustrates how these grades are arrived at.

Additionally a mark below 0 will produce a "MARK TOO LOW" error message, and a mark over 100 will produce a "MARK TOO HIGH" error message.

Remember that an equivalent group of inputs should all produce the same output. How many equivalent groups can you identify? There are in fact eight equivalent input groups.

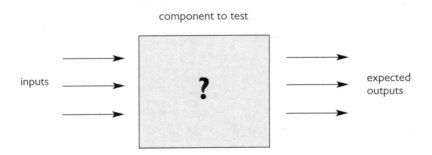

Fig 8.3   The black box approach to testing

1. marks from 70 to 100 are equivalent as they all produce the grade 'A';
2. marks from 60 to 69 are equivalent as they all produce the grade 'B';
3. marks from 50 to 59 are equivalent as they all produce the grade 'C';
4. marks from 40 to 49 are equivalent as they all produce the grade 'D';
5. marks from 30 to 39 are equivalent as they all produce the grade 'E';
6. marks from 0 to 29 are equivalent as they all produce the grade, 'F';
7. marks below 0 are equivalent as they all produce a "MARK TOO LOW" error message;
8. marks above 100 are equivalent as they all produce a "MARK TOO HIGH" error message.

When testing this method you should test *at least one mark* from each equivalent group. Figure 8.4 illustrates one possible set of test data generated in this way.

If a given mark from an equivalence group produces the correct result, you may be tempted to assume that all marks within that group are correct. Remember though that a sample can never *guarantee* that all test cases are correct, they can just *increase your confidence* that the code is correct.

If the code fails to produce the correct result despite having tested a sample from each equivalent group, often the error lies on the boundaries of such equivalent groups. The marks 69, 70 and 71, for example, lie around the boundary between the grade 'A' group of marks and the grade 'B' group of marks.

Therefore, in addition to taking sample test cases from each equivalent group, the boundary values in particular should be tested. In this case the following boundary values should all be tested as well as the sample from each equivalent group identified earlier:

−1, 0, 1, 29, 30, 31, 39, 40, 41, 49, 50, 51, 59, 60, 61, 69, 70, 71, 99, 100, 101

Table 8.1 Student grades	
marks 70 and above	grade 'A'
marks in the 60's	grade 'B'
marks in the 50's	grade 'C'
marks in the 40's	grade 'D'
marks in the 30's	grade 'E'
marks below 30	grade 'F'

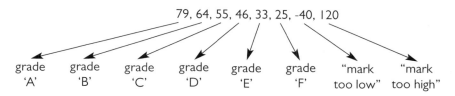

79, 64, 55, 46, 33, 25, -40, 120

grade 'A'   grade 'B'   grade 'C'   grade 'D'   grade 'E'   grade 'F'   "mark too low"   "mark too high"

Fig 8.4   Test data generated by examining equivalent groups of input

If your test cases include a sample from each equivalent group of inputs and all those values that lie on the boundary of those inputs, you are fairly likely to locate any errors that you may have in your code.

8.3.4   White box testing

White box testing is a test generation strategy that treats a software component like a transparent box into which test designers can peek while designing a test case.

Test designers can take advantage of their knowledge of the component's implementation to design tests that will cover all possible paths of execution through the component (see figure 8.5). You can see in figure 8.5 that a **while** loop is being used, so tests should be generated to allow the **while** loop to be executed:

* zero times;
* once;
* more than once.

Inside the loop there is a series of **if** statements; test cases should be selected so that:

* each **if** condition is executed;
* each **else** condition is executed.

Note that the test cases you use following a black box approach will be the same whatever implementation you have arrived at for your component, but the test cases produced as a result of white box testing may vary from implementation to implementation.

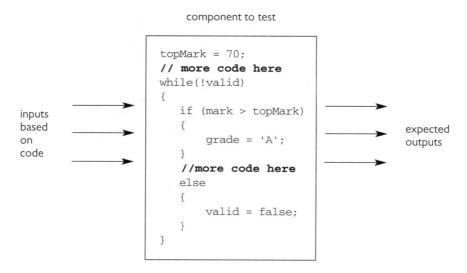

Fig 8.5   The white box approach to testing

8.3.5 The test log

Once a strategy is chosen, the test results should be logged in a **test log**. A test log is a document that records the testing that took place during system development.

Each test case associates an *input* with an *expected output*. The aim of the test is to find a case where the expected output is *not produced*. When such a case is found the reasons for the error have to be identified. A test log needs to record the action associated with entering a given input, the expected result of that action and then the outcome (pass or fail). If the output is not as expected, reasons for this error have to be identified and recorded in the log. Figure 8.6 illustrates a typical test log used to document the testing of the StudentList class.

The test log indicates that an error has been identified when an incorrect grade is displayed. In such a case the reason for the error is investigated and logged. The error has been caused by an incorrect **if** statement as follows:

```
if (mark > topMark)
{
   grade = 'A';
}
```

TEST LOG			
Purpose: To test the STUDENTLIST class			
Run Number: 1	**Date: 17th March 2000**		
Action	**Expected Output**	**Pass/Fail**	**Reason for failure**
Add student ("Ade")	message "student entered"	✓	
set mark to 69	no message expected	✓	
get grade	'B'	✓	
Add student ("Madhu")	message "student entered"	✓	
set mark to 70	no message expected	✓	
get grade	'A'	✗	Displays 'B' instead of 'A'. Due to error in **if** statement
other tests			

Fig 8.6   A test log is used to document the testing process

This will not produce a PASS when the mark is *exactly* 70 (the value of topMark). Here is one way to fix the error:

```
if (mark > topMark-1)
{
   grade = 'A';
}
```

Now a mark of 70 would produce an 'A' grade. As soon as an error is encountered the test run is stopped while the error is fixed. When an amendment has been made to your code, **all** the test cases need to be re-executed.

The reason for this is that modifications to your code could cause an error where previously there was no error. For example, if we had used real numbers to store marks, the above modification would produce a grade 'A' for a mark of 69.4 where previously it had accurately displayed this to be a grade 'B' mark.

This form of testing is known as **regression testing**. A new test log is filled in each time a program is run. Figure 8.7 illustrates test run number 2.

You may need a number of test runs before you clear all errors. Your test documentation should include *all* these test runs.

8.4   *Robustness*

A program is said to **crash** when it terminates unexpectedly. A **robust** program is one that doesn't crash even if it receives unexpected input values. For instance, if you were playing a

TEST LOG			
Purpose: To test the STUDENTQUEUE class			
Run Number: 2	**Date: 17th March 2000**		
Action	**Expected Output**	**Pass/Fail**	**Reason for failure**
Add student ("Ade")	message "student entered"	✓	
set mark to 69	no message expected	✓	
get grade	'A'	✓	
set mark to 70	no message expected	✓	
get grade	'B'	✓	
other tests			

Fig 8.7   The testing process may involve many test runs.

computer game that allowed you to move falling blocks left or right using the arrow keys on your keyboard, you wouldn't want that game to suddenly stop if you hit the wrong key!

In chapter 3 we introduced you to the idea of *input validation* to deal with such unexpected values. Generally, whenever a value is received to be processed, it should be checked before processing continues, if an unexpected value could cause the program to crash. This is not only the case when the user enters a value, but also when a method receives a value as a parameter.

As an example, consider a car showroom (cars4U) that employs two sales staff. Each week, the number of cars sold for each employee is recorded and bonus payments are calculated.

A class, SalesStaff, has been developed for this purpose as follows:

THE *SalesStaff* CLASS

```
class SalesStaff
{
  private int [] staff; // to hold weekly sales figures for staff
  private static final int MAX = 2; // maximum number of staff
  private double bonus;

  public SalesStaff(double bonusIn) // parameter to set bonus rate
  {
    staff = new int[MAX]; // create array
    for (int i = 0; i<staff.length;i++)
    {
      staff[i] = 0; // set figures to zero
    }
    bonus = bonusIn;
  }

  // method allows a sales figure for a given salesperson to be set
  public void setFigure(int numberIn, int valueIn)
  { // remember array indices begin at zero
    staff[numberIn-1] = valueIn;
  }
  // method to calculate bonus
  public double getBonus(int numberIn)
  {
    return (staff[numberIn-1]*bonus);
  }

  // method to return the maximum number of sales staff
  public int getMAX()
  {
    return MAX;
  }
}
```

As it stands, this class is not particularly robust. For example, look again at the setFigure method:

```
public void setFigure(int numberIn, int valueIn)
{
   staff[numberIn-1] = valueIn;
}
```

Can you see why this method might cause a program to crash? Well, the reason that this method could cause the program to crash is because it uses the value of one of the parameters, numberIn, to access an element within the hidden array attribute, staff.

```
public void setFigure(int numberIn, int valueIn)
{

staff[numberIn-1] = valueIn;

}
```

If you look back at the SalesStaff class you will see that this is an array with just two elements indexed, therefore, from 0 to 1. Any attempt to access an element at index 2, for example, would be an error and would cause your program to crash. To illustrate this, program 8.2 is a simple driver written to push the SalesStaff class to its limits.

PROGRAM 8.2

```
public class PushToLimitSalesStaff
{
  public static void main(String[] args)
  {
    int value;
    double bonus;
    System.out.println("Bonus paid for each car sold ? ");
    bonus = EasyIn.getDouble();
    SalesStaff cars4U = new SalesStaff(bonus); // create object
    // loop to fill up list
    for (int i = 1; i<=3; i++) //counter going up to 3 is an error!
    {
      System.out.println ("enter sales for employee " + i);
      value = EasyIn.getInt();
      cars4U.setFigure(i, value);
    }
```

```
    // display bonuses
    for (int i = 1; i<3; i++) // this time loop counter is ok
    {
      System.out.print("bonus for employee " + i + " = ");
      System.out.println(cars4U.getBonus(i));
    }
    EasyIn.pause("press <Enter> to quit");
  }
}
```

This form of testing, where you push a component to its limits (fill up the array in this case), is referred to as **stress testing**. If you were to run this driver, the program would crash as an attempt is made to enter a third value into an array that can only hold two values (see figure 8.8).

When the program crashes it throws out the following error message explaining the reason for the crash:

```
java.lang.ArrayIndexOutOfBoundsException: 2
```

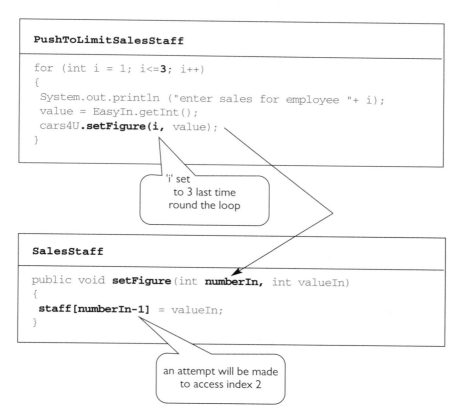

Fig 8.8   A program will crash if an illegal array index is used

As you can see, the error message is quite descriptive: it's telling you that there is a problem with the *array index*. Also the offending array index (2) is displayed. In Java this type of error is referred to as an **exception** as it is a situation that is out of the norm. The Java system is aware of many exceptional circumstances that can occur during the life of a program and, should such an error occur, the correct exception is reported. This process of reporting an exception is known as **throwing an exception**.

In Java, one way of dealing with an exception when it is thrown is to **catch** it before it causes any damage. However, the details of how you carry this out are a bit too complex for your first semester! For now, you should write your code so that the program does not throw such an exception in the first place. In this case you would need to ensure that an array index is valid before you use it.

The responsibility to check this value could be given to the class in which the method that *supplies* the parameter is contained. While this check may indeed take place, the principle of *encapsulation* requires no assumptions about the calling environment to be made, so it cannot be *assumed* that this parameter has been validated. The setFigure method still has a responsibility to check the value of the parameter, which it could do as follows:

```
public void setFigure(int numberIn, int valueIn)
{ // check index will be valid before accessing array
  if (numberIn <= staff.length)
  {
    staff[numberIn-1] = valueIn;
  }
}
```

Now, the array access is protected inside an **if** statement. This is better as the program will no longer crash when an attempt is made to access array indices greater than 1. However, the caller of this method would have no idea that the given sales figure was not entered. An alternative approach would be to display an error message as follows:

```
public void setFigure(int numberIn, int valueIn)
{
  if(numberIn <= staff.length)
  {
    staff[numberIn-1] = valueIn;
  }
  else // display error message when index is invalid
  {
    System.out.println("error queue is full");
  }
}
```

The problem with this approach is that we have put the error message in the setFigure method. However, you cannot predict whether the user of this class would be using a *text screen* for input/output or a *graphics window*, or how the user would wish to report the error – if at all. It should be the *user* of this method that decides on how to *deal with the error*, not the method itself. We can get around this by sending back a **boolean** value indicating success or failure of the method as follows:

```
public boolean setFigure(int numberIn, int valueIn)
{
  if (numberIn <= staff.length)
  {
    staff[numberIn-1] = valueIn;
    return true; // method successful
  }
  else
  {
    return false; // method unsuccessful
  }
}
```

The user of this method is then free to check the value returned and take appropriate action. For example, back in the PushToLimitSalesStaff driver, the following amendment could be made:

```
for (int i = 1; i<=3; i++)
{
  System.out.println ("enter sales for employee " + i);
  value = EasyIn.getInt();
  // call method and check returned boolean value
  boolean ok = cars4U.setFigure(i, value);
  if (!ok) // unable to set figure successfully
  {
    System.out.println("ERROR:last figure not entered ");
  }
}
```

This loop would will no longer cause the setFigure method of SalesStaff to lead to a program crash, even though an attempt is made to access an illegal array index.

8.5   *Usability*

The **usability** of a program refers to the ease with which users of your application can interact with your program. A program that crashes all the time when receiving unexpected inputs is far from usable, so one way of ensuring that your program is easy to use is to make sure that it is robust. A user- manual can also help make your programs easier to follow. The manual forms another important part of the documentation of your system. Such a manual could include:

- details how of how to install your application;
- details of how to use your application once installed;
- a trouble-shooting section where common errors that users are likely to make are identified and their solutions given.

Many applications today simply have the first of these in printed form so that the application can be installed. All additional information is then provided within the application in the form of help files. Figure 8.9, for example, illustrates the user documentation built into the JBuilder IDE.

When designing your programs, you too could think about including user advice in the form of help screens. One way of adding such help files into the types of programs that we have developed so far is to include a HELP option on a menu screen. We refer to the way the user interacts with an application as the **HCI (Human Computer Interaction)** of the program. Menu- based systems offer a much more friendly way of interacting with a user than a simple series of prompts.

As an example, let's go back and look at program 8.1 (the driver for the Reactor class). We said at the time that this driver wasn't as user-friendly as it could be. Here is a sample test run of the driver as it was originally written to explain what we mean:

```
current temperature is 0
temperature after increase is 1
test some more (y/n)? y
current temperature is 1
temperature after increase is 2
test some more (y/n)? y
current temperature is 2
temperature after increase is 3
test some more (y/n)? n
```

Fig 8.9   An example of built-in user documentation in the form of help files

Not very exciting, is it? Apart from the fact that this interface doesn't look very interesting, it's also very rigid. For example, if we wanted to add in some HELP information (to include details of what happens when an attempt is made to increase the reactor temperature above the maximum), where would we add this? Maybe we could include it at the beginning of the program, but then what if the user needs some help later on in the program? Would we have to keep offering help at every stage? By using a menu system, much of this rigidity can be removed. Here is an example of one possible menu interface for the program:

```
*** REACTOR SYSTEM ***

[1] Get current temperature
[2] Increase temperature
[3] HELP
[4] Quit

enter choice [1,2,3,4]: _
```

We've already shown you many examples of such menu- driven programs so you should be able to rewrite program 8.1 yourself to give it such an interface. With this interface the user could now, if he or she chose, increase the temperature many times (by repeatedly choosing option 1) and only then decide to get the current temperature (by choosing option 2). Or the user could get the temperature after each increase. The choice is left up to the user – not the program. Also, notice that a HELP option is always available.

Another issue you should think about, when considering the usability of your programs, is the number of actions a user has to carry out in order to achieve a particular task. For example, if the user chooses the 'Quit' option on a menu, adding a further pause in your program and insisting that the user then press the 'Enter' key in order to quit could be quite irritating! As another illustration of this problem let's go back to program 8.2 (the driver for the SalesStaff class). Here is a sample test run, assuming that the alterations discussed in section 8.4 have been made:

```
Bonus paid for each car sold ?
8
enter sales for employee 1
10
enter sales for employee 2
5
enter sales for employee 3
9
ERROR: too many figures
bonus for employee 1 = 80.0
bonus for employee 2 = 40.0
press <Enter> to quit
```

This interface could do with a title and some line spaces; we'll deal with these issues in a while. For now, look at the error message that was raised when an attempt was made to enter details of a third employee:

enter sales for employee 3
9
ERROR: too many figures

As you can see, the error was raised *after* the sales figure (9) had been entered by the user. This entry of the last sales figure was wasted effort for the user as the figure was never used. The reason the user was asked to enter this figure was that the error was detected only after the figure was sent to the setFigure method:

```
for (int i = 1; i<=3; i++)
{
  System.out.println ("enter sales for employee " + i);
  // value entered before error checking
  value = EasyIn.getInt();
  // method to set figure called
  boolean ok = cars4U.setFigure(i, value);
  // now error checking is taking place here
  if (!ok)
  {
    System.out.println("ERROR:last figure not entered ");
  }
}
```

The user would probably prefer the error checking to take *place* before he or she enters the sales figure. This can be achieved by checking the maximum number of employees *before* asking the user to enter a sales figure as follows:

```
for (int i = 1; i<=3; i++)
{
  System.out.println ("enter sales for employee " + i);
  // check if all employee figures entered
  if (i> cars4U.getMAX())
  {
    // produce error message if no more figures to enter
    System.out.println("!!!!!!!!!!!!!");
    System.out.println(" ERROR:only "+ cars4U.getMAX() +" employees");
    System.out.println("!!!!!!!!!!!!!");
  }
  // ok to enter more sales figures
  else
  {
    // get the figure
    value = EasyIn.getInt();
    // can now enter the figure without further error checking
    cars4U.setFigure(i, value);
  }
}
```

Now, here is another sample test run of program 8.2 after this amendment has been made:

```
Bonus paid for each car sold ?
8
enter sales for employee 1
10
enter sales for employee 2
5
enter sales for employee 3
!!!!!!!!!!!!
ERROR:only 2 employees
!!!!!!!!!!!!
bonus for employee 1 = 80.0
bonus for employee 2 = 40.0
press <Enter> to quit
```

As you can see, this time, the user did not need to enter a sales figure for a third employee. The error was raised immediately.

8.5.1   Text formatting

Look back at the test runs for the programs discussed earlier in this chapter. To make such output attractive to users, careful use of space can be extremely useful. For example, the line space between the title and the menu options of the `Reactor` class tester makes both the title and the options stand out.

In our example programs so far, we've shown you one way to create such space: just use an empty `println()` command as follows:

```
System.out.println("some output");
System.out.println( ); // creates blank line on screen
System.out.println("more output here");
```

The need to add such space is so common that special formatting characters exist in Java to simplify this task. These characters can be added into strings to include such information as "add a new line", and "create a tab space". These special formatting characters are known as **escape sequences**. An escape sequence always consists of a backslash character '\' followed by a special formatting character. For example, to force a new line the '\n' escape sequence can be embedded into a string. Below we use '\n' escape to achieve the same blank line result above (we have emboldened the escape sequence).

```
System.out.println("some output\n");
System.out.println("more output here");
```

Table 8.2	Some useful escape sequences
\t	add a tab space
\"	add a double quote
\'	add a single quote
\\	add a backslash

Note that there is no need to include spaces around the escape sequence, in this case it is added directly onto the end of the first message.

In fact, escape sequences can be added anywhere in a string; for example, the following command achieves exactly the same result as the two output statements above by embedding the new line commands in the middle of a single string (again we have emboldened them for you).

```
System.out.println("some output\n\nmore output here");
```

Notice that in this case we needed two new-line commands, one new line to print the string over two lines, and the other line break to create a blank line between the two messages.

Table 8.2 lists a few other useful escape sequences.

Careful use of such escape sequences can help in producing output that is clearer and easier to follow.

One other output problem we have come up against, with our sample programs, is the formatting of decimal output. As an illustration of this problem let's go back to program 8.2 (the driver for the SalesStaff class). Here is another sample test run, assuming that the alterations discussed in this chapter have been made:

```
Bonus paid for each car sold ?
5.3
enter sales for employee 1
9
enter sales for employee 2
4
enter sales for employee 3
!!!!!!!!!!!!!
ERROR:only 2 employees
!!!!!!!!!!!!!
bonus for employee 1 = 47.699999999999996
bonus for employee 2 = 21.2
press <Enter> to quit
```

Look back at the output of the bonus payments. They don't look too pretty, do they?

Table 8.3 Special DecimalFormat characters	
Character	**Meaning**
.	insert a decimal point
,	insert a comma
0	display a single digit
#	display a single digit or empty if no digit present

Typically, monetary values have two digits after the decimal point. The first bonus payment, however, has *sixteen* digits and the second bonus payment only *one*! You can't blame the Java system for this as it has no idea that these numbers represent monetary values, or how we would like such monetary values to be displayed. Don't worry though, Java has a predefined class, `DecimalFormat`, that you can use to let the program know how you wish to format the display of particular decimal numbers. This class resides in the `java.text` package so to access it you need to add the following **import** statement to the top of your program:

```
import java.text.*;
```

Once you have access to this class you can create `DecimalFormat` objects in your program. These objects can then be used to format decimal numbers for you. As always, you use the **new** operator along with the object constructor to create an object. The `DecimalFormat` constructor has one parameter, the *format* string. This string instructs the object on how you wish to format a given decimal number. Some of the important elements of such a string are given in table 8.3.

For example, look at the following construction of a `DecimalFormat` object:

```
DecimalFormat df = new DecimalFormat( "000,000.000");
```

Here the decimal format object, `df`, that is constructed is being informed on how to format any decimal numbers that may be given to it (see figure 8.10).

The format string "`000,000.000`" indicates that the number should be truncated to three decimal places, and a comma should be used between the hundred and thousand columns. Also, the number displayed will always have six significant digits (digits to the left of the decimal point) and three digits after.

At the moment we have just created a `DecimalFormat` object and informed it how to format a given decimal number. We haven't given it any number to format! We do this by using the `format` method of the `DecimalFormat` class. For example:

```
DecimalFormat df = new DecimalFormat("000,000.000");
double someNumber = 12345.6789;
System.out.println("before\t" + someNumber);
System.out.println("after\t" + df.format(someNumber));
```

Since the `format` method returns the formatted number as a `String`, its returned value can be printed directly to the screen with a `System.out` command (notice also the addition of a tab space with '\t'). The instructions above would lead to the following values being displayed:

```
before      12345.6789
after       012,345.679
```

As you can see, not only has the number been truncated to three decimal places, but it has also been rounded up. In this case the format string insisted on having six significant digits so the formatted number has a leading zero added.

Replacing a zero in a format string with a hash (#) would mean that the digit was optional, not compulsory.

For example, look at the following piece of code:

```
DecimalFormat df = new DecimalFormat( "#00,000.000");
double someNumber = 12345.6789;
System.out.println("before\t" + someNumber);
System.out.println("after\t" + df.format(someNumber));
```

This would result in the following output:

```
before      12345.6789
after       12,345.679
```

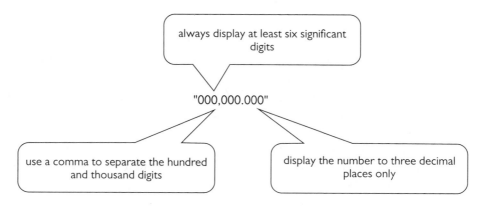

Fig 8.10 A format string used with the *DecimalFormat* class

In case you are wondering, if the decimal number that was to be formatted had *more* than six significant digits, all the extra digits would automatically be displayed. So, only use zeros for digits you insist on displaying, and use hashes for optional formatting.[2]

Bearing all this in mind, how would you format currency values? Well, such values will always have to be given to two decimal places, and they must all have at least one significant digit, so the following format string is required:

```
DecimalFormat df = new DecimalFormat("0.00");
```

Program 8.3 rewrites the PushToLimitSalesStaff driver by including the amendments we discussed in this chapter and improving the text formatting of output.

PROGRAM 8.3

```
import java.text.*; // for DecimalFormat
public class PushToLimitSalesStaff2
{
  public static void main(String[] args)
  {
    int value;
    double bonus;
    // title added
    System.out.println("\n\t\t*** BONUS CALCULATOR ***\n\n");
    // to set bonus rate
    System.out.print("\t Bonus paid for each car sold ?\t");
    bonus = EasyIn.getDouble();
    SalesStaff cars4U = new SalesStaff(bonus);
    // get figures
    System.out.print("\n\n\t enter sales figures\n\n");
    for (int i = 1; i<=3; i++)
    {
      System.out.print("\t employee " + i + "\t");

      // only enter data if required
      if (i> cars4U.getMAX())
      {
        System.out.print("ERROR:only " +cars4U.getMAX()
                                          +" employees");

      }
      else
      {
```

---

[2] There are several other classes in the java.text package that provide useful formatting methods. The NumberFormat class, for example, contains a getCurrencyInstance method that allows you to format a given real number in the currency format of the local country.

```
            value = EasyIn.getInt();
            cars4U.setFigure(i, value);
        }
    }
    // display bonuses
    System.out.print("\n\n\t bonus payments\n\n");
    for (int i = 1; i<3; i++) // this time loop counter is ok
    { // notice the use of DecimalFormat class
        DecimalFormat df = new DecimalFormat( "0.00");
        System.out.print("\t employee " + i + " =\t");
        System.out.println(df.format(cars4U.getBonus(i)));
    }
    EasyIn.pause("\n\n\t press <Enter> to quit");
    }
}
```

Here is a sample test run (we have included an actual screen shot here so that you can fully appreciate the effect of the tab and space formatting).

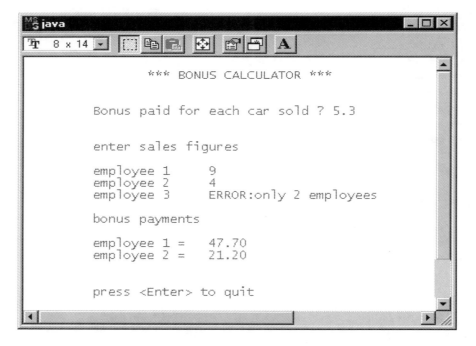

Look back at program 8.3 and compare it with this screen shot to see the effect of the various text formatting instructions.

8.5.2   Graphical user interfaces

So far in this book, we haven't talked very much about how to create visual, graphical interfaces of the type illustrated in figure 8.11. Figure 8.11 is the Print screen from Microsoft's *Word for Windows* application. Such interfaces are often referred to as **GUIs** (**Graphical User Interfaces**). Most applications that you buy today include such an interface.

Interfaces like this are by far the friendliest and easiest for users to operate. Up until now we haven't looked at how to develop such interfaces because you had to get to know about the basics of software development in Java first. But, now we have covered these basics with you, we think you are ready! In the next chapter we show you not only how to create such interfaces but also how to use them with your existing classes.

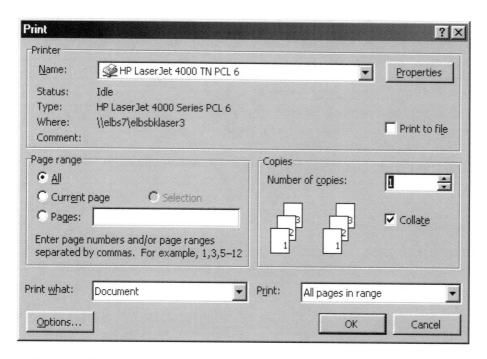

Fig 8.11   A typical GUI interface

Tutorial exercises

1. Identify the documentation required during the following phases of software development:
   - specification/design;
   - implementation;
   - testing;
   - installation and operation.
2. How does the concept of *encapsulation* contribute to the maintainability of applications?
3. Distinguish between the terms *unit testing, integration testing, black box testing* and *white box testing*.
4. In section 8.2 a dummy Student class was developed in order to allow the StudentList class to be tested. Now look back at at chapter 6 where you developed a StudentList-Tester class. How would the dummy Student class need to be amended in order for this tester to work?
5. Look once again at the SalesStaff class. Assume that the getBonus method has been amended so that sales of five cars or fewer receive the usual bonus, sales of six to 15 cars receive double the usual bonus, and sales of more than fifteen 15 cars receive triple the usual bonus. Now:
   (a) write a list of suitable sales figures to test, using both *boundary analysis* and *equivalence test-ing*;
   (b) devise a *test log* based upon these test values.
6. Use escape sequences to print out the following strings:
   (a) I enjoy reading "Java in two Semesters"
   (b) I keep important files at C:\MyDocuments\ImportantFiles
   (c) please press the 'alt' key

Practical work

1. You have been asked to maintain the Reactor class by providing an additional method: decreaseTemp. This method reduces the reactor temperature by one degree. If an attempt is made to reduce the temperature below zero an alarm is raised but the temperature is maintained at zero. Now:
   (a) modify the Reactor class accordingly;
   (b) develop a NewReactorTester class that is run from the following menu screen:

```
         *** REACTOR TESTER ***

    [1]  Increase temperature

    [2]  Decrease temperature

    [3]  Display current temperature

    [4]  HELP

    [5]  Quit
```

(c) develop a suitable test log, with inputs and expected outputs, to test the functionality of the new Reactor class;

(d) run the NewReactorTester class and complete the test log above.

2. Implement the dummy Student class discussed in tutorial question 4 and then combine this class with the StudentList class and the StudentListTester class to check whether testing can proceed.

3. Look back at the SalesStaff class and then:

(a) maintain this system so that the number of employees is increased to ten;

(b) implement the changes to the getBonus method discussed in tutorial question 5;

(c) amend this method so that it cannot throw an ArrayIndexOutOfBounds exception;

(d) rewrite program 8.3 to test whether or not this method still throws the ArrayIndex-OutOfBounds exception.

4. Look again at program 2.3 in chapter 2, which calculates and displays the price of a product after sales tax has been added. Amend the program so that:

(a) all currency values are displayed to two decimal places;

(b) line and tab spaces are used to improve the layout of the information displayed.

GRAPHICS AND EVENT-DRIVEN PROGRAMS

LEARNING OBJECTIVES

By the end of this chapter you should be able to:

➤ explain the structure of the **Abstract Window Toolkit (AWT)**;

➤ program graphics components to handle mouse-click events;

➤ add standard AWT components to a frame;

➤ describe the role of **layout managers**;

➤ use the `FlowLayout` and `BorderLayout` managers;

➤ make use of compound containers.

9.1 Introduction

Do you remember the `SmileyFace` class? So far it is the only graphics class we have developed. So now it is time to learn more about graphics programming – and when we have done that we can start to move away from that rather uninteresting text screen we have been using and build attractive windows programs for our input and output.

In order to do this we are going to be using the core Java graphics package, the **Abstract Window Toolkit**, or **AWT** for short. This package provides the graphics tools and components that you need to produce the sort of windows programs that we have all become used to.

So the first thing we are going to do in this chapter is to explore the Abstract Window Toolkit; after that we can go on to develop our first interactive graphical applications.

9.2   *The Abstract Window Toolkit*

The AWT provides graphics classes that are based on an inheritance structure. This is shown in figure 9.1 – you can see from this diagram that at the top of this hierarchy is a basic Component class. This class contains a number of useful methods, which are inherited by the eight subclasses that you see in the diagram. Most of these, like Button or Checkbox, provide the code for creating and manipulating the basic graphics components that you are used to seeing in windows applications.

Notice that two of the classes, Container and TextComponent (which are abstract classes), are further subclassed to provide additional classes. You will explore some of these as you progress through the chapter and develop more and more complex graphical applications. The appendix on the website provides a description of some of the common AWT components and their methods.

Some examples of these common components can be seen in figure 9.2, which shows a Frame containing a Button, a Checkbox and a Scrollbar.

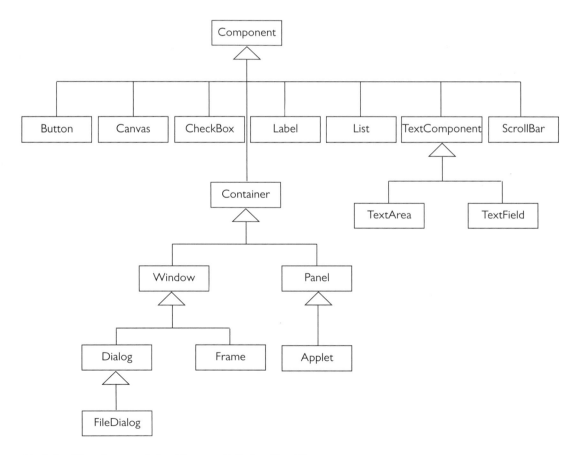

Fig 9.1   The classes of the Abstract Window Toolkit

9.3   *The SmileyFace class revisited*

Do you remember the SmileyFace class that we introduced in chapter 4? When we ran it in a frame it produced a display like the one shown in figure 9.3.

In this chapter we are going to make a few changes to it – but first a reminder of the code:

THE *SmileyFace* CLASS

```java
import java.awt.*;

class SmileyFace extends Panel
{
  public void paint(Graphics g)
  {
    g.setColor(Color.red);
    g.drawOval(85,45,75,75);
    g.setColor(Color.blue);
    g.drawOval(100,65,10,10);
    g.drawOval(135,65,10,10);
    g.drawArc(102,85,40,25,0,-180);
    g.drawString("Smiley Face", 90,155);
  }
}
```

The code for running this class in a frame appears opposite (program 9.1).

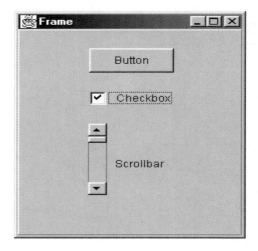

Fig 9.2   A frame containing a button, a checkbox and a scrollbar

PROGRAM 9.1

```java
import java.awt.*;

public class RunFace
{
  public static void main(String[] args)
  {
    Frame frame = new Frame();
    SmileyFace face = new SmileyFace();
    frame.setSize(250,200);
    frame.setBackground(Color.yellow);
    frame.add(face);
    frame.setVisible(true);
  }
}
```

9.4 The EasyFrame *class*

Do you remember the slight problem with the above program when it was first introduced in chapter 4? The simple frame doesn't close when we click on the crosshairs in the top right-hand corner! To adapt the frame so that it closes requires a bit of code that is a little too complicated for the first semester.

So rather than trouble you with it at this stage we have provided you with an EasyFrame class which you can download or copy from the CD-ROM. From now on we will use this frame in our classes and there will be no problems with closing your windows when you are done. The new program for running the SmileyFace class with EasyFrame is now shown in program 9.2.

Fig 9.3   The *SmileyFace* class running in a frame

PROGRAM 9.2

```
import java.awt.*;

public class RunFace
{
  public static void main(String[] args)
  {
    EasyFrame frame = new EasyFrame(); // we are now using EasyFrame
    SmileyFace face = new SmileyFace();
    frame.setSize(250,200);
    frame.setBackground(Color.yellow);
    frame.add(face);
    frame.setVisible(true);
  }
}
```

9.5   The ChangingFace *class*

Now we are going to try to change our SmileyFace class into a ChangingFace class that can change its mood so it can be sad as well as happy. The first thing we are going to do is to add a couple of buttons, as shown in figure 9.4.

You can see that we have now changed our caption from "Smiley Face" to "Changing Face" – because when we have finished we will be able to click on the Frown button and get the face to look like the one you see in figure 9.5.

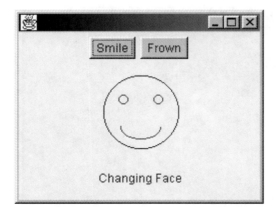

Fig 9.4   The *ChangingFace* class (still smiling)

We will build the ChangingFace class in two stages. The first step is to add the buttons: this is shown below; we have called this class ChangingFaceStep1. The new lines, which are all concerned with adding the buttons, have been emboldened.

THE *ChangingFaceStep1* CLASS

```java
import java.awt.*;
import java.awt.event.*;

class ChangingFaceStep1 extends Panel
{
    private Button happyButton = new Button("Smile");
    private Button sadButton = new Button("Frown");

    public ChangingFaceStep1()
    {
        add(happyButton);
        add(sadButton);
    }

    public void paint(Graphics g)
    {
        g.setColor(Color.red);
        g.drawOval(85,45,75,75);
        g.setColor(Color.blue);
        g.drawOval(100,65,10,10);
        g.drawOval(135,65,10,10);
        g.drawString("Changing Face", 80,155);
        g.drawArc(102,85,40,25,0,-180);
    }
}
```

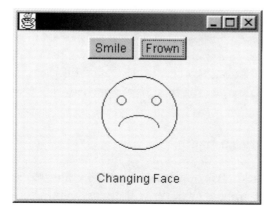

Fig 9.5   The *ChangingFace* class (frowning)

Let's take a closer look at these new lines.

First, we declare the buttons as attributes of the class, and initialize them at the same time:

```
private Button happyButton = new Button("Smile");
private Button sadButton = new Button("Frown");
```

We are creating new objects of the `Button` class; this class has a constructor that allows us to create the buttons with the required caption by sending in this caption as a parameter.

Now that we have created the buttons we have to add them to the panel. We are going to add the buttons at the time an object is created, in other words via the constructor.

```
public ChangingFaceStep1()
{
   add(happyButton);
   add(sadButton);
}
```

We use the `add` method, which is a method of the `Container` class and is therefore available to all derived classes such as `Panel`.

In actual fact these lines are short for:

```
this.add(happyButton);
this.add(sadButton);
```

The keyword **this** is used when a class method refers to the object itself – in this case an object of the `ChangingFaceStep1` class; it can often be omitted.

A container, like our `ChangingFace` (which extends `Panel`), always has a `layout` policy attached to it – this policy determines the way in which components are added to it. The default policy is called `FlowLayout` which means that the components are just placed in the order in which they were added. When one row fills up then the next row starts to be filled. There are other layout policies that we can choose, and these are discussed in section 9.10.

If we were to run the class in a frame then we would get the output shown in figure 9.5 – but of course pressing the buttons would not have any effect; we need to write the code to bring about the desired result when the buttons are pressed. This is called **event-handling**.

9.6   *Event-handling in Java*

The complete `ChangingFace` class appears below. The code that is to do with the event-handling routines has been emboldened. We will discuss them after you have taken a look at the complete code for the class.

THE *ChangingFace* CLASS

```java
import java.awt.*;
import java.awt.event.*;

class ChangingFace extends Panel implements ActionListener
{
  private boolean isHappy;
  private Button happyButton = new Button("Smile");
  private Button sadButton = new Button("Frown");

  public ChangingFace()
  {
    add(happyButton);
    add(sadButton);
    isHappy = true;
    happyButton.addActionListener(this);
    sadButton.addActionListener(this);
  }

  public void paint(Graphics g)
  {

    g.setColor(Color.red);
    g.drawOval(85,45,75,75);
    g.setColor(Color.blue);
    g.drawOval(100,65,10,10);
    g.drawOval(135,65,10,10);
    g.drawString("Changing Face", 80,155);
    if(isHappy == true)
    {
      // draw a smiling mouth
      g.drawArc(102,85,40,25,0,-180);
    }
    else
    {
      // draw a frowning mouth
      g.drawArc(102,85,40,25,0,180);
    }
  }

  // this is where we code the event-handling routines
  public void actionPerformed(ActionEvent e)
  {

    if(e.getSource() == happyButton)
    {
      isHappy = true;
      repaint();
    }
```

```
    if(e.getSource() == sadButton)
    {
      isHappy = false;
      repaint();
    }
  }
}
```

We can now analyse this line by line. The first line of interest is the class header:

```
class ChangingFace extends Panel implements ActionListener
```

Notice how we have appended the words implements ActionListener to our class header. The ActionListener class is a special class called an **interface**; these classes contain abstract methods which, you will remember from chapter 7, means that we are forced to code them. In this case the ActionListener class insists that we code a method called actionPerformed to handle our events. We will see how this is done in a moment.

Before we do that, take a look at this new attribute we have included:

```
private boolean isHappy;
```

You can probably guess how we are going to use this – it will be set to **true** when the Smile button is pressed and **false** when the Frown button is pressed; the face will then be repainted with the appropriate expression.

Now let's look at our new constructor:

```
public ChangingFace()
{
  add(happyButton);
  add(sadButton);
  isHappy = true;
  happyButton.addActionListener(this);
  sadButton.addActionListener(this);
}
```

After adding the buttons we set isHappy to **true**, so that the face starts off happy.

The next two lines are important. When we use the keyword **implements** with an interface class like ActionListener we achieve an effect very similar to that achieved by inheritance – our class actually becomes *a kind of* ActionListener, just as if it were a subclass of some superclass, created with the keyword **extends**. The Buttons, like all subclasses of component, have a method called addActionListener that receives an object of the ActionListener class as a parameter – and since our class is now a kind of ActionListener we can send it to the addActionListener method of a Button. We do it with the keyword **this**; effectively we are registering this panel with the button, which will then wait for an **event** – normally a mouse-click – and then do something to the panel.

The "something" that it does is determined by coding a special routine for that button – this routine is called an **event-handler**.

Before we come to that, however, you need to look at the new bit of the paint method:

```
if(isHappy == true)
{
   g.drawArc(102,85,40,25,0,-180);
}
else
{
   g.drawArc(102,85,40,25,0,180);
}
```

You should remember from chapter 5 how the drawArc method of a Graphic object works. If you look back at this section you will see that by changing the very last parameter from a negative value to a positive value the arc will be drawn clockwise instead of anti-clockwise – this will make the mouth frown instead of smile! So if the isHappy attribute is set to **true** the mouth will smile – if not it will frown!

Now at last we come to our event-handlers:

```
public void actionPerformed(ActionEvent e)
{
   if(e.getSource() == happyButton)
   {
      isHappy = true;
      repaint();
   }
   if(e.getSource() == sadButton)
   {
      isHappy = false;
      repaint();
   }
}
```

We determine what happens when the mouse-button is clicked by coding the actionPerformed method that is required by the ActionListener interface. When the mouse is clicked, this method is automatically sent an object of the class ActionEvent. This class has a method called getSource that returns the name of the object that was clicked on. We use this method in the condition of the **if** statement to find out which button was clicked. You can see that if it was the happyButton that was pressed, then isHappy is set to **true** and then a special method – repaint – is called. This causes the paint method to be called again so that the screen is repainted. The sadButton works in the same way, but sets isHappy to **false**. Take one more look at the paint method to remind yourself how this works.

The ChangingFace class can be run in a frame as shown in program 9.3.

PROGRAM 9.3

```java
import java.awt.*;
public class RunChangingFace
{
  public static void main(String[] args)
  {
    EasyFrame frame = new EasyFrame();
    ChangingFace face = new ChangingFace();
    frame.setSize(250,200);
    frame.setBackground(Color.yellow);
    frame.add(face);
    frame.setVisible(true);
  }
}
```

9.7   *An interactive graphics class*

The next class – which we have called PushMe – that we are going to develop is the first class that allows the user to input information via a graphics screen. The program isn't all that sophisticated, but it introduces the basic elements that you need to build interactive graphics classes.

This program allows the user to enter some text and then, by clicking on a button, to see the text that was entered displayed in the graphics window. You can see what it looks like in figure 9.6.

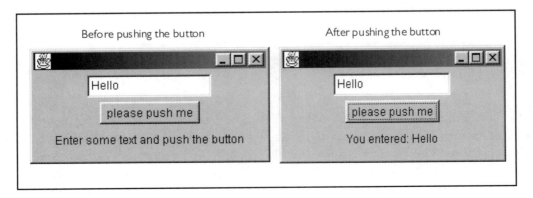

Fig 9.6   The *PushMe* class running in a frame

As usual we will show you the code first and discuss it afterwards:

THE *PushMe* CLASS

```java
import java.awt.*;
import java.awt.event.*;

class PushMe extends Panel implements ActionListener
{
   private TextField myTextField = new TextField(15);
   private Button myButton = new Button("please push me");
   private Label myLabel =
                        new Label("Enter some text and push the button",1);
   // the constructor (adds the components and the ActionListener)
   public PushMe()
   {
     add(myTextField);
     add(myButton);
     add(myLabel);
     myButton.addActionListener(this);
   }

   // the event-handler
   public void actionPerformed(ActionEvent e)
   {
     if(e.getSource() == myButton)
     {
       String myText;
       myText = myTextField.getText();
       myLabel.setText("You entered: " + myText);
     }
   }
}
```

As you can see, there are three components involved here, and we have declared them all as attributes of the class and initialized them at the same time:

```java
private TextField myTextField = new TextField(15);
private Button myButton = new Button("please push me");
private Label myLabel
                  = new Label("Enter some text and push the button",1);
```

The first of the above three components is a TextField – we have used the fact that it has a constructor that accepts an integer value (in this case 15) that allows you to specify the length of the text field to be displayed (a TextContainer consists of rows and columns of characters).

Next we declare the button, which, as before, we have initialized with the required caption ("please push me").

Finally we have declared and instantiated a `Label`. The constructor that we are utilizing here takes two parameters: the text to be displayed and an integer value which determines the alignment of the text – 0 for left, 1 for centre and 2 for right; these can also be entered as `Label.LEFT`, `Label.CENTER` and `Label.RIGHT`.

All of these components also have empty constructors (and others) which that you can use if you wish. You can change the properties later using the various methods that exist; for example, the `setLabel` method of the `Button` class, the `setColumns` method of the `TextField` class or the `setText` method of the `Label` class. Some selected methods of these and other components are provided in the appendix on the website.

Next comes the constructor where we add the buttons to the panel and the `ActionListener` to the button.

```
public PushMe()
{
   add(myTextField);
   add(myButton);
   add(myLabel);
   myButton.addActionListener(this);
}
```

Finally we have the event-handling routine:

```
public void actionPerformed(ActionEvent e)
{
   if(e.getSource() == myButton)
   {
     String myText;
     myText = myTextField.getText();
     myLabel.setText("You entered: " + myText);
   }
}
```

Notice how we are using the `getText` method of the `TextField` class to read the current "value" of the text in `myTextField`, and then using the `setText` method of the `Label` class to "transfer" it to `myLabel`.

Program 9.4 provides the code for running the class in a light grey frame measuring 250 by 120.

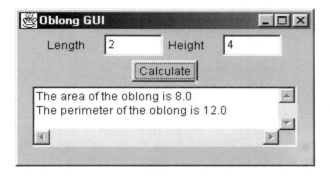

Fig 9.7   A GUI for the *Oblong* class

PROGRAM 9.4

```
import java.awt.*;

public class RunPushMe
{
  public static void main(String[] args)
  {
    EasyFrame frame = new EasyFrame();
    PushMe pushme = new PushMe();
    frame.setSize(250,120);
    frame.setBackground(Color.lightGray);
    frame.add(pushme);
    frame.setVisible(true);
  }
}
```

9.8   *A graphical user interface (GUI) for the* Oblong *class*

Up until now, when we have wanted to write programs that utilize our classes, we have written text-based programs. Now that we know how to write graphics programs we can, if we wish, write graphical user interfaces for our classes. Let's do this for the Oblong class we developed in chapter 5. The sort of interface we are talking about is shown in figure 9.7.

Here is the code for the GUI:

THE GRAPHICAL USER INTERFACE FOR THE *Oblong* CLASS

```
import java.awt.*;
import java.awt.event.*;

class OblongGui extends Panel implements ActionListener
{
```

```
   // declare a new oblong with a length and height of zero
   private Oblong oblong = new Oblong(0,0);

   // now declare the graphics components
   private Label lengthLabel = new Label("Length");
   private TextField lengthField = new TextField(5);
   private Label heightLabel = new Label("Height");
   private TextField heightField = new TextField(5);
   private Button calcButton = new Button("Calculate");
   private TextArea displayArea = new TextArea(3,35);

   public OblongGui()
   {
     // add the graphics components
     add(lengthLabel);
     add(lengthField);
     add(heightLabel);
     add(heightField);
     add(calcButton);
     add(displayArea);

     // now add the ActionListener to the calcButton
     calcButton.addActionListener(this);
   }

   /* finally write the code for handling a mouse-click on the calcButton */
   public void actionPerformed(ActionEvent e)
   {
     String lengthEntered = lengthField.getText();
     String heightEntered = heightField.getText();
     if(e.getSource() == calcButton)
     {
       // make sure the fields aren't blank
       if(lengthEntered.length() == 0 || heightEntered.length() == 0)
       {
       displayArea.setText("Length and height must be entered");
     }
     else
     {
       // we have to convert the input strings to doubles
       oblong.setLength(Double.parseDouble(lengthEntered));
       oblong.setHeight(Double.parseDouble(heightEntered));
       displayArea.setText("The area of the oblong is "
                           + oblong.calculateArea()
                           + "\n"
                           + "The perimeter of the oblong is "
                           + oblong.calculatePerimeter());
     }
    }
   }
  }
}
```

You can see that the first attribute that we declare is an `Oblong` object, `oblong`, which we initialize as a new `Oblong` with a length and height of zero (since the user hasn't entered anything yet):

```
private Oblong oblong = new Oblong(0,0);
```

After this we declare the graphics components; the only one of these that you have not yet come across is the `TextArea`, which is the large text area that you see in figure 9.7, where the area and perimeter of the oblong are displayed. As you can see, it is a useful component for entering and displaying text. We declared it like this:

```
private TextArea displayArea = new TextArea(3,35);
```

You can see that it has a constructor that allows you to fix the size by entering values for the number of rows and columns (in that order, by the way!).

After declaring and initializing the components, we have coded the constructor which is straightforward — it simply adds these components to the panel, and then adds the `ActionListener` to the `calcButton`.

Next we have the event-handling routing for the `calcButton`; this is worth taking a look at:

```
public void actionPerformed(ActionEvent e)
{
   String lengthEntered = lengthField.getText();
   String heightEntered = heightField.getText();
   if(e.getSource() == calcButton)
   {
     // make sure the fields aren't blank
     if(lengthEntered.length() == 0 || heightEntered.length() == 0)
     {
       displayArea.setText("Length and height must be entered");
     }
     else
     {
       oblong.setLength(Double.parseDouble(lengthEntered));
       oblong.setHeight(Double.parseDouble(heightEntered));
       displayArea.setText("The area of the oblong is "
                       + oblong.calculateArea()
                       + "\n"
                       + "The perimeter of the oblong is "
                       + oblong.calculatePerimeter());
     }
   }
}
```

We have declared two local variables, lengthEntered and heightEntered, to hold the values entered by the user; these values are read using the getText method of TextField. Then we check that these are not of length zero (that is, that something has been entered). If one of the fields is empty we display an error message. Otherwise we use the calculateArea and calculatePerimeter methods of Oblong to display the area and perimeter of the oblong in the text area. We have used the setText method of TextArea to do this; we could also have used the append method — the difference is that this does not clear what was previously written in the area, whereas the setText method does.

The program for running the interface in an EasyFrame appears in program 9.5 below.

PROGRAM 9.5

```java
import java.awt.*;

public class GuiDriver
{
  public static void main(String[] args)
  {
    EasyFrame frame = new EasyFrame();
    frame.setTitle("Oblong GUI");
    OblongGui gui = new OblongGui();
    frame.setSize(300,170);
    frame.setBackground(Color.lightGray);
    frame.add(gui);
    frame.setVisible(true);
  }
}
```

9.9   A metric converter

We thought that our next example would be a pretty useful one. Most of the world uses the metric system; however, if you are in the United Kingdom like we are, then you will still be only half-way there — sometimes using kilograms and kilometres, sometimes pounds and miles; or buying petrol in litres and then converting into gallons in your mind! And of course if you are in the USA (and you are not a scientist or an engineer) you will still be using the old imperial values for everything. Some might say it's time that the UK and the USA caught up with the rest of the world, but until that happens this little program, which converts back and forth from metric to imperial, is going to be very handy.

We will be building a MetricConverter class — program 9.6 provides the code for running our converter in an EasyFrame measuring 350 × 255, which we have again coloured light grey.

PROGRAM 9.6

```java
import java.awt.*;

public class RunConverter
{
  public static void main(String[] args)
  {
    EasyFrame frame = new EasyFrame();
    frame.setTitle("Metric Converter");
    MetricConverter converter = new MetricConverter();
    frame.setSize(350,225);
    frame.setBackground(Color.lightGray);
    frame.add(converter);
    frame.setVisible(true);
  }
}
```

Figure 9.8 shows the result of running this program.

The MetricConverter class is now presented; it looks quite long, but most of it is just more of what you already know. There are, however, two concepts, **layout policies** and **compound containers**, that we need to discuss in some depth, and we do this straight after showing you the code.

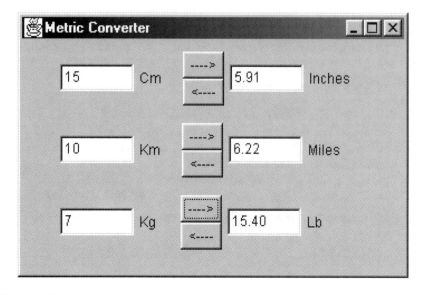

Fig 9.8   The metric converter running in a frame

THE *MetricConverter* CLASS

```java
import java.awt.*;
import java.awt.event.*;
import java.text.*; // required for the DecimalFormat class

class MetricConverter extends Panel implements ActionListener
{
    // we declare the various components as attributes

    /* first the components for converting back and forth from inches
    to centimetres */

    private TextField cmText = new TextField(6);
    private Label cmLabel = new Label("Cm");
    private Button cmToInchButton = new Button("---->");
    private Button inchToCmButton = new Button("<----");
    private Panel inchCmButtons = new Panel(); // compound container
    private TextField inchText = new TextField(6);
    private Label inchLabel = new Label("Inches");
    private Panel inchCmPanel = new Panel(); // compound container

    /* next the components for converting back and forth from miles
    to kilometres */

    private TextField kmText = new TextField(6);
    private Label kmLabel = new Label("Km");
    private Button kmToMileButton = new Button("---->");
    private Button mileToKmButton = new Button("<----");
    private Panel mileKmButtons = new Panel(); // compound container
    private TextField mileText = new TextField(6);
    private Label mileLabel = new Label("Miles ");
    private Panel mileKmPanel = new Panel(); // compound container

    /* finally the components for converting back and forth from pounds
    to kilograms */

    private TextField kgText = new TextField(6);
    private Label kgLabel = new Label("Kg ");
    private Button kgToPoundButton = new Button("---->");
    private Button poundToKgButton = new Button("<----");
    private Panel poundKgButtons = new Panel(); // compound container
    private TextField poundText = new TextField(6);
    private Label poundLabel = new Label("Lb ");
    private Panel poundKgPanel = new Panel(); // compound container

    /* the constructor adds the components to the object at the time
    it is created */

    public MetricConverter()
    {
```

```
      inchCmButtons.setLayout(new BorderLayout()); // see section 9.9
      inchCmButtons.add("North",cmToInchButton);
      inchCmButtons.add("South",inchToCmButton);
      inchCmPanel.add(cmText);
      inchCmPanel.add(cmLabel);
      inchCmPanel.add(inchCmButtons);
      inchCmPanel.add(inchText);
      inchCmPanel.add(inchLabel);

      mileKmButtons.setLayout(new BorderLayout()); // see section 9.9
      mileKmButtons.add("North",kmToMileButton);
      mileKmButtons.add("South",mileToKmButton);
      mileKmPanel.add(kmText);
      mileKmPanel.add(kmLabel);
      mileKmPanel.add(mileKmButtons);
      mileKmPanel.add(mileText);
      mileKmPanel.add(mileLabel);

      poundKgButtons.setLayout(new BorderLayout()); // see section 9.9
      poundKgButtons.add("North",kgToPoundButton);
      poundKgButtons.add("South",poundToKgButton);
      poundKgPanel.add(kgText);
      poundKgPanel.add(kgLabel);
      poundKgPanel.add(poundKgButtons);
      poundKgPanel.add(poundText);
      poundKgPanel.add(poundLabel);

      add(inchCmPanel);
      add(mileKmPanel);
      add(poundKgPanel);
      cmToInchButton.addActionListener(this);
      inchToCmButton.addActionListener(this);
      kmToMileButton.addActionListener(this);
      mileToKmButton.addActionListener(this);
      kgToPoundButton.addActionListener(this);
      poundToKgButton.addActionListener(this);
}

// now we code the event-handlers

public void actionPerformed(ActionEvent e)
{
   double d;
   String s;
   DecimalFormat df = new DecimalFormat("#####0.0#");
   if(e.getSource() == cmToInchButton)
   {
```

```
        s = new String(cmText.getText());
        d = Double.parseDouble(s);
        d = d / 2.54;
        s = df.format(d);
        inchText.setText(s);
      }
      if(e.getSource() == inchToCmButton)
      {
        s = new String(inchText.getText());
        d = Double.parseDouble(s);
        d = d * 2.54;
        s = df.format(d);
        cmText.setText(s);
      }
      if(e.getSource() == kmToMileButton)
      {
        s = new String(kmText.getText());
        d = Double.parseDouble(s);
        d = d / 1.609;
        s = df.format(d);
        mileText.setText(s);
      }
      if(e.getSource() == mileToKmButton)
      {
        s = new String(mileText.getText());
        d = Double.parseDouble(s);
        d = d * 1.609;
        s = df.format(d);
        kmText.setText(s);
      }
      if(e.getSource() == kgToPoundButton)
      {
        s = new String(kgText.getText());
        d = Double.parseDouble(s);
        d = d * 2.2;
        s = df.format(d);
        poundText.setText(s);
      }
      if(e.getSource() == poundToKgButton)
      {
        s = new String(poundText.getText());
        d = Double.parseDouble(s);
        d = d / 2.2;
        s = df.format(d);
        kgText.setText(s);
      }
    }
  }
}
```

9.10 *Layout policies*

We have already described the default layout policy, FlowLayout. But in addition to this policy the AWT package provides a number of other classes called **layout managers**. We can create an object of one of these classes and attach it to a container, and thereafter that container will lay out the components it contains according to the policy of that layout manager. The strategy of the only layout manager we have seen so far, FlowLayout, is simply to arrange the components in the order that they were added, starting a new row when necessary. If the window is resized the items move about accordingly, as shown in figure 9.9.

Another commonly-used layout manager is BorderLayout. Here the window is divided into five regions called North, South, East, West and Center as shown in figure 9.10.

If we use a border layout the components don't get moved around when the window is resized, as you can see from figure 9.11.

The MetricConverter class uses a border layout for some of its components, as explained in the next section. The example below, taken from the MetricConverter, shows how components are placed in the different regions.

First, the setLayout method is used to add a new BorderLayout to a component called inchCmButtons (this is in fact a Panel as explained in section 9.9):

```
inchCmButtons.setLayout(new BorderLayout());
```

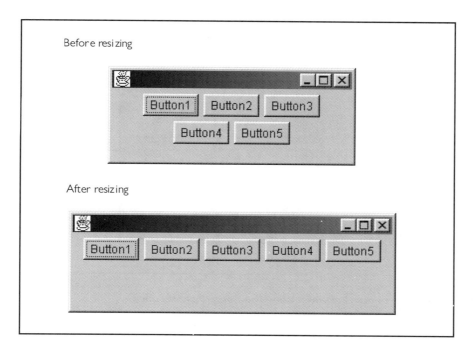

Fig 9.9   The effect of resizing when using the *FlowLayout* Policy

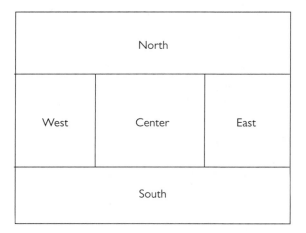

Fig 9.10   The *BorderLayout* Policy

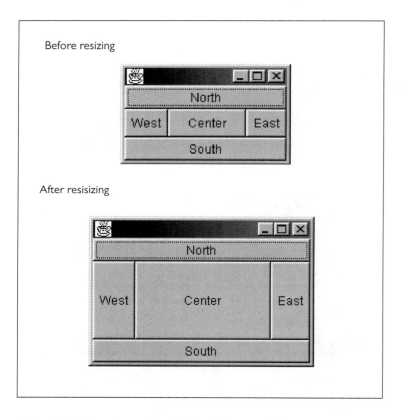

Fig 9.11   The effect of resizing when using the *BorderLayout* Policy

Next we place the cmToInchButton in the North region:

```
inchCmButtons.add("North", cmToInchButton);
```

There are a number of other layout managers that can be used such as GridLayout and CardLayout; you can look these up if you like, but we are not going to introduce them to you in this first semester.

9.11   Compound containers

A **compound** container is, as its name suggests, a container that contains other containers. Each container can use a different layout manager. One of the most useful components that we can use when we build graphics programs is a Panel. This is a component that we don't actually see, but which can be used to hold other components. We have used panels in the MetricConverter. Figure 9.12 shows how each component is named and how we make use of compound containers by constructing the MetricConverter with three panels named inchCmPanel, mileKmPanel and poundKgPanel. The various components are added to these panels which are then added to the MetricConverter itself. In each case one of these components is a panel which contains the two buttons used to make the conversions (the ones with the arrows on them); these panels (inchCmButtons, mileKmButtons and poundKgButtons) have a BorderLayout policy so that the buttons remain one on top of the other however the window is sized.

Look carefully at figure 9.12 and then look back at the code to see how we build up the components that make up the class.

9.12   GUIs for collections of objects

When we developed the GUI for our Oblong class in section 9.8, we connected the GUI to a single instance of an Oblong by declaring an Oblong object as an attribute of the GUI class; you can use a similar technique for the Reactor class in question 4 of the practical examples that follow.

Many real-world examples will of course require you to manipulate more than one object – for example students, employees etc. One way to handle this would be to declare an array of objects as an attribute of the GUI class – you might want to try this out. The disadvantage of this approach, however, is that that you would have to include in the event-handlers all the code for moving through the array (for example to search it or to display items).

Another approach is to use a collection class and to declare an object of this class as an attribute of the GUI class. This is the approach that we have taken in the next two chapters in which we develop a case study that deals with a student hostel.

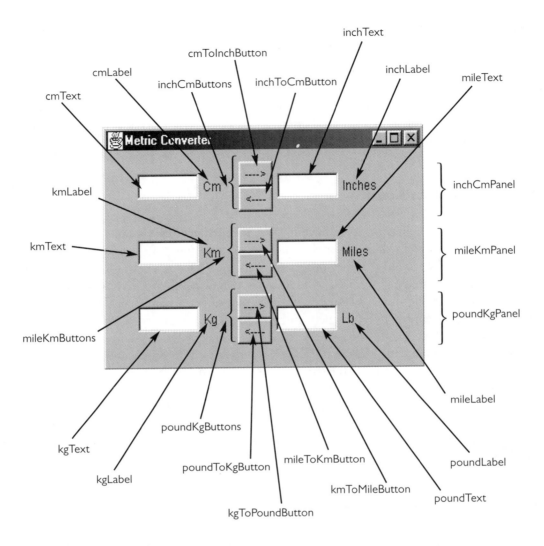

Fig 9.12 The composition of the *MetricConverter* class

Tutorial exercises

1. Explain the difference between the FlowLayout policy and the BorderLayout policy.
2. Consider some changes or additions you could make to the PushMe class. For example, pushing the button could display your text in upper case – or it could say how many letters it contains. Maybe you could add some extra buttons. Think about these changes and sketch out the design and the code.

3. The diagram below shows an application that allows the user to press a button in order to see one of three chosen shapes:

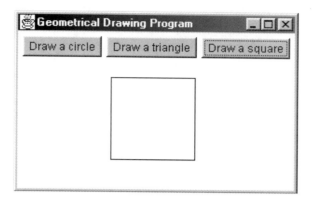

The graphic is written as a class called DrawShapes, and is an extension of the Panel class; it can therefore be added to a Frame in order to view it. The buttons are declared as attributes of the class as follows:

```
private Button circleButton = new Button("Draw a circle");
private Button triangleButton = new Button("Draw a triangle");
private Button squareButton = new Button("Draw a square");
```

(i) Write the code for a constructor for this class which adds these buttons to the Panel and enables them to respond to a mouse-click.

(ii) The program works by setting an integer attribute, typeOfShape, to either 1, 2 or 3 when one of the above shapes – circle, triangle or square – is selected; the graphic is then re-painted. Assuming that the class implements the ActionListener interface, write the code for the actionPerformed method.

4. Below is a variation on the ChangingFace class, which now has a neck and three possible moods!

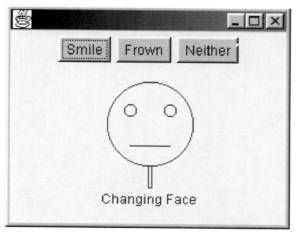

Rewrite the original code to produce this new design.

Hint 1: You will no longer be able to use a **boolean** variable like isHappy, because you need more than two possible values. Can you think of how to deal with this?

Hint 2: There are two useful methods of the Graphics class that you will need:

void drawLine (int x1, int y1, int x2, int y2)
Draws a line from point (x1, y1) to point (x2, y2).

void drawRect (int x, int y, int w, int h)
Draws a rectangle from of width w and height h with the top left-hand corner at point (x, y).

Practical work

1. Implement the changes you have made to the PushMe class.
2. Add some additional features to the MetricConverter – for example Celsius to Fahrenheit or litres to pints.
3. Implement the changes to the ChangingFace class that you made in tutorial question 4.
4. Look back at the final version of the Reactor class that you wrote in the first practical question of chapter 8. Now you can create a graphical user interface for it, instead of a text menu. A suggested interface is shown below, with an explanation of the different components used.

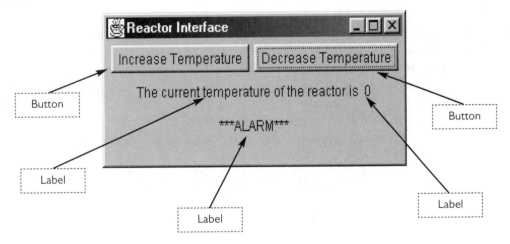

CASE STUDY – PART I

LEARNING OBJECTIVES

By the end of this chapter you should be able to:

➤ develop a Java implementation from a UML specification;

➤ use pseudocode to help develop complex algorithms.

10.1 Introduction

In this and the next chapter we are going to develop a case study that will enable you to get an idea of how a real-world system can be developed from scratch; we start with an informal description of the requirements, and then specify the system using UML notation. From there we go on to design our system and implement it in Java. In this chapter we develop the individual classes required, and test them in the way you learnt in chapter 8; in the next chapter we put them together with a graphical user interface and test out our system as a whole.

The system that we are going to develop will keep records of the residents of a student hostel. In order not to cloud your understanding of the system, we have rather over-simplified things, keeping details of individuals to a minimum, and keeping the functionality fairly basic; you will have the opportunity to improve on what we have done in the tutorial and practical work at the end of each chapter.

The case study demonstrates all the important learning points from previous chapters, and allows you to see how these can be brought together to create a working system; in future, as you learn more advanced techniques, the system can be adapted to become more sophisticated and functional.

10.2 The requirements

The local university requires a program to manage one of its student hostels which contains a number of rooms, each of which can be occupied by a single tenant who pays rent on a monthly basis. The program must keep a list of tenants; the information held for each tenant will consist of a name, a room number and a list of all the payments a tenant has made (month and amount). The program must allow the user to add and delete tenants, to display a list of all tenants, to record a payment for a particular tenant, and to display the payment history of a tenant.

10.3   The specification

Figure 10.1 represents the UML specification of the system; the diagram shows **associations** between the two classes, represented in UML by a single line; in this case a single tenant makes a number of payments – a one-to-many relationship. As was explained in chapter 6 when aggregation was discussed, the "many" side of the relationship is indicated by an asterisk. The "one" side is indicated by a 1.

10.4   The design

We have made a number of design decisions about how the system will be implemented, and these are listed below:

- instances of the Tenant class and instances of the Payment class will each be held in a separate collection class, PaymentList and TenantList respectively;
- the above collection classes will both inherit common features from the generic ObjectList class that we developed in chapter 7;
- The Hostel class which will hold the TenantList will also act as the graphical interface for the system.

The design of the system is shown in figure 10.2. Note that the standard UML notation of underlining a *class* attribute has been used with the maxNoOfPayments attribute of the Tenant class. The Hostel class itself has not yet been designed and this will be left until the next chapter where we consider the overall system design and testing; for this reason it has been drawn with a dotted line.

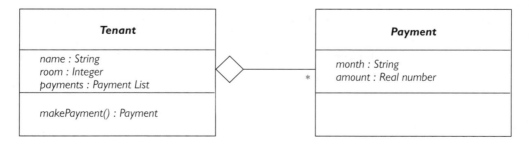

Fig 10.1   The UML specification of the hostel system

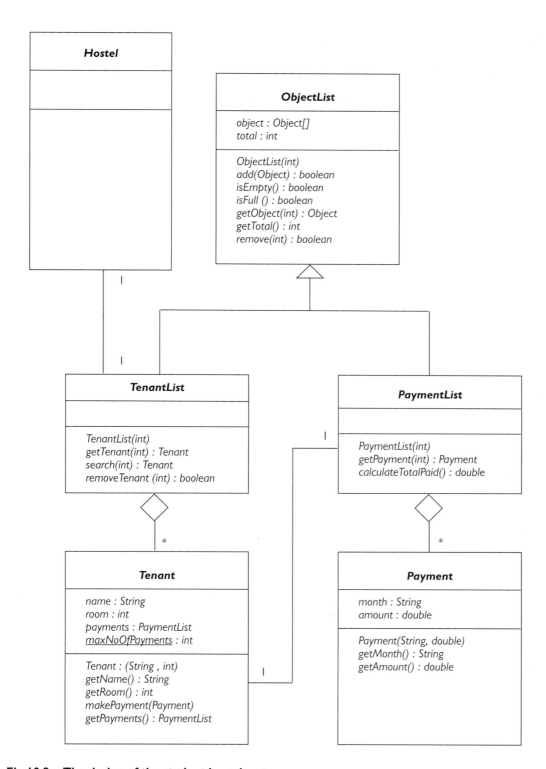

Fig 10.2   The design of the student hostel system

10.5 *Implementing the* Payment *class*

The code for the Payment class is shown below:

THE *Payment* CLASS

```
class Payment
{
  private String month;
  private double amount;

  public Payment(String monthIn, double amountIn)
  {
    month = monthIn;
    amount = amountIn;
  }

  public String getMonth()
  {
    return month;
  }

  public double getAmount()
  {
    return amount;
  }
}
```

As you can see, this class is fairly simple so we won't discuss it any further. A driver to test this class is equally straightforward and we leave it as a practical task at the end of this chapter.

Now let's move on to the more interesting parts of this system. All the remaining classes involve the use of some kind of collection – in each case the type of collection is a list.

This system requires us to develop two kinds of list, a PaymentList and a TenantList. Rather than develop the same code twice we are going to reuse the ObjectList class that we developed in chapter 7, and then use inheritance to add the specific attributes and methods that we need for a PaymentList and a TenantList. If you look back at the UML design in figure 10.2 you can see that after inheriting details from the ObjectList class, there is not a lot of extra work to be done to code the PaymentList class. We present the complete code for this class below, after which we discuss it.

THE *PaymentList* CLASS

```
class PaymentList extends ObjectList // inherit from ObjectList
{
  public PaymentList(int sizeIn)
  { // call ObjectList constructor
    super(sizeIn);
  }

  public Payment getPayment(int indexIn)
  { // call inherited method and type cast
    return (Payment) getObject(indexIn);
  }

  public double calculateTotalPaid()
  {
    double totalPaid = 0; // initialize totalPaid
    // loop through all payments
    for (int i=1; i<= getTotal();i++)
    { // add current payment to running total
      totalPaid = totalPaid + getPayment(i).getAmount();
    }
    return totalPaid;
  }
}
```

As you can see, this class requires no additional attributes and, apart from the new constructor, only two additional methods – getPayment and calculateTotalPaid. Let's have a look at each of these methods in turn.

The getPayment method is simply a wrapper for the getObject method from the inherited ObjectList class. If you remember from chapter 7, we said that generic container classes can be used to store items of *any* type, but when returning such items from the container they must be type cast back to the appropriate type. The getPayment method carries out this task of type casting the returned item back to an object of type Payment.

```
return (Payment) getObject(indexIn);
```

The advantage of this is that responsibility for type casting is taken away from the calling method, and given to getPayment itself. An example of the use of this method can be seen in the calculateTotalPaid method.

The calculateTotalPaid method uses a standard **algorithm** for computing sums from a list of items. An **algorithm** is an often-used term in computing texts, and means a set of instructions for achieving a task (such as a recipe). This algorithm can be expressed in pseudocode as follows:

```
SET totalPaid TO 0
LOOP FROM 1st item in list TO last item in list
BEGIN
  SET totalPaid TO totalPaid + amount of current payment
END
return totalPaid
```

As with the remove method we discussed in chapter 6, this algorithm can be implemented in Java with the use of a **for** loop. Notice how the position of the last item in the list is determined by the getTotal method; remember that we do not have access to the total attribute, since this was declared as **private** in the superclass.

```
double totalPaid = 0;
for (int i=1; i<= getTotal();i++)
{
   totalPaid = totalPaid + getPayment(i).getAmount();
}
return totalPaid;
```

The body of the loop takes the amount associated with the current payment and adds it to the running total. As you can see, the getPayment method is used to return the current payment and the getAmount method is used to find out the amount associated with that payment.

getPayment(i).getAmount()

returns current payment

returns amount of a given payment

Before we move on, it is important to test this PaymentList class in order to ensure that it is functioning correctly. Program 10.1 provides a menu-driven interface for this test driver. Notice the careful use of the new line, '\n', and tab, '\t', escape sequences to improve the display of information on the screen.

PROGRAM 10.1

```
public class PaymentListTester
{
  public static void main(String[] args)
  {
    char choice;
    int total;
    // declare PaymentList object to test
    PaymentList pl;
    // get size of list
    System.out.print("\nMaximum number of payments? ");
    total = EasyIn.getInt();
    // create PaymentList object to test
    pl = new PaymentList(total);
    // menu
    do
    {
      // display options
      System.out.println("\n[1] Add a payment");
      System.out.println("[2] List all payments");
      System.out.println("[3] Get number of payments made");
      System.out.println("[4] Get total payments made");
      System.out.println("[5] Quit");
      System.out.print("\nEnter a choice [1,2,3,4,5]: ");
      // get choice
      choice = EasyIn.getChar();
      // process choice
      switch(choice)
      {
        case '1': option1(pl); break;
        case '2': option2(pl); break;
        case '3': option3(pl); break;
        case '4': option4(pl); break;
        case '5': System.out.print("\n\nBYE"); break;
        default: System.out.print("\n1-5 only");
      }
    } while (choice != '5');
  }

  // static worker methods
  // add payment
  private static void option1(PaymentList listIn)
  {
    if (!listIn.isFull()) // only add if list has space
    {
```

```
            System.out.print("\nenter month:\t");
            String month = EasyIn.getString();
            System.out.print("enter amount:\t");
            double amount = EasyIn.getDouble();
            listIn.add(new Payment (month, amount));
        }
        else // error message if list is full
        {
            System.out.println("\n!!!SORRY, LIST IS FULL!!!");
        }
    }

    // display payments
    private static void option2(PaymentList listIn)
    {
        System.out.print("\nMONTH \tAMOUNT\n"); // header
        // loop through payments in list
        for (int i =1; i <= listIn.getTotal();i++)
        {
            Payment p = listIn.getPayment(i);
            System.out.print(p.getMonth());
            System.out.println("\t" + p.getAmount());
        }
    }

    // get total number of payments
    private static void option3(PaymentList listIn)
    {
        System.out.print("\ntotal number payments made: ");
        System.out.println(listIn.getTotal());
    }

    // get total of payments made
    private static void option4(PaymentList listIn)
    {
        System.out.print("\ntotal sum of payments made: ");
        System.out.println(listIn.calculateTotalPaid());
    }
}
```

To make this driver more readable, menu options have been implemented inside **static** worker methods. There is nothing particularly new here so let's look at a sample test run of this driver program:

Maximum number of payments? **2**

[1] Add a payment
[2] List all payments
[3] Get number of payments made
[4] Get total payments made
[5] Quit

Enter a choice [1,2,3,4,5]: **1**

enter month: Jan
enter amount: 240

[1] Add a payment
[2] List all payments
[3] Get number of payments made
[4] Get total payments made
[5] Quit

Enter a choice [1,2,3,4,5]: **1**

enter month: Feb
enter amount: 225

[1] Add a payment
[2] List all payments
[3] Get number of payments made
[4] Get total payments made
[5] Quit

Enter a choice [1,2,3,4,5]: **2**

MONTH AMOUNT
Jan 240.0
Feb 225.0

[1] Add a payment
[2] List all payments
[3] Get number of payments made
[4] Get total payments made
[5] Quit

Enter a choice [1,2,3,4,5]: **3**

total number payments made: 2

```
[1] Add a payment
[2] List all payments
[3] Get number of payments made
[4] Get total payments made
[5] Quit

Enter a choice [1,2,3,4,5]: 4

total sum of payments made: 465.0

[1] Add a payment
[2] List all payments
[3] Get number of payments made
[4] Get total payments made
[5] Quit

Enter a choice [1,2,3,4,5]: 1

!!!SORRY, LIST IS FULL!!!

[1] Add a payment
[2] List all payments
[3] Get number of payments made
[4] Get total payments made
[5] Quit

Enter a choice [1,2,3,4,5]: 5

BYE
```

Although some aspects of the interface could be improved, the PaymentList class appears to be functioning properly. In order to be more confident, more rigorous testing would need to be carried out. For now though, this amount of testing is sufficient so let's move on to the Tenant class.

10.6   *Implementing the Tenant class*

As you can see from the UML diagram of figure 10.2, the Tenant class contains four attributes: name, room, payments, maxNoOfPayments.

The first two of these represent the name and the room of the tenant respectively. The third attribute, payments, is to be implemented as a PaymentList object and the last attribute, maxNoOfPayments, is to be implemented as a **static** class attribute. The maxNoOfPayments attribute will also be implemented as a *constant* as we are assuming that tenants make a *fixed* number of payments in a year (twelve – one for each month). Below is the code for the Tenant class.

THE *Tenant* CLASS

```
class Tenant
{
  private String name;
  private int room;
  private PaymentList payments;
  private static final int maxNoOfPayments = 12;

  Tenant(String nameIn, int roomIn)
  {
    name = new String(nameIn);
    room = roomIn;
    payments = new PaymentList(maxNoOfPayments);
  }
  public String getName()
  {
    return name;
  }
  public int getRoom()
  {
    return room;
  }
  public void makePayment(Payment paymentIn)
  { // call PaymentList method
    payments.add(paymentIn);
  }
  public PaymentList getPayments()
  {
    return payments;
  }
}
```

As there is nothing very new in this class, we don't really need to discuss it any further other than to point out that the payments attribute, being of type PaymentList, can respond to any of the PaymentList methods we discussed in section 10.5. The makePayment method illustrates this by calling the add method of PaymentList.

```
public void makePayment(Payment paymentIn)
{ // add method of PaymentList called
  payments.add(paymentIn);
}
```

The implementation of a driver to test this class will be very similar to program 10.1 and is left as a practical exercise at the end of this chapter.

10.7 *Implementing the* **TenantList** *class*

The `TenantList` class, like the `PaymentList` class of section 10.5, inherits from the generic `ObjectList` class. As you can see from diagram 10.2, the `TenantList` class requires no new attributes and, apart from the constructor, has only three new methods:

- `getTenant`;
- `search`;
- `removeTenant`.

The `getTenant` method behaves in much the same way as the `getPayment` method of the `PaymentList` class. That is, it acts as a wrapper for the `getObject` method of the generic `ObjectList` class and type casts the returned item back to an object of the correct type, which in this case is an object of type `Tenant`.

```
public Tenant getTenant(int indexIn)
{ // call inherited method and type cast
   return (Tenant)getObject(indexIn);
}
```

The search method is unique to the `TenantList` class. Here is a reminder of its interface:

```
search (int): Tenant
```

The integer parameter represents the room number of the tenant that this method is searching for. The tenant returned is the tenant living in that particular room; if no tenant is found in that room then `null` is returned. From this interface we can derive the method header:

```
public Tenant search (int roomIn)
{
   // code for method goes here
}
```

Searching through a list for a given item is a common activity and many algorithms exist for this purpose. An algorithm is an often-used term in computing texts, and means a set of instructions for achieving a task. Here is a fairly standard search algorithm expressed in pseudocode:

```
LOOP FROM first item TO last item
BEGIN
  IF current item = roomIn
  BEGIN
    EXIT loop with current item
  END
END
indicate item not found
```

A **for** loop can be used to implement this algorithm as follows:

```
for(int i=1;i<=getTotal();i++)
{
    // body of loop
}
return null; // no tenant found with given room number
```

The body of the loop can in turn be implemented using a simple **if** statement. The condition of the selection requires us to check whether the current item is the item we are looking for. We can do this by checking the room number of the current tenant against the room number we are searching for, roomIn, as follows:

```
if(getTenant(i).getRoom() == roomIn)
{
    // body of if statement
}
```

Finally, the body of the **if** statement requires us to exit the loop with the given tenant. The **return** statement allows us to exit with a value so the following statement would be appropriate:

```
return getTenant(i);
```

Notice that as soon as this **return** statement is executed the loop will terminate and the method will be complete. Finally, let's look at the removeTenant method. The interface for this method is given as follows:

```
removeTenant(int): boolean
```

Here the integer parameter represents the room number of the tenant who is to be removed from the list and the **boolean** return value indicates whether or not such a tenant has been removed successfully. From this interface we get the following method header:

```
public boolean removeTenant (int roomIn)
{
   // code for methods goes here
}
```

Most of the work of this method is going to be carried out by the remove method of the ObjectList class. The job of the removeTenant method is to determine which tenant to delete before calling the remove method. This once again requires a *search* so we will use the basis of the search algorithm we presented earlier to devise an algorithm for this method.

```
LOOP FROM first item TO last item
BEGIN
   IF current item = roomIn
   BEGIN
      remove current item from list
      EXIT from loop and indicate success
   END
END
indicate failure (item not found)
```

Remembering that we will use **boolean** values **true** and **false** to indicate success or failure in this method, we arrive at the following implementation for the body of the removeTenant method:

```
for(int i=1;i<=getTotal();i++)
{ // remove tenant with given room number
   if(getTenant(i).getRoom() == roomIn)
   {
      remove(i); // call remove method of ObjectList
      return true; // indicate success
   }
}
return false; // indicate failure
```

The complete code for the TenantList class is now presented below.

THE *TenantList* **CLASS**

```
class TenantList extends ObjectList
{
  public TenantList(int sizeIn)
  { // call ObjectList constructor
    super(sizeIn);
  }

  public Tenant getTenant(int indexIn)
  { // call inherited method and type cast
    return (Tenant)getObject(indexIn);
  }

  public Tenant search(int roomIn)
  {
    for(int i=1;i<=getTotal();i++)
    { // find tenant with given room number
      if(getTenant(i).getRoom() == roomIn)
      {
        return getTenant(i);
      }
    }
    return null; // no tenant found with given room number
  }

  public boolean removeTenant(int roomIn)
  {
    for(int i=1;i<=getTotal();i++)
    { // remove tenant with given room number
      if(getTenant(i).getRoom() == roomIn)
      {
        remove(i);
        return true;
      }
    }
    return false; // no tenant found with given room number
  }
}
```

Program 10.2 is a driver to test the TenantList class. Once again, notice the use of escape sequences to help format output on the screen.

PROGRAM 10.2

```java
public class TenantListTester
{
  public static void main(String[] args)
  { // declare variables
    char choice;
    int total;
    TenantList tl;
    // get size of list
    System.out.print("\nHow many tenants will there be ? ");
    total = EasyIn.getInt();
    // create list
    tl = new TenantList(total);
    // menu
    do
    { // display options
      System.out.println("\n[1] Add a tenant");
      System.out.println("[2] List all tenants");
      System.out.println("[3] Add a payment");
      System.out.println("[4] List payments");
      System.out.println("[5] Remove a tenant");
      System.out.println("[6] Quit");
      System.out.print("\nEnter a choice [1,2,3,4,5,6]: ");
      choice = EasyIn.getChar();// get choice
      // process choice
      switch(choice)
      {
        case '1':option1(tl); break;
        case '2':option2(tl); break;
        case '3':option3(tl); break;
        case '4':option4(tl); break;
        case '5':option5(tl); break;
        case '6':System.out.print("\n\nBYE"); break;
        default: System.out.print("\n1-5 only");
      }
    } while (choice != '6');
  }

  private static void option1(TenantList listIn)
  {
    if (!listIn.isFull()) // only add if list is not full
    {
      System.out.print("\nenter name:\t");
      String name = EasyIn.getString();
      System.out.print("enter room:\t");
      int room = EasyIn.getInt();
      listIn.add(new Tenant (name, room));
```

```java
      }
    else // error message if list is full
    {
      System.out.println("\n!!!SORRY, LIST IS FULL!!! \n");
    }
  }

  private static void option2(TenantList listIn)
  {
    System.out.print("\nNAME \tROOM\n"); // header
    // loop through tenants in list
    for (int i =1; i <= listIn.getTotal();i++)
    {
      Tenant t = listIn.getTenant(i);
      System.out.print(t.getName());
      System.out.println("\t" + t.getRoom());
    }
  }

  private static void option3(TenantList listIn)
  { // get room number of tenant
    System.out.print("\nenter room number of tenant:\t");
    int room = EasyIn.getInt();
    // find relevant tenant
    Tenant t = listIn.search(room);
    if (t != null) // check tenant exists before adding payment
    {
      System.out.print("\nenter month:\t");
      String month = EasyIn.getString();
      System.out.print("enter amount:\t");
      double amount = EasyIn.getDouble();
      Payment p = new Payment (month, amount);
      t.makePayment(p);
    }
    else // no tenant with given room number found
    {
      System.out.print("\n!!!NO TENANT IN THIS ROOM!!! \n");
    }
  }
  private static void option4(TenantList listIn)
  { // get room number of tenant
    System.out.print("\nenter room number of tenant:\t");
    int room = EasyIn.getInt();
    // find relevant tenant
    Tenant t = listIn.search(room);
    if (t != null) // check such a tenant exists before displaying
    {
```

```
      PaymentList pl = t.getPayments();
      System.out.print("\nMONTH \tAMOUNT\n");// header
      // loop through payments in list
      for (int i =1; i <= pl.getTotal();i++)
      {
        Payment p = pl.getPayment(i);
        System.out.print(p.getMonth());
        System.out.println("\t" + p.getAmount());
      }
      // display total amount paid
      System.out.print("\nTOTAL PAID:\t");
      System.out.println(pl.calculateTotalPaid());
    }
    else // no tenant with given room number found
    {
      System.out.print("\n!!!NO TENANT IN THIS ROOM!!! \n");
    }
  }

  private static void option5(TenantList listIn)
  { // get room number of tenant
    System.out.print("\nenter room number of tenant:\t");
    int room = EasyIn.getInt();
    // check tenant exists
    Tenant t = listIn.search(room);
    if (t != null) // only remove if tenant exists
    {
      listIn.removeTenant(room);
    }
    else // no tenant in given room
    {
      System.out.print("\n!!! NO TENANT IN THIS ROOM!!! \n");
    }
  }
}
```

By now, such a menu system should be familiar to you. We just draw your attention to the validation that we have added to some of these menu options.

Option 1 allows the user to add a tenant to the list. We have ensured that a tenant is only added if the list is currently *not full*.

```
if (!listIn.isFull()) // only add if list is not full
{
   // code to get tenant details and add
}
else // error message if list is full
{
   System.out.println("\n!!!SORRY, LIST IS FULL!!! \n");
}
```

Notice we haven't carried out any error checking on the rooms at this stage. Responsibility for ensuring that tenants do not occupy the same room has not been given to the TenantList class so should not be tested here. This job will be given to the Hostel class that we will develop in the next chapter.

Option 3 allows the user to record the payment for a tenant in a given room. We have ensured that a tenant actually exists in that room before recording the payment.

```
int room = EasyIn.getInt();
// find relevant tenant
Tenant t = listIn.search(room);
// check tenant exists before adding payment
if (t != null)
{
   // code to get and record payment goes here
}
else // no tenant with given room number found
{
   System.out.print("\n!!!NO TENANT IN THIS ROOM!!! \n");
}
```

Options 4 and 5 both include similar validation as both require a tenant to exist in a given room before further action can be taken. Below is a sample test run of program 10.2 – examine it closely as we will ask you a question about it in the tutorial section at the end of this chapter.

> How many tenants will there be? **2**
>
> [1] Add a tenant
> [2] List all tenants
> [3] Add a payment
> [4] List payments
> [5] Remove a tenant
> [6] Quit

Enter a choice [1,2,3,4,5,6]: **1**

enter name: **Bart**
enter room: **3**

[1] Add a tenant
[2] List all tenants
[3] Add a payment
[4] List payments
[5] Remove a tenant
[6] Quit

Enter a choice [1,2,3,4,5,6]: **1**

enter name: **Louise**
enter room: **1**

[1] Add a tenant
[2] List all tenants
[3] Add a payment
[4] List payments
[5] Remove a tenant
[6] Quit

Enter a choice [1,2,3,4,5,6]: **2**

NAME ROOM
Bart 3
Louise 1

[1] Add a tenant
[2] List all tenants
[3] Add a payment
[4] List payments
[5] Remove a tenant
[6] Quit

Enter a choice [1,2,3,4,5,6]: **1**

!!!SORRY, LIST IS FULL!!!

[1] Add a tenant
[2] List all tenants
[3] Add a payment
[4] List payments
[5] Remove a tenant
[6] Quit

Enter a choice [1,2,3,4,5,6]: **3**

enter room number of tenant: **5**

!!!NO TENANT IN THIS ROOM!!!

[1] Add a tenant
[2] List all tenants
[3] Add a payment
[4] List payments
[5] Remove a tenant
[6] Quit

Enter a choice [1,2,3,4,5,6]: **3**

enter room number of tenant: **3**

enter month: Jan
enter amount: 240

[1] Add a tenant
[2] List all tenants
[3] Add a payment
[4] List payments
[5] Remove a tenant
[6] Quit

Enter a choice [1,2,3,4,5,6]: **3**

enter room number of tenant: **3**

enter month: Feb
enter amount: 225

[1] Add a tenant
[2] List all tenants
[3] Add a payment
[4] List payments
[5] Remove a tenant
[6] Quit

Enter a choice [1,2,3,4,5,6]: **4**

enter room number of tenant: **2**

!!!NO TENANT IN THIS ROOM!!!

[1] Add a tenant

[2] List all tenants

[3] Add a payment

[4] List payments

[5] Remove a tenant

[6] Quit

Enter a choice [1,2,3,4,5,6]: **4**

enter room number of tenant: **3**

MONTH AMOUNT

Jan 240.0

Feb 225.0

TOTAL PAID: 465.0

[1] Add a tenant

[2] List all tenants

[3] Add a payment

[4] List payments

[5] Remove a tenant

[6] Quit

Enter a choice [1,2,3,4,5,6]: **5**

enter room number of tenant: **7**

!!! NO TENANT IN THIS ROOM!!!

[1] Add a tenant

[2] List all tenants

[3] Add a payment

[4] List payments

[5] Remove a tenant

[6] Quit

Enter a choice [1,2,3,4,5,6]: **5**

enter room number of tenant: **3**

[1] Add a tenant

[2] List all tenants

[3] Add a payment

[4] List payments

[5] Remove a tenant

[6] Quit

```
Enter a choice [1,2,3,4,5,6]: 2

NAME ROOM
Louise 1

[1] Add a tenant
[2] List all tenants
[3] Add a payment
[4] List payments
[5] Remove a tenant
[6] Quit

Enter a choice [1,2,3,4,5,6]: 6

BYE
```

Tutorial exercises

1. What advantages did the use of inheritance have in the student hostel case study?
2. What is the meaning of an underlined attribute in a UML diagram and how should such an attribute be implemented in Java?
3. What is the purpose of returning a **null** value from the search method of section 10.7?
4. Here is an alternative algorithm for the search method of section 10.7.

```
SET found TO false
SET position TO 1
WHILE found = false AND more items to check
BEGIN
   IF current item = roomIn
     SET found TO true
   ELSE
      increment position
   ENDIF
END
IF found = true
   RETURN tenant at current position
ELSE
   RETURN null
ENDIF
```

Develop Java code for this alternative search method.
5. Look back at the sample test run of program 10.2. Complete a test log so that this test run could be repeated with the same inputs and the same expected results.

Practical work

1. Test the Payment class of section 10.5 by implementing a suitable driver class.
2. Amend the driver from practical task 1 above so that instead of the user entering a month directly, another menu is displayed with the 12 months listed as follows:

```
[1]   January
[2]   February
[3]   March
[4]   April
[5]   May
[6]   June
[7]   July
[8]   August
[9]   September
[10]  October
[11]  November
[12]  December

enter month [1 to 12]:
```

3. Test the Tenant class by implementing a suitable driver class.
4. Implement the TenantList class but replace the original search method with that developed in tutorial question 4.
5. Implement and run program 10.2 to test the amended TenantList tester class developed in task 4 above using the test log you created on in tutorial question 5.
6. Amend program 10.2 so that all monetary values are displayed to two decimal places. (Hint: Look back at the DecimalFormat class discussed in chapter 8.)

CASE STUDY – PART 2

LEARNING OBJECTIVES

By the end of this chapter you should be able to:

➤ use your knowledge of software development to create a small integrated application;

➤ design and implement an attractive graphical user interface.

11.1 Introduction

All that remains for us to do to complete our case study is to design, implement and test the Hostel class which will not only keep track of the tenants but will also act as the graphical user interface for the system.

11.2 Keeping permanent records

In practice, an application such as the Student Hostel System would not be much use if we had no way of keeping permanent records – in other words, of saving a file to disk. However, reading and writing files is something that you will not learn until your second semester (chapter 18). So, in the meantime, in order to make it possible to keep a permanent record of your data we have created a special class for you to use; we have called this class TenantFileHandler. It has two **static** methods: the first, saveRecords, needs to be sent two parameters, an integer value indicating the number of rooms in the hostel, and a TenantList, which is a reference to the list to be saved; the second, readRecords, requires only a reference to a TenantList so that it knows where to store the information that is read from the file.

The class can be copied from the CD-ROM or downloaded from the authors' website; the readRecords method will be called when the application is first loaded (so this method call will therefore be coded into the constructor), and the saveRecords method will be called when we finish the application (and will therefore be coded into the event-handler of a "Save and Quit" button). We will also provide the option of exiting without saving, just in case, for any reason, the user should want to abandon any changes.

11.3   Design of the GUI

There will be two aspects to the design of the graphical interface. First, we need to design the visual side of things; then we need to design the algorithms for our event-handling routines so that the buttons do the jobs we want them to, like adding or displaying tenants.

Let's start with the visual design. We need to choose which graphics components we are going to use and how to lay them out. One way to do this is to make a preliminary sketch such as the one shown in figure 11.1. We have named our components so that it is obvious what kind of component we are talking about; for example, roomLabel is a Label, nameField is a Field, addButton is a Button and displayArea is a TextArea.

We are going to use a simple FlowLayout policy, so to get our components where we want

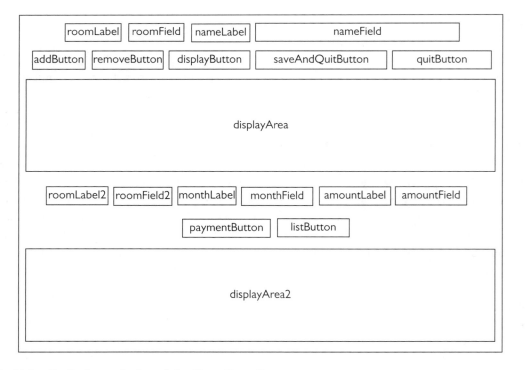

Fig 11.1   Preliminary design of the _Hostel_ interface

them we will have to play about with the size of the components and the size of the frame. To help you see what we are aiming at, we have, with figure 11.2, "cheated" and let you look ahead at the end result. This shows the effect of running our `Hostel` interface in a 570 × 500 frame.

Now that we know the components we need it is an easy matter to complete the UML class diagram. Each of the components must be declared as an attribute of the class – and, in addition, there are two more attributes that we will need. First, we will need to hold information about the number of rooms available in the hostel, so we must declare an attribute of type **int** for this purpose; we have called our attribute noOfRooms. Second, we must, of course, declare an attribute of type `TenantList` (which we have called `list`) to keep track of the tenants in residence.

We are going to need only two methods: a constructor to add the components and read the

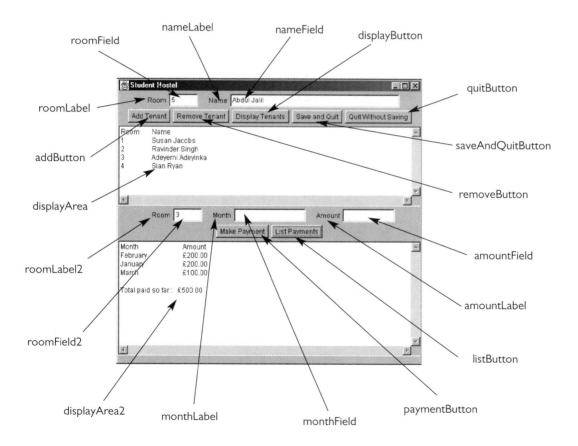

Fig 11.2   The *Hostel* class running in a frame

data from the file, and an `actionPerformed` method for the event-handling routines.
   The class design is shown in figure 11.3.

11.4   *Designing the event-handlers*

As you can see, there are seven buttons that need to be coded so that they respond in the correct way when pressed. Our code for the `actionPerformed` method will therefore take the following form:

```
                          Hostel
─────────────────────────────────────────────
    noOfRooms : int
    list : TenantList
    addButton : Button
    removeButton : Button
    displayButton : Button
    saveAndQuitButton : Button
    quitButton : Button
    roomLabel : Label
    roomField :TextField
    nameLabel : Label
    nameField : TextField
    displayArea : TextArea
    displayArea2 : TextArea
    roomLabel2 : Label
    roomField2 : TextField
    monthLabel : Label
    monthField : TextField
    amountLabel : Label
    amountField : TextField
    paymentButton : Button
    listButton : Button
─────────────────────────────────────────────
    Hostel(int)
    actionPerformed(ActionEvent)
```

Fig 11.3   The *Hostel* class

```
public void actionPerformed(ActionEvent e)
{
  if(e.getSource() == addButton)
  {
    // code for add button goes here
  }

  if(e.getSource() == displayButton)
  {
    // code for display button goes here
  }

  if(e.getSource() == removeButton)
  {
    // code for remove button goes here
  }

  if(e.getSource() == paymentButton)
  {
    // code for payment button goes here
  }

  if(e.getSource() == listButton)
  {
    // code for list button goes here
  }

  if(e.getSource() == saveAndQuitButton)
  {
    // code for saveAndQuit button goes here
  }
  if(e.getSource() == quitButton)
  {
    // code for quit button goes here
  }
}
```

We have summarized below the task that each button must perform, and then gone on to design our algorithms using pseudocode.

The *addButton*

The purpose of this button is to add a new Tenant to the list. The values entered in roomField and nameField must be validated; first of all, they must not be blank; second, the room number must not be greater than the number of rooms available (or less than 1!); finally, the room must not be occupied. If all this is okay, then the new tenant is added (we will make use of the add method of TenantList to do this) and a message should be displayed in displayArea. We can express this in pseudocode as follows:

```
read roomField
read nameField
IF roomField blank OR nameField blank
   display blank field error in displayArea
ELSE IF roomField value <1 OR roomField value> noOfRooms
   display invalid room number error in displayArea
ELSE IF tenant found in room
   display room occupied error in displayArea
ELSE
BEGIN
   add tenant
   blank roomField
   blank nameField
   display message to confirm success in displayArea
END
```

The *displayButton*

Pressing this button will display the full list of tenants (room number and name) in displayArea.

If all the rooms are vacant a suitable message should be displayed; otherwise the list of tenants' rooms and names should appear under appropriate headings as can be seen in figure 11.2. This can be expressed in pseudocode as follows:

```
IF list is empty
   display rooms empty error in displayArea
ELSE
BEGIN
   display header in displayArea
   LOOP FROM first item TO last item in list
   BEGIN
     append tenant room and name to displayArea
   END
END
```

The *removeButton*

Clicking on this button will remove the tenant whose room number has been entered in roomField.

As with the `addButton`, the room number entered must be validated; if the number is a valid one then the tenant is removed from the list (we will make use of the `remove` method of `TenantList` to do this) and a confirmation message is displayed. The pseudocode for this event-handler is given as follows:

```
read roomField
IF roomField blank
   display blank field error in displayArea
ELSE IF roomField value < 1 OR roomField value > noOfRooms
   display invalid room number error in displayArea
ELSE IF no tenant found in room
   display room empty error in displayArea
ELSE
BEGIN
   remove tenant from list
   display message to confirm success in displayArea
END
```

The *paymentButton*

This button records payments made by an individual tenant whose room number is entered in `roomField2`. The values entered in `roomField2`, `monthField` and `amountField` must be validated to ensure that none of the fields is blank, that the room number is a valid one and, if so, that it is currently occupied.

If everything is okay then a new payment record is added to that tenant's list of payments (we will make use of the `makePayment` method of `PaymentList` to do this) and a confirmation message is displayed in `displayArea2`. This design is expressed in pseudocode as follows:

```
read roomField2
read monthField
read amountField
IF roomField2 blank OR monthField blank OR amountField blank
   display fields empty error in displayArea2
ELSE IF roomField2 value<1 OR roomField2 value>noOfRooms
   display invalid room number error in displayArea2
ELSE IF no tenant found in room
   display room empty error in displayArea2
ELSE
BEGIN
   create payment from amountField value and monthField value
   add payment into list
   display message to confirm success in displayArea2
END
```

The *listButton*

Pressing this button causes a list of payments (month and amount) made by the tenant whose room number is entered in roomField2 to be displayed in displayArea2.

After validating the values entered, each record in the tenant's payment list is displayed. Finally, the total amount paid by that tenant is displayed (we will make use of the calculateTotalPaid method of PaymentList to do this). The pseudocode is given as follows:

```
read roomField2
IF roomField2 blank
   display room field empty error in displayArea2
ELSE IF roomField2 value<1 OR roomField2 value>noOfRooms
   display invalid room number error in displayArea2
ELSE IF no tenant found in room
   display room empty error in displayArea2
ELSE
BEGIN
  find tenant in given room
  get payments of tenant
  IF payments = 0
    display no payments error in displayArea2
  ELSE
  BEGIN
    display header in displayArea2
    LOOP FROM first payment TO last payment
    BEGIN
      append amount and month to displayArea2
    END
    display total paid in displayArea2
    blank monthField
    blank amountField
  END
END
```

The *saveAndQuitButton*

Pressing this button causes all the records to be saved to a file (here we make use of the saveRecords method of the TenantFileHandler class that we talked about in section 11.2); it then closes the frame, terminating the program.

It contains only two lines of code and we have therefore not written pseudocode for it.

The *quitButton*

Pressing this button terminates the program without saving the changes.

11.5 *Implementation*

The complete code for the Hostel class now appears below. When you come to reading the code, you should notice that we have utilized the NumberFormat class (which is to be found in the java.text package) to print the amounts in the local currency. Also note the use of the parseInt method of the Integer class to convert the room values, entered as text, into integer values.

There is very little new in this Hostel class apart from some formatting detail, which has been explained by means of comments throughout the code. Study the code carefully and compare it with the pseudocode to make sure you understand it.

THE *Hostel* CLASS

```java
import java.awt.*;
import java.awt.event.*;
import java.text.*;

class Hostel extends Panel implements ActionListener   .
{
    // the attributes
    private int noOfRooms;
    private TenantList list;
    private Button addButton = new Button("Add Tenant");
    private Button displayButton = new Button("Display Tenants");
    private Button removeButton = new Button("Remove Tenant");
    private Label roomLabel = new Label("Room");
    private TextField roomField = new TextField(4);
    private Label nameLabel = new Label("Name");
    private TextField nameField = new TextField(40);
    private Button saveAndQuitButton = new Button("Save and Quit");
    private Button quitButton = new Button("Quit Without Saving");
    private TextArea displayArea = new TextArea(8,75);
    private TextArea displayArea2 = new TextArea(12,75);
    private Label roomLabel2 = new Label("Room");
    private TextField roomField2 = new TextField(4);
    private Label monthLabel = new Label("Month");
    private TextField monthField = new TextField(15);
    private Label amountLabel = new Label("Amount");
    private TextField amountField = new TextField(10);
    private Button paymentButton = new Button("Make Payment");
    private Button listButton = new Button("List Payments");
```

```java
// the constructor
public Hostel(int numberIn)
{
   noOfRooms = numberIn;
   list = new TenantList(noOfRooms);
   add(roomLabel);
   /* We are using the setAlignment method of the Label class to get our
   text lined up to the right. Possible values of the parameter to this
   method are Label.LEFT, Label.CENTER and Label.RIGHT */
   roomLabel.setAlignment(Label.RIGHT);
   add(roomField);
   add(nameLabel);
   nameLabel.setAlignment(Label.RIGHT);
   add(nameField);
   add(addButton);
   add(displayButton);
   add(removeButton);
   add(saveAndQuitButton);
   add(quitButton);
   add(displayArea);
   add(roomLabel2);
   roomLabel2.setAlignment(Label.RIGHT);
   add(roomField2);
   add(monthLabel);
   monthLabel.setAlignment(Label.RIGHT);
   add(monthField);
   add(amountLabel);
   amountLabel.setAlignment(Label.RIGHT);
   add(amountField);
   add(paymentButton);
   add(listButton);
   add(displayArea2);

   // add ActionListeners to the buttons
   addButton.addActionListener(this);
   displayButton.addActionListener(this);
   paymentButton.addActionListener(this);
   listButton.addActionListener(this);
   removeButton.addActionListener(this);
   listButton.addActionListener(this);
   saveAndQuitButton.addActionListener(this);
   quitButton.addActionListener(this);

   // read the records file from disk
   TenantFileHandler.readRecords(list);
}
```

```java
// the event-handlers
public void actionPerformed(ActionEvent e)
{
  if(e.getSource() == addButton)
  {
    String roomEntered = roomField.getText();
    String nameEntered = nameField.getText();

    // if room number or name not entered
    if(roomEntered.length()==0 || nameEntered.length()==0)
    {
      displayArea.setText
                    ("Room number and name must be entered");
    }

    // if room number is out of range
    else if(Integer.parseInt(roomEntered)< 1
              || Integer.parseInt(roomEntered)>noOfRooms)
    {
      displayArea.setText("There are only " + noOfRooms
                                        + " rooms");
    }

    // if the room is occupied
    else if(list.search(Integer.parseInt(roomEntered)) != null)
    {
      displayArea.setText("Room number "
                      + Integer.parseInt(roomEntered)
                      + " is occupied");
    }

    // if everything is okay then add new tenant
    else
    {
      Tenant t = new
        Tenant(nameEntered,Integer.parseInt(roomEntered));
      list.add(t);
      roomField.setText("");
      nameField.setText("");
      displayArea.setText("New tenant in room "
                              + roomEntered
                              + " successfully added");
    }
  }

  if(e.getSource() == displayButton)
  {
    int i;
```

```
      // if the list is empty
      if(list.isEmpty())
      {
        displayArea.setText("All rooms are empty");
      }

      // if the list is not empty then display the tenants
      else
      {
        // display a heading
        displayArea.setText("Room" + "\t" + "Name" + "\n");

        // display each tenant in turn
        for(i= 1; i <= list.getTotal(); i++)
        {
          displayArea.append(list.getTenant(i).getRoom()
                    + "\t"
                    + list.getTenant(i).getName() + "\n");
        }
      }
    }

  if(e.getSource() == removeButton)
  {
    String roomEntered = roomField.getText();

    // if the room number is not entered
    if(roomEntered.length()==0)
    {
      displayArea.setText("Room number must be entered");
    }

    // if the room number is out of range
    else if(Integer.parseInt(roomEntered) < 1
              || Integer.parseInt(roomEntered)>noOfRooms)
    {
      displayArea.setText("Invalid room number");
    }

    // if the room is empty
    else if(list.search(Integer.parseInt(roomEntered)) == null)
    {
      displayArea.setText("Room number " + roomEntered
                                  + " is empty");
    }

    // if everything is okay then remove the tenant
    else
    {
```

```
      list.removeTenant(Integer.parseInt(roomEntered));
      displayArea.setText("Tenant removed from room "
                        + Integer.parseInt(roomEntered));
   }
}

if(e.getSource() == paymentButton)
{
   String roomEntered = roomField2.getText();
   String monthEntered = monthField.getText();
   String amountEntered = amountField.getText();

   // if room number, month or amount not entered
   if(roomEntered.length()==0 || monthEntered.length()==0
                        || amountEntered.length()==0)
   {
      displayArea2.setText
         ("Room number, month and amount must all be entered");
   }

   // if room number out of range
   else if(Integer.parseInt(roomEntered) < 1
           || Integer.parseInt(roomEntered) > noOfRooms)
   {
      displayArea2.setText("Invalid room number");
   }

   // if room is empty
   else if(list.search(Integer.parseInt(roomEntered)) == null)
   {
      displayArea2.setText("Room number " + roomEntered
                              + " is empty");
   }

   // if everything is okay then add the new payment
   else
   {
      Payment p = new
      Payment(monthEntered,Double.parseDouble(amountEntered);
      list.search(Integer.parseInt(roomEntered)).
                                    makePayment(p);
      displayArea2.setText("Payment recorded");
   }
}

if(e.getSource() == listButton)
{
   int i;
   String roomEntered = roomField2.getText();
```

```
// if room number not entered
if(roomEntered.length()==0)
{
  displayArea2.setText("Room number must be entered");
}

// if room number out of range
else if(Integer.parseInt(roomEntered) < 1
        || Integer.parseInt(roomEntered) > noOfRooms)
{
  displayArea2.setText("Invalid room number");
}

// if room is empty
  else if(list.search(Integer.parseInt(roomEntered)) == null)
  {
    displayArea2.setText("Room number "
                   + Integer.parseInt(roomEntered)
                   + " is empty");
  }

  // if everything is okay then list the payments
  else
  {
    Tenant t =
            list.search(Integer.parseInt(roomEntered));
    PaymentList p = t.getPayments();
    if(t.getPayments().getTotal() == 0)
    {
      displayArea2.setText
                     ("No payments made for this tenant");
    }

    else
    {
      /* The NumberFormat class is similar to the DecimalFormat
         class that we used previously. The getCurrencyInstance
         method of this class reads the system values to find out
         which country we are in, then uses the correct currency
         symbol */

      NumberFormat nf =
      NumberFormat.getCurrencyInstance();
      String s;

      // display a heading
      displayArea2.setText("Month" + "\t\t"
                                + "Amount"
                                + "\n");
```

```
                // display each payment in turn
                for(i = 1; i <= p.getTotal(); i++)
                {
                   s = nf.format(p.getPayment(i).getAmount());
                   displayArea2.append(" "
                                       + p.getPayment(i).getMonth()
                                       + "\t\t"
                                       + s
                                       + "\n");
                }
                displayArea2.append("\n" + "Total paid so far : "
                             + nf.format(p.calculateTotalPaid()));
                monthField.setText(" ");
                amountField.setText(" ");
             }
          }
       }

    if(e.getSource() == saveAndQuitButton)
    {
       // save the records to file
       TenantFileHandler.saveRecords(noOfRooms, list);
       // terminate the program
       System.exit (0);
    }

    if(e.getSource() == quitButton)
    {
       //terminate the program without saving the records
       System.exit (0);
    }
  }
}
```

The code needed to run the Hostel class appears below as program 11.1. This program creates a hostel with five rooms; in the tutorial questions you will be given the opportunity to adapt this program so that the number of rooms can be entered by the user.

Notice that we are not using the EasyFrame class here, as we do not want the cross-hairs to work; the user should always exit by choosing either the "Save and Quit" button or the "Quit without Saving" button.

PROGRAM 11.1

```java
import java.awt.*;

public class RunHostel
{
  public static void main(String[] args)
  {
    Frame frame = new Frame();
    frame.setTitle("Student Hostel");
    // assume only 5 rooms available
    Hostel property = new Hostel(5);
    frame.setSize(550,500);
    frame.setBackground(Color.lightGray);
    frame.add(property);
    frame.setVisible(true);
  }
}
```

Before concluding this case study we shall consider how to test the application to ensure that it conforms to the original specification.

11.6   *Testing the system*

If you look back at the Hostel class you can see that much of the event-handling code is related to the validation of data entered from the graphical interface. Much of the testing for such a system will, therefore, be geared around ensuring such validation is effective. This is a form of *white box* testing as we are looking at the implementation to determine this validation; it is not made explicit in the specification.

Among the types of validation we need to test is the display of suitable error messages when input text fields are left blank, or when inappropriate data has been entered into these text fields. Of course, as well as input validation, we also need to test the basic functionality of the system. The specification can be used to determine suitable test data in this case and so a form of *black box* testing may also be appropriate.

Figure 11.4 is one possible test log that may be developed for the purpose of testing the Hostel class. As we will be running this program in the UK, we have defined the expected currency output to be displayed with a pound symbol (£); obviously you should replace this currency symbol with that of your own country.

We include a few sample screen shots produced from running program 11.1 against this test log in figures 11.5–11.8. We will leave the complete task of running program 11.1 against the test log as a practical exercise at the end of this chapter.

TEST LOG			
Purpose: To test the HOSTEL class			
Run Number:	**Date:**		
Action	**Expected Output**	**Pass/ Fail**	**Reason for Failure**
Display tenants	"Empty list" message		
Add tenant: Patel, Room Number blank	"Blank field" message		
Add tenant: blank, Room Number 1	"Blank field" message		
Add tenant: Patel, Room Number 1	Confirmation message		
Add tenant: Jones, Room Number 6	Error message: there are only 5 rooms		
Add tenant: Jones, Room Number 1	Error message: Room 1 is occupied		
Add tenant: Jones, Room Number 2	Confirmation message		
Display tenants	ROOM NAME 1 Patel 2 Jones		
List payments, Room Number 1	"Empty list" message		
Make payment: Room blank, Month January, Amount 100	"Blank field" message		
Make Payment: Room 1, Month blank, Amount 100	"Blank field" message		
Make payment: Room 1, Month January, Amount blank	"Blank field" message		
Make payment: Room 1, Month January, Amount 100	Confirmation message		
Make payment: Room 1, Month February, Amount 200	Confirmation message		
List payments: Room Number blank	"Blank field" message		

Fig 11.4   A test log to ensure the reliability of the *Hostel* class

TEST LOG (continued)			
Purpose: To test the HOSTEL class			
Run Number:	Date:		
Action	Expected Output	Pass/ Fail	Reason for Failure
List payments, Room Number 1	MONTH AMOUNT January £100 February £200 Total paid so far £300		
List payments: Room Number 2	"Empty list" message		
List payments: Room Number 5	"Room Empty" message		
Remove tenant: Room Number blank	"Blank field" message		
Remove tenant: Room Number 1	Confirmation message		
Display tenants	2 Jones		
List payments: Room Number 1	"Room Empty" message		

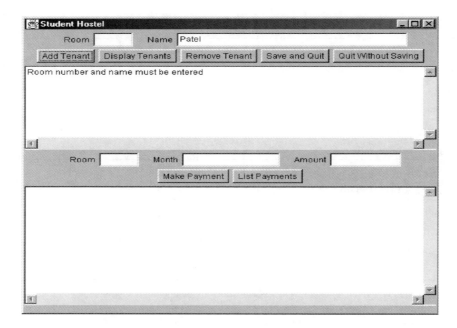

Fig 11.5   Error messages are produced in the *displayArea*. In this case an attempt is made to add a tenant without filling in the *roomField*

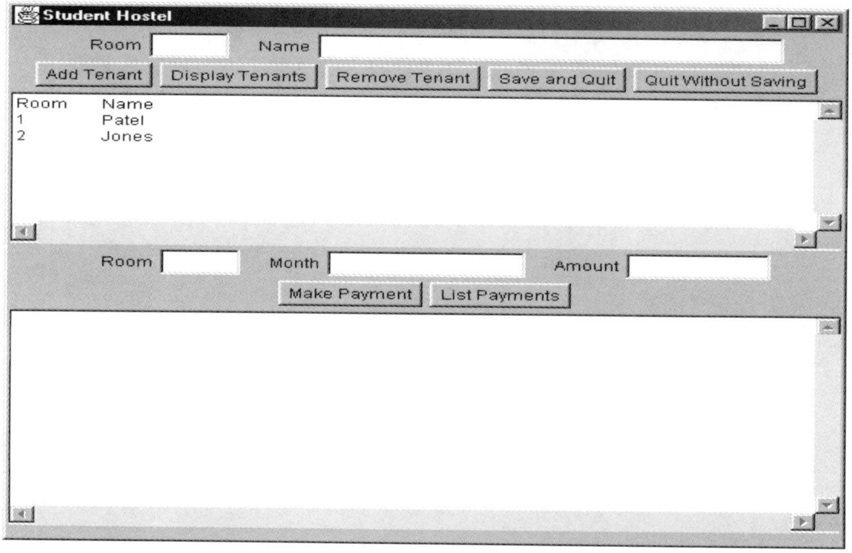

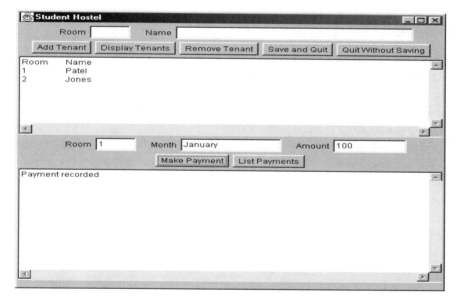

Fig 11.6 The *displayArea* is also used to display a list of tenants entered

Fig 11.7 A payment is recorded for the tenant in room 1

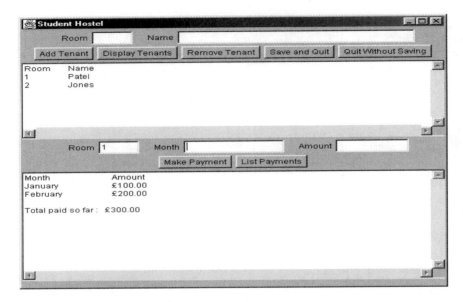

Fig 11.8 **Details of payments are displayed in *displayArea2* when the *ListPayments* button is pressed**

Tutorial exercises

1. Consider the addition of a search button that displays the details (name and room number) of a tenant in a room entered in the `roomField` text box. The details are to be displayed in the `displayArea`.
   (a) What would be a suitable name for this visual component?
   (b) Develop pseudocode for the event-handler of this button.
   (c) Modify the test log in figure 11.4 to include the testing of this event-handler.
2. Look at the test data given in the test log of figure 11.4. Pick out three test cases that are:
   (a) examples of black box testing;
   (b) examples of white box testing.
   In each case, justify your answers above.
3. Rewrite program 11.1 so that instead of fixing the number of rooms to 5, the user is asked how many rooms the hostel is to have.
4. Make a list of any shortcomings of the Student Hostel system, and think of ways in which the system could be enhanced and improved.

Practical work

You will need to download the entire suite of classes that make up the student hostel system from our website (or copy from the CD-ROM).

1. Run program 11.1 against the test log given in figure 11.4.
2. Modify the `Hostel` class by adding the search button as defined in tutorial question 1.
3. Re-run program 11.1 with the modified `Hostel` class against the modified test log developed in tutorial question 1(c).

12 PROGRAMMING FOR THE WORLD WIDE WEB

LEARNING OBJECTIVES

By the end of this chapter you should be able to:

➤ explain the difference between an **application** and an **applet**;

➤ write the HTML code needed to load an applet into a browser;

➤ pass parameters to an applet from an HTML file;

➤ explain the purpose of the **init**, **start**, **stop** and **destroy** methods;

➤ implement the `MouseListener` and the `MouseMotionListener` interfaces.

12.1 Introduction

As you have seen throughout this book, a Java program is made up of a number of classes; so far in this book we have made our classes runnable by providing a main method; a program that contains a class with a main method is called an **application**. The main method provides the overall means of controlling the program.

In the case of the graphical applications that we have developed, the other principal function of the main method, in addition to providing the overall control, was to create a frame in which to run the program. In each case we needed to add our class to the frame and we therefore made our classes extensions of the Java AWT component Panel – because a panel can be added to a frame. Another component that can be added to a frame is an applet. But there is something much more interesting and important about an applet. An applet (a little application) can run in a browser such as Internet Explorer or Netscape. Control of the applet then becomes the responsibility of the browser and there is no need for a main method – if there were a main method in the class, it would simply be ignored when the applet runs.

You will have observed that in this book, apart from the earlier very simple text-based programs, we have organized things in such a way that the main method is never included in the functional class, but instead is placed in a separate "driver" or "tester" class. Other textbooks you come across will often "mix up" the main method in the class itself – but for three reasons we don't like this approach. First, it can be a very confusing way of doing things for somebody who is just starting to program. Second, we believe that our approach is more in the spirit of object-oriented development, because it makes classes more autonomous and able to be easily "plugged in" to any system. Finally, and most relevant to this chapter, is the fact that, as you will soon see, our graphics classes can be converted to applets with very little effort.

12.2 *Running an applet in a browser*

In order to run an applet in a browser (or in one of the applet viewers provided with most Java IDEs), we need to include an instruction in a web page that tells the browser to load the applet and run it. Web pages are written in a special language known as **Hypertext Markup Language (HTML)**. HTML code is interpreted by browsers such as Netscape and Internet Explorer to produce the formatted text and graphics that we are used to seeing.

We are not going to go into any detail here about how to write HTML; we will talk only about the commands you need in order to get your applets running. Commands in HTML are called **tags** and are enclosed in angle brackets. The tag that we are interested in here is the one that tells the browser to load and run a Java class. This uses the key word **applet**, as we shall see in a moment.

Cast your mind back to the ChangingFace class from chapter 9. We are going to make a few small changes. First, we are going to import the java.applet package that provides the support we need for running applets. Second, we are going to make our class extend Applet instead of Panel. Third, we are going to replace the constructor with a special method called init (short for *initialize*). The code that we originally had in the constructor will now be placed in this special init method. We will explain more about this in the next section. Finally, we are going to declare the class as **public** so that it is accessible from outside any package.

The ChangingFaceApplet class is shown below:

THE *ChangingFaceApplet* CLASS

```
import java.awt.*;
import java.applet.*;
import java.awt.event.*;

// the class is declared as public

public class ChangingFaceApplet extends Applet implements ActionListener
{
  private boolean isHappy;
  private Button happyButton = new Button("Smile");
  private Button sadButton = new Button("Frown");
```

```
// the constructor is replaced with an init method
public void init()
{
  add(happyButton);
  add(sadButton);
  isHappy = true;
  happyButton.addActionListener(this);
  sadButton.addActionListener(this);
}

public void paint(Graphics g)
{
  g.setColor(Color.red);
  g.drawOval(85,45,75,75);
  g.setColor(Color.blue);
  g.drawOval(100,65,10,10);
  g.drawOval(135,65,10,10);
  g.drawString("Changing Face", 80,155);
  if(isHappy == true)
  {
    g.drawArc(102,85,40,25,0,-180);
  }
  else
  {
    g.drawArc(102,85,40,25,0,180);
  }
}

public void actionPerformed(ActionEvent e)
{
  if(e.getSource() == happyButton)
  {
    isHappy = true;
    repaint();
  }
  if(e.getSource() == sadButton)
  {
    isHappy = false;
    repaint();
  }
}
}
```

We have provided below the bare minimum HTML code that will load and run this class in a browser; it doesn't add any headings, or attempt to produce a pretty web page – those of you who know HTML will be able to add those features if you wish:

```
<HTML>
<APPLET CODE = "ChangingFaceApplet.class" WIDTH = "250" HEIGHT = "175" >
</APPLET>
</HTML>
```

As some of you might know, HTML tags often have an opening and a closing version, the latter starting with a forward slash (/). The relevant text is contained within these tags. So in our example the HTML tags tell the browser that the text contained represents an HTML page. The text within the APPLET tags provides the information about the applet that needs to be loaded; this is done with special words (called *attributes* just to confuse us!) which are part of the tag. In this case we provide the name of the class (with the CODE attribute) and the dimensions of the applet window (with the attributes WIDTH and HEIGHT).

Figure 12.1 shows the ChangingFace class running in a browser.

Of course it is necessary to have the correct file (in this case ChangingFaceApplet.class) in the same directory as the HTML file; alternatively it is possible to make absolute references to directories in the HTML code, but you should look at books on HTML in order to find out more about this. Do notice, however, that it is the compiled byte code that you need (that is, the file with the .class extension), and not the Java source code.

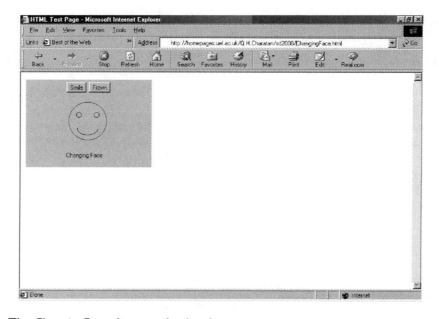

Fig 12.1   The *ChangingFace* class running in a browser

12.3   *Guidelines for creating applets*

When creating applets as opposed to applications there are a few differences that you need to be aware of. These are explained below.

1. Make sure you import the correct package with the line:

    ```
    import java.applet.*;
    ```

2. Ensure that your class extends the `Applet` class.
3. As we have stated above, you should place any initialization routines, such as setting initial values, in an `init` method rather than in a constructor. As we explain in section 12.5, this method is a special method and is called each time the applet is loaded or reloaded by the browser.
4. Do not include any `main` method, as any code in the `main` method is ignored by the browser.
5. Make sure that any input and output goes through the AWT interface – the user will not normally see the text console when using a browser.
6. Do not include any buttons or other controls that attempt to terminate the program – applets terminate when the page is closed in the browser.
7. Always declare your class as **public**.

12.4   *Passing parameters from an HTML file*

Cast your mind back to chapter 9 again. Remember the `OblongGUI` class we developed? First, of all we are going to modify this so that it can be run as an applet – once again, the way we have designed it means that there is no `main` method to worry about, so we don't have to do very much to it. All we have to do, in fact, is to import the `java.applet` package, extend `Applet` rather than `Panel`, make our class **public**, and to change the constructor to an `init` method. Here is the new class:

THE *OblongApplet* CLASS

```java
import java.awt.*;
import java.awt.event.*;
import java.applet.*;

// make sure the class is declared public
public class OblongApplet extends Applet implements ActionListener
{

  // declare a new oblong with a length and height of zero
  private Oblong oblong = new Oblong(0,0);

  // now declare the graphics components
  private Label lengthLabel = new Label("Length");
  private TextField lengthField = new TextField(5);
  private Label heightLabel = new Label("Height");
  private TextField heightField = new TextField(5);
  private Button calcButton = new Button("Calculate");
  private TextArea displayArea = new TextArea(3,35);

  //replace the constructor with an init method
  public void init()
  {
    add(lengthLabel);
    add(lengthField);
    add(heightLabel);
    add(heightField);
    add(calcButton);
    add(displayArea);
    calcButton.addActionListener(this);
  }

  public void actionPerformed(ActionEvent e)
  {
    //as before
  }
}
```

The following HTML code is just sufficient to load and run the applet in a 300 × 150 window:

```html
<HTML>
<APPLET CODE = "OblongApplet.class"
WIDTH = "300"
HEIGHT= "150" >
</APPLET>
</HTML>
```

The result of running the applet is shown in figure 12.2; this time, for a change, we are showing it running in an applet viewer provided with one of the common Java IDEs.

In previous programs you have seen how parameters are passed to class methods from other classes. Now, it is also possible to pass values from an HTML file to a class. Consider the following HTML code which loads and runs a class that we have called `ParameterizedOblongApplet`:

```
<HTML>
<APPLET CODE = "ParameterizedOblongApplet.class"
WIDTH = "300"
HEIGHT="150" >
<PARAM NAME = rows VALUE = "5">
<PARAM NAME = columns VALUE = "28">
</APPLET>
</HTML>
```

You can see that we have used the PARAM tag and the associated NAME and VALUE attributes to name and give values to two variables which will be passed to the applet; notice that they must be defined as `Strings`. We are going to use these values to set the size of the `TextArea` that we use to display the area and perimeter of the oblong. The changes that we have made in our applet in order to get it to use these parameters are shown below in bold and are explained afterwards.

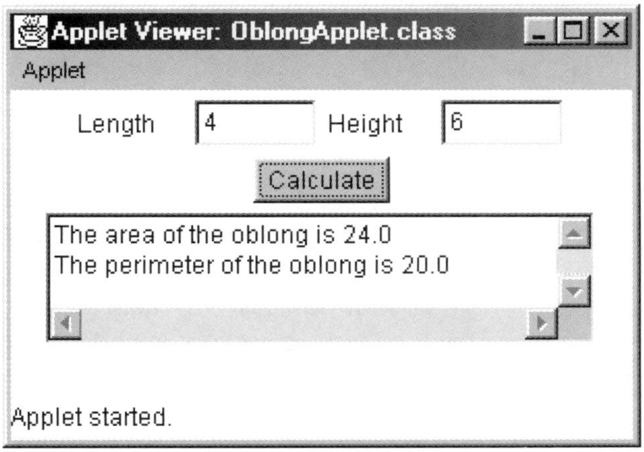

Fig 12.2   The *Oblong* applet running in an applet viewer

THE *ParameterizedOblongApplet* CLASS

```java
import java.awt.*;
import java.awt.event.*;
import java.applet.*;

public class ParameterizedOblongApplet extends Applet
                                        implements ActionListener
{
  // declare a new oblong with a length and height of zero
  private Oblong oblong = new Oblong(0,0);

  // now declare the graphics components
  private Label lengthLabel = new Label("Length");
  private TextField lengthField = new TextField(5);
  private Label heightLabel = new Label("Height");
  private TextField heightField = new TextField(5);
  private Button calcButton = new Button("Calculate");
  private TextArea displayArea;

  public void init()
  {
    displayArea = new TextArea(
      Integer.parseInt(getParameter("rows")),
      Integer.parseInt(getParameter("columns"))
                );
    add(lengthLabel);
    add(lengthField);
    add(heightLabel);
    add(heightField);
    add(calcButton);
    add(displayArea);
    calcButton.addActionListener(this);
  }
  public void actionPerformed(ActionEvent e)
  {
    //as before
  }
}
```

As you can see, we have used the getParameter method of the Applet class (which returns a String) to read a value from the HTML file. However, we cannot do this at the same time as we declare the attributes, so the code has now been placed in the init method; notice that now when we declare the TextArea variable, displayArea, we do not initialize it; this is now done in the init method as follows:

```java
displayArea =
  new TextArea(Integer.parseInt(getParameter("rows")),
    Integer.parseInt(getParameter("columns")));
```

With the values as stated in the HTML code above (5 and 28) we get the output shown in figure 12.3. You can see that because the length of the `TextArea` has been reduced the components have moved around – that is because we have used the default `FlowLayout` manager.

12.5   Special applet methods

In addition to the init method there are three other special applet methods that you can code if you wish; `start`, `stop` and `destroy`. Together with the `paint` method these are automatically called in a special order which is explained in Table 12.1 below.

Table 12.1 The special applet methods (working with the paint method)	
Method	**Invocation**
`init`	Invoked the first time the applet is loaded (or reloaded) by a browser
`start`	Invoked after `init` when the applet is first loaded (or reloaded) and then invoked each time the applet is made visible again by returning to the page
`paint`	Invoked immediately after `start`
`stop`	Invoked when the applet is hidden (by pointing the browser at a different page)
`destroy`	Invoked after `stop` when the applet is abandoned (by closing the browser)

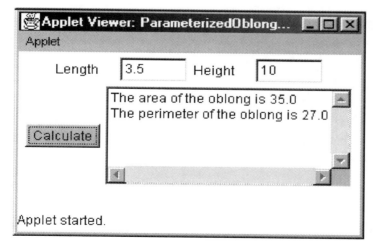

Fig 12.3   The *ParameterizedOblongApplet*

12.6   *The* RedCircle *applet*

The next applet is one that you can use to amuse your friends. Figure 12.4 shows how it looks when it runs in a browser. We have called it – rather unimaginatively – the RedCircle applet; a red circle always moves away from the cursor so you can never click on it, despite being told to do so! And if in desperation you start to click the mouse, the words "Keep Trying" flash onto the screen!

As well as being a bit of fun it also introduces something new, namely the way to program a response to different mouse events like moving and dragging as well as just clicking; this will involve using two new interface classes instead of the single ActionListener interface that we have used before.

Here is the code for the applet:

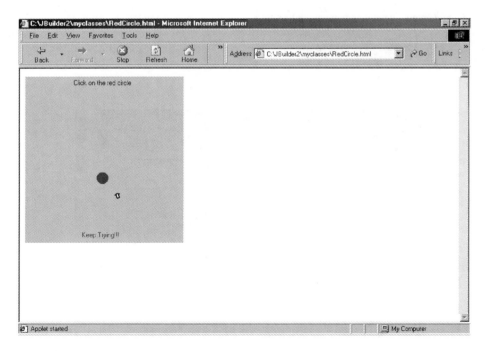

Fig 12.4   The *RedCircle* **applet running in a browser**

THE *RedCircle* APPLET

```java
import java.awt.*;
import java.applet.*;
import java.awt.event.*;

public class RedCircle extends Applet
                        implements MouseMotionListener, MouseListener
{
  private int xPos;
  private int yPos;
  private int winWidth;
  private int winHeight;
  boolean mouseDown = false;

  // the init method
  public void init()
  {
    addMouseMotionListener(this);
    addMouseListener(this);
    /* get the width and height of the applet window from the HTML file */
    winWidth = Integer.parseInt(getParameter("windowWidth"));
    winHeight = Integer.parseInt(getParameter("windowHeight"));
  }

  // the start method
  public void start()
  {
    xPos = winWidth/2 - 20;
    yPos = winHeight/2 - 20;
  }

  // the paint method
  public void paint(Graphics g)
  {
    g.drawString("Click on the red circle",85,15);
    g.setColor(Color.red);
    g.fillOval(xPos,yPos,20,20);
    if(mouseDown)
    {
      g.drawString("Keep Trying!!!", winWidth/2 - 40, winHeight - 10);
    }
  }

  /* The next two methods define what happens when the mouse is moved or
  dragged. They are part of the MouseMotionListener interface. The red
  circle always stays 50 pixels above and 50 pixels to the left of the
  cursor*/
```

```
  public void mouseMoved(MouseEvent e)
  {
    xPos = e.getX() - 50;
    yPos = e.getY() - 50;
    repaint();
  }

  public void mouseDragged(MouseEvent e)
  {
    xPos = e.getX() - 50;
    yPos = e.getY() - 50;
    repaint();
  }

  /* The next two methods define what happens when the mouse button is
  pressed or released. They are part of the MouseListener interface*/

  public void mousePressed(MouseEvent e)
  {
    mouseDown = true;
    repaint();
  }

  public void mouseReleased(MouseEvent e)
  {
    mouseDown = false;
    repaint();
  }

  /* The MouseListener interface also insists that we implement the next
  three methods. We are not actually going to use them here, so we have just
  left them blank */

  public void mouseClicked(MouseEvent e)
  {
  }

  public void mouseEntered(MouseEvent e)
  {
  }

  public void mouseExited(MouseEvent e)
  {
  }
}
```

You can see that here we are implementing two interface classes, MouseListener and MouseMotionListener; notice that the syntax is to separate them by a comma.

```
public class RedCircle extends Applet implements
                              MouseMotionListener, MouseListener
```

Both of these interface classes will of course have abstract methods which we then have to implement. The first one, MouseMotionListener, has two such methods, MouseMoved and MouseDragged. The second, MouseListener, has five, MousePressed, MouseReleased, MouseClicked, MouseEntered and MouseExited. The last three of these are not used in this applet so we have just left them blank. You may be interested to know their purpose, however, so you can use them in future programs; MouseClicked is invoked when the mouse is clicked on a component, MouseEntered is invoked when the cursor enters a component and MouseExited is invoked when the cursor leaves a component.

The declaration of the attributes is shown below; the first two integer attributes xPos and yPos will be used to keep track of the position of the red circle. The next two attributes, winWidth and winHeight, will be used to hold the width and the height of the applet window as determined by the HTML code. The other attribute, mouseDown, is a **boolean** variable and will be set to **true** while the left-hand button of the mouse is depressed, and **false** once it is released; it is therefore initialized as **false**.

```
private int xPos;
private int yPos;
private int winWidth;
private int winHeight;
boolean mouseDown = false;
```

Next we have the init method:

```
public void init()
{
   addMouseMotionListener(this);
   addMouseListener(this);
   winWidth = Integer.parseInt(getParameter("windowWidth"));
   winHeight = Integer.parseInt(getParameter("windowHeight"));
}
```

Remember that this method is invoked when the applet is loaded (or reloaded) into the browser; its purpose, as you can see, is first to add the two listeners to the applet itself; remember that writing the method names without attaching them to an object is actually attaching them to **this** object, and is short for:

```
this.addMouseMotionListener(this);
this.addMouseListener(this);
```

Its other purpose is to read the dimensions of the applet window from the HTML file with the getParameter method, and assign them to winWidth and winHeight.

Now we define a start method:

```
public void start()
{
   xPos = Integer.parseInt(getParameter("windowWidth"))/2 - 20;
   yPos = Integer.parseInt(getParameter("windowWidth"))/2 - 20;
}
```

Remember that this is the method that gets called every time the applet becomes visible; so it will be called after the init method when the applet is first loaded and then again each time we return from viewing another page. The idea is to get the circle to appear in the centre of the window each time the applet becomes visible. So we get the width and the height of the window from the HTML file using the getParameter method; we convert these to integers and then halve them to find the central point of the window; to get the centre of the circle dead in the middle we subtract 20 (the radius of the circle) from the width and the height – remind yourself of the drawOval method in chapter 9 to understand why we have done this.

After the start method has finished doing its job, the paint method is called, and this is the one that we have coded next:

```
public void paint(Graphics g)
{
  g.drawString("Click on the red circle",85,15);
  g.setColor(Color.red);
  g.fillOval(xPos,yPos,20,20);
  if(mouseDown)
  {
    g.drawString("Keep Trying!!!",winWidth/2 - 40, winHeight - 10);
  }
}
```

After drawing the initial string that tells the user to click on the circle, we set the colour to red, and then draw the circle, this time using fillOval instead of drawOval to get a solid circle. The circle is drawn at position (xPos, yPos). Remember, this method not only gets called after the start method, but also every time the program encounters a repaint command, and as we shall see in a moment this happens every time the mouse moves; and each time the screen gets repainted xPos and yPos will have changed. After the circle is drawn, the status of the mouse-button is tested by checking the value of mouseDown; as we said earlier, this attribute is going to be set to **true** if the left mouse-button is down, and **false** if not. If it is **true** the words "Keep Trying!!!" are drawn on the screen. We have tried to organize things so that this is drawn centred near the bottom of the window; you can see that we have used the dimensions of the applet window to do this – we have set the x-coordinate to be half the window width minus 40. The value of 40 is what we have estimated to be half the number of pixels taken up by the phrase "Keep Trying!!!". There are actually more accurate ways of doing this using font metrics, but we want to keep things simple at the moment, so we just had a go to see what it looks like, then tried again until we got it right! Similarly we have set the y-coordinate to be 10 pixels higher than the bottom of the window, and, as you can see from figure 12.4, this looks pretty good.

Now we come to the event-handling routines. This time, as we have mentioned, we are not using the `ActionListener` interface but are using two new interface classes, `MouseMotionListener` and `MouseListener`. The first method we implement, `mouseMoved`, is one of the two abstract methods of `MouseMotionListener`:

```
public void mouseMoved(MouseEvent e)
{
   xPos = e.getX() - 50;
   yPos = e.getY() - 50;
   repaint();
}
```

This method is continually invoked while the mouse is moving; each time it is invoked xPos and yPos are assigned new values. The value assigned to each of them is always the value of the current coordinate of the cursor minus 50. After every assignment the window is repainted; thus, as the cursor moves, the circle moves too – always staying just north-west of it. Notice that the method is automatically sent an object of the `MouseEvent` class and that we use the getX and getY methods of the `this` class to obtain the current coordinates of the cursor.

The other method of the `MouseMotionListener` interface, `mouseDragged`, determines what happens when the mouse is moved with the button held down (dragged). We have coded it in exactly the same way, so that dragging the mouse has the same effect as above.

The next two methods are declared in the `MouseListener` class and determine what happens when the mouse-button is pressed and released. You can see the that we have defined them so that when the button is pressed, the `mouseDown` attribute is set to **true** and the window is repainted; when the button is released it is set to **false**, and the window is repainted once again.

```
public void mousePressed(MouseEvent e)
{
   mouseDown = true;
   repaint();
}

public void mouseReleased(MouseEvent e)
{
   mouseDown = false;
   repaint();
}
```

The `MouseListener` interface also insists that we implement the `mouseClicked`, `mouseEntered` and `mouseExited` methods. We are not actually going to use these here, so as you can see from the code we have just left them blank.

Now that we have completed the code, we just need to write the HTML code to load it into a browser. The code below runs the applet in a 280 × 300 window:

```
<HTML>
<APPLET CODE = "RedCircle.class" WIDTH = "280" HEIGHT="300">
<PARAM NAME = "windowWidth" VALUE = "280">
<PARAM NAME = "windowHeight" VALUE = "300">
</APPLET>
</HTML>
```

12.7   *What next?*

Congratulations – you have now completed your first semester in programming; we hope you have enjoyed it. Many of you will be going on to at least one more semester of software development and programming – so what lies ahead?

Well, you have probably realized that there are still a few gaps in your knowledge and that some of the stuff that you have learnt can be developed further to give you the power to write multi-functional programs. Think, for example, about the case study we developed in the last two chapters; you will need to write the code that stores the information permanently on a disk; also, the user interface could be made to look a bit more attractive; and it would be helpful if our collection classes didn't make us decide in advance how many records we are allowed to have, so something a bit better than simple arrays would be useful.

And there is lots more; the standard Java packages provide classes for many different purposes; there is more to learn about inheritance and interfaces, and about dealing with errors and exceptions; and you need to know how to write programs that can perform a number of tasks at the same time.

Does all this sound exciting? We think so – and we hope that you enjoy your next semester as much as we have enjoyed helping you through this one.

Tutorial exercises

1. Explain the purpose of the following applet methods:
    - init;
    - start;
    - stop;
    - destroy.
2. Look at the `MetricConverter` class that we developed in chapter 9. What changes would you need to make to this class in order to run it as an applet?

3. Identify some improvements that could be made to the RedCircle applet.
4. Look back at tutorial question 3 in chapter 9, and then answer the following questions.
   (a) What changes would you need to make to the DrawShapes class in order to run it as an applet in a browser?
   (b) Write a fragment of HTML code that would run the applet in a 300 × 200 window.
   (c) Imagine that it is required that the applet is modified so that a single integer value can be embedded into the HTML code and passed to the applet in order to set the value of the diameter of the circle, the base of the triangle or the side of the square. Describe the modifications that would need to be made to the HTML code and to the applet in order to achieve this.

Practical work

1. Implement some of the applets from this chapter (ChangingFace, OblongGUI, ParameterizedOblongApplet and RedCircle); write the appropriate HTML code and load it into a browser. If you have your own website, upload the HTML page and the class so you can run it remotely.
2. Apply the changes to the MetricConverter class that you identified in tutorial question 2.
3. Implement the improvements to the RedCircle applet that you identified in tutorial question 3.

SEMESTER TWO

PACKAGES

LEARNING OBJECTIVES

By the end of this chapter you should be able to:

➤ identify the role of **packages** in organizing classes;

➤ distinguish between **class files** and **source files**;

➤ create your own packages in Java;

➤ access classes residing in your own packages;

➤ explain how the **CLASSPATH** environment variable us used to locate class files;

➤ identify the core packages in the **Java API**.

13.1   Introduction

Welcome back to the second semester of our programming course. We spent the first semester laying the foundations of the skills you would require to develop programs in Java. During that time you came a long way. You learnt about the idea of variables and control structures, and then went on to develop your own classes. Finally you developed applications consisting of many classes working closely together and interacting with users via attractive graphical interfaces. Along the way you also learnt about the UML methodology and issues affecting software quality and running Java applets over the web. At the beginning of that semester you probably didn't expect to come as far as you have. Well, the second semester might look equally challenging but, with some help from us along the way, you will be eagerly awaiting new and more advanced challenges.

The first thing we are going to do this semester is to take a more in-depth look at Java's package concept.

13.2   *Understanding packages*

A **package**, in Java, is simply a *named collection of related classes*. Of course, you have already come across the idea of a package in your first semester. To draw some components, such as a Button or a TextField, onto a screen you accessed classes belonging to the awt package. To format some text you used classes in the text package. Giving meaningful names to a set of related classes in this way makes it easy for programmers to locate these classes when required.

Packages can themselves contain other packages. For example, as well as containing related visual component classes, the awt package also contains the event package, since these groups of classes are still logically related to Java's Abstract Window Toolkit.

The package name actually corresponds to the *name of the directory* (or folder as some operating systems call it) in which all the given classes reside. All predefined Java packages themselves reside in a global Java directory, named simply java. This directory is not itself a package but a store for other packages. Figure 13.1 illustrates this hierarchy of packages.

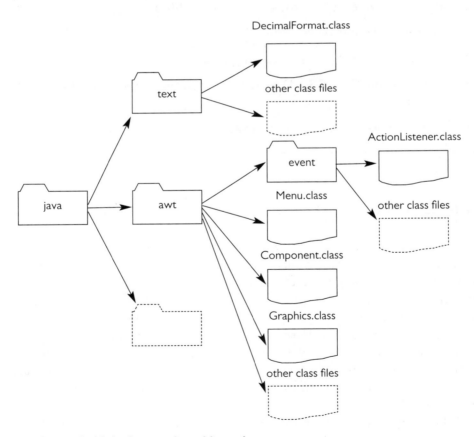

Fig 13.1   A sample of the Java package hierarchy

As you can see from figure 13.1, packages contain **class files** (that is the compiled Java byte code), not **source files** (the original Java instructions). This means the location of the original Java source files is unimportant here. They may be in the same directory as the class files, in another directory or, as in the case of the predefined Java packages, they may even no longer be available!

Suppose you are writing the code for a new class. Can you recall how you can give it access to a class contained within a package? Just referencing the class won't work. For example, let's assume a class you are writing needs a `TextField` component:

```
class SomeClass
{
  private TextField someAttribute;  // will not compile
}
```

This won't compile because the compiler won't be able to find a class called `TextField`. One way to tell the compiler where this class file resides is, as you already know, to add an **import** statement above the class:

```
import java.awt.*; // allows the compiler to find the TextField.class file

class SomeClass
{
  private TextField someAttribute;  // now this will compile
}
```

As we mentioned in chapter 4, the asterisk allows you to have access to *all* class files in the given package. Can you see how the **import** statement matches the directory structure we illustrated in figure 13.1? Effectively the compiler is being told to look for classes in the awt directory (package), which in turn is in the java directory (whose location is already known to the Java runtime system). The location of a file is often referred to as the **path** to that file. In the Windows operating systems this path would be expressed as follows:

> java\awt\

In other operating systems forward slashes may be used instead of backward slashes. The Java **import** statement simply expresses this path but uses dots instead of backward (or forward) slashes.

Note that there can only ever be one '.*' in an **import** statement and the '.*' must follow a package name, but you can have as many **import** statements as you require.

```
import java.*.*;        // illegal as contains more than one '.*'
import java.*;          // illegal as 'java' is not a package
import java.awt.*;      // fine, allows access to awt classes
import java.awt.event.*; // fine, allows access to event classes
```

If you want, you could list a *specific* class file instead of accessing *all* the files in a package as follows:

```
import java.awt.TextField; // access only to the TextField class
```

However, as there is no overhead in allowing access to all files in a package, specific file naming is not very common. Keeping this information in mind, let's develop a small application to explore this package notation further.

13.3   The "Magic Robot" application

The application we are going to show you is a program for children, where a robot carries out simple calculations via a magic belly button! Figures 13.2 and 13.3 show you some *before* and *after* screen shots, to illustrate how the program works.

As you can see, not only does the robot carry out the given calculation but its belly button also changes according to the type of calculation carried out!

We have written a utility class (that is a class that is there simply to provide some useful methods) to assist in the drawing of the robot's belly button. We have called this class `Button`. You might be concerned at this choice of class name as there is already a `Button` class in the awt package. Let's see if this does indeed cause any problems.

Our utility class contains just one **static** method, `drawBellyButton`, that draws a belly button of a given size, with a given symbol inside it, at a given location. First look at the code and then we'll discuss it.

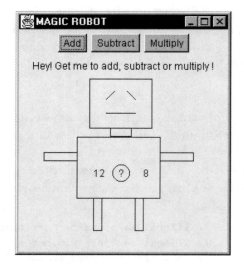

Fig 13.2   The Magic Robot before pressing any buttons

OUR NEW *Button* CLASS

```
import java.awt.*; // to access the Graphics class

class Button
{
  public static void drawBellyButton (Graphics g, String symbol,
                                      int x, int y, int w, int h)
  {
    g.drawOval(x,y,w,h); // draw the belly button
    g.drawString(symbol, x+7, y+15); // place symbol inside belly button
  }
}
```

As you can see the **static** method, drawBellyButton, takes six parameters. The first is a Graphics object and for this we need access to the awt package. You will see in a moment that the Graphics object will be sent to the methods of the Button class from a paint method. Remember that an object of the Graphics class is sent automatically to a paint method and will contain information about the component on which the painting is to take place; the Graphics class also contains the methods such as drawString and drawOval with which to do the painting.

The second parameter is the symbol to be drawn in the middle of the belly button – sent as a String. The last four parameters are required by the drawOval method (that we discussed with you in chapter 5) to determine the x and y coordinates of the belly button, and its width and height respectively.

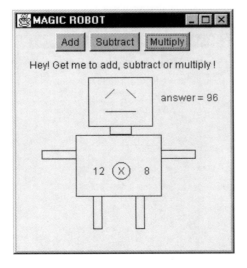

Fig 13.3   The Magic Robot after pressing the 'Multiply' button

Although this class has the same name as a class in awt package it will actually compile without any errors, creating a class file called Button.class. Now let's consider the MagicRobot class. Figure 13.4 demonstrates that the graphical components required in this class are three buttons and one label.

We will call the add, subtract and multiply buttons, addButton, subtractButton and multButton respectively, and the label instructionbLbl.

In order to create these buttons and this label, and in order to draw the robot, we will need to import the awt package. Also in order to respond to events, we need to import the event package (that itself resides in the awt package). This gives us the following class outline so far:

```
import java.awt.*; // for visual components and Graphics
import java.awt.event.*; // for ActionListener class

class MagicRobot extends Panel implements ActionListener
{
    // class attributes go here
    // class methods go here
}
```

Now let's think about how we declare the four graphical components to be attributes of the MagicRobot class. The obvious way is to declare them in the way we have always declared graphical components:

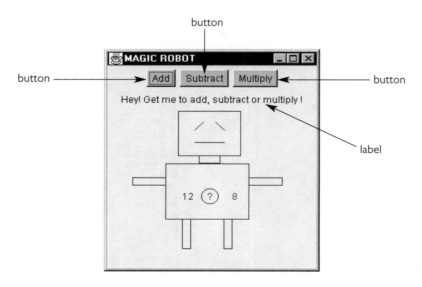

Fig 13.4   The graphical components required in the 'Magic Robot' class

```
// try this to create three button attributes and one label?
private Button addButton = new Button("Add");
private Button subtractButton = new Button("Subtract");
private Button multButton = new Button("Multiply");
private Label instructionLabel = new Label
    ("Hey! Get me to add, subtract or multiply!");
```

Unfortunately these lines will result in compiler errors. Can you think why? The problem is that there are now *two* Button classes that our application will be referring to! There is the utility Button class that we just wrote and then there is the Button class that is a subclass of the awt Component class. For example, later on in this MagicRobot class we will draw a belly button with the following instruction

```
// the intention here is to access our utility 'Button' class
Button.drawBellyButton(g,"?",113,165,20,20);
```

Clearly the intention here is to use our utility Button class, whereas the intention in our attribute declaration was to use the visual awt component class Button. However, the compiler cannot guess a programmer's intentions!

The instructions that declare the three button attributes are the ones that cause the compiler errors, not the line that makes reference to our utility class.

```
// these are the lines that cause compiler errors
private Button addButton = new Button("Add");
private Button subtractButton = new Button("Subtract");
private Button multButton = new Button("Multiply");
```

The reason for this is that, when compiling a class, *the Java compiler always looks for classes in the same directory as the current class file, before looking for classes in other package directories.* So in this case it thinks *all* references to the Button class are to the utility class we just developed. But as these lines are not the correct way to use our utility class they lead to compiler errors!

One way to avoid such a problem is to ensure names of classes never clash. Unfortunately, it will be difficult always to come up with completely original class names. The second approach is to make use of Java's package notation.

Packages not only allow for related classes to be kept together and given a meaningful name, they also allow classes within them to be given *unique* names. This is done by appending the class name onto the package path. For example, here is another way to refer to the TextField class that resides in the awt package:

```
class SomeClass
{
   private java.awt.TextField someAttribute;
}
```

Note that this will compile even without an '**import** java.awt.*' statement at the top of the class! The **import** statement is used only to prevent programmers having to use this long form of class names. Most of the time, when an **import** statement is used, the long class name need never be used. However, when there is a name conflict between a local class and a package class (as there is between our utility Button class and the awt Button class), the long class names can be used for package classes to distinguish them from local classes. So, to remove our original compiler errors, we just have to change the declaration of the Button attributes as follows:

```
private java.awt.Button addButton = new java.awt.Button("Add");
private java.awt.Button subtractButton = new java.awt.Button("Subtract");
private java.awt.Button multButton = new java.awt.Button("Multiply");
```

The complete code for the MagicRobot class is now presented below.

THE MagicRobot CLASS

```
import java.awt.*; //for visual components and Graphics
import java.awt.event.*; // for ActionListener class

class MagicRobot extends Panel implements ActionListener
{
   // numbers in calculation
   private int number1;
   private int number2;
   private int answer;
   // button choice
   private int choice = 0;

   // visual components
   /* the class name is appended to the package name in order to avoid
      confusion with the local 'Button' class we defined ourselves */
   private java.awt.Button addButton = new java.awt.Button("Add");
   private java.awt.Button subtractButton = new java.awt.Button("Subtract");
   private java.awt.Button multButton = new java.awt.Button("Multiply");
   // as there is no local Label class there is no problem here
   private Label instructionLbl = new Label
      ("Hey! Get me to add, subtract or multiply !");
```

```
  // constructor
  public MagicRobot(int first, int second) // parameters for calculation
  {
    // set value of numbers
    number1 = first;
    number2 = second;
    // add visual components
    add(addButton);
    add(subtractButton);
    add(multButton);
    add (instruction);
    // add listeners to buttons
    addButton.addActionListener(this);
    subtractButton.addActionListener(this);
    multButton.addActionListener(this);
  }

  // draw robot
  public void paint(Graphics g)
  {
    g.setColor(Color.red);
    g.drawRect( 85,60,75,60); // head
    g.drawRect(110,120,25,10); // neck
    // eyes
    g.drawLine(105,85,115,75);
    g.drawLine(130,75,140,85);
    g.drawLine(105,102,140,102); // mouth
    g.drawRect(70,131,100,75); // body
    // arms
    g.drawRect(30,150,40,10);
    g.drawRect(170,150,40,10);
    // legs
    g.drawRect(90,206,10,40);
    g.drawRect(140,206,10,40);
    // belly
    g.drawString(number1+"",90,180);
    g.drawString(number2+"",150,180);

    // draws correct belly button and displays answer when necessary
    switch (choice)
    {
      // here we are calling our utility 'Button' class
      case 0: Button.drawBellyButton(g,"?",113,165,20,20);
              break;
      case 1: Button.drawBellyButton(g,"+",113,165,20,20);
              g.drawString("answer = " +answer,170, 90);
              break;
```

```
        case 2: Button.drawBellyButton(g," ",113,165,20,20);
                g.drawString("answer = "+answer,170, 90);
                break;
        case 3: Button.drawBellyButton(g,"X",113,165,20,20);
                g.drawString("answer = "+answer,170, 90);
                break;
    }
}

// process response events
public void actionPerformed(ActionEvent e)
{
    if(e.getSource() == addButton)
    {
        choice = 1;
        answer = number1 + number2;
        repaint();
    }
    if(e.getSource() == subtractButton)
    {
        choice = 2;
        answer = number1 - number2;
        repaint();
    }
    if(e.getSource() == multButton)
    {
        choice = 3;
        answer = number1 * number2;
        repaint();
    }
}
}
```

By making use of the package notation we have avoided name conflicts between classes in packages and our own classes. Program 13.1 now provides a frame in which to run this MagicRobot class:

PROGRAM 13.1

```java
import java.awt.*;

public class RunMagicRobot
{
   public static void main(String[] args)
   {
      // two numbers used in calculations are sent in as parameters
      MagicRobot robot = new MagicRobot(12,8);
      Frame frame = new Frame();
      frame.setSize(260,300);
      frame.setBackground(Color.yellow);
      frame.setTitle("MAGIC ROBOT");
      frame.add(robot);
      frame.setVisible(true);
   }
}
```

13.4 Developing your own packages

You might be surprised to know that all the classes that you have developed so far already reside in a *single* package. This may seem strange as you didn't instruct the compiler to add your classes to any package. Well, what actually happens is that if you don't specifically ask your classes to be put in a package – they all get added to some large unnamed package. What this effectively means is that all your class files will have been saved in a single directory, no matter where you wrote the original source files. If you don't believe us, take a look for yourself on your machine!

Up until now this didn't cause any problems as we were careful to name all our classes uniquely. During this second semester, however, you will start to write more and more Java applications, involving more and more classes and you may, possibly, start working in conjunction with other people also developing their own classes. When this happens there will always be danger that, sooner or later, two classes are going to be developed with *the same name*. Two classes within a package cannot have the same name. To solve this problem, you could keep classes in your own packages when appropriate.

Remember, a package is nothing more than a directory in which to keep your classes. At the moment all your classes are kept in one directory. Think of the difficulty that this could cause when you come to look for the class files for one application amongst a long list of all your class files!

Let's create a unique package in which to put our `MagicRobot` application class files – we will call this package `robot`. The two classes that make up this application are our utility class, `Button`, and the `MagicRobot` class itself. To instruct the compiler that you wish to add these classes to a package called `robot`, simply add the following line at the top of each of the two original source files

```
package robot;
```

This line instructs the compiler that the class file created from this source file must be put in a package called robot. Here is the utility Button class with this **package** line added

```
package robot; // instructs compiler to add class file to package 'robot'
import java.awt.*;

class Button
{
   // as before
}
```

You should ensure that a directory called robot actually exists for the class file to be added to. This directory might have been created for you by your Java IDE. If not, you must create it yourself. We have created it within the directory that contains all our class files. On our machine, which uses a Windows operating system, our class files are kept in a directory called myclasses, which is itself in a directory called JBuilder3 (which is a root directory on our hard drive). Figure 13.5 illustrates the directory structure that needs to be set up in this case.

You will obviously need to adjust this for the set-up on your machine. Once this is done, compile the MagicRobot and Button classes. If your Java set-up doesn't automatically place the resulting class files in your robot directory, you may have to move them manually.

Now the last step, showing you how to import this robot package into programs like any other package. If you had developed your robot package in this way, and then written program 13.1 as normal (outside of a package), the program would no longer compile. Here are the important lines:

```
import java.awt.*;

public class RunMagicRobot
{
   public static void main(String[] args)
   {
      MagicRobot robot = new MagicRobot(12,8); // will cause an error
      // other code as before
   }
}
```

The instruction that makes reference to the MagicRobot class will cause an error because that class no longer lives in the same directory as every other class file, but instead lives in its own package directory − robot. The obvious answer is to import that package into this file as follows:

```
import robot.* // try this?
import java.awt.*;

public class RunMagicRobot
{
  public static void main(String[] args)
  {
   MagicRobot robot = new MagicRobot(12,8);
   // as before
  }
}
```

This seems to make sense as this should provide access to both classes in the robot package. Unfortunately this will still lead to a compiler error.

One reason for this is that the *classes can be made visible outside of their package only if they are declared as* **public**. Unless they are declared as **public** classes by default have only **package** scope. That is they are visible only to other classes within the same package.

Note that not all classes in the package need be declared as **public** as some classes may be part of the implementation only and the developer may not wish them to be made available to the client. In this way, packages provide an extra layer of security for your classes.

In this case, the utility class Button need not be made **public** as it was developed only to assist in our implementation of the MagicRobot. This means we have only to make the MagicRobot class **public** as follows.

```
package robot;
import java.awt.*;
import java.awt.event.*;

// must ensure this class is declared as public
public class MagicRobot extends Panel implements ActionListener
{
  // code as before
}
```

Fig 13.5   The directory structure for the 'robot' package

If after this the program still does not compile, it will be because the Java interpreter will not know where to look for this robot package.

If this were the case here, we would have to inform the operating system that packages we have written can be found within the myclasses directory, which in turn can be found in the JBuilder3 directory. You may well have a different set up of which to inform the system.

You inform the operating system of such information by setting a special **environment variable**. Environment variables provide your operating system with information such as the location of important files in your system. The special environment variable related to the location of Java packages is the **CLASSPATH** variable.

13.5   *Setting the CLASSPATH environment variable*

The details of how the CLASSPATH environment variable is set will differ from one operating system to another. In Windows, for example, you could modify the autoexec.bat file using an application like Microsoft NotePad, whereas if you are working in a UNIX environment you would use the setenv command. Check with your tutor the exact method to use.

In our case we would set the CLASSPATH with the following line in our autoexec.bat file:[1]

```
SET CLASSPATH = C:\JBuilder3\myclasses;
```

Note that the CLASSPATH is not the location of *classes* in packages, but the location of *packages* themselves. It would be wrong to set the CLASSPATH as follows:

```
SET CLASSPATH = C:\JBuilder3\myclasses\robot;
```

This is because the robot directory does not contain a package – it *is* a package! Also note that the CLASSPATH may already have some settings, in which case we would just add this path to the current settings. For example, if the CLASSPATH were set as follows:

```
SET CLASSPATH=C:\Java\lib;
```

then the new path could be appended in the following way:

```
SET CLASSPATH=C:\Java\lib; C:\JBuilder3\myclasses;
```

Most operating systems will require a system reboot in order for this new setting to take effect.

Once the CLASSPATH is set correctly and the MagicRobot class been declared as **public**, this system will function properly with the following added advantages

1. name clashes with classes in the robot package can be avoided;
2. classes in the robot package can easily be located and imported into other programs;
3. the Button class can be kept hidden from the client.

---

[1] We are working with a Windows operating system; check with your tutor about the correct syntax for your system.

13.6   *Running applications from the command line*

Way back in chapter 1 we discussed the process of compiling and running Java programs. If you remember, we said that if you are working within a Java IDE you may have simple icons to click in order to carry out these procedures. If, however, you are working from a command line, like a DOS prompt for example, you would use the **javac** command (followed by the name of the source file) to compile a source file and **java** (followed by the name of a class) to run an application. When you run a class that resides in a package you must amend this slightly.

As an example let's once gain consider the MagicRobot application. When you run an application you must run the class that contains the main method. Program 13.1 provided such a class for running the MagicRobot application. We called this class RunMagicRobot. This class file was *not* part of a package, so it can be run simply from the command line (assuming it has already been compiled) as follows:[2]

```
java RunMagicRobot
```

Notice that the .class extension is not added to the name of the class. Now let's assume that we provided a similar class, with a main method, as part of our robot package. This class will be identical to RunMagicRobot, but will send two different numbers to the MagicRobot class for the calculation. It's called RunMagicRobotFromPackage. The code is presented in program 13.2 below.

PROGRAM 13.2

```java
package robot; // this class is part of the robot package
import java.awt.*;

// this class must be made 'public' to be accessible outside of its package
public class RunMagicRobotFromPackage
{
  public static void main(String[] args)
  {
    // parameters are different from the ones used in 'RunMagicRobot'
    MagicRobot robot = new MagicRobot(10,4);
    // rest of the lines the same as 'RunMagicRobot'
    frame = new Frame();
    frame.setSize(260,300);
    frame.setBackground(Color.yellow);
    frame.setTitle("MAGIC ROBOT");
    frame.add(robot);
    frame.setVisible(true);
  }
}
```

---

[2] Typing the given command at the command line might not necessarily run the application for you. If you are working with a Java IDE, various environment settings may need to be made before running from the command line is possible. Consult the documentation accompanying your IDE.

Now, to run this class from the command line we could try the following:

```
java RunMagicRobotFromPackage
```

Unfortunately this won't work as the Java interpreter won't be able to find a class of the given name. In order to run a class that is contained within a package you must append the class name onto the name of the package. So, in this case you can run this class by using the following command:

```
java robot.RunMagicRobotFromPackage
```

Note that even if this class had the same name as the original program, RunMagicRobot, the package name would have allowed the correct class file to have been found and executed.

Before we move on let's just stop and have a look at the parameter that we always give to main methods:

```
public static void main(String[] args)
```

As you know, this means that main is given an array of String objects as a parameter. How are these String objects passed on to main? Up until now we have not discussed them at all. Well, these strings can be passed to main when you run the given class from the command line. Often there is no need to pass any such strings and this array of strings is effectively empty. Sometimes, however, it is useful to send in such parameters. They are sent to main from the command line by listing the strings, one after the other after the name of the class as follows:

```
java ClassName firstString secondString otherStrings
```

As you can see, the strings are separated by spaces. Any number of strings can be sent in this way. For example if a program were called ProcessNames, two names could be sent to it as follows:

```
java ProcessNames Aaron Quentin
```

Notice that the strings do not need to be enclosed in quotes, but if the strings contained spaces they must be enclosed in quotes:

```
java ProcessNames "Aaron Kans" "Quentin Charatan"
```

These strings will be placed into main's array parameter (args), with the first string being at args[0], the second at args[1] and so on. The number of strings sent to main is variable. The main method can always determine the number of strings sent by checking the length of the array (args.length). Program 13.3 is a simple implementation of the ProcessNames class.

PROGRAM 13.3

```java
public class ProcessNames
{
  public static void main(String[] args)
  {
    // loop through all elements in the 'args' array
    for (int i = 0; i<args.length; i++)
    {
      // access individual strings in array
      System.out.println("hello " + args[i]);
    }
  }
}
```

We deliberately left out the final `EasyIn.pause` that we usually put at the end of our text-based program as we will run this program from the command line. You do not have to worry about the window closing as soon as the program finishes if the program is run from the command line. We can run this program from the command line as follows:

java "Batman and Robin" Superman

Notice "Batman and Robin" needed to be surrounded by quotes as it has spaces in it, whereas `Superman` does not. Running this program would produce the obvious result:

```
hello Batman and Robin
hello Superman
```

13.7   An overview of the core Java API packages

Before we end this chapter, we will provide a brief overview of the complete group of predefined Java packages, sometimes referred to as the **Java API** (Application Programming Interface). It is important to become familiar with these packages, and the classes provided within them, to avoid any unnecessary duplication of work on your part. For example, you wouldn't want to bother defining a `TextField` class when one is already available to you would you!

Table 13.1 provides a list of the core Java packages with some information about the family of classes they provided.

We will be exploring many of these packages in more depth throughout this semester.

Table 13.1 Core packages in the Java API Package	
Package Name	**Description**
java.applet	Contains the Applet class, and the interfaces an applet uses to communicate with its applet context (see chapter 12).
java.awt	Contains classes such as Graphics that allow simple shapes to be drawn, as well as classes such as Button, Label and Frame for managing and creating visual components. We have already discussed this class in chapter 9, and we will be looking further into it in chapters 17 and 19.
java.awt.event	Contains classes and interfaces such as ActionListener and MouseListener for handling events triggered by AWT components. in graphics programming. We discussed this class in chapter 9, and we will be looking further into it in chapters 17 and 19.
java.beans	Contains classes such as Beans, that relate to rapid application development with Java Beans. We will examine this package in chapter 23.
java.io	Contains classes such as BufferedReader and File for system input and output through data streams, and files. We will examine this package in chapter 18.
java.lang	Contains the key Java classes such as System, Object and String. Consequently, this package is implicitly imported into every Java program.
java.text	Contains classes such as DecimalFormat for formatting of information (see chapter 8).
java.util	Contains many utility classes, such as Random, and collection classes such as HashTable and Vector. We will examine this package in chapter 16.
javax.swing	A recent addition to the Java API provides classes such as JButton and JLabel for managing visual components that aim to be more platform independent than their AWT counterparts. We will examine this package in chapter 19.
The following three packages are outside of the scope of this book. They are provided for reference only.	
java.net	Contains classes for implementing networking applications.
java.rmi	Contains classes for remote method calling.
java.sql	Contains classes for querying databases.

Tutorial exercises

1. Name three benefits of creating packages for your applications.
2. Distinguish between a class file and a source file in Java.
3. What is the meaning of a class having **package scope**?
4. Look back at the Hostel application we developed in chapters 10 and 11. Modify these classes so that they are added to a package called hostelApp.
5. Look back at figure 13.4 that illustrates the directory structure of our robot class. Now assume that this directory structure changes so that we keep all our packages in a directory called javaBook, as follows:

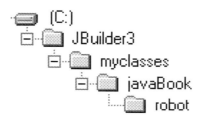

   (a) How could this change be accommodated by modifying the CLASSPATH only?
   (b) If the CLASSPATH is not changed how else could this change be accommodated?
6. What changes would need to be made to the MagicRobot class if all the **import** statements were removed?
7. At the moment program 13.2 (RunMagicRobotFromPackage) fixes the two numbers to be passed on to the MagicRobot class as 10 and 4 respectively:
   (a) amend this class so that the two numbers could be sent in as command line parameters;
   (b) write the command to run this application from the command line with parameters 9 and 3.

Practical work

1. In chapter 6 we developed an IntegerStack class. In fact, there is a predefined Stack class inside the util package. Browse through your Java documentation to find out more about this package and then use it, instead of the IntegerStack class, in program 6.3.
2. Implement the robot package on your machine and then write program 13.1 to run the application.
3. Implement program 13.2 and make the amendments you developed in tutorial question 7a.
4. The lang package contains a class called Math, which has a **static** method called random to generate random numbers. There is also a random number class, Random, in the util package. Browse your Java documentation to find out more about these random number generation techniques. Then rewrite the amended program 13.2 (as discussed in practical

task 3), and then amend the program further so that if no command line parameters are sent to this class, the two numbers are produced by randomly generating numbers from 1 to 10 using:

(a) the **static** random method of the Math class in the lang package;

(b) the random number class, Random, in the util package.

5   Go back and look at program 11.1 (the RunHostel class) from the case study. Amend this program so that the size of the tenant list can be set from a command line parameter.

ABSTRACTION, INHERITANCE AND INTERFACES

14.1 Introduction

In your first semester you were introduced to a number of important concepts in connection with object-oriented development. In this chapter we will pull together some of those ideas and provide you with a better understanding of the object-oriented way of doing things.

The chapter begins by exploring the idea of **abstraction** and **abstract data types**. It then goes on to examine in more depth the concepts of inheritance and polymorphism that you learnt about in the first semester and relates these to this whole notion of abstraction. We then look more closely at abstract classes and methods, and give you the chance to increase your understanding of interfaces by means of some useful and interesting examples.

14.2 Abstraction

The concept of **abstraction** is an important theme in object-oriented development; it is the idea of focussing on what an object does, without worrying about the detail of how it does it.

It is therefore particularly relevant at the analysis stage when we are trying to determine exactly what it is that we want our system to do. The more abstract our specification, the more likely we are to build a system that is flexible and maintainable, because we do not tie ourselves down to one particular design.

Do you remember the UML notation we used throughout the first semester for specifying a class? At the specification stage we didn't concern ourselves with unnecessary detail, and we didn't use types that were specific to one particular programming language. An example that we used in chapter 5 is reproduced in figure 14.1, which shows the specification of the `Oblong` class.

A class template such as this is often referred to as an **abstract data type**, because normally all that is available to the user of such a type is the method descriptions (inputs and outputs) as opposed to information about the data (attributes). Object-oriented programming languages differ from earlier languages in that the principal data types that they manipulate are abstract data types (objects of a class) rather than the simple (intrinsic) types such as **int** and **char**.

Central to all this is the idea that we can broadly define a class, specifying its fundamental behaviour, and concentrating on the important details that make the class what it is. Part of the process of analysis involves *abstracting* the relevant details of a system and discarding irrelevant details. For example, if we are analysing a system that is concerned with keeping student records, we do not need to worry about cleaning the classrooms or serving the coffee in the breaks – important as these activities might be, they are not relevant to our system.

You have already seen how it is possible at the analysis stage to describe classes in very general terms simply by describing the class methods together with their inputs and outputs. We do not worry about how these methods perform their duties until we start to think about the design and implementation of our system.

A very useful technique in all of this, and crucial to the object-oriented way of doing things, is the technique of defining a class in terms of what we already know and making it possible to extend these definitions later.

We have already come across a number of techniques that help us to achieve this: inheritance, polymorphism, abstract classes and interfaces. We will now explore these in more detail.

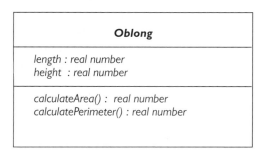

Fig 14.1   The specification of the *Oblong* class

14.3   *More on inheritance and polymorphism*

Cast your mind back to chapter 7 and the `Employee` hierarchy we developed there. The design of the class is shown again in figure 14.2. Do you remember the `getStatus` method? This method was declared as an **abstract** method in the superclass (the `Employee` class) and then overridden in the subclasses (`FullTimeEmployee` and `PartTimeEmployee`). Calling this method causes a `String` to be returned – "Full-Time" for a `FullTimeEmployee` object, and "Part-Time" in the case of a `PartTimeEmployee` object.

In order to help you to understand some further important concepts connected with inheritance and polymorphism we are going to show you another very useful example of how this method could be used. We are going to create an array – and our array is going to hold a

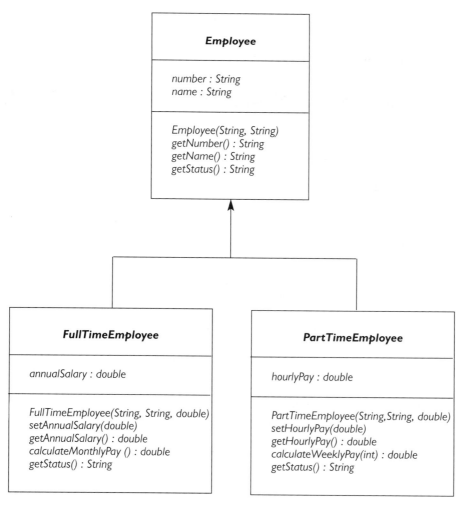

Fig 14.2   The *Employee* hierarchy

mixture of different objects at the same time – some full-time employees and some part-time employees.

So, we are going to have an array that at some particular time could look like the one shown below in figure 14.3.

Program 14.1 allows a user to create a list like this and test it out by displaying the details of the employee's number, name and status on the screen.

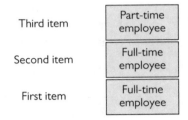

Third item   Part-time employee

Second item   Full-time employee

First item   Full-time employee

Fig 14.3   An array holding items of different types

PROGRAM 14.1

```java
public class MixedListTester
{
  public static void main(String[] args)
  {
    // declare an array big enough for three employees
    Employee[] employeeList = new Employee[3];
    // declare local variables to hold values entered by user
    String num, name;
    double pay;
    char status;
    // get the user to enter the employees' details
    for(int i = 0; i < employeeList.length; i++)
    {
      System.out.print("Enter the employee number: ");
      num = EasyIn.getString();
      System.out.print("Enter the employee's name: ");
      name = EasyIn.getString();
      System.out.print("<F>ull-time or <P>art-time? ");
      status = EasyIn.getChar();
      if(status == 'f' || status == 'F')
      {
        System.out.print("Enter the annual salary: ");
      }
      else
      {
```

```
         System.out.print("Enter the hourly pay: ");
      }
      pay = EasyIn.getDouble();
      if(status == 'f' || status == 'F')
      {
        employeeList[i] = new FullTimeEmployee(num, name, pay);
      }
      else
      {
        employeeList[i] = new PartTimeEmployee(num, name, pay);
      }
   }
   System.out.println();
   for(int i = 0; i < employeeList.length; i++)
   {
      // display employee's number, name, and status
      System.out.println("Employee number: "
                              + employeeList[i].getNumber());
      System.out.println("Employee name: "
                              + employeeList[i].getName());
      System.out.println("Status: " + employeeList[i].getStatus());
      System.out.println();
   }
   EasyIn.pause();
  }
}
```

Let's take a look at what's going on here. We create an array big enough to hold three Employee objects with this line of code:

```
Employee [] employeeList = new Employee[3];
```

Then, after declaring some local variables, we use a **for** loop to get the user to enter the details of each of the three employees. The first part of the loop therefore looks like this:

```
for(int i = 0; i < employeeList.length; i++)
{
  System.out.print("Enter the employee number: ");
  num = EasyIn.getString();
  System.out.print("Enter the employee's name: ");
  name = EasyIn.getString();
  System.out.print("<F>ull-time or <P>art-time? ");
  status = EasyIn.getChar();
  if(status == 'f' || status == 'F')
  {
    System.out.print("Enter the annual salary: ");
  }
  else
  {
    System.out.print("Enter the hourly pay: ");
  }
  pay = EasyIn.getDouble();
```

Notice that once we have established whether the employee is full- or part-time we are able to choose the appropriate message requesting the employee's pay (annual salary for a full-time employee, hourly pay for a part-time employee).

The **for** loop continues and we create our new employee, either full-time or part-time depending on the value of the status variable:

```
if(status == 'f' || status == 'F')
{
  employeeList[i] = new FullTimeEmployee(num, name, pay);
}
else
{
  employeeList[i] = new PartTimeEmployee(num, name, pay);
}
System.out.println();
}
```

Now comes the clever bit!

```
for(int i = 0; i < employeeList.length; i++)
{
  // display employee's number, name, and status
  System.out.println("Employee number: " + employeeList[i].getNumber());
  System.out.println("Employee name: " + employeeList[i].getName());
  System.out.println("Status: " + employeeList[i].getStatus());
  System.out.println();
}
```

We are navigating through the array and, by calling on the getNumber, getName and getStatus method of each object, we are displaying the number, name and status of each employee. And the clever thing is that the correct status is displayed, even though we didn't decide on the status of the employee until the program was run! Here is a sample test run:

```
Enter the employee number: 1
Enter the employee's name: Jones
<F>ull-time or <P>art-time? f
Enter the annual salary: 30000

Enter the employee number: 2
Enter the employee's name: Agdeboye
<F>ull-time or <P>art-time? f
Enter the annual salary: 35000

Enter the employee number: 3
Enter the employee's name: Sharma
<F>ull-time or <P>art-time? p
Enter the hourly pay: 15

Employee number: 1
Employee name: Jones
Status: Full-Time

Employee number: 2
Employee name: Agdeboye
Status: Full-Time

Employee number: 3
Employee name: Sharma
Status: Part-Time
```

You will remember that the getStatus method was *overridden* in each subclass, so that when a message is sent to a FullTimeEmployee object requesting its status, the string "Full-Time" is returned, whereas in the case of a PartTimeEmployee object the string "Part-Time" is returned. As we navigate through the array the appropriate message is returned depending on the type of employee stored at each location.

But how does this work? When the program is compiled it is not known whether, on each iteration of the loop, the employee will be full-time or part-time; this is decided by the user each time the program is run. The technique which makes it possible for this decision to be made is known as **run-time binding** or **dynamic binding**. Let's investigate this a bit more.

First, let's consider what would happen in the case of a language that did not use run-time binding, but instead used **compile-time** or **static binding**. In this case, when the code for a class was compiled the code for each of its methods would simply be compiled alongside it; the compiler would ensure that every time an object of that class received a message to invoke that method, the control of the program would jump to the place where the code for the method was stored – the instructions in that method would then be executed, and the program control would then return to the place where it left off.

But as you can see, that wouldn't work in a case like the MixedListTester (program 14.1) where we don't know until run-time what sort of object we are dealing with. In our final loop we had the following line:

```
System.out.println("Status: " + employeeList[i].getStatus());
```

Where should the program jump to? The compiler can't write the instruction to jump to a particular place, because there is more than one possible place for it to go; it could jump to the place where the instructions for the full-time getStatus method is located – or it could jump to the place where the part-time getStatus method is located. This decision is made not at the time the program is compiled, but at the time it is run. So what has to happen is that every time a new object is created, it must hold information about where its methods are stored; in this way the decision about which actual method is called can be postponed until run-time. This is the technique that constitutes run-time binding.

So Java normally uses dynamic (run-time) binding. However, as you can probably tell, dynamic binding involves a bit more processing and a bit more storage space than does static binding, so it might be useful not to use it unless it's necessary; and of course it is necessary only if a method might be overridden. Therefore if you know that a method is not going to be overridden you can use the **final** modifier with a method, meaning that this method cannot be overridden; if you do that, then static binding will be used.

Notice that there is one thing we did not do in the previous example – we didn't display the employee's pay; to do this we would have to use a method that was specific to one of the two employee types: getAnnualSalary in the case of a full-time employee and getHourlyPay in the case of a part-time employee. We would need, therefore, to type cast back to the appropriate employee type – we could use the getStatus method in order to determine which type of employee we are dealing with and type cast accordingly. This is left as a tutorial exercise.

Before moving on, let's make sure you understand the difference between method *overriding* and method *overloading*. Both are forms of *polymorphism*, a concept you came across in the first semester. Overriding, which we have just used, involves redefining a superclass method in a subclass. Overloading on the other hand, when applied to methods, means having many methods with the same name, distinguished from one another by the parameter list. We saw several examples of this in the first semester – one of the most frequent uses is to provide a number of different constructors for a single class.

14.4   *Abstract classes and interfaces*

You should recall from chapter 7 that the superclass Employee is declared as **abstract**, meaning that you are not permitted to create instances of this class; also, one of its methods, getStatus, is an abstract method, meaning that only the header is defined here – every subclass must have its own version of the method.

Now it is possible to have a class in which *all* methods are abstract; such a class is called an **interface**. You have already come across interfaces such as ActionListener and MouseListener which are provided as part of the java.awt.event package; but it is perfectly possible to create your own interfaces.

Let's consider an example to illustrate the use of interfaces. Imagine that we are producing a program that could be used by different organizations; we would like to place the organization's logo somewhere on the screen. It would be useful if we could produce a class that we could customize later with a particular logo – that way the class is re-usable, because we just have to attach the right logo at the time.

Now we can think back to our earlier discussion about abstraction, and see how the notion of interfaces helps us out here. What is it that would make a class *attachable*? Let's think about this in very abstract terms – in other words let's try to identify the essence of the thing that makes something attachable, and ignore everything else. Well, it would seem that the obvious answer to our question is that it would need to have an *attach* method! Having such a method would make our class attachable – whatever else it has is its own business, but we want to make sure it has this particular method. Interfaces allow us to do this. To see what we mean let's define an Attachable interface:

THE *Attachable* INTERFACE

```
import java.awt.*;

interface Attachable
{
   public void attach(Component c, int xPos, int yPos);
}
```

Do you see what we've done here? We have defined an interface, Attachable, with a single method attach. The method is abstract so it is not actually defined here – that is left to the particular class that implements Attachable. Incidentally, we do not have to use the **abstract** modifier here because all interface methods are abstract by definition.

Implementing an interface is very much like inheriting a class; the class that implements Attachable, for example, becomes a *kind of* Attachable – and it will of course "inherit" and redefine the attach method.

Notice that we have defined our method header to accept three parameters – the Component that the logo should attach itself to (hence the need to import the AWT package), and two co-ordinates to enable the user of the class to decide where it is to be attached.

Let's look at an example; say we wanted any class that had anything to do with our books to bear a *Charatan and Kans* logo. A CAndKLogo class must be *attachable* so it could look like this:

THE *CAndKLogo* CLASS

```java
import java.awt.*;

class CAndKLogo implements Attachable
{
  public void attach(Component c, int xPos, int yPos)
  {
    Graphics g = c.getGraphics();
    g.setFont(new Font("Serif", Font.BOLD,15));
    g.setColor(Color.red);
    g.fillRect(xPos,yPos,125,20);
    g.setColor(Color.yellow);
    g.drawString("Charatan & Kans",xPos + 3, yPos + 15);
  }
}
```

We have seen before the use of the word **implements**, which is used with interfaces and has a similar effect to **extends**, which is used with classes. You can see that the class now defines its own version of the attach method, as required by the Attachable interface.

The method itself consists of code for drawing stuff on the component. The first line looks like this:

```java
Graphics g = c.getGraphics();
```

When we have used Graphics objects in the past we have done so within a component's paint method – a Graphics object is automatically sent to this method, and contains the information about the component that is needed by other methods such as drawString or setColor. In this case we need to generate a Graphics object which will contain this information with respect to the component in question (which is received as a parameter to the attach method). We do this with the getGraphics method of Component – we refer to this process as *getting the graphics context*. Once we have done this, we use various methods of the Graphics class to produce our logo, using the co-ordinates that were received as parameters to position it in the right place. One such method is this one:

```
g.setFont(new Font("Serif", Font.BOLD,15));
```

You can see here that we have created our own font and then set the component's font to this new font. You will find more about this in chapter 19.

Now this logo – or indeed any other `Attachable` – can be attached to a `Graphics` component, for example a `Panel`. This is done in the example that follows, which we have called `LogoPanel`.

THE *LogoPanel* CLASS

```
import java.awt.*;

class LogoPanel extends Panel
{
    // the attributes - an attachable object and its co-ordinates
    private Attachable logo;
    private int xPos;
    private int yPos;

    // the constructor
    public LogoPanel(Attachable logoIn, int xIn, int yIn)
    {
        logo = logoIn;
        xPos = xIn;
        yPos = yIn;
    }

    // the paint method
    public void paint(Graphics g)
    {
        // call the attach method of the attachable object
        logo.attach(this, xPos, yPos);
    }
}
```

You can see that this class has three attributes – an `Attachable` object, and two integers representing the position of that object. Of course this `Panel` could have other attributes and do other things – indeed in practice it certainly would do; but all we are interested in is how to get a logo attached to it.

Now let's take a closer look at the constructor:

```
public LogoPanel(Attachable logoIn, int xIn, int yIn)
{
   logo = logoIn;
   xPos = xIn;
   yPos = yIn;
}
```

The nice thing about this is that the particular Attachable object to be added doesn't have to be specified here — it is passed in as a parameter. But because it is Attachable we know that it will have an attach method — and we are therefore able to use it to paint the component:

```
public void paint(Graphics g)
{
   logo.attach(this, xPos, yPos);
}
```

Now it is an easy matter to add our LogoPanel to a frame; program 14.2 does just this, choosing the *Charatan and Kans* logo which is added at co-ordinates (10,5), roughly in the top left-hand corner. We have also introduced the use of the setLocation method of Component (and inherited by Frame) to position the frame on the screen.

PROGRAM 14.2

```
public class LogoTester
{
   public static void main(String[] args)
   {
      // create a frame
      EasyFrame f = new EasyFrame();
      // create a CAndKLogo
      CAndKLogo logo = new CAndKLogo();
      // create a LogoPanel to display the CAndKLogo
      LogoPanel loPanel = new LogoPanel(logo, 10, 5);
      // add the LogoPanel to the Frame
      f.add(loPanel);
      f.setSize(250,250);
      f.setLocation(200,200);
      f.setVisible(true);
   }
}
```

The result of running this program can be seen in figure 14.4.

Fig 14.4   The *Charatan and Kans* logo

Of course, it would now be a simple matter to change our logo; all we would have to do is send in a different logo as a parameter. Even our arch-rivals *Bharatan and Bans* could devise a logo which could be added very easily, as shown in program 14.3, which in this case displays it in the right hand corner (co-ordinates (110,5)).

PROGRAM 14.3

```
public class LogoTester2
{
  public static void main(String[] args)
  {
    // create a frame
    EasyFrame f = new EasyFrame();
    // create a BAndBLogo
    BAndBLogo logo = new BAndBLogo();
    // create a LogoPanel to display the BAndBLogo
    LogoPanel loPanel = new LogoPanel(logo, 110, 5);
    // add the LogoPanel to the Frame
    f.add(loPanel);
    f.setSize(250,250);
    f.setLocation(200,200);
    f.setVisible(true);
  }
}
```

The result of displaying their logo is shown in figure 14.5.

Fig 14.5 The *Bharatan and Bans* logo

You will no doubt agree that their logo isn't nearly as good as ours! However just in case you want to see how *not* to do it, here is the code for their logo:

THE *BandBLogo* CLASS

```java
import java.awt.*;

class BAndBLogo implements Attachable
{
  public void attach(Component c, int xPos, int yPos)
  {
    Graphics g = c.getGraphics();
    g.setFont(new Font("SansSerif", Font.ITALIC +Font.BOLD,15));
    g.setColor(Color.blue);
    g.fillRect(xPos, yPos, 125, 20);
    g.setColor(Color.yellow);
    g.drawString("Bharatan & Bans",xPos + 3,yPos + 15);
  }
}
```

14.5 *Analysis of the* EasyFrame *class*

Now that you fully understand the concept of an interface, we can take a look at the EasyFrame class that we have been using since chapter 9. You will remember that the standard Frame that is provided as part of the AWT doesn't close when you click on the cross-hairs, and that we developed EasyFrame to get round this problem. This is what the EasyFrame class looks like:

THE *EasyFrame* CLASS

```java
import java.awt.*;
import java.awt.event.*;

public class EasyFrame extends Frame implements WindowListener
{
  /* two constructors are provided - the second gives the option of
     including a caption */
  public EasyFrame()
  {
    addWindowListener(this);
  }
  public EasyFrame(String msg)
  {
    super(msg);
    addWindowListener(this);
  }

  /* the frame is disposed of when the cursor is clicked on the
     crosshairs */
  public void windowClosing(WindowEvent e)
  {
    dispose();
  }

  // when the window closes the program is shut down
  public void windowClosed(WindowEvent e)
  {
    System.exit(0);
  }

  /* the remaining methods are required by the WindowListener interface */
  public void windowDeactivated(WindowEvent e)
  {
  }

  public void windowActivated(WindowEvent e)
  {
  }

  public void windowDeiconified(WindowEvent e)
  {
  }

  public void windowIconified(WindowEvent e)
  {
  }

  public void windowOpened(WindowEvent e)
  {
  }
}
```

You can see that the `EasyFrame` extends a "normal" `Frame`, and also implements an interface called `WindowListener`, which listens for events and provides methods to determine what happens when these events occur. We have provided two constructors. The first one simply adds a `WindowListener` to the frame:

```
public EasyFrame()
{
   addWindowListener(this);
}
```

The second gives us the opportunity of also providing a caption, by calling the constructor of the superclass, `Frame`:

```
public EasyFrame(String msg)
{
   super(msg);
   addWindowListener(this);
}
```

The `WindowListener` expects us to code a number of methods – only two of them are necessary for our purposes – the rest, as you can see, have been left blank. The first, `windowClosing`, determines what happens when somebody clicks on the cross-hairs in the right-hand corner. In our case we have called the single method `dispose` which the frame inherits from the `Window` class:

```
public void windowClosing(WindowEvent e)
{
   dispose();
}
```

This method – as its name suggests – causes the frame to be disposed of and any resources that it has used (such as memory) to be "reclaimed" by the operating system.

The other method we have coded is the `windowClosed` method. This determines what happens once the window has closed. In the case of `EasyFrame` we have decided that when the frame is closed the system should shut down altogether; if, however, you were developing a system in which more than one frame was involved you might want to adapt this so that there is only one "master" window which shuts the whole system down when closed. The instruction to shut the system down is `System.exit(0)`:

```
public void windowClosed(WindowEvent e)
{
    System.exit(0);
}
```

14.6 Adapters

As you can see from the above example, using an interface means that we have to code all the interface methods, even those we are not interested in — for example in the EasyFrame class we have had to include methods such as windowOpened, which we have simply left blank.

There is a way around this, which is to use an adapter. An adapter is a special class that acts as an intermediary between our class and the interface, making it unnecessary to code all the methods; an adapter is provided for every interface that comes with the standard Java packages. To illustrate this we will explore an alternative method of providing a closable frame like our EasyFrame. The first thing to note is that an adapter has to be inherited — so our EasyFrame class can't simply inherit the adapter because Java does not allow multiple inheritance (that is, inheritance from more than one class),[1] and EasyFrame already inherits Frame. We will need to find another strategy.

If we want an object to respond to a window event such as clicking on the cross-hairs, then we have two things to consider:

- we must be able to add a WindowListener object to it, so that it "listens" for the event;
- we must tell it where to look for the instructions once the event has taken place.

In the case of EasyFrame this was all done in the same class. Because it inherited from Frame (and therefore Window) we could add a WindowListener to it by invoking the method addWindowListener; and because it implemented WindowListener, thus itself becoming a kind of WindowListener, we were able to write the instructions within the class itself, by coding the windowClosing and windowClosed methods.

Now we are going to use the WindowAdapter, and because we cannot inherit from more than one class, we will have to write a new class to add to a Frame later on. Let's call this EasyListener.

---

[1] There is good reason for this – think of the confusion that could arise if the two superclasses had methods of the same name!

THE *EasyListener* CLASS

```java
import java.awt.*;
import java.awt.event.*;

class EasyListener extends WindowAdapter
{
  public void windowClosing(WindowEvent e)
  {
    // determine which window caused the event
    Window win = e.getWindow();
    // dispose of that window
    win.dispose();
  }
  public void windowClosed(WindowEvent e)
  {
    // close down the whole system
    System.exit(0);
  }
}
```

Let's take a look at the windowClosing method:

```java
public void windowClosing(WindowEvent e)
{
  Window win = e.getWindow();
  win.dispose();
}
```

The windowClosing method is automatically sent an object of the WindowEvent class. One of the methods of this class is the getWindow method, which returns the details of the particular window that caused the event, and therefore lets us know which one to dispose of. We need to do this here because our EasyListener is not associated with any particular window. Once we have determined this, we use the dispose method of Window as before.

Now that we have our EasyListener we can add it to a frame:

PROGRAM 14.4

```
import java.awt.event.*;
import java.awt.*;

public class WindowTester
{
  public static void main(String[] args)
  {
    Frame frame = new Frame();
    frame.setSize(250,200);
    // add an EasyListener to the frame
    frame.addWindowListener(new EasyListener());
    frame.setVisible(true);
  }
}
```

All this program will do, of course, is to produce an empty frame – but it will close when you click on the cross-hairs because we have added an EasyListener to it.

There is another way of doing this. We could actually declare our EasyListener class within the code that runs the program; a class declared in this way is referred to as an **inner class**. You can see how this is done in program 14.5.

PROGRAM 14.5

```java
import java.awt.event.*;
import java.awt.*;

public class WindowTester2
{
  public static void main(String[] args)
  {
    // declare an inner class
    class EasyListener extends WindowAdapter
    {
      public void windowClosing(WindowEvent e)
      {
        Window win = e.getWindow();
        win.dispose();
      }
      public void windowClosed(WindowEvent e)
      {
        System.exit(0);
      }
    }
    Frame frame = new Frame();
    frame.setSize(250,200);
    frame.addWindowListener(new EasyListener());
    frame.setVisible(true);
  }
}
```

14.7 *The toString method*

In chapter 7 you found out that, in Java, every class is inherited from a "super superclass" called Object. In other words every object of every class is a kind of Object. The Object class has a method called toString that returns a String, and that can be overridden by subclasses of Object – in other words by any other class. Methods of other classes can be set up to use this method – some classes in the standard Java packages have methods (for example print and println) which take an Object object as a parameter and use its toString method; we could also write such methods in our own classes.

An example will show you how useful this is. Let's look at our BankAccount class, which we developed in chapter 5. We will add a toString method as defined below, thus overriding the toString method of the Object class which BankAccount, like all other classes, inherits:

```
public String toString()
{
  return "Account Number: "
            + accountNumber
            + "\nAccount Name: "
            + accountName
            + "\nCurrent Balance: "
            + balance
            + "\n";
}
```

Now look at program 14.6:

PROGRAM 14.6

```
public class RunAccount
{
  public static void main(String[] args)
  {
    BankAccount account1 = new BankAccount("001", "Sarah Patel");
    BankAccount account2 = new BankAccount("002", "Robinder Grewel");
    System.out.println(account1);
    System.out.println(account2);
    EasyIn.pause();
  }
}
```

Do you see that in each case the parameter to the `println` method is just the name of the object? This is possible because, as we indicated earlier, there is a version of `println` provided that accepts an object and outputs the return value of the object's `toString` method. Since we have overridden the `toString` method in our `BankAccount` class as shown, the output from this program will be:

```
Account Number: 001
Account Name: Sarah Patel
Current Balance: 0.0

Account Number: 002
Account Name: Robinder Grewel
Current Balance: 0.0
```

As you are aware, other versions of `print` and `println` also exist. For example, the `print` method that takes an intrinsic type (such as an `int`) as a parameter will have been set up to convert this to its equivalent wrapper class (`Integer`) and print the `toString` method of that class – which will have been designed to return the `String` representation of the relevant type.

We could create our own methods which receive Objects and make use of toString. In the following example we have created a class called EasyText which extends the standard AWT component TextArea and gives it a display method:

THE *EasyText* CLASS

```java
import java.awt.*;
class EasyText extends TextArea
{
  public void display(Object objectIn)
  {
    super.setText(objectIn.toString());
  }
}
```

Notice that in this display method we use the keyword **super** to call the setText method of the superclass, TextArea.

We test out this class with a BankAccount object in program 14.7.

PROGRAM 14.7

```java
import java.awt.*;

public class EasyTextTester
{
  public static void main(String[] args)
  {
    EasyFrame frame = new EasyFrame();
    BankAccount account = new BankAccount("001", "Bill Tin-Wardrobe");
    EasyText eText = new EasyText();
    frame.setSize(300,170);
    frame.setBackground(Color.lightGray);
    frame.add(eText);
    frame.setVisible(true);
    eText.display(account);
  }
}
```

The result of running this program is shown in figure 14.5.

Fig 14.5   Using the *display* method of *EasyText*

Tutorial exercises

1. Explain the meaning of the following terms:
   - abstraction;
   - abstract data type;
   - method overloading;
   - method overriding;
   - dynamic (run-time) binding;
   - static (compile-time) binding.
2. Adapt program 14.1 so that it displays the employee's pay – the annual salary if it is a full-time employee or the hourly pay if it is a part-time employee. You may need to re-read the whole of section 14.3 in order to do this.
3. Write a new version of the EasyFrame class which has a constructor that accepts a parameter, the value of which determines whether or not the entire system shuts down when the frame closes.
4. As mentioned in section 14.6, Java does not support multiple inheritance. Think of examples that illustrate the fact that multiple inheritance could lead to confusion and ambiguity within a program.

Practical work

1. Implement the new version of program 14.1 that you devised in tutorial question 2.
2. Implement and test out the new version of EasyFrame that you designed in tutorial question 3.

EXCEPTIONS

15.1 Introduction

One way in which to write a program is to assume that everything proceeds smoothly and as expected – users input values at the correct time and of the correct format, files are never corrupt, array indices are always valid and so on. Of course this view of the world is very rarely true. In reality, unexpected situations arise that could compromise the correct functioning of your program.

We said in chapter 8 that you should aim to write programs that are robust, that is: programs that continue to function even if such unexpected situations should arise. For the most part, this can be achieved by techniques that we have already discussed with you; carefully constructed **if** statements, the sending back of error flags when appropriate and so on. However, in some circumstances, these forms of protection against undesirable situations prove inadequate. In such cases Java's *exception handling* facility must be used.

15.2   *Pre-defined exception classes in Java*

An **exception** is an event that occurs, during the life of a program, that could cause that program to behave unreliably. You can see that the events we described in the introduction fall into this category. For example, accessing an array with an invalid index could cause that program to terminate. In many programming languages, the responsibility of monitoring for such events is purely on the programmer. Luckily, Java has a very powerful exception handling facility that simplifies the detection and safe handling of these dangerous events.

Most events that can lead to an exception are *already known* to the Java system. This means that the programmer is freed from the burden of having to write the code to detect such an event and instead only needs to write the code that deals with the response to such an event taking place. Each type of event that could lead to an exception is associated with a pre-defined *exception class* in Java. When a given event occurs, the Java runtime environment determines which exception has occurred and an object of the given exception class is generated. This process is known as **throwing** an exception. These exception classes have been named to reflect the nature of the exception. For example as you have already seen in chapter 8, when an array is accessed with an illegal index, an object of the `ArrayIndexOutOfBoundsException` class is thrown.

All exception classes inherit from the base class `Throwable` which is found in the `java.lang` package. These subclasses of `Throwable` are found in various packages and are then further categorized depending upon the type of exception. For example, the exception associated with a given file not being found (`FileNotFoundException`) and the exception associated with an end of file having been reached (`EOFException`) are both types of input/output exceptions (`IOException`), which reside in the `java.io` package. Figure 15.1 illustrates part of this hierarchy.

As you can see from figure 15.1, there are two immediate subclasses of `Throwable`: `Exception` and `Error`. The `Error` class describes internal system errors that are very unlikely ever to occur (so called "hard" errors). For example, one subclass of `Error` is `VirtualMachineError` where some error in the JVM has been detected. There is little that can be done in way of recovery from such errors other than to end the program as gracefully as possible. All other exceptions are subclasses of the `Exception` class and it is these exceptions that programmers deal with in their programs. The `Exception` class can be further subdivided. The two most important subdivisions are shown in figure 15.1, `IOException` and `RuntimeException`.

The `RuntimeException` class deals with program errors that arise when executing a program. For example, accessing an array using an illegal index (`ArrayIndexOutOf-BoundsException`), trying to convert a `String` into a number when the `String` contains non-numeric characters (`NumberFormatException`) and so on. Generally, avoiding these events are within the control of the programmer.

The `IOException` class deals with external errors that could affect the program during periods of input and output. Such errors could include the keyboard locking, or an external file being corrupted. Generally, these events are outside of the control of the programmer.

As nearly any Java instruction could result in `RuntimeException` errors, the Java compiler does not insist that all these potential exceptions are dealt with by the programmer. Whether or not they are is entirely up to the programmer. Consequently this class of errors are known as **unchecked** exceptions. However, since a programmer cannot control `IOException` errors, the Java compiler does insist that programmers deal with such errors when statements that could potentially result in such errors are used. Consequently, these kinds of errors are known as **checked exceptions**.

15.3   *Handling exceptions*

Consider a simple program that allows the user to enter an aptitude test mark at the keyboard; the program then informs the user if they have passed the test and been allowed on a given course. We could use the `EasyIn` method, `getInt`, to allow the user to enter this mark. However, in order to show you how exceptions can be dealt with in your programs, we will not use `EasyIn` methods – we will devise our own class, `TestException`, that will contain a class method called `getInteger`. We will code this `getInteger` method using standard Java methods rather than `EasyIn` methods. Before we do that here is the outline of the `main` application:

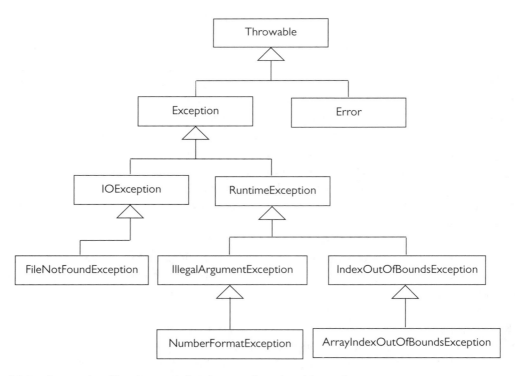

Fig 15.1   A sample of Java's pre-defined exception class hierarchy

```
class AptitudeTest
{
  public static void main (String[] args)
  {
    int score;
    System.out.print("Enter aptitude test score: ");
    score = TestException.getInteger( ); // calling class method
    // test score here
  }
}
```

Now let's look at an outline for the TestException class

```
class TestException
{
  // this method is declared 'static' as it is a class method
  public static int getInteger()
  {
    // code for method goes here
  }
}
```

The getInteger method must allow the user to enter an integer at the keyboard and then to return that integer. There is no simple routine that does this for you in Java. Instead we must allow the integer to be entered as a string and then we must convert this string into an integer. We will use a method called read in the System.in object to help us carry this out. So far we have used the System.out object to display information on the screen but we have not explored the System.in object. This object is not automatically available like the System.out object. It is contained within the java.io package so the following **import** statement is required at the top of the TestException class:

```
import java.io.*;
```

You will remember from week 2 that each character on the keyboard is represented by a Unicode number. For countries in which the standard western alphabet is used the lower case letters 'a' through to 'z' are represented by the Unicode values 97 through to 122 inclusive. Special characters also have Unicode values, for example the 'Enter' key has a Unicode value 13.

The read method of the System.in object is a bit like the getString method of EasyIn except that it treats the string as a series of Unicode numbers. Each number is considered to be of type **byte** so that the string itself is considered an array of bytes. Figure 15.2 illustrates the effect of the read method when someone enters the word "hello" at the keyboard.

Notice that the array of bytes is not returned as a value. Instead they are placed into the parameter. Also note that the end of a line is marked by a Unicode value of 10.

The getInteger method will first have to take this array of bytes and convert it into a string. Luckily a version of the String constructor returns a String object from an array of bytes. We then remove any trailing spaces at the end of the String, this can be done with the String method trim as follows :

```
byte [] buffer = new byte[512]; // declare a large byte array
System.in.read(buffer); // characters entered stored in array
String s = new String (buffer); // make string from byte array
s = s.trim(); // trim string
```

Now, finally, we have to convert this string into an integer. We can use the parseInt method of the Integer class to allow us to do this:

```
int num = Integer.parseInt(s); // converts string to an 'int'
```

Our TestException class now looks like this:

```
// this is a first attempt, it will not compile!
import java.io.*;
class TestException
{
  public static int getInteger()
  {
    byte [] buffer = new byte[512];
    System.in.read(buffer);
    String s = new String (buffer);
    s = s.trim();
    int num = Integer.parseInt(s);
    return num; // send back the integer value
  }
}
```

Unfortunately, as things stand, this class will not compile. The cause of the error is in the getInteger method, in particular the way we used the read method of System.in. Whenever this method is used the Java compiler insists that we be very careful. To understand this better take a look at the header for this read method, in particular the part we have emboldened:[1]

---

[1] You can find the headers of pre-defined Java methods in your Java documentation.

```
public int read (byte[] b) throws IOException
```

Up until now you have not seen a method header of this form. The words **throws** IOException are the new bits in this method header. In Java this is known as a method **claiming an exception**.

15.3.1 Claiming an exception

The term **claiming an exception** refers to a given method, warning that it *could* cause an exception in your program. So the term **throws** IOException means that the method *could* cause an input/output exception in your program. The type of error that could take place while data is being read includes a file being corrupted or the keyboard locking, for example.

Remember, when an exception occurs, an exception object is created. This is an unwanted object that could cause your program to fail or behave unpredictably, and so should be dealt with and not ignored! Rather than dealing with this exception object *within* the read method, the Java people decided it would be better if callers of this method dealt with the exception object in whatever way they felt was suitable. In effect, they *passed the error* onto the caller of the method (see Figure 15.3).

As the type of exception generated (IOException) is not a subclass of RuntimeException, it is an example of a *checked exception*. In other words, the compiler *insists* that if the read method is used, the programmer deals with this exception in some way, and does not just ignore it as we did originally. That is why we had a compiler error initially.

There are always two ways to deal with an exception:

1. deal with the exception within the method;
2. pass on the exception out of the method.

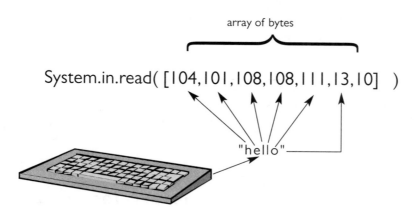

Fig 15.2 **The 'System.in.read' method stores characters entered at the keyboard as an array of bytes.**

The developers of the read method decided to pass on the exception, so now our getInteger method has to decide what to do with this exception. In a while we will show you how to deal with an exception within a method, but for now we will just make our getInteger method pass on the exception too! We do this by simply adding a **throws** clause to our method:

```
private static int getInteger( ) throws IOException
{
    // as before
}
```

Now this method will compile as we have not just *ignored* the exception, we have made a *conscious decision* to pass the exception on to any method that calls this getInteger method. Now, let's look at the AptitudeTest class again.

```
// something wrong here!
class AptitudeTest
{
  public static void main (String[] args)
  {
    int score;
    System.out.print("Enter aptitude test score: ");
    score = TestException.getInteger( ); // calling class method
    // test score here
  }
}
```

Can you see what the problem with this application is? Well, this application will not compile as the main method makes a call to our getInteger method, and remember this method throws an exception of the type IOException. The main method now has to deal with

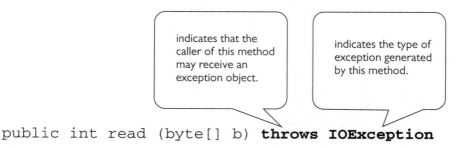

Fig 15.3   The 'throws' clause can be added to a method header to indicate that the method may generate an exception

this exception and not just ignore it! To keep the compiler happy, we will just let the main method throw this exception as well! Here is the code:

```java
import java.io.*; // for IOException
class AptitudeTest
{
  // this main method will throw out any IOExceptions
  public static void main (String[] args) throws IOException
  {
    int score;
    System.out.print("Enter aptitude test score: ");
    // the 'getInteger' method may throw an IOException
    score = TestException.getInteger( );
    if (score >= 50)
    {
      System.out.println("You have a place on the course!");
    }
    else
    {
      System.out.println("Sorry, you failed your test");
    }
    EasyIn.pause("press <Enter> to quit");
  }
}
```

Notice that the `java.io` package needs to be imported to make reference to the `IOException` class. Dealing with the exception in the way we have is not a very good idea. We have effectively continually passed on the exception object until it gets thrown out of our program to the operating system! This may cause the program to terminate when such an exception occurs. Before we deal with this problem let us show you a test run. Take a look at it as something very interesting happens!

```
Enter aptitude test score: 12w
java.lang.NumberFormatException: 12w
    at java.lang.Integer.parseInt(Integer.java:418)
    at java.lang.Integer.parseInt(Integer.java:458)
    at TestException.getInteger(TestException.java:10)
    at AptitudeTest.main(AptitudeTest.java:11)
```

As you can see, when asked to enter an integer, the user inadvertently added a character into the number (12**w**). This has led to an exception being generated and thrown out of our program. Again looking at the output generated, you can see that when an exception is generated in this way the Java system gives you quite a lot of information. This information includes the name of the method that threw the exception, the class that the method belongs to, the line numbers in these source files where the error arose, and the type of exception that was thrown.

Look at the name of the exception that is thrown. It's not the one we were worried about, `IOException`, but `NumberFormatException`. This exception is raised when trying to convert a string into a number when the string contains non-numeric characters, as we were trying to do in this case within our `getInteger` method:

```
public static int getInteger() throws IOException
{
   // some code here
   int num = Integer.parseInt(s); /* will cause a NumberFormatException, if
                                      string s, contains non-numeric
                                      characters*/

}
```

Why didn't the compiler warn us about this when we first used the `parseInt` method in our implementation of `getInteger`? Well, the reason is that the exception that could arise (`NumberFormatException`) is a subclass of `RuntimeException` and so is unchecked!

Notice that runtime exceptions do not need to be claimed in method headers in order for them to be thrown. For example, although the following is valid in Java, it is not *necessary* to claim the `NumberFormatException` in the header.

```
/* multiple exceptions can be claimed in method header as follows by
   separating exception names with commas, however run-time exceptions do
   not need to be claimed in this way */
public static int getInteger() throws IOException, NumberFormatException
{
   // some code here
}
```

However, it is always useful to make explicit in method headers all exceptions that could be thrown. You obviously have to be careful when using methods that could lead to runtime exceptions as the compiler will not flag these exceptions for you.

The way we have dealt with exceptions so far has not been very effective. As you can see from the test run of program 15.1, continually throwing exceptions up to the calling method does not really solve the problem. It may keep the compiler happy, but eventually it means exception objects will escape from your programs and cause them to terminate. Instead, it is better at some point to handle an exception object rather than throw it. In Java this is known as **catching an exception**.

15.3.2 Catching an exception

One route for an exception object is *out* of the current method and *up to* the calling method. That's the approach we used in the previous section. Another way out for an exception object, however, is into a **catch** block. Once an exception object is trapped in a **catch** block, and that block ends, the exception object is effectively terminated! In order to trap the exception object in a **catch** block you must surround the code that could generate the exception in a **try** block. The syntax for using a **try** and **catch** block is given as follows:

```
try
{
   // code that could generate an exception
}
catch (Exception e) // type of exception being caught is given in brackets
{
   // action to be taken when an exception occurs
}
// other instructions could be placed here
```

There are a few things to note before we show you this **try catch** idea in action. First, any number of lines could be within the **try** block, and more than one of them could cause an exception. If none of them causes an exception the **catch** block is missed and the lines following the **catch** block are executed. If any one of them causes an exception the program will leave the **try** block and look for a **catch** block that deals with that exception.

Once such a **catch** clause is found, the statements within it will be executed and the program will then *continue* with any statements that follow the **catch** clause — it will *not* return to the code in the **try** clause. Look carefully at the syntax for the **catch** block:

```
catch (Exception e)
{
   // action to be taken when an exception occurs
}
```

This looks very similar to a method header. You can see that the **catch** block header has one parameter: an object, that we called e, of type Exception. Since *all* exceptions are subclasses of the Exception class, this will catch *any* exception that should arise. However, it is better to replace this exception class with the *specific* class that you are catching so that you can be certain *which* exception you have caught. As there may be more than one exception generated within a method, there may be more than one **catch** block below a **try** block — each dealing with a different exception. When an exception is thrown in a **try** block, the **catch** blocks are inspected in order — the first matching **catch** block is the one that will handle the exception.

Within the **catch** block, programmers can interrogate the exception object if they choose using some Exception methods. For example, the method getMessage returns a string with a brief description of the exception. Alternatively, a more detailed description of the problem can be obtained by calling the toString method.

With this information in mind we can deal with the exceptions in the previous section in a different way. All we have to decide is where to catch the exception object. For now we will leave the getInteger method as it is and catch offending exception objects in the main method of Program 15.2.

PROGRAM 15.2

```java
class AptitudeTest2
{
  public static void main (String[] args)
  {
    try
    {
      int score;
      System.out.print("Enter aptitude test score: ");
      //'getInteger' may throw IOException or NumberFormatException
      score = TestException.getInteger( );
      if (score >= 50)
      {
        System.out.println("You have a place on the course!");
      }
      else
      {
        System.out.println("Sorry, you failed your test");
      }
    }
    // if something does go wrong!
    catch (NumberFormatException e)
    {
      System.out.println("You entered an invalid number!");
    }
    catch (IOException e)
    {
      System.out.println(e.getMessage());
    }
    // even if no exception thrown/caught, this line will be executed
    EasyIn.pause("press <Enter> to quit");
  }
}
```

Notice that by catching an offending exception object there is no need to pass that object out of the method by raising that exception in the method header. Since we catch the IOException here, the throws IOException clause can be removed from the header of main. In program 15.2 we have chosen to print out a summary of the exception if an IOException is raised (by calling the getMessage method), whereas we have chosen to print our own message if a `NumberFormatException` is raised. Now look at a sample test run of program 10.2

```
Enter aptitude test score: 12w
You entered an invalid number!
press <Enter> to quit
```

As you can see the user once again entered an invalid integer, but this time the program did not terminate. Instead the exception was handled with a clear message to the user, after which the program continued to operate normally.

Whenever you are dealing with exceptions you always have a decision to make – whose responsibility should it be to catch an exception? Do you remember how you used our original `EasyIn` methods? You didn't have to deal with any exceptions coming out of them, did you? If we had written them in the way we developed the `getInteger` method so far, you would have had to deal with exceptions in your program the way we dealt with them in program 15.2. We thought this would be a bit too much in your first semester – we bet you agree! So, instead of throwing exceptions from our methods for you to catch, we caught them in the methods themselves. Here's our actual implementation of the `getInt` method in the `EasyIn` class for example:

```java
public static int getInt()
{ int i;
  String s ;
  boolean ok = false; // error flag
  while(!ok) // keep on allowing input while errors occur
  {
    byte[] b = new byte[512];
    try
    {
      System.in.read(b);
      s = new String(b);
      s = s.trim();
      i = Integer.parseInt(s);
      ok = true; // indicate success
    }
    catch(NumberFormatException e)
    {
      System.out.println("Make sure you enter an integer!");
    }
    catch(IOException e)
    {
      System.out.println(e.getMessage());
    }
  } // continue in loop to allow for re-entry
  return i; // sends back value only when valid
}
```

As you can see we have put the **try catch** block in the method itself. To allow for re-entry of data if an exception occurs, we have placed this **try catch** block in a **while** loop that keeps repeating until a valid value has been entered. The user of this method is kept hidden from the exceptions that may have been thrown.

15.4 *Exceptions in GUI applications*

In the previous section we showed you how the parseInt method could potentially result in a NumberFormatException being thrown. If this wasn't handled at some point, the exception object would escape out of your program and cause the program to terminate. However, this isn't the first time that you used the parseInt method. You often had to use it when implementing GUI applications. In such applications all user input is initially considered a string, in order to retrieve integer values from these strings you used the parseInt method (and to retrieve decimal values you used parseDouble). At the time, you never considered handling these exceptions, and your applications never seemed to terminate as a result of invalid data entry! For example, do you remember the Hostel case study of chapters 10

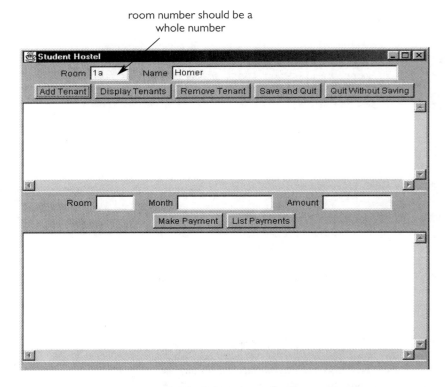

Fig 15.4 **A sample screen shot from the 'Hostel' case study illustrating an invalid room number having been entered**

and 11? Figure 15.4 illustrates a sample screen shot when a user enters an invalid room number.

When such an event occurred within a GUI application, the application seemed to *continue operating regardless*. After our discussion on exceptions this might seem surprising as the text entered is being processed by a `parseInt` method. To remind you, here is a fragment from the event handler:

```
if(e.getSource() == addButton)
{
   // some code here
   String roomEntered = roomField.getText(); // read text entered
   // could cause an exception!
   if(Integer.parseInt(roomEntered)< 1
                     || Integer.parseInt(roomEntered)>noOfRooms)
   {
      displayArea.setText("There are only " + noOfRooms + " rooms");
   }
   // some code here
}
```

In fact, when an invalid number is entered as illustrated in figure 15.4, a `NumberFormat-Exception` occurs but

- you will not see details of the exception in your graphics screen since they will always be displayed on your black console window (which may be hidden during the running of your application);
- exceptions do not terminate GUI applications; however they may make them behave unpredictably.

So, if you uncover your black console screen you will see a list of exceptions that have been thrown during the running of your GUI applications – you may be surprised to see how many are actually thrown when you thought your program was operating correctly! This black console screen is also available when running applets in browsers. It is kept hidden but can be made visible.

Often, graphical programs will continue to operate normally in the face of exceptions, but to be sure of this you can still add exception handling code into your GUI applications. For example, we could amend the event handler above as follows:

```
if(e.getSource() == addButton)
{
  try
  {
    // previous add button code goes here
  }
  // if any lines throw NumberFormatException this handler is activated
  catch (NumberFormatException nfe)
  {
    // display error message and clear original text in room field
    displayArea.setText(nfe.getMessage() + " is not a valid room number"
                            + "\nEnter whole numbers only!");
    roomField.setText("");
  }
}
```

error message displayed   text field cleared

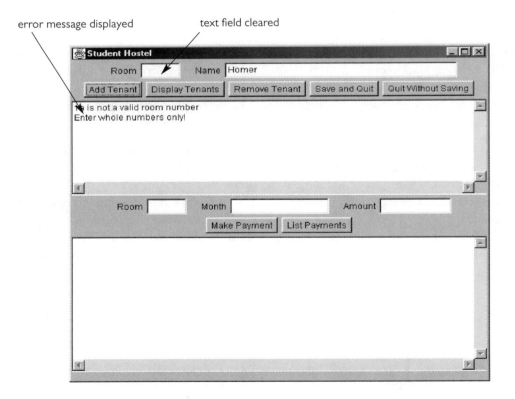

Fig 15.5   Exceptions can still be dealt with in GUI applications

Notice we had to pick a different name for our exception object. We chose nfe (for **NumberFormatException**) rather than just e as before, as we already have an object called e in this event handler. Now if we run the application again, with the same input as depicted in figure 15.4 we get the response given in figure 15.5.

15.5 *Unavoidable exceptions in your own classes*

So far we have mainly been dealing with how to handle exceptions that are thrown by predefined Java methods, such as read and parseInt. Up until now, the methods you have been writing yourself have not had to deal with exceptions unless they themselves used a Java method that throws an exception.

We have managed to avoid the need for exceptions by using **if** statements to monitor dangerous situations, and to send back boolean error values when appropriate, to warn users of our methods that something went wrong. In this way, exceptions never arose. As an example, think back to the IntegerStack class of chapter 6. The important parts of this class are presented again below.

THE *IntegerStack* CLASS

```
class IntegerStack
{
  private int[] stack ; // to hold the stack of integers
  private int total; // to track number of items

  public IntegerStack(int sizeIn) // constructor
  {
    stack = new int[sizeIn];
    total = 0;
  }
  public boolean push(int j)
  {
    if( isFull() == false ) // checks if space in stack
    {
      stack[total] = j;
      total++;
      return true;
    }
    else
    {
      return false;
    }
  }
  public boolean pop()
    {
    if( isEmpty() == false)
    {
```

```
        total--;
        return true;
      }
      else
      {
        return false;
      }
  }
  public boolean isEmpty()
  {
      // code to check if stack is empty goes here
  }
  public boolean isFull()
  {
      // code to check if stack is full goes here

  }
  public int getItem(int i)
  {
      return stack[i-1]; // ith item at position i-1
  }
  public int getTotal()
  {
      return total;
  }
}
```

Look carefully at the push method from this class:

```
public boolean push(int j)
{
  if( isFull() == false ) // checks if space in stack
  {
    stack[total] = j;
    total++;
    return true;
  }
  else
  {
    return false;
  }
}
```

As you can see the instructions within this method are placed within an **if else** selection and a **boolean** value is returned from this method. An item was added into the array attribute only if space existed; the **boolean** value indicated whether or not this method had successfully added the item.

The selection prevented any illegal array access being attempted with an invalid array index. For example, if the maximum size of the array were 5, the value of total would be 5. But the array indices run from 0 to 4. An attempt to add an item into stack[5] would cause an error.

You already know, from chapter 8, that the error that is caused is an ArrayIndexOut-OfBoundsException. This exception is avoided, in the pop method, by placing the array access in a selection, and the user of this method is informed of something going wrong by returning a **boolean** value.

Wherever possible, this is always the best approach – avoid exceptions rather than throw and catch them, and report errors with **return** values. This is a preferable approach because throwing exceptions involves extra resource demands on your program. However, sometimes the technique of avoidance and reporting of errors in **return** values does not work and exception handling techniques have to be used.

To illustrate this take a closer look at the getItem method of the IntegerStack class.

```
public int getItem(int i)
{
   return stack[i-1]; // ith item at position i-1
}
```

This method can still throw an ArrayIndexOutOfBoundsException! If there are only five positions in the array an attempt to get the eighth item will cause this exception to be thrown. How can this be avoided? Well, we could use an **if** statement as with the pop method to ensure we only get a valid position. Here's a first attempt:

```
public int getItem(int i) // first attempt at avoiding an exception
{
   if (i>=1 && i <= total)
   {
      return stack[i-1]; // will only use valid array indices
   }
}
```

While this avoids the exception being raised, it causes another problem. If the index is invalid (and the statements in the **if** block are skipped), no value is returned from this method. But this method *must* return an integer, so this will lead to a compiler error. How can we ensure that an integer is always returned, even if an illegal position were sent in as a parameter? Well, there is no completely satisfactory answer to this. We could send back an integer value that we could use to indicate failure, for example –999.

```
public int getItem(int i) // second attempt at avoiding an exception
{
  if (i>=1 && i <= total)
  {
    return stack[i-1];
  }
  else // when position is invalid
  {
    return -999; // indicates failure
  }
}
```

This is better than our first attempt, as this method will now compile. If there were no possibility of −999 being a value in the stack then this may be completely fine. However, our stack can hold any integer including −999. The caller of this method could not tell if the −999 was a value in the stack or an indication of error! In this case the only way to report the error will be by throwing an exception.

Here's another method with a similar problem – the constructor:

```
public IntegerStack(int sizeIn)
{
  stack = new int[sizeIn]; // could throw exception if 'size' is negative
  total = 0;
}
```

As the comment explains, this constructor could throw an exception if an attempt is made to size an array with a negative number. The name of the exception that is thrown can always be tested by writing a small **try catch** block in a main method. Program 15.3 is one such simple tester program:

PROGRAM 15.3

```
* the purpose of this class is just to test which exception is thrown when a
  negative array size is entered */
public class TestException
{
  public static void main(String[] args)
  {
    try
    {
      // here write the code you are testing
      System.out.println("Enter size");
      int size = EasyIn.getInt();
      int[] list = new int[size];
    }
    catch (Exception e) // this will catch any exception that is thrown
    {
      System.out.println(e); // will display the name of the exception
    }
    EasyIn.pause();
  }
}
```

Notice that since all exceptions are of type Exception, the **catch** clause above will catch any exception that occurs. When testing your applications it might be a good idea to place the instructions inside main in such a **try catch** block. Here is a sample test run:

> *Enter size*
>
> *-5*
>
> *java.lang.NegativeArraySizeException:*

As you can see, this results in a NegativeArraySizeException. Now that you know your constructor could also throw this exception what could you do? Avoiding it would be a good idea and that is simple:

```
public IntegerStack(int sizeIn) // try this method of avoiding exception
{
  if (sizeIn >= 0)
  {
    stack = new int[sizeIn]; // only positive number used
    total = 0;
  }
}
```

Note that an array size of zero is legal. The problem we are left with now is how to report back to the caller that a problem occurred. In other methods we could try to use a **return** value, but constructors have no return value! The only way to report back errors from constructors is to use exceptions. Okay, we've shown how exceptions can be a useful error checking technique; let's now look at how to incorporate exceptions into the methods of your classes.

15.6   *Throwing exceptions*

One way of indicating that a method may throw an exception is to add the exception to the method header in a **throws** clause. So we could amend the IntegerStack class as follows:

```
class IntegerStack
{
  // attributes as before

  // warn that the constructor may throw an exception
  public IntegerStack(int sizeIn) throws NegativeArraySizeException
  {
    stack = new int[sizeIn];
    total = 0;
  }

  // warn that 'getItem' method may throw an exception
  public int getItem(int i) throws ArrayIndexOutOfBoundException
  {
    return stack[i-1];
  }

  // other methods as before
}
```

This would work but has several drawbacks:

- both exceptions are unchecked (as they are subclasses of RuntimeException), so the compiler will not remind the developers who call this method that an exception must be dealt with;
- the names of the exceptions give away the fact that an array is being used to implement a stack. This is undesirable as the purpose of this class was to hide the array from the user. Also, if in future a decision was made to replace the array representation with another representation, these exception names will not be valid.

Both of these problems could be solved by throwing a general exception (of type Exception), rather than a specific exception (like NegativeArraySizeException for example). A general exception will be checked by the compiler, forcing the caller to deal with this exception and not ignore it, and the exception name does not reveal the underlying representation. Here's how the header for the constructor would be amended if this were the chosen strategy:

```
public IntegerStack (int sizeIn) throws Exception
{
   // some code in here
}
```

Unfortunately this approach does require some modifications to the actual body of the method. While the Java system will automatically detect and throw a specific exception object (of type NegativeArrayIndexException for example), there is no event that will lead to a general exception object (of type Exception) being thrown. In order to throw a general exception object you must

- detect the situation when such an exception should be thrown and then;
- write an instruction explicitly to throw the exception using the **throw** command;
- use the **new** command to generate an object of type Exception.

In the case of the constructor, the exception object will be thrown when the array size is less than zero. Here is the amended constructor:

```
public IntegerStack throws Exception
{
   if (sizeIn < 0) // throw exception object under this condition
   {
      throw new Exception ("cannot set a negative size");
   }
   else
   {
      stack = new int[sizeIn];
      total = 0;
   }
}
```

Notice that when you explicitly throw an exception object you may also pass along a message as a parameter as we did in this case:

```
throw new Exception ("cannot set a negative size");
```

This message can be retrieved by the receiver of this exception object. For example here are the relevant lines from the IntegerStackTester class from chapter 6:

```
public class IntegerStackTester
{
  public static void main(String[] args)
  {
    try
    { // some code here
      IntegerStackTester s = new IntegerStackTester(size)
      // rest of code here
    }
    catch (Exception e)
    {
      System.out.println(e.getMessage());
    }
  }
// other static methods here
```

Notice how throwing an exception object, from the IntegerStack constructor, forced us in the IntegerStackTester class to deal with the error – it could not be ignored. A similar exception object could of course be thrown from the getItem method. Here is a sample test run of the amended IntegerStackTester class:

```
maximum number of items on stack?
-5
cannot set a negative size
```

Notice how the error message no longer reveals the underlying array representation. This approach of throwing general exceptions, while adequate, also has its drawbacks:

- the name of the exception does not explain the source of the problem; the getMessage method must be used to determine that;
- if we amend the getItem method in the same way as the constructor, the resulting exception object will also be caught in this **catch** clause, but we may wish to handle that exception in a different way to the constructor exception;
- the catch clause we used to deal with the resulting exception object will catch *any* exception that is thrown as all exceptions are derived from the exception class!

If these issues affect your application you will have to create your own exception classes rather than throwing general exceptions.

15.7   *Creating your own exception classes*

You can create your own exception class by inheriting from the class Exception. In the IntegerStack class we identified two methods that required exceptions to be thrown. The constructor and the getItem method. First of all we will define our own exception class to use in the constructor. Remember, the problem that arose there was the possibility of a negative size, so we will call this exception `NegativeSizeException`. Look at the code first and then we will discuss it.

THE *NegativeSizeException* CLASS

```
class NegativeSizeException extends Exception
{
  public NegativeSizeException () // constructor without parameter
  {
    super("cannot set a negative size");
  }
  public NegativeSizeException (String message)
                        // constructor with parameter
  {
    super (message);
  }
}
```

As well as inheriting from the class `Exception`, user-defined exception classes should have two constructors defined within them. One that takes no parameter and simply calls the exception constructor with a message of your choosing is:

```
public NegativeSizeException ()
{
  super("cannot set a negative size"); // calls Exception constructor
}
```

The other constructor allows a user defined message to be supplied with the exception object:

```
public NegativeSizeException (String message)
{
  super (message); // message supplied as parameter
}
```

Now let's turn to an exception for the `getItem` method. In this method the problem is that an invalid position could be supplied so let's call this exception class `InvalidStackPositionException`. Here is the code:

THE *InvalidStackPositionException* CLASS

```
class InvalidStackPositionException extends Exception
{
  public InvalidStackPositionException()
  {
    super("an invalid stack position was provided");
  }
  public InvalidStackPositionException(String message)
  {
    super(message);
  }
}
```

Notice that both of these exceptions will be checked exceptions as they are not subclasses of RuntimeException. This means that the compiler will insist exception objects of this type are not ignored. Now, here is an IntegerStackWithExceptions class. As the name suggests, it is similar to IntegerStack except it uses the exceptions we have just defined.

THE *IntegerStackWithExceptions* CLASS

```
class IntegerStackWithExceptions
{
  // same attributes as before
  private int[] stack ;
  private int total;

  // constructor throws user-defined exception
  public IntegerStackWithExceptions(int size)
                        throws NegativeSizeException
  {
    if (size < 0)
    {
      throw new NegativeSizeException();
    }
    else
    {
      stack = new int[size];
      total = 0;
    }
  }

  // this method also throws a user-defined exception
  public int getItem(int i) throws InvalidStackPositionException
  {
    if (i<1 || i > total)
    {
      throw new InvalidStackPositionException ();
    }
```

```
    else
    {
      return stack[i-1];
    }
  }

  public boolean push(int j)
  {
    // same as IntegerStack
  }

  public boolean pop()
  {
    // same as IntegerStack
  }
  public boolean isEmpty()
  {
    // same as IntegerStack
  }

  public boolean isFull()
  {
    // same as IntegerStack
  }

  public int getSize()
  {
    // same as IntegerStack
  }
}
```

Program 15.4 is a tester program to check the methods throwing an exception.

PROGRAM 15.4

```
public class TestIntegerStackWithExceptions
{
  public static void main(String[] args)
  {
    try
    { char choice;
      System.out.print("Maximum number of elements on stack?: ");
      int size = EasyIn.getInt();
      // the next line could throw an exception
      IntegerStackWithExceptions s = new IntegerStackWithExceptions(size);
      do
      {
```

```
        // offer menu and process choice
        System.out.println("\n1. Push item onto stack");
        System.out.println("2. Get any item from the stack");
        System.out.println("3. Quit");
        System.out.print("\nEnter choice: ");
        choice = EasyIn.getChar();
        switch(choice)
        {
          case '1': option1(s);break;
          case '2': option2(s);break;  //this method could throw an exception
          case '3': break;
          default : System.out.println("Invalid entry");
        }
     }while(choice!='3');
   }

catch (NegativeSizeException e) // from stack constructor call
{ // source and type of error displayed
   System.out.println(e.getMessage());
   System.out.println("due to error created by stack constructor");
}
catch (InvalidStackPositionException e) // from 'option2' method call
{ // source and type of error displayed
   System.out.println(e.getMessage());
   System.out.println("due to error created by call to 2nd menu option");
}
catch (Exception e) // just in case any other exception is thrown
{
    System.out.println("This exception was not considered");
    System.out.println(e.getMessage());
   }
   EasyIn.pause("\nPress <Enter > to quit program");
}

private static void option1(IntegerStackWithExceptions stackIn)
{
   System.out.print("\nEnter number: ");
   int num = EasyIn.getInt();
   boolean ok = stackIn.push(num);
   if(!ok)
   {
     System.out.println
       ("You are trying to push a number onto a full stack");
   }
}
```

```
// this method throws out any InvalidStackPositionException
  private static void option2(IntegerStackWithExceptions stackIn)
                throws InvalidStackPositionException
  {
    System.out.print("\nWhich position would you like to get? ");
    int position = EasyIn.getInt();
    System.out.println("This item is: " + stackIn.getItem(position));
    System.out.println();
  }
}
```

Notice how we added an extra **catch** clause to catch any exceptions that we might not yet have considered. During testing this is always a good strategy. Here is one test run of program 15.4:

> *Maximum number of elements on stack?: **−5***
> *cannot set a negative size*
> *due to error created by stack constructor*
>
> *Press <Enter> to quit program*

Here, a negative size was set so the NegativeSizeException was raised and caught. Here is another test run of program 15.4

> *Maximum number of elements on stack?: **5***
>
> *1. Push item onto stack*
> *2. Get any item from the stack*
> *3. Quit*
>
> *Enter choice: **1***
>
> *Enter number: **99***
>
> *1. Push item onto stack*
> *2. Get any item from the stack*
> *3. Quit*
>
> *Enter choice: **2***
>
> *Which position would you like to get? **1***
> *This item is: **99***
>
> *1. Push item onto stack*
> *2. Get any item from the stack*
> *3. Quit*

Enter choice: **2**

Which position would you like to get? **4**
an invalid stack position was provided
due to error created by call to 2nd menu option

Press <Enter> to quit program

Here, the program continued operating until an attempt was made to get an item at position 4 when only one item was in the stack. This resulted in an exception being thrown and caught of the type `InvalidStackPositionException`.

Of course, this tester could be improved by allowing re-entry of invalid inputs — but this is left as a practical exercise at the end of this chapter.

15.8   *Re-throwing exceptions*

Ordinarily, when an exception is caught in a **catch** block, that exception has been dealt with. It is, however, possible to throw an exception from within a **catch** block. For example, look back at the `getItem` method of the `IntegerStackWithExceptions`

```
public int getItem(int i) throws InvalidStackPositionException
{
   if (i<1 || i > total)
   {
     throw new InvalidStackPositionException ();
   }
   else
   {
     return stack[i-1];
   }
}
```

Here, an **if** statement was used to determine when to throw an exception object. We could, instead, have allowed an `ArrayIndexOutOfBoundsException` to be thrown and then thrown our own `InvalidStackPositionException` in a **catch** block as follows:

```
public int getItem(int i) throws InvalidStackPositionException
{
  try // check for exceptions
  {
    return stack[i-1];
  }
  catch (ArrayIndexOutOfBoundsException e) // allow this to be caught
  {
    // then throw our own exception
    throw new InvalidStackPositionException ();
  }
}
```

This technique might be useful if the condition required for the **if** statement were difficult to formulate, or where there were several points in a method where an exception could be thrown. In the latter case all these possible points of error could be included in a single **try** block.

Tutorial exercises

1. Explain the difference between a checked and unchecked exception.
2. Look at program 15.5 and then answer the questions that follow:

PROGRAM 15.5

```
public class SomeClassWithExceptions
{
  public static void main(String [] args)
  {
    int someArray = [12,9,3,11];
    int position = getPosition();
    display (someArray, position);
    EasyIn.pause("press <Enter> to quit");
  }
  private static int getPosition()
  {
    System.out.println("Enter array position to display");
    String positionEntered = EasyIn.getString();
    return Integer.parseInt(positionEntered);
  }
  private static void display (int[] arrayIn, int posIn)
  {
    System.out.println("Item at this position is: " + arrayIn[posIn]);
  }
}
```

(a) Will this result in any compiler errors?

(b) Which exceptions will this program throw?

(c) Re-write the getPosition method so that it throws any exception it may encounter back to main;

(d) Re-write the display method so that it also throws any exception it may encounter back to main;

(e) Re-write main so that it catches any exceptions it may now throw by displaying a message on the screen indicating the exception thrown;

(f) Add an additional **catch** clause in main to catch any unaccounted for exceptions;

(g) Create your own exception class InvalidArrayPositionException (ensure that it is a checked exception);

(h) Re-write the display method so that it throws the InvalidArrayPositionException in a **catch** block.

(i) Re-write main to take account of this amended display method.

3. Look back at tutorial question 7 and practical task 3 of chapter 13. You developed a RunMagicRobotFromPackage class so that it would accept command line parameters. At the moment this program can throw an exception. Re-write this class so that the exception is caught, allowing the two random numbers to be passed on to the MagicRobot class.

Practical work

1. Code the IntegerStackWithExceptions class and Program 15.4 (the TestInteger-StackWithExceptions class). Now

(a) Re-write the TestIntegerStackWithExceptions class so that option2 method now catches the InvalidStackPositionException and continually allows the user to re-enter a valid position.

(b) Amend the TestIntegerStackWithExceptions class further so that the user is continually allowed to enter the size of a stack until no NegativeStackSizeException is thrown.

2. Implement program 15.5 from tutorial question 2 and make all the amendments discussed in parts a–g of that tutorial question.

3. Implement the changes to the RunMagicRobotFromPackage class discussed in tutorial question 3.

4. Go back and look at the case study classes from chapters 10 and 11 and then:

(a) Define the following two exception classes: NegativeSizeException and Invalid-PositionException.

(b) Re-write the PaymentList class so that the NegativeSizeException is thrown when a negative value is sent to the constructor and an InvalidPositionException is thrown when an invalid position is sent to the getPayment method.

(c) Re-write the TenantList class so that the NegativeSizeException is thrown when a negative value is sent to the constructor and an InvalidPositionException is thrown when an invalid position is sent to the getTenant method.

(d) Re-write the Hostel class so that all exceptions thrown are caught with suitable error messages on the graphical user interface.

(e) Re-write the amended version of program 11.1 (the RunHostel class), as discussed in practical task 5 of chapter 13, so that any exceptions thrown are caught.

MORE ON ARRAYS AND COLLECTION CLASSES

LEARNING OBJECTIVES

By the end of this chapter you should be able to:

➤ create a **two-dimensional** array;

➤ use loops to process a two-dimensional array;

➤ develop collection classes using Java's `Vector` class;

➤ develop collection classes using Java's `Hashtable` class;

➤ use an `Enumeration` object.

16.1 Introduction

Back in chapter 6 we introduced you to the idea of an array. An array is a useful type that allows a collection of values to be stored together. We also showed you how to use an array to build your own collection classes. In this chapter we examine arrays in a bit more detail and take a look at some pre-defined collection classes that are available to you in the `java.util` package.

16.2 Multi-dimensional arrays

Do you remember the temperature reading example we used in chapter 6? There we used an array to hold seven temperature readings (one for each day of the week):

```
double[] temperature; // declare array reference
temperature = new double [7]; // create array of 7 double values
```

Creating an array allowed us to use loops when processing these values, rather than having to repeat the same bit of code seven times – once for each different temperature variable. Now consider the situation where temperatures were required for the four weeks of a month. We could create four arrays as follows:

```
double[] temperature1 = new int [7]; // to hold week 1 temperatures
double[] temperature2 = new int [7]; // to hold week 2 temperatures
double[] temperature3 = new int [7]; // to hold week 3 temperatures
double[] temperature4 = new int [7]; // to hold week 4 temperatures
```

How would the temperatures for these four months be entered? The obvious solution would be to write four loops, one to process each array:

```
// enter week 1 temperature
for (int i = 0; i< temperature1.length; i++)
{
   System.out.println("Enter temperature for week 1 day " + (i+1));
   temperature1[i] =EasyIn.getDouble();
}
// repeat this three more times for the remaining three arrays
```

While this would work, imagine what you would have to do if you had to enter temperatures for 52 weeks! Luckily there is an alternative approach – create a **multi-dimensional** array.

A multi-dimensional array is an array that has *more than one* subscript. So far the arrays that we have shown you have had only one subscript – for this reason they are very often referred to as **one-dimensional** arrays. However, an array may have as many subscripts as is necessary (up to the limit of the memory on your machine). Usually, no more than two subscripts will ever need to be used. An array with two subscripts is called a **two-dimensional** array. To create a two-dimensional (2D) array simply provide the size of both subscripts. In this example we have four lots of seven temperatures:

```
double [][] temperature ; // declares a 2D array
temperature = new double [4][7]; // creates memory for a 4 by 7 array
```

Whereas you would think of a one-dimensional array as a list, you would probably think of a two-dimensional array as a table (although actually it is implemented in Java as an array of arrays). The name of each item in a two-dimensional array is the array name, plus the row and column index (see figure 16.1).

Note again that both row and column indices begin at zero. With a two-dimensional array, nested loops are required to process each element – one loop for each array index. As it is normal to think of days and weeks beginning at one and not zero, in the following code fragment we've started our day and week counters at 1, and then taken one off these counters to get back to the appropriate array index:

```
// the outer loop controls the week row
for (int week = 1; week <= temperature.length; week++)
{
   // the inner loop controls the day column
   for (int day = 1; day <=temperature[week].length; day++)
   {
      System.out.println("enter temperature for week " + week
                      + " and day " + day);
      /* as array indices start at zero not 1, we must take one off the loop
         counters */
      temperature[week-1][day-1] = EasyIn.getDouble();
   }
}
```

Notice that in a multi-dimensional array, the `length` attribute returns the length of the first index (that is what you would think of as a the number of rows):

```
// here, the length attribute returns 4 (the number of rows)
for (int week = 1; week <= temperature.length; week++)
```

The number of columns is determined by examining the length of a particular row:

```
// the length of a row returns the number of columns (7 in this case)
for (int day = 1; day <=temperature[week].length; day++)
```

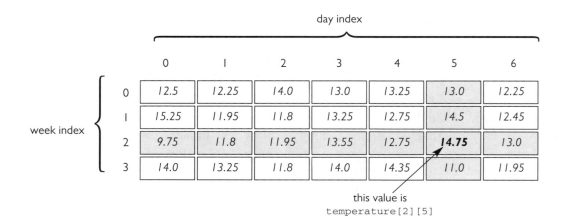

Fig 16.1   To access an element in a 2D array requires both a row and a column index

16.3   *The NoughtsAndCrosses class*

Noughts and crosses (Tic Tac Toe) is a traditional two-player game for children, that involves a three by three grid of squares. A player wins a game when they get a line of noughts, or crosses. Figure 16.2 provides some screen shots of this game being played.

As you can see from figure 16.2, the game consists of a board with nine squares. Each of these squares is, in fact, an `awt Button`. The layout suggests that a two dimensional array of buttons would be a good way to implement this board, so that's exactly what we'll do. An array of visual components is perfectly valid. We would create this array in the obvious way:

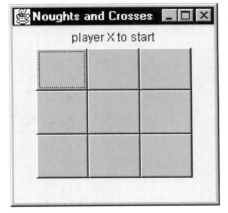

a) initially player X is asked to move.

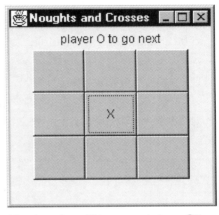

b) when player X has moved player O is asked to move.

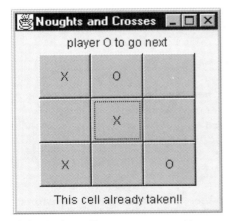

c) here, player O attempts to move into the centre cell that is already taken by player X.

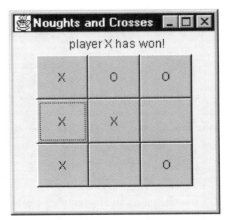

d) player X has won this game because she has completed a line of 3 X's.

Fig 16.2   Some sample screen shots from a game of noughts and crosses

```
Button [][] cell; // declare 'cell' to be a 2D array of buttons
cell = new Button [3][3]; // create memory for a 3 by 3 array of buttons
```

Unlike the array we used in section 16.2, this array is an array of objects. To add a `Button` object into this array we have to use the `Button` constructor to create such a button. In this game, the button's label indicates a particular player (X or O) occupying that given cell. Initially no cell will be occupied, so a blank label is required. For example:

```
cell[0][0] = new Button();
```

Each button also needs to respond to a mouse click and therefore requires an `Action-Listener` to be added to it. For example:

```
cell[0][0].addActionListener(this);
```

Finally, to achieve the desired layout we will add each button to a `Panel`. Assuming this panel is called `board` we get the following:

```
board.add(cell[0][0]);
```

We will discuss the layout policy of this panel later. Obviously, we need to create nine new buttons, add nine `ActionListeners` and add each of these nine buttons to the board. Rather than repeat the above lines nine times, we use nested loops as follows:

```
for (int i = 0; i<3; i++) // row index
{
  for (int j=0; j<3;j++) // column index
  {
    cell[i][j] = new Button(); // create new button
    cell[i][j].addActionListener(this); // add listener
    board.add(cell[i][j]); // add to board
  }
}
```

As you can see, using a 2D array of buttons (rather than creating nine individual buttons) allowed us to use loops to reduce the coding effort. This array will also be useful when processing the mouse click events from each button. Rather than having to have nine **if** statements to capture the appropriate mouse click event, we can now just use a single **if** statement and place that **if** statement within a pair of nested loops:

```
public void actionPerformed(ActionEvent e)
{
  for (int i = 0; i<3; i++)
  {
    for (int j=0; j<3;j++)
    {
      if (e.getSource()== cell[i][j])
      {
        // code to process event here
      }
    }
  }
}
```

The code for this noughts and crosses class is now presented below. Examine it carefully, and then we will discuss it in more detail:

THE *NoughtsAndCrosses* CLASS

```
import java.awt.*;
import java.awt.event.*;

public class NoughtsAndCrosses extends Panel implements ActionListener
{
  private boolean gameOver; // to keep track of the game status
  private String player; // to keep track of the current player
  private Panel board = new Panel(); // to hold the nine cells
  private Button [][]cell= new Button [3][3]; // the cells
  // these next two labels provide a border around the cells
  private Label blankL = new Label(" ");
  private Label blankR = new Label(" ");
  // the next two labels are centre aligned
  private Label error = new Label (" ",1);
  private Label info = new Label ("player X to start", 1);

  // the constructor
  public NoughtsAndCrosses()
  {
    gameOver = false;
    player = "X"; // player X to start the game
    board.setLayout(new GridLayout(3,3)); // discussed later
    // creates and adds nine buttons to the board
    for (int i = 0; i<3; i++)
    {
      for (int j=0; j<3;j++)
      {
```

```
      cell[i][j] = new Button();
      cell[i][j].addActionListener(this);
      board.add(cell[i][j]);
    }
  }
  // positions the items on the screen
  setLayout(new BorderLayout());
  add("Center",board);
  add ("West", blankL);
  add("East", blankR);
  add("North", info);
  add("South",error);
}

public void actionPerformed(ActionEvent e)
{
  if (!gameOver) // process mouse click only if game is not over
  {
    for (int i = 0; i<3; i++)
    {
      for (int j=0; j<3;j++)
      {
        if (e.getSource()== cell[i][j])
        {
          processEvent(i,j); // call worker method to process event
        }
      }
    }
  }
}

// worker method to process a given button press
private void processEvent(int i, int j)
{
  // check no attempt made to move into an occupied cell
  if (cell[i][j].getLabel().equals("X") ||
              cell[i][j].getLabel().equals("O"))
  {
    error.setText("This cell already taken!!");
  }
  else
  {
    // clear any error messages
    error.setText(" ");
    // change button label to current player
    cell[i][j].setLabel(player);
```

```java
    // check whether this moves results in game over
    if (hasWon(i, j)) // process game over
    {
      info.setText(" player " + player + " has won!");
      gameOver = true;
    }
    else // process game not over
    {
      // change player
      if (player.equals("X"))
      {
        player = "O";
      }
      else
      {
        player = "X";
      }
      info.setText("player " +player+" to go next");
    }
  }
}

// worker method to check if game over
private boolean hasWon(int i, int j)
{
  boolean won;
  // check current row
  won = true;
  for(int col = 0; col<3; col++)
  {
      if (!cell[i][col].getLabel().equals(player))
      {
        won = false;
      }
  }
  if (!won)
  {
    // check current column
    won = true;
    for(int row = 0; row<3; row++)
    {
      if (!cell[row][j].getLabel().equals(player))
      {
        won = false;
      }
    }
  }
```

```
      if (!won)
      {
        // check left diagonal
        won = true;
        for(int num = 0; num<3; num++)
        {
          if (!cell[num][num].getLabel().equals(player))
          {
            won = false;
          }
        }
      }
      if (!won)
      {
        // check right diagonal
        won = true;
        for(int num = 0; num<3; num++)
        {
          if (!cell[2-num][num].getLabel().equals(player))
          {
            won = false;
          }
        }
      }
      return won;
    }
}
```

First of all, let's go back and consider the board panel. We are using this panel to hold the nine buttons and we would like the buttons to appear as a three by three grid. An easy way to achieve this is to give the panel a **grid layout**. This is a layout policy that we have not discussed yet. A grid layout policy allows you to specify the number of rows and columns for the items you wish to add. In this case we require three rows and three columns of buttons so we specify the layout as follows:

```
board.setLayout(new GridLayout(3,3));
```

This layout policy ensures that once three buttons are added to the panel, the next three would be on the next row, and the last three on the final row. Now, let's go back and examine the actionPerformed method in a bit more detail. You can see that this method calls a worker method, processEvent, which processes a mouse click event for a given button. Initially, the label of the given button is checked to ensure that the player has not moved into an occupied square. A square is occupied when its label is set to "X" or "O".

```
if (cell[i][j].getLabel().equals("X") || cell[i][j].getLabel().equals("O"))
{ // 'error' label used to display error messages
  error.setText("This cell already taken!!");
}
```

If the cell is not taken the move is allowed to go ahead. This involves clearing any error messages that may have been displayed and re-setting the cell's label to the current player:

```
error.setText("");
cell[i][j].setLabel(player);
```

Two possibilities now arise; either the player has won the game, in which case a congratulatory message is displayed, or the game has not been won and the current player changes to the next player:

```
if (hasWon(i, j)) // calls another worker method
{
   // code to set congratulatory message and gameOver status
}
else
{
   // code to change player and inform them of their go
}
```

Again, this method calls another worker method, hasWon, to determine whether or not a player has won the game.

There are four ways in which a player can win a game:

* the player completes a row;
* the player completes a column;
* the player completes the left diagonal;
* the player completes the right diagonal.

Figure 16.3 illustrates a player having won a game by completing a row. Here the last move was at 'i' position 1, and 'j' position 2. In order to check this row we must check the labels of cell[1][0], cell[1][1] and cell[1][2] and see if they are all set to the current player ("X"). If at least one label is not set to the current player, then the player has not won this game by completing a row. As you can see, in order to do this, the original 'i' position (1 in this case) of each button remains the same, while the 'j' position changes. This can be achieved by fixing the row number to the current row and using a loop to check every column in that row:

```
won = true; // assume the player has won
for(int col = 0; col<3; col++) // move through the columns
{
    // keep the row fixed at 'i'
    if (!cell[i][col].getLabel().equals(player)) // check label
    {
        won = false; // indicate failure to win
    }
}
```

At the end of this loop, if the value of 'won' is **true** the player has won, otherwise other possibilities for winning must be checked. If a player wins a game by completing a column, then the column index will be fixed to the current column:

```
won = true;
for(int row = 0; row<3; row++)
{
    // column index remains fixed
    if (!cell[row][j].getLabel().equals(player))
    {
        won = false;
    }
}
```

The final two possibilities for winning a game are if the player completes a left or right diagonal. Figure 16.4 illustrates a player winning by completing a left diagonal.

You can see from figure 16.4, that to check the left diagonal we need to check `cell[0][0]`, `cell[1][1]` and `cell[2][2]` and that in each case the row index is the same as the column index. Once again, a loop can be used to check this for us:

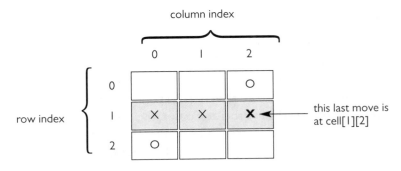

Fig 16.3   When a player wins the game by completing a row, the row index for each winning cell remains the same

```
won = true;
for(int num = 0; num<3; num++)
{ // keep row and column index the same
   if (!cell[num][num].getLabel().equals(player))
   {
      won = false;
   }
}
```

Finally, when checking the right diagonal, the cells to check are `cell[2][0]`, `cell[1][1]` and `cell[0][2]`. You can see that the column index moves up from 0 to 2. The row index can then be calculated by subtracting the row index from 2.

Program 16.1 now runs this game in an `EasyFrame`.

PROGRAM 16.1

```
import java.awt.*;
public class RunNoughtsAndCrosses
{
   public static void main(String[] args)
   {
      EasyFrame gameFrame = new EasyFrame();
      gameFrame.setTitle("Noughts and Crosses");
      NoughtsAndCrosses game = new NoughtsAndCrosses();
      gameFrame.setSize(210,210);
      gameFrame.add(game);
      gameFrame.setBackground(Color.yellow);
      gameFrame.setVisible(true);
   }
}
```

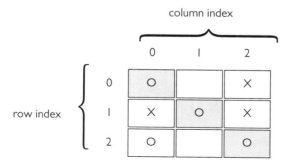

Fig 16.4 **When a player has won the game by completing a left diagonal, the row and column index for each winning cell is the same**

16.4   *The* **Vector** *class*

An array is a very useful type in Java but it has its restrictions:

- once an array is created it must be sized, and this size is fixed;
- it contains very few useful pre-defined methods.

Think back to the `StringList` class of chapter 6. We used an array to implement this class. In doing so we had to put an upper limit to the size of this list. Sometimes, however, an upper limit is not known. Just creating a very big array is very wasteful of memory – and what happens if even this very big array proves to be too small? Also, to carry out any interesting processing (like searching the array) required us to write complex algorithms.

One solution to the first problem would be to create a reasonably sized array and, when the array is full, copy this array into a slightly bigger array and use this new array and continue doing this every time the array gets full. A solution to the second problem would be to do as we did with the `ObjectList` class in chapter 7, that is wrap the array in a generic collection class and provide useful array methods like searching in this wrapper class.

Luckily we do not need to go to such lengths, the Java people have already done this for us! They've developed a generic collection class that contains an array but can grow as more elements are added to it, and this class provides lots of useful methods. The name of this class is `Vector`. It is to be found in the `java.util` package. Table 16.1 describes some of the most useful methods of the `Vector` class.

Table 16.1 contains just a selection of vector methods. A more comprehensive list can be found at www.mcgraw-hill.co.uk/textbooks/charatan.

As you can see, several methods have two implementations. For example, to add an element into a vector you may use `add` or `addElement`. The more concise names (such as `add` and `get`) have been added into recent versions of Java to be more consistent with other Java collection classes. We will use these concise names in our examples; if you have an older compiler you should replace these methods with their longer name counterparts.

The `StringList` class of chapter 6 was developed to store a list of fruit names. At the time we used an array to implement this class. Look how much simpler this would be if we use a vector instead. First, we create a vector object, `list` say, to contain the list of fruit:

```
Vector list = new Vector();
```

This syntax is much less messy than the array syntax, and there is no need to specify any upper limit. Of course, in order to have access to the `Vector` class we need to import the `java.util` package at the top of the program:

```
import java.util.*;
```

Table 16.1   Some *Vector* methods

Method	Description	Inputs	Outputs
`Vector`	Creates a new empty vector.	None	None
`add`	Adds the given item to the end of the vector (available since Java version 1.2). This method always returns **true**.[1]	An item of type `Object`	An item of type **boolean**
`addElement`	Identical in functionality to the `add` method.	An item of type `Object`	None
`get`	Returns a reference to the item at a given position in the vector. The position acts like an array subscript. As with arrays, positions begin at zero (available since Java 1.2).	An item of type **int**	An item of type `Object`
`elementAt`	Identical in functionality to the `get` method.	An item of type **int**	An item of type `Object`
`remove`	Removes the first occurrence of the given element from the vector. Return **true** if the element was in the vector and **false** otherwise (available since Java 1.2).	An item of type `Object`	An item of type **boolean**
`removeElement`	Identical in functionality to the `remove` method.	An item of type `Object`	An item of type **boolean**
`contains`	Returns **true** if the vector contains the given element, and **false** otherwise.	An item of type `Object`	An item of type **boolean**
`isEmpty`	Returns **true** if the vector is empty, and **false** otherwise.	None	An item of type **boolean**
`toString`	Returns a string representation of all the elements in the vector.	None	An item of type `String`
`size`	Returns the number of elements within the vector	None	An item of type **int**

[1] From Java 1.2 onwards, a `List` interface is introduced, which contains several useful list methods. The `Vector` class has been extended to implement this interface. In order to do so, an add method had to be implemented to send back a **boolean** value (usually used to indicate success or otherwise of adding the element into the list). As a value can *always* be added into a vector, this method always returns a value of **true**.

Now, we can add some fruit to the list:

```
list.add("Apple");
list.add("Pear");
list.add("Orange");
```

Again, no need to keep track of where to add these items, and if the list should ever become full – the Vector class takes care of this for us by automatically expanding to accommodate extra values.

Since the Vector class has a toString method, we can print the entire vector out on the screen with a println statement:[2]

```
System.out.println(list); // implicitly calls the toString method of Vector
```

When a vector is converted to a string it is enclosed in square brackets as follows:

```
[Apple, Pear, Orange]
```

Removing items from a vector is easy – just use the remove method:[3]

```
list.remove("Pear");
```

Now, if we printed out the vector again we would get the following:

```
[Apple, Orange]
```

As you can see, the methods provided with the Vector class are very useful and considerably reduce your coding effort when compared to an array. The only thing you have to be careful of is to remember that Vector is a *generic* collection class. This is great when it comes to adding items to a list, as vectors can be used to hold items of *any* class, but when the vector returns items it always returns the item as an object of type Object. Just as with the generic collection class we developed in chapter 7 (ObjectList), items returned from such a collection need to be type cast back to their appropriate type. So, to return the first item in our list of fruit names, we could use the get method, but we must type cast the returned item back to an item of type String:

```
System.out.print("the first item in the list is ");
System.out.print( (String) list.get(0)); // first item at position zero
```

---

[2] For the vector to be converted to a string effectively, the contained class must also have a toString method defined. The String class has such a method.

[3] For the remove method to work effectively, the contained class must override the equals method of Object. The String class provides such a method.

Another drawback that you must remember with all generic collection classes like Vector, when compared to an array, is that they can only hold *objects* not items of scalar type.

16.5   *The IdSet class*

Consider a company that wishes each of its employees to have a unique name when logging on to their systems. Such a name is often called an identity (ID). This unique ID can be combined with a company domain name to provide users with unique e-mail addresses. We will develop an application that keeps track of all IDs, so that no two identical IDs are ever created. Effectively this will require us to implement a collection of IDs in which there are no *repetitions*. Mathematically, a collection without repetitions is often called a **set**, so we will call this class IdSet.

When developing this class we will assume that IDs are stored as strings and that there are restrictions on the size of the ID name. Also, we will use a vector to implement this set. The UML design for this class is given in figure 16.5.

The methods specified in figure 16.5 are the minimum we would need to code in order to develop this application (more could clearly be added). A description of each of these methods is given below:

IdSet(int, int, String)
This constructor takes two integer parameters that are used to set the minimum and maximum size of valid IDs, as well as a string representing the global domain name. The set of id names is initially an empty vector.

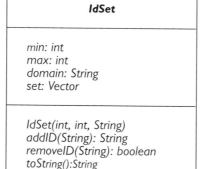

Fig 16.5   The *IdSet* class

addID(String): String

This method takes an ID as a parameter and adds that ID to the set of current ID names, returning the appropriate e-mail address for this user as a string. If a user name is given as a parameter invalid (either because it already exists, is too short or is too long) an InvalidUserNameException is thrown.

removeID(String): boolean

This method removes the given ID from the set of ID names. A value of **true** is returned if the given ID was removed successfully, or **false** otherwise.

toString(): String

This method returns a string representation of the list of user IDs.

Before we present the code for this class to you, we need to code the InvalidUserName-Exception class:

THE *InvalidUserNameException* CLASS

```
class InvalidUserNameException extends Exception
{
  public InvalidUserNameException()
  {
    super ("this user name is not valid");
  }

  public InvalidUserNameException(String message)
  {
    super (message);
  }
}
```

There is nothing new in this class so let's now turn to the code for the IdSet class. Examine it closely and then we will discuss it:

```
import java.util.*; // for the Vector class
class IdSet
{
  private int min;
  private int max;
  private String domain;
  private Vector set;

  public IdSet(int minIn, int maxIn, String domainIn )
  {
    min = minIn;
    max = maxIn;
    domain = domainIn;
    set = new Vector(); // this Vector constructor creates an empty vector
  }

  public String addID(String idIn) throws InvalidUserNameException
  {
    if (idIn.length()< min) // ID name too short
    {
      throw new InvalidUserNameException
        ("user name must have a minimum of " + min + " characters");
    }
    if (idIn.length()>max) // ID name too long
    {
      throw new InvalidUserNameException
        ("user name can have a maximum of " + max + " characters");
    }
    if (set.contains(idIn)) // ID name already taken
    {
      throw new InvalidUserNameException
        ("this user name is already taken");
    }
    else
    {
      set.add(idIn); // call 'add' method of Vector
      return(idIn+"@"+domain); // send back e-mail address
    }
  }

  public boolean removeID(Object idIn)
  {
    return set.remove(idIn); // call 'remove' method of Vector
  }

  public String toString ()
  {
    return set.toString(); // call 'toString' method of Vector
  }
}
```

As you can see from the code above, this class really acts like a wrapper class around the Vector class. Let's take a closer look at the addID method. This provides a wrapper for the add method of Vector. Before the ID is added however, a check is made to ensure that, first, the ID name is not too short or too long.

```
if (idIn.length()< min) // ID name too short
{
   throw new InvalidUserNameException
   ("user name must have a minimum of " + min + " characters");
}
if (idIn.length()>max) // ID name too long
{
   throw new InvalidUserNameException
      ("user name can have a maximum of " + max + " characters");
}
```

The final check before adding the ID name is to ensure that the name is not already taken. The contains method of Vector allows us to check whether an item exists within the vector:[4]

```
if (set.contains(idIn)) // calling the 'contains' method of Vector
{
   throw new InvalidUserNameException("this user name is already taken");
}
```

If none of these exceptions is thrown, the ID is added to the set, by calling the add method of Vector, and an e-mail address is generated (by adding the ID onto the domain name) and returned.

```
set.add(idIn);
return(idIn+"@"+domain);
```

Figures 16.6–16.9 illustrate this class running in a GUI, assuming a domain name of *JavaRules.com*.

The code to create this GUI and run it in an EasyFrame can be found at www.mcgraw-hill.co.uk/textbooks/charatan or copied from the accompanying CD-ROM.

---

[4] Like the remove method of Vector, the contains method requires the contained class to have an equals method defined. Again the String class has such a method.

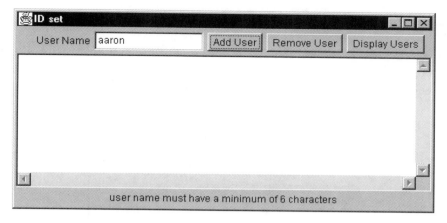

Fig 16.6   Here, an attempt is made to add an invalid user name

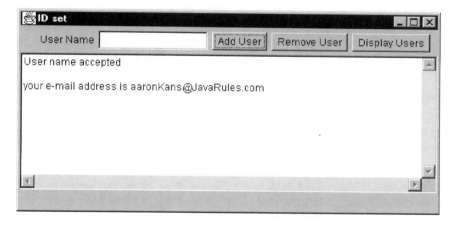

Fig 16.7   Here a user name is successfully added

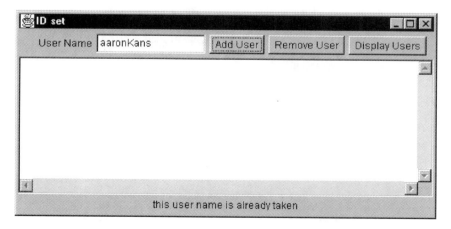

Fig 16.8   Here a new user name has been picked that has already been taken

16.6 *Enhancing the user ID application*

Let's consider the user ID application a little further. Assume now that each user, as well as choosing an ID, must also choose a password. Table 16.2 illustrates some passwords that may have been chosen for the users depicted in figure 16.9.

Table 16.2 Each user chooses a password	
User ID	**Password**
aaronKans	popcorn
quentin	television
godfried	elephant

How could we implement this association between a user ID and a password? There are several possibilities.

We could use a 2D array of strings. Alternatively, we could try using a pair of vectors. Vectors have an advantage over arrays in that they do not have an upper limit on their size, so we would not have to put an upper limit on the number of users we could process. However, both arrays and vectors prove cumbersome when having to deal with associations between values.

For example, think about how you would check a user's password in a 2D array. You would have to step through the array and look for a given user ID to determine that user's index in the array, and then look at the password column to find the corresponding password at that index. As vectors use the same indexing system as arrays, the same process applies to vectors.

The ideal solution would be to have a collection class that is something like a vector (so no upper limit on the size is required), but where the items used to look up values are not continuous numbers but *any object*. In this case we would like to have user IDs as a means of looking up passwords.

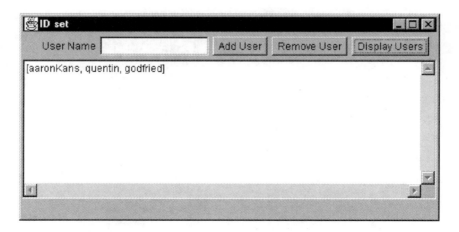

Fig 16.9   Once a number of users have been added they are displayed

The `java.util` package provides two such collection classes, one is the `HashMap` class and the other the `Hashtable` class. Both classes provide very similar methods but the `HashMap` class is available only with newer versions of the Java, so we will take a look at the `Hashtable` class.

16.7   *The Hashtable class*

A **hash table** is a well known concept in the field of computing. It is often referred to as a *look up* table. It consists of a list of entries, each of which consists of a **key** and **value**. A value in the hash table is *looked up* (accessed) by submitting a *key*. For example, the bank details of an account holder can be looked up by entering an account number. For this to work, the keys in a hash table must all be unique.

Whereas array and vector values are looked up by means of an index *number*, values in a hash table are looked up by means of an *object* (of any class). Returning to the account holder example, this would mean that the hash table key could be a `String` object (representing the account number) but not a primitive type such as `int`.[5] Table 16.3 lists some of the methods found in the `Hashtable` class, a more comprehensive list can be found at www.mcgraw-hill.co.uk/textbooks/charatan.

As you can see from table 16.3, the `Hashtable` class provides some powerful methods. Try and imagine the amount of work that would have had to go into implementing similar methods if an array or vector had been used. With a hash table you get them all for free!

Returning to the ID example, a user ID (which is unique for each user) could be the key to the hash table. We will use a `String` type for the user ID. The password would then be the value looked up by this key. We could create a hash table of users as follows:

```
Hashtable users = new Hashtable();
```

To add a user ID and password to this hash table we use the `put` method as follows:

```
users.put("aaronKans", "popcorn");
```

Note that the `put` method treats the first parameter as a key item and the second parameter as its associated value. Really, we should be a bit more careful before we add user IDs and passwords into this hash table – only user IDs that are not already taken should be added. If we did not check this, we would end up overwriting a previous user's password. The `containsKey` method allows us to check this:

---

[5] If a primitive type is required as a hash table key, the corresponding wrapper class should be used.

Method	Description	Inputs	Outputs
Hashtable	Creates a new empty hash table.	None	None
put	Adds the given key and value pair to the hash table. This method returns the previous value of the specified key in this hash table, or **null** if it did not have one.	Two items of type Object	An item of type Object
get	Returns the value associated with the given key. Returns **null** if this key is not in the hash table.	An item of type Object	An item of type Object
remove	Removes the given key (if it exists) and its corresponding value from this hash table. Like the put method, this method returns the previous value of the specified key in this hash table, or **null** if it did not have one.	An item of type Object	An item of type Object
containsKey	Returns **true** if the specified object is a key in this hash table, and **false** otherwise.	An item of type Object	An item of type **boolean**
isEmpty	Returns **true** if the hash table is empty, and **false** otherwise.	None	An item of type **boolean**
toString	Returns a string representation of all the elements in the hash table.	None	An item of type String
size	Returns the number of keys in this hash table.	None	An item of type **int**

Table 16.3   Some Hashtable methods

```
if (!users.containsKey("aaronKans")) // check ID not already taken
{
   users.put("aaronKans", "popcorn");
}
```

Later, a user might be asked to enter his or her ID and password before being able to access company resources. The get method can be used to check whether or not the correct password has been entered:

```
System.out.print("enter user ID ");
String idIn = EasyIn.getString();
System.out.print("enter password ");
String passwordIn = EasyIn.getString();
// find out recorded password for this user (type cast required)
String getPassword = (String) users.get(idIn);
if ( getPassword.equals(passwordIn)) // check password entered is correct
{
    // allow access to company resources
}
```

As with all generic collections, when an item is returned from the hash table (using the get method), that item is of type Object. This item has to be type cast back to the appropriate type – in this case String.

```
// 'get' method returns item of type 'Object', must be type cast to String
String getPassword = (String) users.get(idIn);
```

Like the Vector class, the Hashtable class provides a toString method so that the items in the hash table can be displayed:

```
System.out.print(users); // implicitly calls 'toString' method of Hashtable
```

Key and value pairs are displayed in braces. If we assume that ID and password values are entered as given in table 16.2, in the same order as given in table 16.2, this would produce the following output:

```
{godfried = elephant, aaronKans = popcorn, quentin = television}
```

As you can see, the ordering of the elements when displayed does not match the ordering in which they were added. That is because (unlike a Vector) a Hashtable is an *unordered* collection class. The physical order of items does not correspond to any logical ordering of keys or input. In this example that is not a problem as we are not interested in the order in which items were entered.

There is another problem though. We might wish to step through all the elements within a collection in order to process them. With both a vector and an array this is easy; each item has a number index so we can use a **for** loop to scan through the elements. However items within a hash table do not have a number index.

To get around this problem, the Hashtable class provides two methods, keys and elements, to scan through the elements of the hash table. Both methods return a special object, called an Enumeration object, for this purpose.

16.8 *Enumeration objects*

An Enumeration object provides methods that are given in the Enumeration interface. The Enumeration interface consists of just two methods:

THE *Enumeration* INTERFACE

```
interface Enumeration
{
  public boolean hasMoreElements();
  public Object nextElement();
}
```

These two methods should work as follows:

- The hasMoreElements method determines whether there are any more elements in the collection to scan through.
- The nextElement method effectively pulls out another element in the collection and returns a reference to it (the order in which items are returned from a collection do not correspond to the order in which they were added). Because the collection is generic, the type of this element is Object, it must be type cast to the appropriate type to be of use.

To fully appreciate how this works, we need to show you how to use this Enumeration object in practice. As we mentioned in the last section, the Hashtable class provides two methods that return Enumeration objects:

- keys: returns an Enumeration object to scan through the keys of the hash table;
- elements: returns an Enumeration object to scan through the values of the hash table.

So, for example, if we wished to display a list of user IDs from the users hash table of section 16.7, we would call the keys method as follows:

```
Enumeration idList = users.keys(); // 'keys' returns the key collection
```

The Enumeration object that we created above, idList, can respond to the two Enumeration methods hasMoreElements and nextElement. These two methods should always be used in tandem. The next element should never be retrieved (with the nextElement method) before first ensuring such an element exists (with the hasMoreElements) method. Often the two methods are combined in a **while** loop as follows:

```
while (idList.hasMoreElements()) // ensure more elements exist to scan
{
    String currentID = (String) idList.nextElement(); // pick next element
    System.out.println(currentID); // process element as required
}
```

Note the need to type cast the returned element back to String. When the end of a collection has been reached, there is no method to return to the beginning of that collection. To revisit the elements within a collection a new Enumeration object needs to be created.

By the way, the Vector class also has a method that returns an Enumeration object. This method is also called elements and it allows you to scan through the items of the vector. However, with a vector a **for** loop may be more useful as the order of the items is controlled by the loop, whereas the items returned by an Enumeration object are unordered.[6]

16.9   *The BookTable class*

Consider an application to store and search the details of books held in a shop. The initial UML design for this application is given in figure 16.10. As you can see, the type of the BookTable attribute, 'books', has yet to be decided.

Before we consider the BookTable class, here is the code for the Book class.

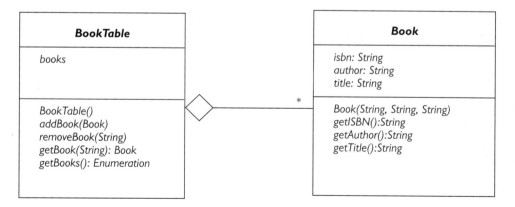

Fig 16.10   Initial design for the book store application

---

[6] Some of the newer collection classes in the java.util package provide Iterator objects to scan through the elements of a collection. Iterator objects implement the Iterator interface which is exactly like the Enumeration interface except it includes an extra method, remove, to remove the current item from the list.

THE *Book* CLASS

```
class Book
{
  private String isbn;
  private String title;
  private String author;

  public Book(String isbnIn, String titleIn, String authorIn)
  {
    isbn = isbnIn;
    title = titleIn;
    author = authorIn;
  }

  public String getISBN()
  {
    return isbn;
  }

  public String getTitle()
  {
    return title;
  }

  public String getAuthor()
  {
    return author;
  }
}
```

The isbn attribute represents a book's International Standard Book Number (ISBN). This is a unique number allocated to all published books.[7] The code for this class is fairly straightforward so let's now turn to the BookTable class.

From figure 16.10 you can see that the BookTable attribute, books, is acting as a container for Book objects. We need to decide on the Java type for this attribute. We could use an array but adding and removing books becomes a complex task. A vector is better here, but searching is still difficult. A hash table would simplify both tasks by taking care of the details of adding, removing and searching.

Now, what do you think should be the *key* for the hash table? Well, keys have to be unique, so ISBNs would be sensible.

What then would be the *value* associated with this key? Logically, at this point, it may make sense to think of the value as being the remaining book details (author and title). However, this would require us to define a new class (BookDetails say) that contained just these two

---

[7] The current recognized standard for an ISBN is a 10 digit number. In a real application, the format of ISBNs submitted should be checked against this standard.

attributes. Not only would this waste the effort we spent on implementing the Book class, it would also introduce a class that has no real-world counterpart. We don't really observe BookDetail objects but we do observe Book objects. For this reason it makes sense for a complete Book object to be the value that is returned from the hash table, even though its ISBN number is also a key. Before we implement the BookTable class, here is a description of each of its methods:

BookTable()
This constructor creates an empty book list.

addBook(Book)
Adds the given book into the book list. If the ISBN provided is already in the list an InvalidISBNException is thrown (see below).

removeBook(String)
This method takes a book's ISBN (as a string), and removes the book from the list. If the ISBN provided is not present in the book list an InvalidISBNException is thrown.

getBook(String): Book
This method takes an ISBN of a book in the book list, and returns the given book. If the ISBN provided is not present in the book list an InvalidISBNException is thrown.

getBook(): Enumeration
This method returns an Enumeration object to scan through the books in the book list.

As you can see, we have made use of exceptions to communicate ISBN errors. Here is the code for the InvalidISBNException class.

THE *InvalidISBNException* CLASS

```
class InvalidISBNException extends Exception
{
  public InvalidISBNException()
  {
    super ("ISBN error");
  }
  public InvalidISBNException(String message)
  {
    super (message);
  }
}
```

The code for the BookTable class is now presented below, take a look at it and then we will discuss it.

THE *BookTable* CLASS

```java
import java.util.*; // for Hashtable
class BookTable
{
  private Hashtable books;
  public BookTable()
  {
    books = new Hashtable(); // initially empty
  }

  public void addBook(Book book)throws InvalidISBNException
  {
    String isbn = book.getISBN(); // ISBN extracted for key
    if (books.containsKey(isbn)) // check ISBN not already in use
    {
      throw new InvalidISBNException ("this ISBN is taken");
    }
    books.put(isbn, book); // add book to list with ISBN as key
  }
  public void removeBook (String isbnIn)throws InvalidISBNException
  {
    if (!books.containsKey(isbnIn)) // check ISBN in list
    {
      throw new InvalidISBNException ("this ISBN does not exist");
    }
    books.remove(isbnIn); // removes ISBN and associated book from list
  }

  public Book getBook(String isbnIn)throws InvalidISBNException
  {
    if (!books.containsKey(isbnIn)) // check ISBN in list
    {
      throw new InvalidISBNException ("this ISBN does not exist");
    }
    return (Book)books.get(isbnIn); // get associated book
  }

  public Enumeration getBooks()
  {
    return books.elements(); // returns book list as an enumeration object
  }
}
```

The code in the `BookTable` class should be fairly straightforward to follow. Figures 16.11–16.13 illustrate this class running in a GUI.

Once again, the code for this GUI can be found at www.mcgraw-hill.co.uk/textbooks/charatan or copied from the accompanying CD-ROM. We just draw your attention to the processing of the DISPLAY ALL BOOKS button.

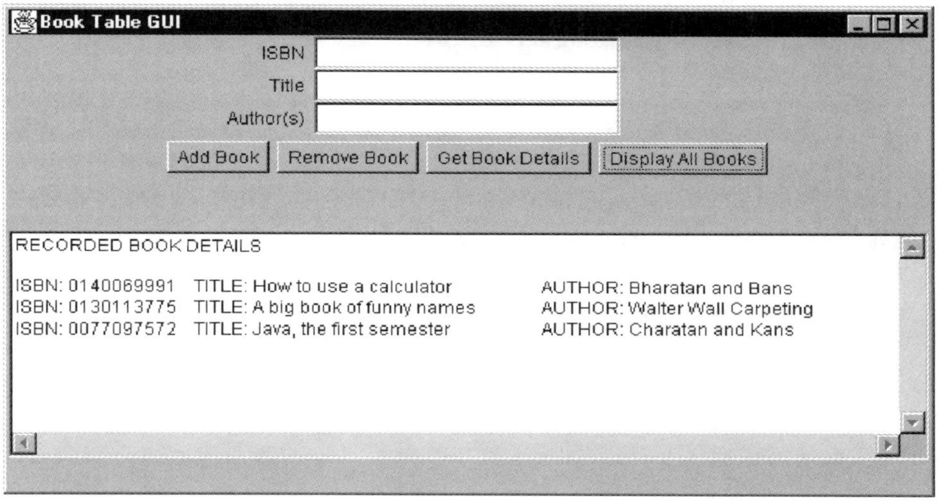

Fig 16.11   After entering three books, the list of books is displayed

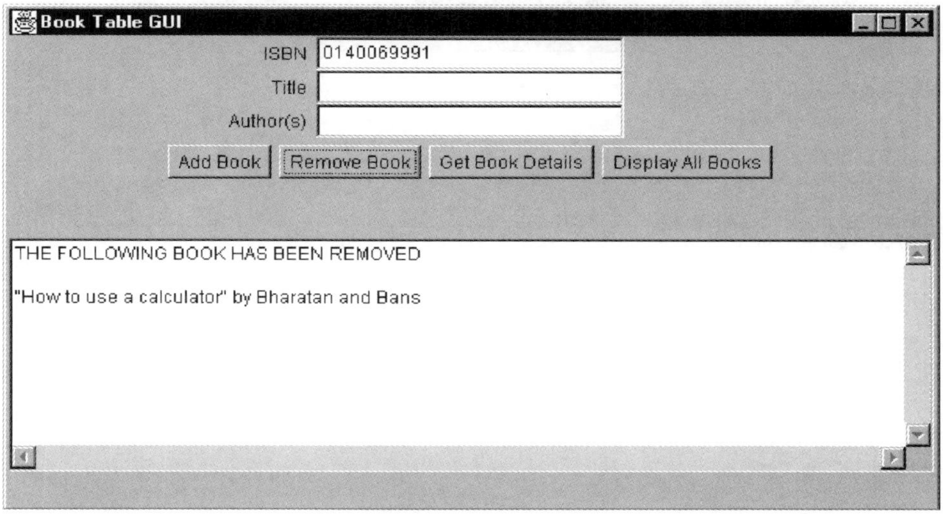

Fig 16.12   Here an unpopular book is removed from the list!

Here is the relevant code:

```
if(e.getSource() == displayButton)
{
  String details = "RECORDED BOOK DETAILS\n"; // string to be displayed
  Enumeration en = shop.getBooks(); // 'shop' is our BookTable object
  while(en.hasMoreElements()) // Enumeration methods used to scan ISBNs
  {
    Book thisBook =(Book)en.nextElement(); // current book
    // Book methods used to extract information
    details = details +"\nISBN: "+thisBook.getISBN();
    details = details +"\t TITLE: "+ thisBook.getTitle();
    details = details +"\t AUTHOR: "+ thisBook.getAuthor();
  }
  displayArea.setText(details); // book details displayed
}
```

As you can see, we are making use of the getBooks method of BookList that returns an Enumeration object to us.

```
Enumeration en = shop.getBooks();
```

This object can be used to scan through the list of books in the book list. A **while** loop of the form we showed you in section 16.8 is then used to scan through the books in the list, by calling methods hasMoreElements and nextElement:

Fig 16.13   Here, an ISBN is entered and the details of that book displayed

```
while(en.hasMoreElements())
{
    // some code here
    Book thisBook =(Book)en.nextElement();
    // some code to process this book here
}
```

Tutorial exercises

1. Consider an application that records the punctuality of a certain train.
   (a) Declare a 2D array, late, to hold the number of times the train was late for each day of the week, and for each week of the year.
   (b) Write a fragment of code that adds up the total number of days in the year when the train was late more than twice in a given day.
2. If you look back at figure 16.9, items in the IdSet object were presented (using the toString method of the vector class) as follows:

   [*aaronKans, quentin, godfried*]

   In standard maths texts, sets are usually presented as being enclosed in curly brackets:

   {aaronKans, quentin, godfried}

   Write the code for an additional IdSet method, toSet, which returns a set representation of the items in the list as a string. This method should make use of an Enumeration object as returned by the elements method of the Vector class.
3. Figure 16.13 gives the UML class design for an address book application:

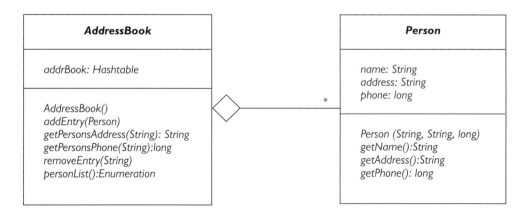

Fig 16.13   UML class design for the address book application

A description of each `AddressBook` method is given below:

AddressBook()
This constructor creates an empty address book.

addEntry(Person): boolean
Adds a given person into the address book. If the name provided is already in the address book an `InvalidNameException` is thrown.

getPersonsAddress(String): String
Takes a person's name and returns that person's address. If the name provided is not in the address book an `InvalidNameException` is thrown.

getPersonsPhone(String): long
Takes a person's name and returns that person's phone number. If the given name is not in the address book an `InvalidNameException` is thrown.

removeEntry(String): boolean
Takes a person's name and removes the associated entry from the address book. If the name was not originally in the address book an `InvalidNameException` is thrown.

personList(): Enumeration
Returns a list of all people in the address book as an `Enumeration` object.

Write the code for this `AddressBook` class.

Practical work

1. Download or copy from the accompanying CD-ROM the `NoughtsAndCrosses` class and program 16.1, which runs this game in an `EasyFrame`. Now, amend the `NoughtsAnd-Crosses` class so that the size of the grid is determined by a value sent to the constructor. Program 16.2 below can be used to test this class:

PROGRAM 16.2

```java
import java.awt.*;

public class RunNoughtsAndCrosses2
{
    public static void main(String[] args)
    {
        EasyFrame gameFrame = new EasyFrame();
        gameFrame.setTitle("Noughts and Crosses");
        System.out.print("how big do you want your grid? ");
        int size = EasyIn.getInt();
        NoughtsAndCrosses game = new NoughtsAndCrosses (size);
        gameFrame.setSize(70*size,70*size);
        gameFrame.add(game);
        gameFrame.setBackground(Color.yellow);
        gameFrame.setVisible(true);
    }
}
```

---

2. Download or copy from the CD-ROM the `InvalidUserNameException` class and amend the `IdSet` class by making the additions you considered in tutorial task 2. Then:
   (a) download or copy from the CD-ROM the classes in appendix 3 that run the `IdSet` class in a GUI;
   (b) change the event-handler for the "Display Users" button by making use of the `toSet` method you developed in tutorial question 2 so that the users are presented in standard set notation.

3. Download or copy from the CD-ROM the `InvalidISBNException` class, the `Book` class and the `BookTable` class. Then:
   (a) download or copy from the CD-ROM the classes that run the `BookTable` GUI in an `EasyFrame`;
   (b) add an extra SEARCH button to the GUI which displays all the books written by a given author(s).

4. From the design given in figure 16.13 implement the `Person` class and then
   (a) implement an `InvalidNameException` class,
   (b) implement the `AddressBook` class you developed from tutorial task 3,
   (c) write an `AddressBookTester` class to test the methods of the `AddressBook` class.

ADVANCED GRAPHICS PROGRAMMING

LEARNING OBJECTIVES

By the end of this chapter you should be able to:

➤ create dialogue windows in Java;

➤ create pull-down and pop-up menus;

➤ use the `FileDialog` class to access the computer's file system;

➤ use a number of methods of the `Graphics` class;

➤ add scrollbars and images to components.

17.1 Introduction

In chapter 9 you learnt how to make use of some of the basic components of the AWT package. In this chapter you are going on to learn how to utilize many more of these components, so that you can add features like menus, dialogues and scrollbars to your graphical interfaces.

It is worth mentioning here that in chapter 19 you will be using an extension of the AWT package called **Swing** – in this package there are a number of components that can be made to look very attractive and are becoming very popular. Some texts have decided to dispense with teaching the AWT components entirely, in favour of Swing. We have decided against that approach because many browsers are not yet Swing-enabled, so that applets that use Swing components won't run. And in fact, once you have become familiar with using the AWT components, you will be able to adapt to Swing very easily.

17.2 The Dialog class

The first new class that we are going to explore is the `Dialog` class. This class exists with the express purpose of providing a separate frame that pops up so as to provide a means of communication between the user and the program. It is useful for those occasions when we do not want a part of a frame or window permanently devoted to this communication because it is only needed at particular times. A good example of this would be a dialogue that asked the user to enter his or her password; once this is done the dialogue window can be disposed of. Another purpose might be to provide the user with a message, such as "you have entered an invalid account number", and to wait for acknowledgement.

In order to demonstrate the use of the Dialog class we are going to adapt the ChangingFace class that we developed in chapter 9. Figure 17.1 shows the new version of ChangingFace – which we have called ChangingFaceWithDialog – with an extra button added. You will see from the code that we have moved everything down a bit to accommodate this additional button.

You will remember that when we developed this class in chapter 9 we didn't set the background colour in the class itself, but left this job to the frame in which it was run. We are now going to take this responsibility away from the frame and give it to the ChangingFace class itself – so now it will be the ChangingFace object that will be painted with the correct background colour rather than the frame. We have designed the program so that it starts off with the default (white) background and then the user can choose the colour by pressing the "Set Background Colour" button. Pressing this button causes a separate dialogue window to be displayed as shown in figure 17.2.

Fig 17.1   The *ChangingFaceWithDialog* class

Fig 17.2   The dialogue for the *ChangingFaceWith Dialog* class

We have designed the program in such a way that the background changes only when the "OK" button is pressed; an alternative approach is described at the end of this section. Let's see how this is done. We have created a class called ColourDialog which extends the Dialog class provided in the AWT; its purpose will be to allow the user to change the background colour of a component. Here is the code:

THE *ColourDialog* CLASS

```java
import java.awt.*;
import java.awt.event.*;

class ColourDialog extends Dialog implements ActionListener
{
  private Button okButton = new Button("OK");
  private Label greenLabel = new Label("Green ",Label.CENTER);
  private Label yellowLabel = new Label("Yellow",Label.CENTER);
  private Label greyLabel = new Label("Grey ",Label.CENTER);

  // create the checkboxes
  private Checkbox greenBox = new Checkbox();
  private Checkbox yellowBox = new Checkbox();
  private Checkbox greyBox = new Checkbox();

  // create a checkbox group to link the checkboxes together
  private CheckboxGroup box = new CheckboxGroup();

  /* declare a reference to the location of the component whose background
     colour is to be changed */
  private Component associatedComponent;

  // the constructor
  public ColourDialog(Frame frameIn, Component componentIn)
  {
    /* call the constructor of Dialog with the associated frame as a
       parameter */
    super(frameIn);

    /* assign the associatedComponent attribute to the component that has
       been sent in as a parameter */

    associatedComponent = componentIn;

    /* set the layout to FlowLayout (BorderLayout is the default for
       Dialogs) */
    setLayout(new FlowLayout());

    // set the background colour of the dialog window
    setBackground(Color.red);

    // assign the checkboxes to a group
    greenBox.setCheckboxGroup(box);
    yellowBox.setCheckboxGroup(box);
    greyBox.setCheckboxGroup(box);
```

```
   // add the components to the Dialog
   add(greenLabel);
   add(greenBox);
   add(yellowLabel);
   add(yellowBox);
   add(greyLabel);
   add(greyBox);
   add(okButton);

   // add the ActionListener
   okButton.addActionListener(this);

   /* set the location of the dialogue window, relative to the top left-
      hand corner of the frame */
   setLocation(300,300);

   // use the pack method to automatically size the dialogue window
   pack();

   // make the dialogue visible
   setVisible(true);
}

/* the actionPerformed method determines what happens when the okButton is
   pressed */
public void actionPerformed(ActionEvent e)
{
   if(greenBox.getState() == true)
   {
      associatedComponent.setBackground(Color.green);
   }

   else if(yellowBox.getState() == true)
   {
      associatedComponent.setBackground(Color.yellow);
   }

   else if(greyBox.getState() == true)
   {
      associatedComponent.setBackground(Color.lightGray);
   }
   // close down the dialogue window
   dispose();
   }
}
```

Let's take a closer look at what's going on here. Although the code is rather lengthy, it's actually quite straightforward. First, we declare as attributes, and simultaneously create, the components that are going to appear on the dialogue box. The first four of these are very familiar to you by now – but then we have some components that you have not seen before:

```
private Checkbox greenBox = new Checkbox();
private Checkbox yellowBox = new Checkbox();
private Checkbox greyBox = new Checkbox();
```

These are the checkboxes that you saw a picture of back in chapter 9; basically they allow you to make a selection by ticking a box. Often it is useful to link a few boxes together, so that only one at a time can be ticked. To do this we need to create a `CheckboxGroup`, which is the next attribute to be declared:

```
private CheckboxGroup box = new CheckboxGroup();
```

You can see from figure 17.2 that when we group checkboxes together they become round instead of square; they are then referred to as *radio buttons*.

There is one more attribute that we need:

```
private Component associatedComponent;
```

As you will see, we are going to use this attribute to hold a reference to the component whose background colour will be affected.

Now we come to the constructor:

```
public ColourDialog(Frame frameIn, Component componentIn)
```

We are sending in two parameters, a `Frame` object and a `Component` object. The frame is necessary when we create a new `Dialog` object; a dialogue always has to be associated with a frame – the frame that generates it – and this has to be sent in as a parameter to the `Dialog` constructor:

```
super(frameIn);
```

The component is the item whose background colour is to be changed – in this case a `ChangingFace` object. We assign our `associatedComponent` attribute to this parameter:

```
associatedComponent = componentIn;
```

The next thing the constructor does is to set the layout to `FlowLayout` (the default for `Dialogs` is `BorderLayout`) and then to set its own background colour (we thought red would look nice).

After this, the three checkboxes are assigned to a group:

```
greenBox.setCheckboxGroup(box);
yellowBox.setCheckboxGroup(box);
greyBox.setCheckboxGroup(box);
```

As we explained before, this makes them work together, with the effect of allowing only one box at a time to be selected.

The rest of the constructor is mostly stuff that you have seen before — adding the components to the `Dialog` (just as we would to a `Frame` or any other `Container`), setting the location and adding an `ActionListener` to the `okButton`. Note the use of the `pack` method here (`pack` is a method of the `Window` class, of which `Dialog` is a subclass) — this method automatically sizes a window based on the components it contains. The final instruction in the constructor makes the dialogue visible.

The only other method of this class is the `ActionPerformed` method, which determines what happens when the `okButton` is pressed — this is the only component that has an `ActionListener` attached to it, so we don't have to worry about determining what caused the event. Our code for this method is therefore very straightforward:

```
public void actionPerformed(ActionEvent e)
{
   if(greenBox.getState() == true)
   {
      associatedComponent.setBackground(Color.green);
   }
   else if(yellowBox.getState() == true)
   {
      associatedComponent.setBackground(Color.yellow);
   }
   else if(greyBox.getState() == true)
   {
      associatedComponent.setBackground(Color.lightGray);
   }
   dispose();
}
```

As you can see, the method makes use of the `getState` method of the `CheckBox` class (this returns a **boolean**) to determine which box is ticked, and then sets the background of the associated component to the appropriate colour. The dialogue box itself is then disposed of.

Now that we have created our ColourDialog class we are in a position to write our new ChangingFaceWithDialog class. Here it is:

THE *ChangingFaceWithDialog* CLASS

```java
import java.awt.*;
import java.awt.event.*;

/* most of this is the same as before; comments have been added only for the
   new bits */

class ChangingFaceWithDialog extends Panel implements ActionListener
{
  private boolean isHappy = true;
  private Button happyButton = new Button("Smile");
  private Button sadButton = new Button("Frown");
  private Button backgroundButton = new Button("Set Background Colour");

  /* we need to know the location of the frame to which the panel will be
     added so that we can send it to the ColourDialog */
  Frame parentFrame;

  public ChangingFaceWithDialog(Frame frameIn)
  {
    /* assign the parentFrame attribute to the frame that has been sent in
       as a parameter */
    parentFrame = frameIn;
    add(happyButton);
    add(sadButton);
    add(backgroundButton);
    happyButton.addActionListener(this);
    sadButton.addActionListener(this);
    backgroundButton.addActionListener(this);
  }

  public void paint(Graphics g)
  {
    g.setColor(Color.red);
    g.drawOval(85,95,75,75);
    g.setColor(Color.blue);
    g.drawOval(100,115,10,10);
    g.drawOval(135,115,10,10);

    g.drawString("Changing Face", 80,205);
    if(isHappy == true)
    {
      g.drawArc(102,135,40,25,0,-180);
    }
    else
    {
```

```
        g.drawArc(102,135,40,25,0,180);
      }
  }
  public void actionPerformed(ActionEvent e)
  {
    if(e.getSource() == happyButton)
    {
      isHappy = true;
      repaint();
    }
    if(e.getSource() == sadButton)
    {
      isHappy = false;
      repaint();
    }

    /* if the backgroundButton is pressed a new ColourDialog is created; the
       parentFrame and this panel itself are sent in as parameters */
    if(e.getSource() == backgroundButton)
    {
      new ColourDialog(parentFrame, this);
    }
  }
}
```

Having put all our new functions in our ColourDialog class there is very little new stuff to worry about in this class. There are two items of interest. The first is the fact that it is now necessary for the ChangingFaceWithDialog class to know the location of the frame it is going to run in; this is because it has to pass this information to a Dialog object each time one is created. So we receive this information in our constructor and assign it to an attribute which we have called parentFrame. The other area of interest is the new option in the actionPerformed method:

```
if(e.getSource() == backgroundButton)
{
    new ColourDialog(parentFrame, this);
}
```

Here we create a new ColourDialog object, sending it the information it requires – a reference to the parent frame and a reference to the panel itself (note the use of the **this** object for this purpose). Notice that here we have not created a reference to this new object as we are not ever going to have to refer to it.

The code for running our new class is shown in below in program 17.1.

PROGRAM 17.1

```
import java.awt.*;

public class RunChangingFaceWithDialog
{
  public static void main(String[] args)
  {
    EasyFrame frame = new EasyFrame();
    ChangingFaceWithDialog face = new ChangingFaceWithDialog(frame);
    frame.setSize(250,250);
    frame.add(face);
    frame.setVisible(true);
  }
}
```

An alternative approach to this application would be to make the background change as soon as the colour is selected. To do this we would need to make the following changes to our ColourDialog class:

1. Make sure that class implements the ItemListener interface as well as the ActionListener interface:

```
class ColourDialog extends Dialog implements ActionListener, ItemListener
```

2. In the constructor, add ItemListeners to each of the checkboxes:

```
greenBox.addItemListener(this);
yellowBox.addItemListener(this);
greyBox.addItemListener(this);
```

3. Implement an itemStateChanged method that will determine what happens when the state of a checkbox is changed:

```
public void itemStateChanged(ItemEvent e)
{
  if(e.getSource()== greenBox)
  {
    associatedComponent.setBackground(Color.green);
  }
  else if(e.getSource() == yellowBox)
  {
    associatedComponent.setBackground(Color.yellow);
  }
  else if(e.getSource() == greyBox)
  {
    associatedComponent.setBackground(Color.lightGray);
  }
}
```

4. Modify the `actionPerformed` method so that all it does is dispose of the dialogue box (when the `okButton` is pressed):

```
public void actionPerformed(ActionEvent e)
{
  dispose();
}
```

17.2.1 Modal and non-modal dialogues

An object of the `Dialog` class can be **modal** or **non-modal**; in the above example, the `Dialog` constructor that we used, which receives only one parameter (a reference to a `Frame`) creates a non-modal dialogue. This means that any listening components on the originating frame are still enabled and we can therefore interact with the frame even while the dialogue is visible. A modal dialogue on the other hand works in such a way as to "freeze" any interaction with the parent frame until the dialogue is disposed of.

To create a modal dialogue you can use a different constructor, which takes a second, **boolean**, parameter; if this parameter is **true** a modal dialogue will be created, if **false** a non-modal dialogue will be created.

Thus, in the constructor of the `ColourDialog`, we could have created a modal dialogue by calling the constructor of the superclass with the line:

```
super(frameIn, true);
```

17.3   *Creating menus*

As you are aware, a very common way to provide choices is via a menu. In the case of graphics based programs, the menu options are provided in one of two ways: either by a bar at the top of the window, usually referred to as a **pull-down menu**; or by a box that pops up as required – a **pop-up menu**.

17.3.1 Pull-down menus

A pull-down menu is shown in figure 17.3, which is our changing face once again, but with the options for both mood and background colour presented in menu form. We have called this class ChangingFaceWithMenu.

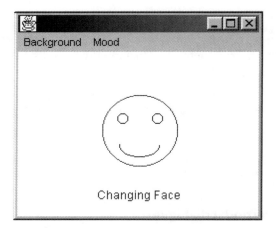

Fig 17.3   The *ChangingFaceWithMenu* class

Fig 17.4   The Background menu of the *ChangingFaceWithMenu* class

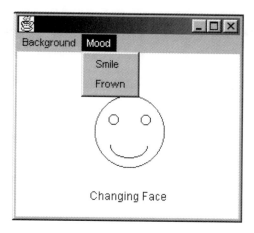

Fig 17.5   The Mood menu of the *ChangingFaceWithMenu* class

Figures 17.4 and 17.5 show the sub-menu of each of the two menu options.

Now there isn't really anything here that is very different to what we have done before, so you should be able to pick most of it up by looking at the code; however we will go through some of the main points after you have had a chance to go through it.

THE *ChangingFaceWithMenu* CLASS

```java
import java.awt.*;
import java.awt.event.*;
class ChangingFaceWithMenu extends Panel implements ActionListener
{
    // declare the menu items as attributes and initialize them
    // the menu bar
    private MenuBar bar = new MenuBar();
    // the top-level menus
    private Menu backgroundMenu = new Menu("Background");
    private Menu moodMenu = new Menu("Mood");

    // the sub-menu items
    private MenuItem greenChoice = new MenuItem("Green");
    private MenuItem yellowChoice = new MenuItem("Yellow");
    private MenuItem greyChoice = new MenuItem("Grey");
    private MenuItem smileChoice = new MenuItem("Smile");
    private MenuItem frownChoice = new MenuItem("Frown");
    private boolean isHappy = true;

    // the constructor
    public ChangingFaceWithMenu(Frame frameIn)
    {
```

```
      /* add the menu bar to the associated frame (which has been passed in as
         a parameter */
      frameIn.setMenuBar(bar);

      // add the top-level menus to the menu bar
      bar.add(backgroundMenu);
      bar.add(moodMenu);

      // add the sub-menu items to the top-level menus
      backgroundMenu.add(greenChoice);
      backgroundMenu.add(yellowChoice);
      backgroundMenu.add(greyChoice);
      moodMenu.add(smileChoice);
      moodMenu.add(frownChoice);

      // add ActionListeners to the menu items
      greenChoice.addActionListener(this);
      yellowChoice.addActionListener(this);
      greyChoice.addActionListener(this);
      smileChoice.addActionListener(this);
      frownChoice.addActionListener(this);
   }
   public void paint(Graphics g)
   {
     g.setColor(Color.red);
     g.drawOval(85,45,75,75);
     g.setColor(Color.blue);
     g.drawOval(100,65,10,10);
     g.drawOval(135,65,10,10);
     g.drawString("Changing Face", 80,155);
     if(isHappy == true)
     {
       g.drawArc(102,85,40,25,0,-180);
     }
     else
     {
       g.drawArc(102,85,40,25,0,180);
     }
   }
   public void actionPerformed(ActionEvent e)
   {
     if(e.getSource() == greenChoice)
     {
       setBackground(Color.green);
     }
     if(e.getSource() == yellowChoice)
     {
```

```
        setBackground(Color.yellow);
    }
    if(e.getSource() == greyChoice)
    {
        setBackground(Color.lightGray);
    }
    if(e.getSource() == smileChoice)
    {
        isHappy = true;
        repaint();
    }

    if(e.getSource() == frownChoice)
    {
        isHappy = false;
        repaint();
    }
    }
}
```

If you take a look at the attributes you will see that there are three aspects to creating a menu – there is the menu bar at the top and then the different menus – and each of these has its own list of menu items:

```
private MenuBar bar = new MenuBar();

private Menu backgroundMenu = new Menu("Background");
private Menu moodMenu = new Menu("Mood");

private MenuItem greenChoice = new MenuItem("Green");
private MenuItem yellowChoice = new MenuItem("Yellow");
private MenuItem greyChoice = new MenuItem("Grey");
private MenuItem smileChoice = new MenuItem("Smile");
private MenuItem frownChoice = new MenuItem("Frown");
```

Figure 17.6 clarifies how each of these items is used to create the menu.

Let's take a quick look at the constructor – notice how once again the frame is passed in as a parameter. The first thing we do is to add a menu bar to the frame with the setMenuBar method of Frame:

```
frameIn.setMenuBar(bar);
```

Now we can add the menus to the menu bar:

```
bar.add(backgroundMenu);
bar.add(moodMenu);
```

To each of these menus we add the appropriate menu items:

```
backgroundMenu.add(greenChoice);
backgroundMenu.add(yellowChoice);
backgroundMenu.add(greyChoice);
moodMenu.add(smileChoice);
moodMenu.add(frownChoice);
```

Finally we add `ActionListeners` to the menu items to enable them to respond to selection via the mouse:

```
greenChoice.addActionListener(this);
yellowChoice.addActionListener(this);
greyChoice.addActionListener(this);
smileChoice.addActionListener(this);
frownChoice.addActionListener(this);
```

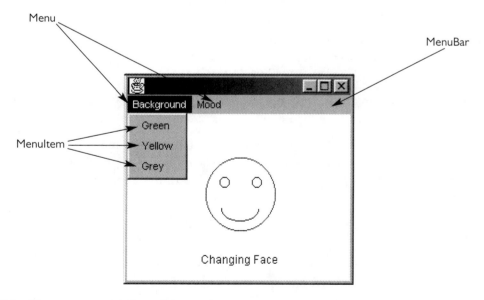

Fig 17.6   The components that make up a menu

The `ActionPerformed` method is straightforward and doesn't need any further discussion – program 17.2 provides the code for running the `ChangingFaceWithMenu` in an `EasyFrame`.

PROGRAM 17.2

```java
import java.awt.*;

public class RunChangingFaceWithMenu
{
  public static void main(String[] args)
  {
    EasyFrame frame = new EasyFrame();
    ChangingFaceWithMenu face = new ChangingFaceWithMenu(frame);
    frame.setSize(250,200);
    frame.add(face);
    frame.setVisible(true);
  }
}
```

17.3.2 Popup Menus

Figure 17.7 shows another variation of the `ChangingFace` class, which we have called `ChangingFaceWithPopup`. As you can see, all the functionality of the changing face – both the option to change the background colour, and the option to change the mood – is now the responsibility of a popup menu that we have arranged to appear in the bottom right-hand corner of the frame.

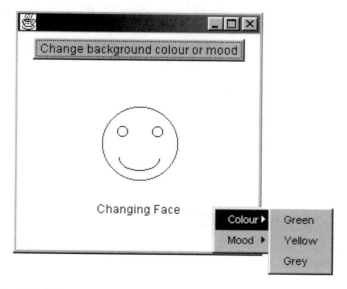

Fig 17.7   The *ChangingFaceWithPopup* Class

There is nothing very new about the creation of this menu itself – it simply makes use of the PopupMenu class that comes with the AWT. We create a FacePopupMenu class which extends PopupMenu; an object of this class is then created when the button is pressed. Now that you have seen the previous examples, inspecting the code should quickly make it clear how to use this class.

There is, however, another issue here that we need to think about. The popup menu behaves in a very similar way to the dialogue that we used previously; now, however, the responsibility for changing the mood, as well as the background colour, lies with the popup menu, so this class needs to have access to the isHappy attribute of the ChangingFaceWithPopup class. So the first thing we need to do is to provide the ChangingFaceWithPopup class with a setHappy method.

But now the associated component that we send in to the constructor of our FacePopupMenu class can no longer be just any old component. Can you see why this is so? The answer is that selecting one of the mood menu options will have to invoke the setHappy method – and a Component object doesn't have one of these! The best way around this is to create an interface. We will call this interface Smileable, and we will give it a setHappy method. Then we can get our ChangingFaceWithPopup class to implement Smileable (thus guaranteeing that it will have a setHappy method), and send a Smileable object into the FacePopupMenu class, where we can confidently use its setHappy method.

We are nearly there – but there is one more thing to consider. The FacePopupMenu class will also need to use the object's setBackground and repaint methods – both of which are inherited from Component. So the Smileable class must also declare these two methods, insisting that any class that implements it must define them. And the ChangingFaceWithPopup class does indeed define these two methods – because it inherits them from Component!

So here is our interface:

THE *Smileable* INTERFACE

```
import java.awt.*;

interface Smileable
{
  public void setHappy(boolean moodIn);
  public void setBackground(Color c);
  public void repaint();
}
```

Now we can present the FacePopupMenu class, which extends the PopupMenu class. We have not provided a discussion afterwards because all the new concepts are explained by the comments and the previous discussion.

THE *FacePopupMenu* CLASS

```java
import java.awt.*;
import java.awt.event.*;

// our class will extend the PopupMenu class
class FacePopupMenu extends PopupMenu implements ActionListener
{
    //declare and initialize the menu items (as attributes)

    private MenuItem greenChoice = new MenuItem("Green");
    private MenuItem yellowChoice = new MenuItem("Yellow");
    private MenuItem greyChoice = new MenuItem("Grey");
    private MenuItem smileChoice = new MenuItem("Smile");
    private MenuItem frownChoice = new MenuItem("Frown");

    private Menu colourMenu = new Menu("Colour");
    private Menu moodMenu = new Menu("Mood");

/* declare a reference to the location of the component whose properties are
   to be changed. This component must implement our Smileable interface */
    private Smileable associatedComponent;

    // the constructor
    public FacePopupMenu(Frame frameIn, Smileable componentIn)
    {
        /* assign the associatedComponent attribute to the component that has
           been sent in as a parameter */

        associatedComponent = componentIn;

        // add the menu items to the menus
        colourMenu.add(greenChoice);
        colourMenu.add(yellowChoice);
        colourMenu.add(greyChoice);
        moodMenu.add(smileChoice);
        moodMenu.add(frownChoice);

        //add the menu items to the popup menu
        add(colourMenu);
        add(moodMenu);
        frameIn.add(this);

        greenChoice.addActionListener(this);
        yellowChoice.addActionListener(this);
        greyChoice.addActionListener(this);
        smileChoice.addActionListener(this);
        frownChoice.addActionListener(this);

        /* make the menu visible on frameIn; the top left-hand corner of the
           frame is the point (0,0) */
        show(frameIn, 200,200);
    }
```

```java
    public void actionPerformed(ActionEvent e)
    {
      // background colour options
      if(e.getSource() == greenChoice)
      {
        associatedComponent.setBackground(Color.green);
      }

      else if(e.getSource() == yellowChoice)
      {
        associatedComponent.setBackground(Color.yellow);
      }

      else if(e.getSource() == greyChoice)
      {
        associatedComponent.setBackground(Color.lightGray);
      }

      // mood options
      else if(e.getSource() == smileChoice)
      {
        associatedComponent.setHappy(true);
        associatedComponent.repaint();
      }

      else if(e.getSource() == frownChoice)
      {
        associatedComponent.setHappy(false);
        associatedComponent.repaint();
      }
    }
}
```

Here is the code for the ChangingFaceWithPopup class:

THE *ChangingFaceWithPopup* CLASS

```java
import java.awt.*;
import java.awt.event.*;

// much of this is similar to the ChangingFace with Dialog class

// the class must implement our Smileable interface
class ChangingFaceWithPopup extends Panel implements
                                    ActionListener, Smileable
{
```

```java
  private boolean isHappy = true;
  private Button backgroundAndMoodButton
                    = new Button("Change background colour or mood");

  private Frame parentFrame;

  public ChangingFaceWithPopup(Frame frameIn)
  {
    parentFrame = frameIn;
    add(backgroundAndMoodButton);
    backgroundAndMoodButton.addActionListener(this);
  }

  /* we need to provide write access to the setHappy attribute so that the
     FacePopupMenu can change the mood */
  public void setHappy(boolean moodIn)
  {
    isHappy = moodIn;
  }

  public void paint(Graphics g)
  {

    g.setColor(Color.red);
    g.drawOval(85,75,75,75);
    g.setColor(Color.blue);
    g.drawOval(100,95,10,10);
    g.drawOval(135,95,10,10);

    g.drawString("Changing Face", 80,185);
    if(isHappy == true)
    {
      g.drawArc(102,115,40,25,0,-180);
    }
    else
    {
      g.drawArc(102,115,40,25,0,180);
    }
  }

  /* all that the actionPerformed method does is to create a new Popup menu.
     Changing the background colour and the mood is left to the FacePopup
     class */

  public void actionPerformed(ActionEvent e)
  {
    new FacePopupMenu(parentFrame, this);
  }
}
```

Finally, program 17.3 runs the class in a frame.

PROGRAM 17.3

```
import java.awt.*;

public class RunChangingFaceWithPopup

{
  public static void main(String[] args)
  {
    EasyFrame frame = new EasyFrame();
    ChangingFaceWithPopup face = new ChangingFaceWithPopup(frame);
    frame.setSize(250,250);
    frame.add(face);
    frame.setVisible(true);
  }
}
```

17.4   *The* Choice *class and the* List *class*

Alternative ways of providing choices are shown in figures 17.8 and 17.9 respectively. The first makes use of the Choice class, the second uses the List class.

The implementation of these classes is left for the practical exercises at the end of the chapter; some help is given there to explain how these classes work – and a description of their methods is given in the appendix on the website.

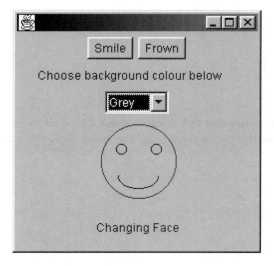

Fig 17.8   Making choices with the *Choice* class

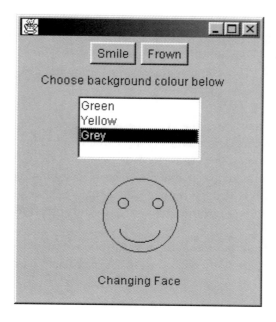

Fig 17.9   Making choices with the *List* class

17.5   *The* **FileDialog** *class*

A quick look back at figure 9.2 will remind you that in the Component hierarchy of the AWT there is a subclass of Dialog called FileDialog. A FileDialog object interacts with your computer's operating system to enable you to search directories and select files. To illustrate the use of this class we will develop a class called FileHandler that we can run in a frame containing a menu bar consisting of a couple of menu options. The application itself is not really very sophisticated – it provides the menu bar and a text area, as shown in figure 17.10.

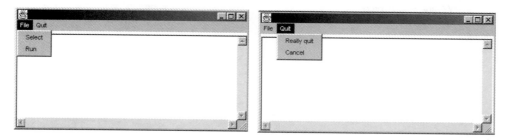

Fig 17.10   The *FileHandler* class

Choosing the *Select* option from the *File* menu will cause a dialogue window to appear – this will look different according to the operating system that you are using – with our Windows system we got the window shown in figure 17.11.

For contrast, figure 17.12 shows the result when running the program in a UNIX environment, connected to an X11 server.

You can see that in figure 17.11 we have chosen the file called *Calc.exe*, which is the calculator program that comes with the Windows operating system. Once we select this file a message appears in our text area, telling us the name of the file chosen, including its full directory path. This is illustrated in figure 17.13.

If the file we have chosen is an executable file, then selecting the *Run* option of the *File* menu will run the program, in this case the Windows calculator. When we get to the next chapter, we will learn more about handling files, and will be able to add an option to our menu which will allow us to look inside a file.

Once again, there is not a huge amount of new stuff here – there is the code for creating the `FileDialog` object, and there is the running of the executable itself. Below is the code for the `FileHandler` class.

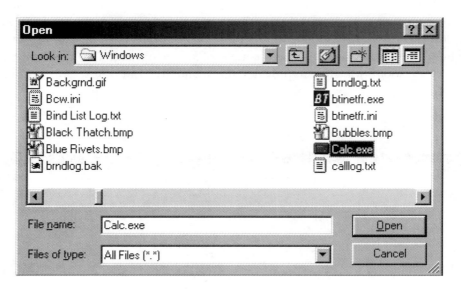

Fig 17.11   The file dialogue presented by a Windows operating system

Fig 17.12   The file dialogue presented by a UNIX system connected to an XII server

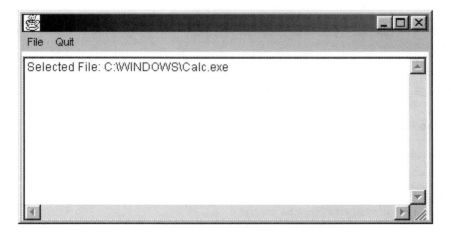

Fig 17.13   The name of the file we select appears in the text area

THE *FileHandler* CLASS

```java
import java.awt.*;
import java.awt.event.*;
import java.io.*;

class FileHandler extends Panel implements ActionListener
{
    // the attributes

    // declare an attribute to hold the location of the associated frame
    private Frame associatedFrame;

    // declare a TextArea
    private TextArea viewArea = new TextArea(10,55);

    // declare the menu components
    private MenuBar bar = new MenuBar();
    private Menu fileMenu = new Menu("File");
    private Menu quitMenu = new Menu("Quit");
    private MenuItem selectChoice = new MenuItem("Select");
    private MenuItem runChoice = new MenuItem("Run");
    private MenuItem reallyQuitChoice = new MenuItem("Really quit");
    private MenuItem cancelChoice = new MenuItem("Cancel");

    /* declare attributes to hold the file name and directory name, initially
       setting them to null */
    private String selectedFile = null;
    private String dir = null;

    // the constructor
    public FileHandler(Frame frameIn)
    {
        associatedFrame = frameIn;
        add(viewArea);

        // add the menus to the menu bar
        bar.add(fileMenu);
        bar.add(quitMenu);

        // add the menu items to the menus
        fileMenu.add(selectChoice);
        fileMenu.add(runChoice);
        quitMenu.add(reallyQuitChoice);
        quitMenu.add(cancelChoice);

        // add the menu bar to the frame
        frameIn.setMenuBar(bar);

        // add the ActionListeners
        selectChoice.addActionListener(this);
        runChoice.addActionListener(this);
        reallyQuitChoice.addActionListener(this);
        cancelChoice.addActionListener(this);
    }
```

```java
public void actionPerformed(ActionEvent e)
{
  if(e.getSource() == selectChoice)
  {
    // create a new FileDialog object and make it visible
    FileDialog fd = new FileDialog(associatedFrame);
    fd.show();

    // get the name of the selected file
    selectedFile = fd.getFile();

    /* get the full name of the directory in which the selected file is
       located */
    dir = fd.getDirectory();

    viewArea.append("Selected File: " + dir + selectedFile + '\n');
  }

  if(e.getSource() == runChoice)
  {

    // create a RunTime object
    Runtime rt = Runtime.getRuntime();
    try
    {
      // run the file
      rt.exec(dir + selectedFile);
    }

    catch(IOException ioe)
    {
      if(selectedFile == null) // no file selected
      {
        viewArea.append("No file selected\n");
      }
      else
      {
        viewArea.append("Not an executable file\n");
      }
    }
  }
  if(e.getSource() == reallyQuitChoice)
  {
    System.exit(0);
  }

  if(e.getSource() == cancelChoice)
  {
    viewArea.append("Quit option cancelled\n");
  }
}
}
```

Let's take a look at the actionPerformed method. First, there is the option associated with choosing the menu item that lets us select a file:

```
if(e.getSource() == selectChoice)
{
  FileDialog fd = new FileDialog(associatedFrame);
  fd.show();
  selectedFile = fd.getFile();
  dir = fd.getDirectory();
  viewArea.append("Selected File: " + dir + selectedFile + '\n');
}
```

We are using various methods of the FileDialog class here. First, the constructor; to which we send the parent frame. We then call the show method to make the dialogue window visible, at which point it waits until a file is selected (look back at figure 17.11). Then we use the getFile and getDirectory methods, which return, respectively, strings representing the name of the selected file and the full path name of the directory where the file resides.

Now the code for the runChoice option, which loads and runs the selected file.

```
if(e.getSource() == runChoice)
{
  Runtime rt = Runtime.getRuntime();
  try
  {
    rt.exec(dir + selectedFile);
  }
  catch(IOException ioe)
  {
    if(selectedFile == null)
    {
      viewArea.append("No file selected\n");
    }
    else
    {
      viewArea.append("Not an executable file\n");
    }
  }
}
```

As you can see we are making use of a standard Java class called RunTime. We create an object of this class and then assign it the return value of the getRuntime method, which is a **static** method of the RunTime class. The object returned by this method contains information about the java application that is currently running. Being armed with information about the current application, the RunTime object is able to execute a command – specific to the particular operating system – as a separate process in the computer's memory. It does this with its exec method, which executes the command that is sent in as a parameter. You can see from the program that we are sending in the name of the selected directory and the file as a single string. If the file is an executable file then, with a Windows, Unix or Linux system, this will load and run the selected file.

You can see that the exec method throws an IOException (hence the need to import the java.io package); we have used the catch block to display an appropriate message (based on the fact that we initially assigned a null value to the file name).

Program 17.4 runs the FileHandler class in a Frame.

```
PROGRAM 17.4

import java.awt.*;

public class RunFileHandler
{
  public static void main(String[] args)
  {
    Frame frame = new Frame();
    FileHandler fh = new FileHandler(frame);
    frame.setSize(415,200);
    frame.add(fh);
    frame.setVisible(true);
  }
}
```

17.6   *Using scrollbars*

Scrollbars (or *Sliders* as they are sometimes called) allow us to view text or images which fill up more than the visible viewing area than is currently available, by dragging a bar with the mouse; they also allow us to control the value of a variable. You have, in fact, already come across them when you used a TextArea component. If you look back at the case study that we developed in chapters 10 and 11, you can see that the two TextArea objects both have horizontal and vertical scrollbars which are "greyed out" until they are needed. If you run the program, allowing something like ten tenants, then you will see that the scrollbars become active when you reach the point where you have to display more tenants than you have room for in the viewing area.

In the next section, when we talk about displaying images from files, you will also see the use of the ScrollPane class, which, as its name suggests, provides a pane with scrollbars automatically attached.

In this section, however, you are going to learn how to attach *individual* scrollbars to a component such as a Panel and use them to increase or decrease a value that can be represented by an integer within a particular range.

The Scrollbar class has a method called getValue that returns an integer representing the distance that the bar has been moved. An example should make it clear how this works; in figure 17.14 we have placed a scrollbar at the top of a panel, and added a label to show the current value returned by getValue – in other words how far along we have moved the bar.

In the first figure we set the minimum value to zero and the maximum to 50, so that there is a total range of 50 units – as we move the bar along the value varies between these limits. In the second diagram we set the range from 100 to 300 – a range of 200 units. The diagrams show how the width of the bar varies according to the range of values that has to be traversed.

Here is the code for this ScrollbarDemo class:

THE *ScrollbarDemo* CLASS

```
import java.awt.*;
import java.awt.event.*;

class ScrollbarDemo extends Panel implements AdjustmentListener
{
    // declare and initialize a horizontal scrollbar
    private Scrollbar bar = new Scrollbar(Scrollbar.HORIZONTAL);

    private Label valueLabel = new Label();

    public ScrollbarDemo (int MinIn, int MaxIn)
    {
        setLayout(new BorderLayout());

        // set the minimum and maximum values for the scrollbar
        bar.setMinimum(MinIn);
        bar.setMaximum(MaxIn);
        // add the scrollbar to the top of the panel
        add("North", bar);

        // set the initial text for the label
        valueLabel.setText("Current value: " + MinIn);

        // add the label to the panel
        add("South", valueLabel);

        // add the listener to the scrollbar
        bar.addAdjustmentListener(this);
    }
    // the event-handler
    public void adjustmentValueChanged(AdjustmentEvent e)
    {
        valueLabel.setText("Current value: " + bar.getValue());
    }
}
```

Most of the code is self-explanatory. There are a few things to point out here, however. First, notice that we have used a BorderLayout policy for the panel and added the scrollbar to the North sector; this means that the scrollbar stretches out to fill the length of the panel. Second, you should observe that the constructor allows us to decide upon the orientation of the scrollbar with a predefined integer parameter that can be either `Scrollbar.HORIZONTAL` or `Scrollbar.VERTICAL`. Third, you should note that the interface that we need to implement in this case is `AdjustmentListener` − the method that handles the event is `adjustmentValueChanged`, which receives an `AdjustmentEvent` object; notice how we report on the movement of the bar by using the `getValue` method:

```java
public void adjustmentValueChanged(AdjustmentEvent e)
{
   valueLabel.setText("Current value: " + bar.getValue());
}
```

You can see that the minimum and maximum values of the scrollbar are received as parameters to the constructor; program 17.5 sets these values, in this case to zero and 100 respectively, and adds the panel to an `EasyFrame`:

PROGRAM 17.5

```java
import java.awt.*;

public class RunScrollBarDemo
{
   public static void main(String[] args)
   {
      final int MIN = 0;
      final int MAX = 100;

      EasyFrame frame = new EasyFrame("ScrollBar Demo");
      ScrollBarDemo demo = new ScrollBarDemo(MIN, MAX);
      frame.setSize(250,100);
      frame.setLocation(250,200);
      frame.add(demo);
      frame.setVisible(true);
   }
}
```

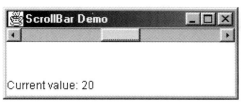

(a) the range is set between 0 and 50

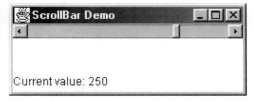

(b) the range is set between 100 and 300

Fig 17.14   Using the *Scrollbar* class

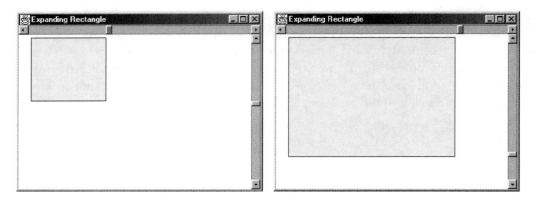

Fig 17.15   Using scrollbars to control the size of a rectangle

Now let's consider an example where we use the `Scrollbar` class in a more interesting way, and which could potentially be very useful. Figure 17.15 shows a program in which a horizontal and vertical scrollbar are added to a panel and used to alter the width and height of a rectangle. To make it a little more interesting, we have made the rectangle yellow surrounded by a black border.

Here is the code for the `ExpandingRectangle` class:

THE *ExpandingRectangle* CLASS

```
import java.awt.*;
import java.awt.event.*;

class ExpandingRectangle extends Panel implements AdjustmentListener
{
  private int width = 0;
  private int height = 0;
  // declare and initialize a horizontal and a vertical scroll bar
  private Scrollbar widthBar = new Scrollbar(Scrollbar.HORIZONTAL);
  private Scrollbar heightBar = new Scrollbar(Scrollbar.VERTICAL);

  public ExpandingRectangle (int frameWidth, int frameHeight)
  {
    // set the maximum value for the scrollbars
    widthBar.setMaximum(frameWidth - 50);
    heightBar.setMaximum(frameHeight - 50);

    /*  a border layout will enable us to position our scrollbars at the
        right and at the top */
    setLayout(new BorderLayout());

    // add the scrollbars to the panel
    add("North", widthBar);
    add("East", heightBar);
```

```
        // add the listeners to the scrollbars
        widthBar.addAdjustmentListener(this);
        heightBar.addAdjustmentListener(this);
    }

    public void paint(Graphics g)
    {
        // draw the outer rectangle in black
        g.drawRect(20,20,width,height);
        // draw the inner rectangle in yellow
        g.setColor(Color.yellow);
        g.fillRect(21,21, width-1, height-1);
    }

    // the event-handlers
    public void adjustmentValueChanged(AdjustmentEvent e)
    {
        if(e.getAdjustable() == widthBar)
        {
            /* set the width of the rectangle to the value of the horizontal
               scrollbar and repaint */
            width = widthBar.getValue();
            repaint();
        }
        if(e.getAdjustable() == heightBar)
        {
            /* set the height of the rectangle to the value of the vertical
               scrollbar and repaint */
            height = heightBar.getValue();
            repaint();
        }
    }
}
}
```

Notice that the constructor accepts the width and height of the frame to which the panel will be added, and sets the maximum value of the horizontal and vertical scrollbars to 50 pixels less than this value. The idea here is to get the rectangle to fit neatly into the frame – the 50 pixels take account of the width of the scrollbars themselves.

Finally, take a look at the event-handling routines, which set the dimensions of the rectangle to the values returned by the scrollbars, and then repaint the panel:

```
public void adjustmentValueChanged(AdjustmentEvent e)
{
  if(e.getAdjustable() == widthBar)
  {
    /* set the width of the rectangle to the value of the horizontal
       scrollbar and repaint */
    width = widthBar.getValue();
    repaint();
  }
  if(e.getAdjustable() == heightBar)
  {
    /* set the height of the rectangle to the value of the vertical
       scrollbar and repaint */
    height = heightBar.getValue();
    repaint();
  }
}
```

Once again we have used a BorderLayout and have added the scrollbars to the "North" and "East" sectors.

Program 17.6 adds the panel to a 400×300 EasyFrame.

PROGRAM 17.6

```
import java.awt.*;

public class RunExpandingRectangle
{
  public static void main(String[] args)
  {
    final int width = 400;
    final int height = 300;
    EasyFrame frame = new EasyFrame("Expanding Rectangle");
    ExpandingRectangle rect = new ExpandingRectangle(width, height);
    frame.setSize(width,height);
    frame.setLocation(250,200);
    frame.add(rect);
    frame.setVisible(true);
  }
}
```

17.7 *Adding images to components*

There are many occasions, particularly when we are programming for the World Wide Web, when we will want to display an image loaded from a file. In Java it is possible to do this with files in either of two formats .GIF (Graphics Interchange Format) or .JPG (Joint Photographic Experts Group).

In order to display an image it is necessary to obtain some information about the system we are working on. The class that does this for us is called `Toolkit`. Its use is demonstrated in the `ImageHolder` class below, which loads an image from a file called "Java.gif" onto a `Canvas` — which is a component of the AWT that provides a blank area onto which we can paint.[1]

THE *ImageHolder* CLASS

```java
import java.awt.*;

class ImageHolder extends Canvas
{
  public void paint(Graphics g)
  {
    Toolkit kit = Toolkit.getDefaultToolkit();
    Image image = kit.getImage("Java.gif");
    g.drawImage(image, 10, 10, this);
  }
}
```

You can see from the above that `Toolkit` has a class method called `getDefaultToolkit` that returns a `Toolkit` object containing the necessary information about our system. We can then use the `getImage` method of this object to load our image from the file.

Once we have loaded the image we display it with the `drawImage` method of the `Graphics` class. As you can see, this method takes four parameters: the first is the image to be displayed, the next two are integer values representing the co-ordinates of the top left-hand corner of the position of the image, and the fourth is the object that is to hold the image (in the above case, it is to be held in *this* object). Program 17.7 displays our image in a 250 × 340 `EasyFrame`.

---

[1] A `Canvas` is very similar to a `Panel`, but is not a subclass of `Container`, so we can't add other components to it.

PROGRAM 17.7

```java
import java.awt.*;

public class RunImageHolder
{
  public static void main(String[] args)
  {
    EasyFrame frame = new EasyFrame("Image display");
    ImageHolder holder = new ImageHolder();
    frame.add(holder);
    frame.setSize(250,340);
    frame.setVisible(true);
  }
}
```

Figure 17.16 shows the result of running the program.

In this case we arranged our frame to be big enough initially to hold the canvas containing the image; however if you reduce the size of the frame you will see that eventually you only get to see part of the image. What would be useful here is for some scrollbars to be available so that we could move the image about within the frame. To do this we can use the `ScrollPane` class. Look at program 17.8

Fig 17.16   Displaying an image from a file

PROGRAM 17.8

```
import java.awt.*;

public class RunImageHolder1
{
  public static void main(String[] args)
  {
    EasyFrame frame = new EasyFrame("Image display");
    ImageHolder holder = new ImageHolder();
    // create a ScrollPane
    ScrollPane pane = new ScrollPane(ScrollPane.SCROLLBARS_ALWAYS);
    // add the holder to the ScrollPane
    pane.add(holder);
    // add the ScrollPane to the frame
    frame.add(pane);
    frame.setSize(250,340);
    frame.setVisible(true);
  }
}
```

You can see that now, instead of adding the ImageHolder directly to the frame, we have created a ScrollPane object, added our ImageHolder to that, and then added the ScrollPane to the frame. The version of the constructor that we have used takes an integer value, which can be entered as one of three pre-defined constants – either ScrollPane.SCROLLBARS_AS_NEEDED, ScrollPane.SCROLLBARS_NEVER or, as we have used here, ScrollPane.SCROLLBARS_ALWAYS. There is also another constructor available, which does not take any parameters; in this case the ScrollPane defaults to ScrollPane.SCROLLBARS_AS_NEEDED.

Figure 17.17 shows the result of running this program, and then reducing the size of the frame with the mouse.

Fig 17.17   Displaying an image using the *ScrollPane* class

Tutorial exercises

1. Explain the difference between a *modal* and a *non-modal* dialogue box.
2. Design the code for the applications shown in figures 17.8 and 17.9 respectively. These will use the `Choice` and `List` classes respectively. Look at the appendix on the website to find out about the methods of these classes.

    The classes you develop will have to implement the `ItemListener` interface and will need to code an `itemStateChanged` method for handling the responses to the various options.

Practical work

1. Download and implement the programs from this chapter.
2. Adapt the `ColorDialog` class so that it creates a modal dialogue – examine the effect of this by using it in conjunction with the `ChangingFaceWithDialog` class.
3. Implement the applications that you designed in tutorial exercise 2.
4. In tutorial question 3 of chapter 16 you wrote the code for a personal address book. Implement this address book and add an attractive graphical interface to the application. Once you have completed the next chapter, you will be able to store your records as permanent files on disk.

WORKING WITH FILES

LEARNING OBJECTIVES

By the end of this chapter you should be able to:

➤ explain the principles of **input** and **output** and identify a number of different input and output devices;

➤ explain the concept of an **I/O stream**;

➤ describe the basic file-handling techniques used in the Java language;

➤ distinguish between **text**, **binary** and **object** encoding of data;

➤ distinguish between **serial** access files and **random** access files;

➤ create and access files in Java using all the above encoding and access methods.

18.1 Introduction

When we developed our case study in chapters 10 and 11 it became apparent that in reality an application such as that one wouldn't be much use unless we had some way of storing our data permanently – even when the program has been terminated and the computer has been switched off. You will remember how in that chapter, because you had not yet learnt how to do this, we provided a special class called `TenantFileHandler` that enabled you to keep permanent records on disk.

Now it is time to learn how to do this yourself. As you are no doubt already aware, a named block of externally stored data is called a **file**.

When we are taking an object-oriented approach, as we have been doing, we tend not to separate the data from the behaviour; however, when it comes to storing information in files then of course it is only the data that we are interested in storing. When referring to data alone it is customary to use the terms **record** and **field**. A record refers to a single data instance – for example a person, a stock-item, a student and so on; a **field** refers to what in the object-oriented world we would normally call an attribute – a name, a stock-number, an exam mark etc.

In this chapter we will learn how to create files, and write information to them, and to read the information back when we need it. We start by looking at this process in the overall context of input and output, or I/O as it is often called; you will then go on to learn a number of different techniques for keeping permanent copies of your data.

18.2   *Input and output*

Any computer system must provide a means of allowing information to come in from the outside world (**input**) and, once it has been processed, to be sent out again (**output**). The whole question of input and output, particularly where files are concerned, can sometimes seem rather complex, especially from the point of view of the programmer.

As with all aspects of a computer system, the processes of input and output are handled by the computer hardware working in conjunction with the system software – that is, the operating system (Windows2000 or Unix for example). The particular application program that is running at the time normally deals with input and output by communicating with the operating system, and getting it to perform these tasks in conjunction with the hardware.

All this involves some very real complexity and involves a lot of low-level details that a programmer is not usually concerned with; for example, the way in which the system writes to external media such as disks, or the way it reconciles the differences between the speed of the processor with the speed of the disk-drive.

18.3   *Input and output devices*

The most common way of getting data input from the outside world is via the keyboard; and the most common way of displaying output data is on the screen. Therefore, most systems are normally set up so that the *standard* input and output devices are the keyboard and the screen respectively. However, there are many other devices that are concerned with input and output: magnetic and optical disks for permanent storage of data; network interface cards and modems for communicating with other computers; and printers for producing hard copies.

We should bear in mind that the process, in one sense, is always the same, no matter what the input or output device. All the data that is processed by the computer's central processing unit in response to program instructions is stored in the computer's main memory or RAM (Random Access Memory). Input is the transfer of data from some external device to main memory whereas output is the transfer of data from main memory to an external device. In order for input or output to take place, it is necessary for a channel of communication to be established between the device and the computer's memory. Such a channel is referred to as a **stream**. The operating system will have established a **standard input stream** and a **standard output stream**, which will normally be the keyboard and screen respectively. In addition to this, there is usually a **standard error stream** where error messages can be displayed; this is normally also set to the screen. All of these default settings for the standard streams can be changed either via the operating system or from within the program itself.

In chapter 15 you saw that the System class has two attributes called in and out – it also has an additional attribute called err; these objects are already set up to provide access to the standard input, output and error streams. In this chapter, instead of dealing with input and output to the standard streams, we are going to be dealing with the input and output of data to external disk drives in the form of files.

18.4 *File-handling*

The output process, which consists of transferring data from memory to a file, is usually referred to as **writing**; the input process, which consists of transferring data from a file to memory, is referred to as **reading**. Both of these involve some low-level detail to do with the way in which data is stored physically on the disk – and as programmers we do not want to have to worry more than is necessary about this process – which, of course, will differ from one machine to the next and from one operating system to the next. Fortunately, Java makes it quite easy for us to deal with these processes. As we shall see, Java provides low-level classes which create **file streams** – input or output streams that handle communication between main memory and a named file on a disk. It also provides higher-level classes which we can "wrap around" the low-level objects, enabling us to use methods that relate more closely to our logical way of thinking about data. In this way we are shielded from having to know too much detail about the way our particular system stores and retrieves data to or from a file.

As we shall see, this whole process enables us to read and write data in terms of units that we understand – for example, in the form of strings, lines of text, or basic types such integers or characters; Java even allows us to store and retrieve whole objects.

18.4.1 Encoding

Java supports three different ways of **encoding** data – that is, representing data on a disk. These are **text**, **binary** and **object**.

Text encoding means that the data on the disk is stored as characters in the form used by the external system – most commonly ASCII. Java, as we know, uses the Unicode character set, so some conversion takes place in the process, but fortunately the programmer does not have to worry about that. As an example, consider saving the number 107 to a text file – it will be saved as the character '1' in ASCII code (or whatever is used by the system) followed by the character '0', followed by the character '7'. A text file is therefore readable by a text editor (such as Windows Notepad).

Binary encoding, on the other hand, means that the data is stored in the same format as the internal representation of the data used by the program to store data in memory. So the number 107 would be saved as the binary number 1101011. A binary file could not be read properly by a text editor as we shall see in section 18.6.

Finally, object-encoding is a powerful mechanism provided by Java whereby a whole object can be input or output with a single command.

You are probably asking yourself which is the best method to use when you start to write applications that read and write to files. Well, if your files are going to be read and written by the same application, then it really makes very little difference how they are encoded! Just use the method that seems the easiest for the type of data you are storing. However, do bear in mind that if you wanted your files to be read by a text editor then you must, of course, use the text encoding method.

18.4.2 Access

The final thing that you need to consider before we show you how to write files in Java is the way in which files are accessed. There are two ways in which this can take place – **serial** access and **random** access. In the first (and more common) method, each item of data is read (or written) in turn. The operating system provides what is known as a **file pointer**, which is really just a location in memory that keeps track of where we have got to in the process of reading or writing to a file.

Another way to access data in a file is to go directly to the record you want – this is known as random access, and is a bit like going straight to the song you want on a CD; whereas serial access is like using an audio tape, where you have to work your way through all the songs to get to the one you want. Java provides a class (`RandomAccessFile`) that we can use for random access. We will start, however, with serial access.

18.5   *Reading and writing to text files*

In this and the following section we are going to use as an example a very simple class called `Car`; the code for this class is given below:

THE _Car_ CLASS

```
class Car
{
  private String registration;
  private String make;
  private double price;

  public Car(String registrationIn, String makeIn, double priceIn)
  {
    registration = registrationIn;
    make = makeIn;
    price = priceIn;
  }

  public String getRegistration()
  {
    return registration;
  }

  public String getMake()
  {
    return make;
  }

  public double getPrice()
  {
    return price;
  }
}
```

Program 18.1 below is a very simple menu-driven program which manipulates a list of cars, held in memory as a Vector; it provides the facility to add new cars to the list, to remove cars from the list and to display the details of all the cars in the list. As it is a demonstration program only, we have not bothered with such things as input validation, or checking if the list is empty before we try to remove an item.

The difference between this and other similar programs that we have discussed before, is that the list is kept as a permanent record – as we mentioned before, we did a similar thing in our case study in chapter 11, but there the process was hidden from you.

The program is designed so that reading and writing to the file takes place as follows: when the quit option is selected, the list is written as a permanent text file called Cars.txt; each time the program is run, this file is read into the list.

The program is presented below; notice that we have provided two worker methods, writeList and readList for the purpose of accessing the file; as we shall explain, the writeList method also deals with creating the file for the first time.

PROGRAM 18.1

```java
import java.util.*; // required for the Vector class
import java.io.*;   // required for handling the IOExceptions
public class TextFileTester
{
  public static void main(String[] args)
  {
    char choice;
    Vector carList = new Vector();
    // read the list when the program starts
    readList(carList);
    do
    {
      System.out.println("\nText File Tester");
      System.out.println("1. Add a car");
      System.out.println("2. Remove a car");
      System.out.println("3. List all cars");
      System.out.println("4. Quit\n");
      choice = EasyIn.getChar();
      System.out.println();
      switch(choice)
      {
        case '1': addCar(carList);
                  break;
        case '2': removeCar(carList);
                  break;
        case '3': listAll(carList);
                  break;
        case '4': writeList(carList);
                  break;
        default: System.out.print
                  ("\nPlease choose a number from 1-4 only\n ");
      }
    }while(choice != '4');
  }

  // method for adding a new car to the list
  private static void addCar(Vector carListIn)
  {
    String tempReg;
    String tempMake;
    double tempPrice;
```

```
    System.out.print("Please enter the registration number: ");
    tempReg = EasyIn.getString();
    System.out.print("Please enter the make: ");
    tempMake = EasyIn.getString();
    System.out.print("Please enter the price: ");
    tempPrice = EasyIn.getDouble();
    carListIn.addElement(new Car(tempReg, tempMake, tempPrice));
}

/* method for removing a car from the list - in a real application this
   would need to include some validation */
private static void removeCar(Vector carListIn)
{
    int pos;
    System.out.print("Enter the position of the car to be removed: ");
    pos = EasyIn.getInt();
    carListIn.removeElementAt(pos - 1);
}

// method for listing details of all cars in the list
private static void listAll(Vector carListIn)
{
    for(int i = 0; i < carListIn.size(); i++)
    {
        /* we have to type cast here because the elementAt method of Vector
           returns an object */
        Car tempCar = (Car) carListIn.elementAt(i);
        System.out.println(tempCar.getRegistration()
                        + " "
                        + tempCar.getMake()
                        + " "
                        + tempCar.getPrice());
    }
    EasyIn.pause("\n Press <enter> to continue");
}

// method for writing the file
private static void writeList(Vector carListIn)
{
    Car tempCar;
    try
    {
        /* create a FileWriter object, carFile, that handles the low-level
           details of writing the list to a file which we have called
           "Cars.txt" */
        FileWriter carFile = new FileWriter("Cars.txt");
```

```
      /* now create a PrintWriter object to wrap around carFile; this allows
         us to use high-level functions such as println */
   PrintWriter carWriter = new PrintWriter(carFile);
   // write each element of the list to the file
   for(int i = 0; i < carListIn.size(); i++)
   {
     tempCar = (Car) carListIn.elementAt(i);
     carWriter.println(tempCar.getRegistration());
     carWriter.println(tempCar.getMake());
     /* println can accept a double, then write it as a text string */
     carWriter.println(tempCar.getPrice());
   }
   /* close the file so that it is no longer accessible to the program */
   carWriter.close();
  }

  // handle the exception thrown by the FileWriter methods
  catch(IOException e)
  {
    System.out.println("There was a problem writing the file");
  }
}

// method for reading the file
private static void readList(Vector carListIn)
{
  String tempReg;
  String tempMake;
  String tempStringPrice;
  double tempDoublePrice;
  try
  {
    /* create a FileReader object, carFile, that handles the low-level
       details of reading the list from the "Cars.txt" file */
    FileReader carFile = new FileReader("Cars.txt");
    /* now create a BufferedReader object to wrap around carFile; this
       allows us to user high-level functions such as readLine */
    BufferedReader carStream = new BufferedReader(carFile);
    // read the first line of the file
    tempReg = carStream.readLine();
    /* read the rest of the first record, then all the rest of the records
       until the end of the file is reached */
    while(tempReg != null) // a null string indicates end of file
    {
      tempMake = carStream.readLine();
      tempStringPrice = carStream.readLine();
```

```
              /* as this is a text file we have to convert the price to double */
              tempDoublePrice = Double.parseDouble(tempStringPrice);
              carListIn.addElement
                        (new Car(tempReg, tempMake, tempDoublePrice));
              tempReg = carStream.readLine();
          }
          /* close the file so that it is no longer accessible to the program */
          carStream.close();
      }

      /* handle the exception that is thrown by the FileReader constructor if
         the file is not found */
      catch(FileNotFoundException e)
      {
          System.out.println("\nNo file was read");
      }

      // handle the exception thrown by the FileReader methods
      catch(IOException e)
      {
          System.out.println("\nThere was a problem reading the file");
      }
    }
}
```

It is only the writeList and readList methods that we need to analyse here – none of the other methods involves anything new. Let's start with writeList. The first thing to notice is that, after declaring a Car object, we enclose everything in a **try** block. This is because all the methods (including the constructor) of the FileWriter class that we are going to use throw IOExceptions to deal with situations in which the file cannot be written (for example if the disk is full).

The first thing we need to do (within the **try** block) is to open a file in which to keep our records. To do this we use the class called FileWriter; this is one of the classes we talked about earlier that provide the low-level communication between the program and the file. By opening a file we establish a *stream* through which we can output data to the file. We create a FileWriter object, carFile, giving it the name of the file to which we want to write the data:

```
FileWriter carFile = new FileWriter("Cars.txt");
```

In this case we have called the file Cars.txt.[1] Creating the new FileWriter object causes the file to be opened in output mode – meaning that it is ready to receive data; if no file of this name exists then one will be created. Opening the file in this way (in output mode) means that

---

[1] As we have not supplied an absolute pathname, the file will be saved in the current directory.

any data that we write to the file will wipe out what was previously there. That is what we need for this particular application, because we are simply going to write the entire list when the program terminates. Sometimes, however, it is necessary to open a file in **append** mode; in this mode any data written to the file would be written after the existing data. To do this we would simply have used another constructor, which takes an additional (`boolean`) parameter indicating whether or not we require append mode:

```
FileWriter carFile = new FileWriter("Cars.txt", true);
```

The next thing we do is create an object, `carWriter`, of the `PrintWriter` class, sending it the `carFile` object as a parameter.

```
PrintWriter carWriter = new PrintWriter(carFile);
```

This object can now communicate with our file via the `carFile` object; `PrintWriter` objects have higher level methods than `FileWriter` objects (for example `print` and `println`) that enable us to write whole strings like we do when we output to the screen.

Now we are ready to write each `Car` in the list to our file – we can use a `for` loop for this:

```
for(int i = 0; i < carListIn.size(); i++)
{
   tempCar = (Car) carListIn.elementAt(i);
   carWriter.println(tempCar.getRegistration());
   carWriter.println(tempCar.getMake());
   carWriter.println(tempCar.getPrice());
}
```

We have declared an object, `tempCar` that is assigned on each iteration to the next object in the list by invoking the `elementAt` method of `Vector` – remembering to type cast the object that this method returns back to a `Car`. And now we can use the `println` method of our `PrintWriter` object, `carWriter`, to write the registration number, the make and the price of the car to the file; `println` converts the price to a `String` before writing it. Notice also that the `println` method inserts a newline character at the end of the string that it prints; if we did not want the newline character to be inserted, we would use the `print` method instead.

Now that we have finished with the file it is most important that we *close* it. Closing the file achieves two things. First, it ensures that a special character, the end-of-file marker,[2] is written at the end of the file. This enables us to detect when the end of the file has been reached when we are reading it – more about this when we explore the `readList` method. Second, closing

---

[2] Most systems use ASCII character 26 as the end-of-file marker.

the file means that it is no longer accessible by the program, and is therefore not susceptible to being written to in error. We close the file by calling the `close` method of `PrintWriter`:

```
carWriter.close();
```

Finally we have to handle the `IOExceptions` thrown by the `FileWriter` methods:

```
catch(IOException e)
{
   System.out.println("There was a problem writing the file");
}
```

In a moment we will explore the code for reading the file. But bear in mind that if we were to run our program and add a few records, and then quit the program we would have saved the data to a text-file called `Cars.txt`, so we should be able to read this file with a text editor. When we did this, we created three cars, and then looked inside the file using Windows Notepad. Figure 18.1 shows the result.

As we have written each field using the `println` statement, each one, as you can see, starts on a new line. If our aim were to view the file with a text editor as we have just done, then this might not be the most suitable format – we might, for example, have wanted to have one record per line; we could also have printed some headings if we had wished. However, it is actually our intention to make our program read the entire file into our list when the program starts – and as we shall now see, one field per line makes reading the text file nice and easy. So let's take a look at our `readList` method.

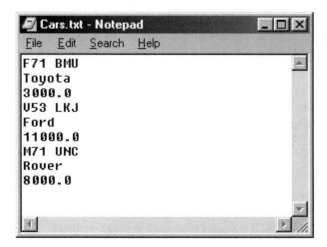

Fig 18.1   Viewing a text file with Windows Notepad

First, we need to declare some variables to hold the value of each field as we progressively read through the file. Remembering that this is a text file we declare three `Strings`:

```
String tempReg;
String tempMake;
String tempStringPrice;
```

But the last of these will have to be converted to a **double** before we store it in the list so we also need a variable to hold this value once it is converted:

```
double tempDoublePrice;
```

Now, as before, we put everything into a **try** block, as we are going to have to deal with the exceptions thrown by the various methods we will be using.

The first thing we need to do is to open the file that we wish to read; we create an object – `carFile` – of the class `FileReader` which deals with the low-level details involved in the process of reading a file. The name of the file, `Cars.txt`, that we wish to read is sent in as a parameter to the constructor; this file is then opened in `read` mode.

```
FileReader carFile = new FileReader("Cars.txt");
```

Now, in order that we can use some higher level read methods, we wrap up our `carFile` object in an object of a class called `BufferedReader`. We have called this new object `CarStream`.

```
BufferedReader carStream = new BufferedReader(carFile);
```

Now we are going to read each field of each record in turn, so we will need some sort of loop. The only problem is to know when to stop – this is because the number of records in the file can be different each time we run the program. There are different ways in which to approach this problem. One very good way (although not the one we have used here), if the same program is responsible for both reading and writing the file, is simply to write the total number of records as the first item when the file is written. Then, when reading the file, this item is the first thing to be read – and once this number is known a simple `for` loop can be used to read the records.

However, it may well be the case that the file was written by another program (such as a text editor). In this case it is necessary to check for the end-of-file marker that we spoke about earlier. In order to help you understand this process we are using this method here, even though we could have used the first (and perhaps simpler) method.

This is what we have to do: we have to read the first field of each record, then check whether that field began with the end-of-file marker. If it did, we must stop reading the file, but if it didn't we have to carry on and read the remaining fields of that record. Then we start the process again for the next record.

Some pseudocode should make the process clear; we have made this pseudocode specific to our particular example:

```
BEGIN
  READ the Registration Number field of the first record
  LOOP while the field just read does not contain the end-of-file marker
  BEGIN
    READ the Make field of the next record
    READ the Price field of the next record
    Convert the Price to a double
    Create a new car with details just read and add it to the list
    READ the Registration Number field of the next record
  END
END
```

The code for this is shown below:

```
tempReg = carStream.readLine();
while(tempReg != null) // a null string indicates end of file
{
  tempMake = carStream.readLine();
  tempStringPrice = carStream.readLine();
  tempDoublePrice = Double.parseDouble(tempStringPrice);
  carListIn.addElement (new Car(tempReg, tempMake, tempDoublePrice));
  tempReg = carStream.readLine();
}
```

Notice that we are using the readLine method of BufferedReader to read each record. This method reads a line of text from the file; a line is considered anything that is terminated by the newline character. The method returns that line as a String (which does not include the newline character). However, if the line read consists of the end-of-file marker, then readLine returns a null, making it very easy for us to check if the end of the file has been reached. In section 18.7 you will be able to contrast this method of BufferedReader with the read method, which reads a single character only.

Once we have finished with the file, we mustn't forget to close it!

```
carStream.close();
```

Finally we must handle the exceptions that are thrown by the methods of `FileReader`; first, the constructor throws a `FileNotFound` exception if the file is not found.

```
catch(FileNotFoundException e)
{
    System.out.println("\nNo file was read");
}
```

All the other methods throw `IOExceptions`:

```
catch(IOException e)
{
    System.out.println("\nThere was a problem reading the file");
}
```

18.6 *Reading and writing to binary files*

In many ways, it makes little difference whether we store our data in text format or binary format; but it is, of course, important to know the sort of file that we are dealing with when we are reading it. For example, in the previous section you saw that we needed to convert a `String` to a **double** when it came to handling the price of a car. However, it is important for you to be familiar with the ways of handling both types of file, so now we will show you how to read and write data to a binary file using exactly the same example as before.

The only difference in our program will be the `writeList` and `readList` methods. First let's look at the code for the new `writeList` method:

```
private static void writeList(Vector carListIn)
{
  Car tempCar;
  try
  {
    FileOutputStream carFile = new FileOutputStream("Cars.bin");
    DataOutputStream carWriter = new DataOutputStream(carFile);
    for(int i = 0; i < carListIn.size(); i++)
    {
      tempCar = (Car) carListIn.elementAt(i);
      carWriter.writeUTF(tempCar.getRegistration());
      carWriter.writeUTF(tempCar.getMake());
      carWriter.writeDouble(tempCar.getPrice());
    }
    carWriter.close();
  }
  catch(IOException e)
  {
    System.out.println("There was a problem writing the file");
  }
}
```

You can see that the process is similar to the one we used to write a text file, but here the two classes that we are using are `FileOutputStream` and `DataOutputStream` which deal with the low-level and high-level processes respectively. The `DataOutputStream` class provides methods such as `writeDouble`, `writeInt` and `writeChar` for writing all the basic scalar types, as well as a method called `writeUTF` for writing strings. The UTF stands for *Unicode Transformation Format*, and the method is so-called because it converts the Unicode characters (which are used in Java) to the more commonly used ASCII format when it writes the string to a file.

Before moving on to the `readList` method it is worth reminding ourselves that a file written in this way – that is, a binary file – cannot be read by a text editor. And to prove the point, figure 18.2 shows the result of trying to read such a file in Windows Notepad.

So now we can look at the `readList` method:

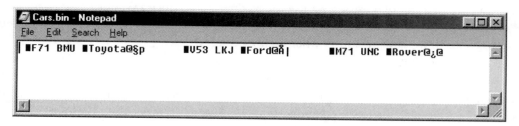

Fig 18.2   Trying to read a binary file with a text editor

```
private static void readList(Vector carListIn)
{
  String tempReg;
  String tempMake;
  double tempPrice;
  boolean endOfFile = false;
  try
  {
    // we have renamed the file 'Cars.bin'
    FileInputStream carFile = new FileInputStream("Cars.bin");
    DataInputStream carStream = new DataInputStream(carFile);
    while(endOfFile == false)
    {
      try
      {
        tempReg = carStream.readUTF();
        tempMake = carStream.readUTF();
        tempPrice = carStream.readDouble();
        carListIn.addElement(new Car(tempReg, tempMake, tempPrice));
      }
      catch(EOFException e)
      {
        endOfFile = true;
      }
    }
    carStream.close();
  }
  catch(FileNotFoundException e)
  {
    System.out.println("\nNo file was read");
  }
  catch(IOException e)
  {
    System.out.println("There was a problem reading the file");
  }
}
```

You can see that the two classes we use for reading binary files are FileInputStream for low-level access and DataInputStream for the higher-level functions; they have equivalent methods to those we saw previously when writing to files.

The most important thing to observe in this method is the way we test whether we have reached the end of the file. In the case of a binary file we can do this by making use of the fact that the DataInputStream methods throw EOFExceptions when an end of file marker has been detected during a read operation. So all we have to do is declare a **boolean** variable, endOfFile, which we initially set to **false**, and we use this as the termination condition in the **while** loop. Then we enclose our read operations in a **try** block, and, when an exception is thrown, fileNotFound is set to **true** within the **catch** block, causing the while loop to terminate.

18.7   *Reading a text file character by character*

As you will have realized by now, there are many ways in which we can deal with handling files, and the methods we choose will depend largely on what it is we want to achieve.

In this section we will show you how to read a text file character by character – this is a useful technique if we do not know anything about the structure of the file. The way we have done this is to add a new option to the FileHandler class that we developed in the previous chapter (section 17.6). We have added a *Display contents* option to the *File* menu. To demonstrate this we created a file called Poem.txt with a text editor, and when we selected it and displayed its contents we got the result shown in figure 18.3.

The technique that we used to do this was to read each character of the file, display it in the viewing area, then move on to the next character. We have designed the program to stop either when the end of the file has been reached or when a stipulated maximum number of characters has been read. We put this last condition in as a safeguard in case the user should try to display a very large file by mistake.

Here is the code for the event handler for the new menu option, which we called displayContentsChoice:

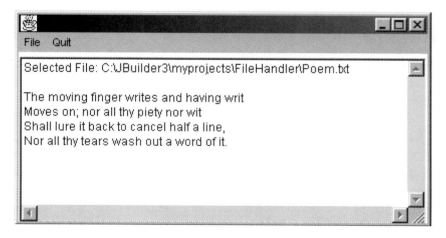

Fig 18.3   Using the *Display contents* option of the *FileHandler* class

```
if(e.getSource() == displayContentsChoice)
{
  try
  {
    final int MAX = 1000;
    FileReader testFile = new FileReader(dir + selectedFile);
    BufferedReader textStream = new BufferedReader(testFile);
    int ch; // to hold the integer (Unicode) value of the character
    char c; // to hold the character when type cast from integer
    int counter = 0; // to count the number of characters read so far
    ch = textStream.read(); // read the first character from the file
    c = (char) ch; // type cast from integer to character
    viewArea.append("\n");
    /* continue through the file until either the end of the file is reached
       (in which case -1 is returned) or the maximum number of characters
       stipulated have been read*/
    while( ch != -1 && counter <= MAX)
    {
      counter++; // increment the counter
      viewArea.append(" " + c); // display the character
      ch = textStream.read(); // read the next character
      c = (char) ch;
    }
    textStream.close();
    viewArea.append("\n");
  }
  catch(IOException ioe)
  {
    if(selectedFile == null) // no file selected
    {
      viewArea.append("No file selected\n");
    }
    else
    {
      viewArea.append("There was a problem reading the file\n");
    }
  }
}
```

The main thing to notice here is that we are using the read method of BufferedReader; this method reads a single character from the file and returns an integer, the Unicode value of the character read. If the character read was the end-of-file marker then it returns −1, making it an easy matter for us to check whether the end of the file has been reached. In the above example, as explained earlier, we stop reading the file if we have reached the end or if more than the maximum number of characters allowed has been read; here we have set that maximum to 1000. You can see that in the above method, after each read operation, we type cast the integer to a character, which we then display in the view area.

18.8   *Stream tokenization*

Let's stick with text files for a moment. In section 18.5 the approach we used was to wrap a high-level BufferedReader object around a low-level FileReader object. Another approach is to make use of a class called StreamTokenizer. Using this class allows us to analyse the contents of a file. The class has a method called nextToken; every time this method is invoked, individual characters are read from the file until a recognizable **token** has been built – a token is basically a word or a number, together with some special characters that indicate such things as an end of line or an end of file.

Once a token has been read, a value is placed in an attribute called ttype. The value of ttype therefore tells us the type of token that has just been read. To make it easier for us, a number of integer constants have been defined within the StreamTokenizer class as follows:

TT_WORD: indicates that a word has been read
TT_NUMBER: indicates that a number has been read
TT_EOF: indicates that an end-of-file marker has been read
TT_EOL: indicates that an end-of-line character has been read; this is not
               recognized unless you have previously called the eolIsSignificant
               method of StreamTokenizer, with a value of **true** as the parameter.

If a character is read that is not going to form part of a word or a number (such as a punctuation mark like a bracket or comma for example) then ttype holds the Unicode value of that character.

Two other important attributes of StreamTokenizer are nval (a **double**) and sval (a String). If the token just read by the nextToken method was a number (that is, ttype has a value TT_NUMBER) then nval will hold the value of the number just read (or null if a number was not read). If the token was a word, then sval holds the value of that word (or null if a word was not read).

It should be noted that nextToken stops reading either when it comes to a special token like an end-of-line marker or when it encounters a character that will not form part of a word or number – most commonly this will be a space. However, if anything is contained within double or single quotes, it will read the entire string and leave its value in sval. If a quoted string has been read, then ttype holds the Unicode value for the double quote or the single quote.

Program 18.2 tests out the StreamTokenizer class for us. The comments should be self-explanatory in the light of the above description, so we won't say too much about it afterwards – apart from showing you the result.

THE *TokenizedReader* **CLASS**

```java
import java.io.*;

public class TokenizedReader
{
  public static void main(String[] args)
  {
    try
    {
      // create a FileReader object, testFile
      FileReader testFile = new FileReader("Test.java");
      // create a StreamTokenizer object to wrap around testFile
      StreamTokenizer tokenTest = new StreamTokenizer(testFile);
      // get the first token
      tokenTest.nextToken();
      // keep reading tokens until the end of the file is reached
      while(tokenTest.ttype != StreamTokenizer.TT_EOF)
      {
        // if the token was a number
        if(tokenTest.ttype == StreamTokenizer.TT_NUMBER)
        {
          System.out.println("Number: " + tokenTest.nval);
        }
        // if the token was a word
        else if(tokenTest.ttype == StreamTokenizer.TT_WORD)
        {
          System.out.println("Word: " + tokenTest.sval);
        }
        // if the token is a quoted string
        else if(tokenTest.ttype == '"'|| tokenTest.ttype == '\'')
        {
          System.out.println("Quoted string: " + tokenTest.sval);
        }
        // if the token is any other character
        else
        {
          System.out.println("Character: " + (char) tokenTest.ttype);
        }
        tokenTest.nextToken();
      }
    }

    catch(FileNotFoundException e)
    {
      System.out.print("\nFile not found");
    }
```

```
      catch(IOException e)
      {
        System.out.print("\nThere was a problem reading the file");
      }
      EasyIn.pause("Press <Enter> to quit");
    }
}
```

You can see that the file that gets analysed is actually a little Java program file called Test.java, which looks like this:

```
public class Test
{
  public static void main(String[] args)
  {
    System.out.print("This is a number: " + 3.987);
  }
}
```

Running program 18.2 gives the following output:

```
Word: public
Word: class
Word: Test
Character: {
Word: public
Word: static
Word: void
Word: main
Character: (
Word: String
Character: [
Character: ]
Word: args
Character: )
Character: {
Word: System.out.print
Character: (
Quoted string: This is a number:
Character: +
Number: 3.987
```

```
Character: )
Character: ;
Character: }
Character: }
Press <Enter> to quit
```

Notice that we did not check for end-of-line characters here – this is left as a practical exercise.

18.9   *Object serialization*

If you are going to be dealing with files that will be accessed only within a Java program, then one of the easiest ways to do this is to make use of two classes called `ObjectInputStream` and `ObjectOutputStream`. These classes have methods called, respectively, `readObject` and `writeObject` that enable us to read and write whole objects from and to files. The process of converting an object into a stream of data suitable for storage on a disk is called **serialization**.

Any class whose objects are to be read and written using the above methods must implement the interface `Serializable`. This is a type of interface that we have not actually come across before – it is known as a **marker** and in fact contains no methods. Its purpose is simply to make an "announcement" to anyone using the class; namely that objects of this class can be read and written as whole objects. In designing a class we can, then, choose not to make our class serializable – we might want to do this for security reasons (for example, to stop whole objects being transportable over the World Wide Web) or to avoid errors in a distributed environment where the code for the class was not present on every machine.

In the case of our `Car` class, we therefore need to declare it in the following way before we could use it in a program that handles whole objects:

```
class Car implements Serializable
```

Note that the `Serializable` interface resides within the `java.io` package, so this package needs to be imported for us to access it.

Now we can re-write the `writeList` and `readList` methods of program 18.1 so that we manipulate whole objects. First the `writeList` method:

```
private static void writeList(Vector carListIn)
{
  try
  {
    // create a FileOutputStream object, carFile
    // notice that we have now called the file 'Cars.obf'
    FileOutputStream carFile = new FileOutputStream("Cars.obf");
    // create an ObjectOutputStream object to wrap around carFile
    ObjectOutputStream carStream = new ObjectOutputStream(carFile);
    for(int i = 0; i < carListIn.size(); i++)
    {
      // save the whole object with the writeObject method
      carStream.writeObject(carListIn.elementAt(i));
    }
    carStream.close();
  }
  catch(IOException e)
  {
    System.out.println("There was a problem writing the file");
  }
}
```

You can see how easy this is — you just need one line to save a whole object to a file by using the writeObject method of ObjectOutputStream.

Now the readList method:

```
private static void readList(Vector carListIn)
{
  boolean endOfFile = false;
  Car tempCar;
  try
  {
    // create a FileInputStream object, carFile
    FileInputStream carFile = new FileInputStream("Cars.obf");
    // create an ObjectInputStream object to wrap around carFile
    ObjectInputStream carStream = new ObjectInputStream(carFile);
    // read the first (whole) object with the readObject method
    tempCar = (Car) carStream.readObject();
    while(endOfFile != true)
    {
      try
      {
        carListIn.addElement(tempCar);
```

```
                // read the next (whole) object
                tempCar = (Car) carStream.readObject();
            }
            /* use the fact that readObject throws an EOFException to check
               whether the end of the file has been reached */
            catch(EOFException e)
            {
                endOfFile = true;
            }
        }
        carStream.close();
    }

    catch(FileNotFoundException e)
    {
        System.out.println("\nNo file was read");
    }

    catch(ClassNotFoundException e)  // thrown by readObject
    {
        System.out.println
                ("\nTrying to read an object of an unknown class");
    }

    catch(StreamCorruptedException e)  // thrown by the constructor
    {
        System.out.println("\nUnreadable file format");
    }

    catch(IOException e)
    {
        System.out.println("There was a problem reading the file");
    }
}
```

Again you can see how easy this is — a whole object is read with the readObject method.

We should draw your attention to a few of the exception handling routines we have used here — first, notice that we have once again made use of the fact that readObject throws an EOFException to check for the end of the file. Second, notice that readObject also throws a ClassNotFoundException which indicates that the object just read does not correspond to any class known to the program. Finally, the constructor throws a StreamCorruptedException which indicates that the input stream given to it was not produced by an ObjectOutputStream object — underlining the fact that reading and writing whole objects are complementary techniques that are specific to Java programs.

One final thing to note — if an attribute of a Serializable class is itself an object of another class, then that class too must be Serializable in order for us to be able to read and write whole objects as we have just done. You will probably have noticed that in the case of the Car class, one of its attributes is a String — fortunately the String class does indeed implement the Serializable interface, which is why we had no problem using it in this way in our example.

Before moving on, it is worth noting that all the Java collection classes such as Hashtable and Vector are themselves serializable. This is discussed more fully in chapter 20.

18.10 *Random access files*

All the programs that we have looked at so far in this chapter have made use of serial access. For small applications this will probably be all you need — however if you were to be writing applications that handled very large data files it would be desirable to use random access methods. Fortunately Java provides us with this facility.

The class that we need is called RandomAccessFile. This enables us to open a file for random access. Random access files can be opened in either read-write mode or in read-only mode; the constructor therefore takes, in addition to the name of the file, an additional String parameter which can be either "rw" or "r", indicating the mode in which the file is to be opened.

In addition to methods similar to those of the DataOutputStream class (such as writeUTF, readDouble and so on), RandomAccessFile has a method called seek. This takes one attribute, of type long, which indicates how many bytes to move the file-pointer before starting a read or write operation.

So now we have the question of how far to move the pointer — we need to be able to calculate the size of each record. If we are dealing only with intrinsic types, this is an easy matter. These types all take up a fixed amount of storage space, as shown in table 18.1.

Table 18.1	Size of the intrinsic types
byte	1 byte
short	2 bytes
char	2 bytes
int	4 bytes
long	8 bytes
float	4 bytes
double	8 bytes
boolean	1 bit[3]

---

[3] Allow for 1 byte when calculating storage space.

The difficulty comes when a record contains `Strings`, as is commonly the case. The size of a `String` object varies according to how many characters it contains. What we have to do is to restrict the length of each string to a given amount; let's take the `Car` class as an example. The data elements of any `Car` object consist of two `Strings` and a **double**. We will make the decision that the two `String` attributes – registration number and make – will be restricted to 10 characters only. Now, any `String` variable will always take up 1 byte for each character, plus two extra bytes (at the beginning) to hold an integer representing the length of the `String`. So now we can calculate the maximum amount of storage space we need for a car as follows:

```
registration (String)     12 bytes
make (String)             12 bytes
price (double)             8 bytes
TOTAL                     32 bytes
```

This still leaves us with one problem – what if one of the `String` attributes entered is actually *less* than 10? The best way to deal with this is to pad the string out with spaces so that it always contains *exactly* 10 characters. This means that the size of every `Car` object will always be exactly 32 bytes – you will see how we have done this when you study program 18.3. This program uses a rather different approach to the one we have used so far in this chapter. Two options (as well as a Quit option) are provided. The first, the option to add a car, simply adds the car to the end of the file. The second, to display the details of a car, asks the user for the position of the car in the file then reads this record directly from the file. You can see that there is now no need for an array or vector to store the list of cars.

Study the program carefully – then we will discuss it.

PROGRAM 18.3

```java
import java.util.*;
import java.io.*;

public class RandomFileTester
{
  private static final int CAR_SIZE = 32; // each record will be 32 bytes
  public static void main(String[] args)
  {
    char choice;
    do
    {
      System.out.println("\nRandom File Tester");
      System.out.println("1. Add a car");
      System.out.println("2. Display a car");
      System.out.println("3. Quit\n");
      choice = EasyIn.getChar();
      System.out.println();
      switch(choice)
      {
```

```
        case '1' : addCar();
                break;
        case '2' : displayCar();
                break;
        case '3' : break;
        default : System.out.print("\nChoose 1-3 only please\n");
      }
   }while(choice != '3');
}

private static void addCar()
{
   String tempReg;
   String tempMake;
   double tempPrice;
   System.out.print("Please enter the registration number: ");
   tempReg = EasyIn.getString();
   // limit the registration number to 10 characters
   if(tempReg.length() > 10)
   {
     System.out.print("Ten characters only - please re-enter: ");
     tempReg = EasyIn.getString();
   }
   // pad the string with spaces to make it exactly 10 characters long
   for(int i = tempReg.length() + 1 ; i <= 10 ; i++)
   {
     tempReg = tempReg.concat(" ");
   }
   System.out.print("Please enter the make: ");
   tempMake = EasyIn.getString();
   //limit the make number to 10 characters
   if(tempMake.length() > 10)
   {
     System.out.print("Ten characters only - please re-enter: ");
     tempMake = EasyIn.getString();
   }
   // pad the string with spaces to make it exactly 10 characters long
   for(int i = tempMake.length() + 1; i <= 10; i++)
   {
     tempMake = tempMake.concat(" ");
   }
   System.out.print("Please enter the price: ");
   tempPrice = EasyIn.getDouble();
   // write the record to the file
   writeRecord(new Car(tempReg, tempMake, tempPrice));
}
```

```
private static void displayCar()
{
   int pos;
   // get the position of the item to be read from the user
   System.out.print("Enter the car's position in the list: ");
   pos = EasyIn.getInt();
   // read the record requested from the file
   Car tempCar = readRecord(pos);
   if(tempCar != null)
   {
      System.out.println(tempCar.getRegistration().trim()
                        + " "
                        + tempCar.getMake().trim()
                        + " "
                        + tempCar.getPrice());
   }
   else
   {
      System.out.println("Invalid position");
   }
   EasyIn.pause("\n Press <enter> to continue");
}

private static void writeRecord(Car tempCar)
{
   try
   {
      // open a RandomAccessFile in read-write mode
      RandomAccessFile carFile = new RandomAccessFile("Cars.rand", "rw");
      // move the pointer to the end of the file
      carFile.seek(carFile.length());
      // write the three fields of the record to the file
      carFile.writeUTF(tempCar.getRegistration());
      carFile.writeUTF(tempCar.getMake());
      carFile.writeDouble(tempCar.getPrice());
      // close the file
      carFile.close();
   }
   catch(IOException e)
   {
      System.out.println("There was a problem writing the file");
   }
}

private static Car readRecord(int pos)
{
```

```
    String tempReg;
    String tempMake;
    double tempPrice;
    Car tempCar = null; /* a null value will be returned if there was a
                           problem reading the record */
    try
    {
      // open a RandomAccessFile in read-only mode
      RandomAccessFile carFile = new RandomAccessFile("Cars.rand","r");
      // move the pointer to the start of the required record
      carFile.seek((pos-1) * CAR_SIZE);
      // read the three fields of the record from the file
      tempReg = carFile.readUTF();
      tempMake = carFile.readUTF();
      tempPrice = carFile.readDouble();
      // close the file
      carFile.close();
      // use the data just read to create a new Car object
      tempCar = new Car(tempReg, tempMake, tempPrice);
    }
    catch(FileNotFoundException e)
    {
      System.out.println("\nNo file was read");
    }

    catch(IOException e)
    {
      System.out.println("There was a problem reading the file");
    }
    // return the record that was read
    return tempCar;
  }
}
```

You can see that in the addCar method we have called writeRecord with a Car object as a parameter. Let's take a closer look at the writeRecord method. First, the line to open the file in read-write mode:

```
RandomAccessFile carFile = new RandomAccessFile("Cars.rand", "rw");
```

Now the instruction to move the file pointer:

```
carFile.seek(carFile.length());
```

You can see how we use the seek method to move the pointer a specific number of bytes; here the correct number of bytes is the size of the file (as we want to write the new record at the end of the file), so we use the `length` method of RandomAccessFile to determine this number.

Now we can move on to look at the readRecord method. You can see that this is called from within the `displayCar` method, with an integer parameter, representing the position of the required record in the file.

The file is opened in read-only mode:

```
RandomAccessFile carFile = new RandomAccessFile("Cars.rand","r");
```

Then the seek method of RandomAccessFile is invoked as follows:

```
carFile.seek((pos-1) * CAR_SIZE);
```

You can see that the number of bytes through which to move the pointer has been calculated by multiplying the size of the record by one less than the position. This is because in order to read the first record we don't move the pointer at all; in order to read the second record we must move it 1 × 32 bytes; for the third record 2 × 32 bytes; and so on.

The final thing to note about program 18.3 is that in the `displayCar` method we have used the `trim` method of String to get rid of the extra spaces that we used to pad out the first two fields of the record.

Here is a test run from the program (starting off with an empty file):

```
Random File Tester
1. Add a car
2. View a car
3. Quit

1

Please enter the registration number: R54 HJK
Please enter the make: Vauxhall
Please enter the price: 7000

Random File Tester
1. Add a car
2. View a car
3. Quit

1
```

```
Please enter the registration number: T87 EFU
Please enter the make: Nissan
Please enter the price: 9000

Random File Tester
1. Add a car
2. View a car
3. Quit

2

Enter the car's position in the list: 2
T87 EFU Nissan 9000.0

Press <enter> to continue
```

Tutorial exercises

1. Explain the differences among text, binary and object encoding of data.
2. Describe the difference between serial file access and random file access.
3. Explain what is meant by the term *object serialization*.

Practical work

You will need to have access to the Car *class, which you can download or copy from this chapter or from the* CD-ROM.

1. Download and run program 18.1 then adapt it so that it handles binary files, as described in section 18.6.
2. Add the *Display Contents* option to the FileHandler class from chapter 17, as described in section 18.7.
3. Download and run program 18.2, then adapt it so that it recognizes the end-of-line character (see section 18.8).
4. Adapt program 18.1 so that it uses object encoding, as explained in section 18.9 (don't forget that the Car class must implement the Serializable interface).
5. Download and run program 18.3.
6. Adapt the address book program that you developed in the last chapter so that it keeps permanent records.

ENHANCING THE USER INTERFACE

19.1 Introduction

The means by which a user communicates with a program is referred to as the **user interface** or **human computer interface**. In chapters 9 and 17 you learnt to create and use the components available in the Abstract Window Toolkit (AWT) package. In this chapter you are going to learn to use an extension of the AWT called **Swing**. You will find that using this package enables you to produce very professional and attractive user interfaces.

At the end of this chapter we explain how you can improve your interfaces even further by creating your own colours and fonts, and we also introduce some additional layout managers.

Finally, we provide some guidelines for good interface design.

19.2   *The Java* **Swing** *package*

The Swing classes build on the AWT classes to provide enhanced functionality and appearance. There is, in fact, so much to the Swing components that we won't be able to cover everything in this book; but instead we will provide what we hope is a useful overview of the many classes in the Swing package, so that you are aware of what is available; and in chapter 21, which builds the GUI for our next case study, you will see even more of ways of using the Swing components.

There is one very important difference between AWT and Swing. To illustrate this we have converted the GUI for the case study that we developed in chapters 10 and 11 to a Swing version. This is shown in figure 19.1.

You can see that this GUI has a rather different look and feel compared to the previous one. In the case of applications developed using the AWT classes you will probably have noticed that the components (buttons, text boxes etc.) look very similar to the ones you are used to seeing on your particular platform. However, whatever platform you were to run the Swing

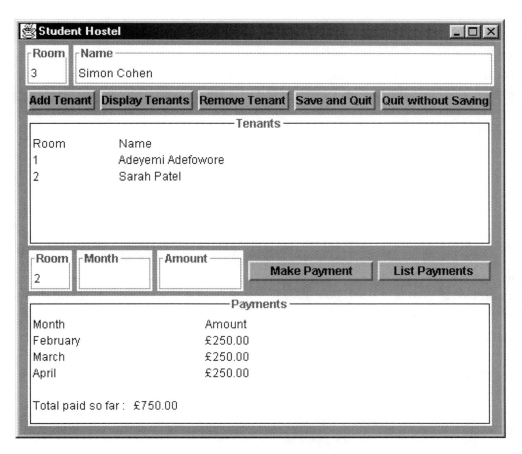

Fig 19.1   The *Swing* version of the *Hostel* GUI

application on it will look exactly the same! This is because the design of the Swing classes involves a very different approach to that of the AWT classes.

When we use the AWT classes, any component that we create is associated with the corresponding component in the native operating system; so for example, when we use methods of an AWT `Button` object, this communicates with a corresponding object – usually referred to as a **peer** – provided by, say, the Windows or Mac operating system. Consequently your button will look like a Windows or a Mac button. Components that rely on the native operating system are described as **heavyweight** components as they make extensive use of the system's resources.

In the case of Swing, however, most of the components are written in Java and all the code is provided as part of the Swing package. Components that are written in Java are called **lightweight** components.

The Swing package, along with the AWT, is part of what is known as the Java Foundation Classes (JFC).

One word of warning about using Swing; any JVM that runs your program needs to be packaged with all the classes of the JFC in order for your Swing programs to work. This is certainly the case with any JVM that comes with any modern development tool, but is not the case with the JVM in many common browsers. It is therefore likely that Swing applets will not be successful, and until all browsers are Swing-enabled, it is a good idea to stick to AWT when building applets.

The Swing classes come in a package called Javax (Java eXtension). When writing Swing programs you must therefore include the **import** statement:

```
import javax.swing.*;
```

As we have said, Swing is an extension of AWT; the primary component of Swing, from which many other Swing classes are derived, is called `JComponent` and is derived from `Component`. Many of the other Swing classes are named simply by putting a J in front of their AWT equivalent. Figure 19.2 shows the relationship between the AWT and Swing classes. All the components that are derived from `JComponent` are lightweight components; the four top-level window classes – `JFrame`, `JWindow`, `JDialog`, `JApplet` – are heavyweight.

You can see from the new version of the `Hostel` GUI that using Swing enables you to produce interfaces that have a very attractive look and feel to them. Some of the other advantages of using Swing are summarized below:

- you can create attractive borders on all the basic components;
- you can easily combine text and graphics on components (using the Icon interface);
- you can add scrolling facilities to *any* component (using the `JScrollPane` class);
- you can easily provide message boxes and input boxes (using the `JOptionPane` class); examples of this can be found in chapter 21;
- the swing equivalent to the AWT `Applet` class – the `JApplet` class – has a method that allows you to add menus to objects of this class.

In order to provide an overview of Swing we will start by studying the JFrame class, and then go on to explore some of the above bullet points, thus giving you examples of the many ways that the potential of Swing can be exploited.

19.3 *The JFrame class*

The new Swing version of the Hostel program that you saw in figure 19.1 was created by converting all the components in the Hostel class to their Swing equivalents – the new class is named HostelSwing, and the complete code is available on the website and the CD-ROM.

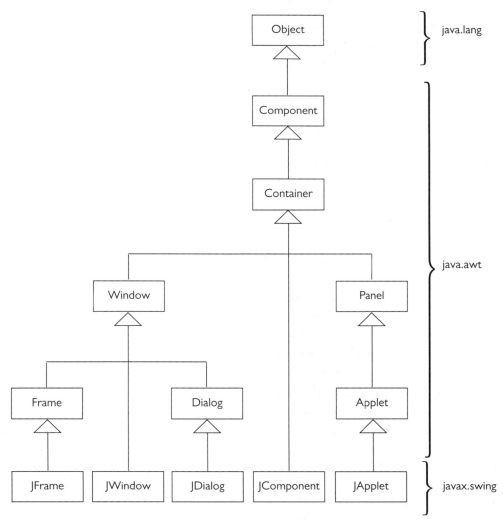

Fig 19.2 The AWT and Swing class hierarchies

Program 19.1 shows how we run this class in the Swing equivalent of a Frame – namely a JFrame. You will notice a few differences.

PROGRAM 19.1

```
import javax.swing.*;
import java.awt.*;

class RunHostelSwing
{
  public static void main(String[] args)
  {
    JFrame frame = new JFrame();
    frame.setDefaultCloseOperation(JFrame.DO_NOTHING_ON_CLOSE);
    frame.setTitle("Student Hostel");
    HostelSwing property = new HostelSwing(20);
    frame.setSize(500,440);
    frame.getContentPane().setBackground(new Color(0,190,170));
    frame.getContentPane().add(property);
    frame.setVisible(true);
  }
}
```

The first thing to notice is the statement that imports the Swing components from the Javax package:

```
import javax.swing.*;
```

Notice that we still need to import the AWT package here because we are using the Color class.

After creating a new JFrame object, frame, the first thing we did was to invoke its setDefaultCloseOperation method:

```
frame.setDefaultCloseOperation(JFrame.DO_NOTHING_ON_CLOSE);
```

You will remember that when we were using the regular AWT frame we couldn't close it by clicking on the cross-hairs. This is not the case with the JFrame; there are three possibilities, which we choose by passing a value into the setDefaultCloseOperation method. The three possible values are JFrame.DO_NOTHING_ON_CLOSE, JFrame.HIDE_ON_CLOSE (the default), or finally JFrame.DISPOSE_ON_CLOSE. We have chosen the first one of these here, because we want the user to be able to close the frame only by choosing the appropriate quit button.

The other thing you will notice here is that when we want to do things to a JFrame like change the background, or add a component, we do not communicate directly with the frame; look at these two lines:

```
frame.getContentPane().setBackground(new Color(0,190,170));
frame.getContentPane().add(property);
```

A JFrame allows more than one container to be added to it: a **content pane**, an optional JMenuBar and a transparent **glass pane** that is positioned above the other components and allows layering. In this book, we will concern ourselves only with the main drawing area, the content pane (in this chapter) and the menu bar (in chapter 21). The above code fragment shows how we use the getContentPane method of the JFrame so that we can add components or change its properties.

19.4   *The Border interface*

One of the most useful aspects of Swing is the fact that you can add a variety of attractive borders to any component. All the basic components such as the JButton or the JLabel are derived from JComponent, and inherit its setBorder method, which can be used to add the border of your choice.

In the javax.swing.border package is a Border interface. In this package there are eight standard border classes that implement this interface. These are:

- BevelBorder;
- SoftBevelBorder;
- LineBorder;
- EtchedBorder;
- TitledBorder;
- MatteBorder;
- CompoundBorder;
- EmptyBorder.

Figure 19.3 shows examples of these borders.

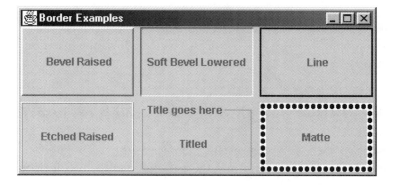

Fig 19.3   Examples of border styles

Each of these border classes has one or more constructors. The following fragment of code, with explanatory comments, shows the constructors that were invoked to produce the borders shown above:

```
BevelBorder bevel = new BevelBorder(BevelBorder.RAISED);
/* the constructor used here takes an integer parameter, the value of which
   can be BevelBorder.RAISED or BevelBorder.LOWERED. There are other
   constructors that allow for the selection of highlight and shadow colours
   */

SoftBevelBorder soft = new SoftBevelBorder(SoftBevelBorder.LOWERED);
/* similar to BevelBorder */

LineBorder line = new LineBorder(Color.black, 2);
/* the first parameter to this constructor defines the colour of the line;
   the second defines the thickness of the line. There is also a constructor
   that accepts one parameter for the colour only, the thickness defaulting
   to 1 */

EtchedBorder etched = new EtchedBorder(EtchedBorder.RAISED);
/* similar to BevelBorder */

TitledBorder titled = new TitledBorder("Title goes here");
/* the String parameter determines the title. A number of other constructors
   exist to allow for positioning of the title. */

MatteBorder matte = new MatteBorder(new ImageIcon("Circle.gif"));
/* the parameter determines the icon used to form the border - see next
   section. There are other constructors that allow adjustment of the
   insets, and a simple coloured line border. */
```

Once created, a border can then be added to a component called, for example, myLabel with the following line of code:

```
myLabel.setBorder(bevel);
```

If you want to create more complex border combinations, you can use the CompoundBorder class in conjunction with the EmptyBorder class (which allows the insertion of empty space around components).

19.5   *Combining text and graphics with the Icon interface*

In the Swing package there is a very useful interface – the Icon interface. Any class that implements this interface can be passed into the setIcon method that is defined for many of the basic Swing components such as JButton or JLabel.

To demonstrate how this works we are going to define a simple class called SquareIcon, which will produce an icon consisting of a red square, the size of which can be passed into the constructor. Here is the code for the class:

THE *SquareIcon* CLASS

```
import javax.swing.*;
import java.awt.*;

class SquareIcon implements Icon
{
  private int size;

  public SquareIcon(int sizeIn)
  {
    size = sizeIn;
  }

  // all the following methods are required by the Icon interface
  public void paintIcon(Component c, Graphics g, int x, int y)
  {
    g.setColor(Color.red);
    g.fillRect(x, y, size, size);
  }

  public int getIconWidth()
  {
    return size;
  }

  public int getIconHeight()
  {
    return size;
  }
}
```

There is a need for only one attribute, which will hold the width (and height) of the square. The constructor sets the value of this to whatever is sent in. The paintIcon method, which we are required to implement, is called automatically when the icon is created, and is automatically sent four attributes:

```
public void paintIcon(Component c, Graphics g, int x, int y)
{
  g.setColor(Color.red);
  g.fillRect(x, y, size, size);
}
```

Methods of the first attribute can be used to find out information (such as the foreground or background colour) of the component on which the icon is painted. The second parameter is the graphics context, and the final two are the co-ordinates at which the icon should be painted. These will have been calculated to take into account any borders that exist on the component.

The getWidth and getHeight methods have to be implemented at the insistence of the Icon interface.

The IconDemo class shown below creates a SquareIcon and adds this, together with some text, to a JButton.

THE *IconDemo* CLASS

```java
import javax.swing.*;
import java.awt.*;
import java.awt.event.*;

class IconDemo extends JPanel implements ActionListener
// adds an icon and text to a component
{
  private JButton button = new JButton();
  private SquareIcon icon = new SquareIcon(30);

  public IconDemo()
  {
    button.setMargin(new Insets(0,0,0,0));
    button.setIcon(icon); // adds the icon to the button
    button.setText(" Quit "); // adds the text to the button
    add(button);
    button.addActionListener(this);
  }
  public void actionPerformed(ActionEvent e)
  {
    System.exit(0);
  }
}
```

You can see that we have used, respectively, the setIcon and setText methods of JButton (inherited from JComponent) to add our icon and then some text to the button.[1] Prior to this we called the setMargin method to set all the insets to zero; this has the effect of making the icon and text fill the whole button.

Program 19.2 creates an IconDemo object and adds it to a frame.

---

[1] There is also a version of the JButton constructor that accepts the desired icon and text as parameters.

PROGRAM 19.2

```
import javax.swing.*;

public class RunIconTest
{
  public static void main(String[] args)
  {

    JFrame frame = new JFrame();
    IconDemo icDemo = new IconDemo();
    frame.getContentPane().add(icDemo);
    frame.setSize(180,100);
    frame.setVisible(true);
  }
}
```

The result of running this program is shown in figure 19.4.

A very useful class that is defined in the Swing package, and that implements the `Icon` interface, is the `IconImage` class. This class allows you to create an icon from a file in `.gif` or `.jpg` format. We took a file called "Quit.gif", which consists of a red circle on a white background, and then, in our `IconDemo` class, replaced this line

```
private SquareIcon icon = new SquareIcon(30);
```

with this one:

```
private ImageIcon icon = new ImageIcon("Quit.gif");
```

The result we got is shown in figure 19.5.

Fig 19.4   A button with an icon and text

Fig 19.5   A button with an icon and text: in this case, the icon was created from a file

19.6   *Creating message boxes and input boxes*

In the Swing package there is a very useful class called JOptionPane. By making use of this class we can provide dialogue boxes of four possible types. These are described in table 19.1; examples of each will be seen in the application that we describe shortly.

To illustrate the use of these dialogues, we are going to create a "Magic Words" application, which could be used as the basis of a children's game. When the program first starts the user is presented with an **option** dialogue as shown in figure 19.6.

The idea of the program (which you could easily adapt to make it a lot more interesting) is to allow the user to enter a word, and then be told whether or not the word entered was a "magic" word. The user can continue to enter words and try to work out the "secret" of what makes a particular word magical – the answer, in fact, is that magic words start and end with the same letter. As you can see here, the user can choose to find out the secret at any time.

Table 19.1 The *JOptionPane* Dialogue Types	
Option	Displays a list of buttons to enable the user to choose an option; see figure 19.6.
Input	Allows the user to enter data via a text field or list. Also provides an "OK" and "Cancel" buttons; see figure 19.7.
Message	Displays a message and an "OK" button; see figures 19.8 and 19.9.
Confirm	Asks the user a question and provides "Yes" and "No" buttons for the answer; see figure 19.10.

Fig 19.6   An Option Dialogue

If the user chooses to enter a word, the **input** dialogue shown in figure 19.7 appears.

Once the "OK" button is pressed a **message** dialogue appears, informing the user whether or not the word entered was a magic word (figure 19.8).

There are different types of message dialogue – the one shown in figure 19.8 is an information message dialogue. If no text had been entered, a different sort of dialogue – showing an error message – would appear as shown in figure 19.9.

If the user chooses the "Find the secret" button from the option dialogue then a **confirm** dialogue appears as shown in figure 19.10.

Choosing the "Yes" button causes another information message box to appear, revealing the secret.

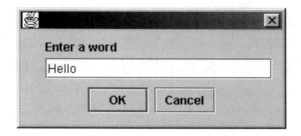

Fig 19.7   An Input Dialogue

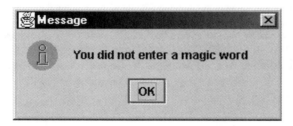

Fig 19.8   A Message Dialogue (information)

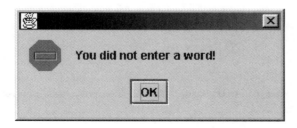

Fig 19.9   A Message Dialogue (error)

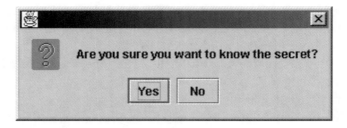

Fig 19.10   A Confirm Dialogue

As you can see, we have designed this program to be a little bit like the old menu-driven programs that you started writing before you knew much about graphics. The JOptionPane class has allowed us to create a similar style of program but using graphical message boxes and input boxes instead of a text screen.

The code for this program is shown below in program 19.3:

PROGRAM 19.3

```java
import javax.swing.*;

class MagicWords
{
  public static void main(String[] args)
  {
    int result;
    do
    {
      // declare an array of strings to represent the choices
      String[] choice = {"Enter a word", "Find the secret", "Quit"};
      /* create an option dialogue; the showOptionDialog method returns an
         integer */
      result = JOptionPane.showOptionDialog
                        (null,
                         "Choose an option",
                         "Magic Words",
                         JOptionPane.DEFAULT_OPTION,
                         JOptionPane.PLAIN_MESSAGE,
                         null,
                         choice,
                         "Enter a word");
      switch(result)
      {
        case 0: // the first button, "Enter a word", was pushed
                enterWord();
                break;
```

```
        case 1: // the second button, "Find the secret", was pushed
                findSecret();
                break;
    }
  }while(result != 2); // continue until the "Quit" button is pushed
  System.exit(0);
}

// worker methods

private static void enterWord()
{
  char first, last;
  String word, message;
  /* create an input dialogue; the showInputDialog method returns a
     string */
  word = JOptionPane.showInputDialog(null,
                                "Enter a word",
                                null,
                                JOptionPane.PLAIN_MESSAGE);
  if(word != null) // the cross-hairs were not clicked on
  {
    if(word.length() != 0)
    {
      word = word.toUpperCase();
      first = word.charAt(0);
      last = word.charAt(word.length() - 1);
      if(first == last)
      {
      message = "You entered a magic word";
      }
      else
      {
        message = "You did not enter a magic word";
      }
      // create a message dialogue, giving information
      JOptionPane.showMessageDialog(null,
                                message,
                                null,
                                JOptionPane.INFORMATION_MESSAGE);
    }
    else
    {
```

```
                    // create a message dialogue, showing an error
                    message = "You did not enter a word!";
                    JOptionPane.showMessageDialog(null,
                                        message,
                                        null,
                                        JOptionPane.ERROR_MESSAGE);
            }
        }
    }

    private static void findSecret()
    {
        /* create a confirm dialogue; the showConfirmDialog method returns an
           integer */
        int answer;
        answer = JOptionPane.showConfirmDialog
                        (null,
                        "Are you sure you want to know the secret?",
                        null,
                        JOptionPane.YES_NO_OPTION,
                        JOptionPane.QUESTION_MESSAGE);
        if(answer == JOptionPane.YES_OPTION)
        {
            /* the message dialog defaults to an information message if the
               following constructor is used */
            JOptionPane.showMessageDialog
                (null, "A magic word starts and ends with the same letter";)
        }
    }
}
```

As you can see, we have used the approach that we took in early chapters whereby a **do . . . while** loop controls the menu and a **switch** statement is used to process the user's choice. Our program is really more for demonstration purposes than anything else, and more commonly the JOptionPane class will be used as part of a more complex graphical application.

Let's take a look at some of the features of JOptionPane that we have used in the above program.

We have used four static methods of JOptionPane to create our dialogues; each of these methods has more than one version, but we will concentrate on the one we have used here – the others simply take a different combination of parameters.

We have begun by declaring an array of Strings, choice, to represent our three options:

```
String[] choice = {"Enter a word", "Find the secret", "Quit"};
```

The first thing that we have done within our **do . . . while** loop is to create an option dialogue (as shown in figure 19.6), for which purpose we use the showOptionDialog method:

```
result = JOptionPane.showOptionDialog
                            (null,
                            "Choose an option",
                            "Magic Words",
                            JOptionPane.DEFAULT_OPTION,
                            JOptionPane.PLAIN_MESSAGE,
                            null,
                            choice,
                            "Enter a word");
```

You can see that the version of this method that we have used takes eight parameters. The first of these is the parent component (that is the component such as a JFrame or JPanel from which the dialogue was generated). In our program the dialogue was not generated from any other component, so this parameter is **null**.

The second parameter is a String – this determines the question or instruction that will appear in the dialogue – in our case "Choose an option".

The third parameter, also a String, determines the title.

The fourth parameter is an integer that will determine which buttons will appear on the dialogue box. Pre-defined constants exist for this purpose. The one we have used here is JOptionPane.DEFAULT_OPTION, which provides different defaults for the different types of dialogues. In the case of an option dialogue, the default is to provide no buttons other than those that determine our choices. However, as you will see below, for other types of dialogues we can choose other options such as JOptionPane.OK_OPTION, JOptionPane.YES_NO_OPTION, or finally, JOptionPane.YES_NO_CANCEL_OPTION.

The fifth parameter determines the icon that is displayed on the box. The possible options are shown in table 19.2.

Table 19.2 Message types available in the *JOptionPane* class	
JOptionPane.PLAIN_MESSAGE	No icon is displayed
JOptionPane.INFORMATION_MESSAGE	An information icon is displayed (see figure 19.8)
JOptionPane.ERROR_MESSAGE	An error icon is displayed (see figure 19.9)
JOptionPane.QUESTION_MESSAGE	A question icon is displayed (see figure 19.10)
JOptionPane.WARNING_MESSAGE	A warning icon is displayed

The sixth parameter can be an Icon of your choice – **null** in our case.

The seventh parameter is the array of Strings that represents our list of options. The final parameter determines the option that is initially highlighted.

The showOptionDialog method returns an integer, which we have assigned to result. The value of this integer represents the option selected – 0 for the first, 1 for the second and so on. In our case, pushing the "Quit" button will cause a value of 2 to be returned, and this is used to terminate the **do . . . while** loop. A return value of 0 causes the enterWord method to be called. Let's take a closer look at this.

After declaring some variables, we create an input dialogue (figure 19.7) by calling the showInputDialogue method of JOptionPane:

```
word = JOptionPane.showInputDialog
                (null, "Enter a word", null, JOptionPane.PLAIN_MESSAGE);
```

The version of this method that we have used here returns the string that was entered, and takes four parameters representing, respectively, the parent component, the message, the title and the message type.

The next bit of this method tests for a **null** return value (caused by closing the dialogue with the cross-hairs) and then, if all is well, goes on to determine whether or not a magic word was entered. It then assigns either the string "You entered a magic word" or the string "You did not enter a magic word" to a String variable, message. If no word was entered it assigns the string "You did not enter a word" to message.

If a word was entered, the showMessageDialogue method of JOptionPane is called:

```
JOptionPane.showMessageDialog
                (null, message, null, JOptionPane.INFORMATION_MESSAGE);
```

This method has the same parameter list as above; you can see that we have used message as the second parameter, and have chosen an information message as the message type. You can see the result in figure 19.8.

If no word was entered we again create a message box, but this time it is an error message (figure 19.9).

If the user had selected the "Find the secret" from the original option dialogue, this would have caused the worker method findSecret to be called. This method calls the showConfirmDialog method of JOptionPane:

```
answer = JOptionPane.showConfirmDialog (null,
                      "Are you sure you want to know the secret?",
                      null,
                      JOptionPane.YES_NO_OPTION,
                      JOptionPane.QUESTION_MESSAGE);
```

Table 19.3 Possible return values from the *showConfirmDialog* method	
JOptionPane.YES_OPTION	The "Yes" button was pressed
JOptionPane.NO_OPTION	The "No" button was pressed
JOptionPane.CANCEL_OPTION	The "Cancel" button was pressed
JOptionPane.OK_OPTION	The "OK" button was pressed
JOptionPane.CLOSED_OPTION	The dialogue was closed by clicking on the cross-hairs

The first three parameters here are the same as above, as is the final one. The one before the last represents the option type required.

The method returns an integer that is assigned to a variable called answer. The possible return values are shown in table 19.3.

You can see from the code that if the "Yes" button were pressed, then an information message box is created, explaining the secret of a magic word.

19.7 *Creating new colours*

Those of you who have studied some elementary physics will know that there are three primary colours, red, green and blue;[2] all other colours can be obtained by mixing these in different proportions.

Mixing red, green and blue in equal intensity produces white light; the colour we know as black is in fact the absence of all three. Mixing equal amounts of red and green (and no blue) produces yellow light; red and blue produce a mauvish colour called magenta; and mixing blue and green produces cyan, a sort of turquoise.

Residing in the AWT package is a class called Color. We have already been using the pre-defined attributes of this class such as red, green, blue, lightGray and so on. However it is perfectly possible to create our own colours. A new colour is created by mixing any of the primary colours, which can be added in different degrees of intensity. This intensity for each colour can range from a minimum of zero to a maximum of 255. So there are 256 possible intensities for each primary colour, so the total number of different colours available to us is $256 \times 256 \times 256$, or 16,777,216. To create our new colour we simply use the constructor of the Color class, which accepts three integer parameters, representing the intensity of red, green and blue respectively.

Program 19.4 tests out a few new colours that we have created as well as demonstrating the principles we mentioned earlier about mixing the primary colours.

[2] Don't confuse this with the mixing of coloured paints, where the rules are different. In the case of mixing coloured lights (as on a computer monitor) we are dealing with reflection of light – in the case of paints we are dealing with absorption, so the primary colours, and the rules for mixing, are different. For paints the primary colours are red, blue and yellow.

PROGRAM 19.4

```java
import java.awt.*;
import java.swing.*;

public class ColourTester
{
  public static void main(String[] args)
  {
    Color magenta = new Color(255,0,255);
    Color cyan = new Color(0,255,255);
    Color black = new Color(0,0,0);
    Color purple = new Color(210,100,210);
    Color orange = new Color(250,150,0);
    Color brown = new Color(200,150,150);

    JFrame frame = new JFrame();
    frame.setSize(150,160);
    frame.setVisible(true);
    Graphics g = frame.getGraphics();
    g.setColor(magenta);
    g.drawString("This is magenta", 10,40);
    g.setColor(cyan);
    g.drawString("This is cyan", 10,60);
    g.setColor(black);
    g.drawString("This is black", 10,80);
    g.setColor(purple);
    g.drawString("This is purple", 10,100);
    g.setColor(orange);
    g.drawString("This is orange", 10,120);
    g.setColor(brown);
    g.drawString("This is brown", 10,140);
  }
}
```

Figure 19.11 shows the result (in monochrome here, of course):

Fig 19.11   Creating new colours

19.8   *Creating new fonts*

Creating our own fonts is a similar process to that of creating colours, this time making use of the Font class which again resides in the AWT package. You saw an example of this in section 14.4, where you saw that the Font constructor takes three attributes – two strings representing a font name and a style respectively, and an integer representing the font size.

The possible font names are "Serif", "SansSerif", "Monospaced", "Dialog" and "DialogInput". The possible styles are Font.PLAIN, Font.BOLD and Font.ITALIC; the last two of these can be combined by using the plus sign. Program 19.5 shows us examples of the different options.

PROGRAM 19.5

```
import java.awt.*;
import javax.swing.*;

public class FontTester
{
  public static void main(String[] args)
  {
    Font font1 = new Font("SansSerif",Font.PLAIN,16);
    Font font2 = new Font("Serif",Font.PLAIN,20);
    Font font3 = new Font("Monospaced",Font.PLAIN,30);
    Font font4 = new Font("Dialog",Font.BOLD,20);
    Font font5 = new Font("DialogInput",Font.BOLD,20);
    Font font6 = new Font("Serif",Font.ITALIC,30);
    Font font7 = new Font("Serif",Font.ITALIC + Font.BOLD,16);
    JFrame frame = new JFrame();
    frame.setSize(260,260);
    frame.setVisible(true);
    Graphics g = frame.getGraphics();
    g.setFont(font1);
    g.drawString("This is font1", 10,47);
    g.setFont(font2);
    g.drawString("This is font2", 10,75);
    g.setFont(font3);
    g.drawString("This is font3", 10,105);
    g.setFont(font4);
    g.drawString("This is font4", 10,135);
    g.setFont(font5);
    g.drawString("This is font5", 10,165);
    g.setFont(font6);
    g.drawString("This is font6", 10,200);
    g.setFont(font7);
    g.drawString("This is font7", 10,230);
  }
}
```

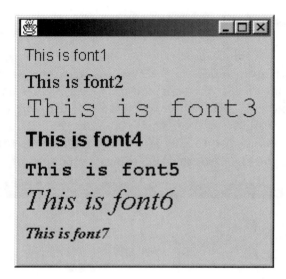

Fig 19.12   Creating new fonts

Figure 19.12 shows the result of running this program.

19.9   *More layout policies*

In chapter 9 you learnt about two layout policies – FlowLayout and BorderLayout. The GridLayout manager was introduced to you in chapter 16. Another very useful layout manager is CardLayout. The components in a container that implements a CardLayout policy are arranged like cards in a pack. The CardLayout class provides five methods that allow you to display each "card" in turn – these are First, Next, Previous, Last and Random. This layout policy is particularly useful when you want to break up a screen into different sections, so that the sections can be shown one at a time. The example that follows provides a possible start-up screen for a game – the screen is divided into three "cards" that allow players to choose their level, then the character they want to be, and finally the imaginary location for the game scenario. Buttons on either side allow the user to go back to a previous screen or to continue.

Fig 19.13 **An example of the *CardLayout* manager, showing three different screens**

The code for this class is shown below (only the "Go back" and "Continue" buttons have been made functional):

THE *Cards* CLASS

```
import javax.swing.*;
import java.awt.*;
import java.awt.event.*;

class Cards extends JPanel implements ActionListener
{
    // create a CardLayout object
    private CardLayout cardLayout = new CardLayout();

    // create a panel to hold the cards
    private JPanel centrePanel = new JPanel();
```

```java
// create the buttons for selecting the next and previous cards
private JButton nextButton = new JButton("Continue");
private JButton previousButton = new JButton(" Go back ");

// create the cards
private JPanel firstCard = new JPanel();
private JPanel secondCard = new JPanel();
private JPanel thirdCard = new JPanel();

// the constructor
public Cards()
{
  setLayout(new BorderLayout());

  // add labels and buttons to the cards
  firstCard.add(new JLabel("Choose your level"));
  firstCard.add(new JButton(" Novice "));
  firstCard.add(new JButton("Regular"));
  firstCard.add(new JButton(" Expert "));
  firstCard.add(new JButton("   Elite   "));
  secondCard.add(new JLabel("Select a character"));
  secondCard.add(new JButton("Zorrkk"));
  secondCard.add(new JButton("Kluggg"));
  secondCard.add(new JButton("Grrogg"));
  secondCard.add(new JButton("Skrank"));
  thirdCard.add(new JLabel("Select a location"));
  thirdCard.add(new JButton("Castle of Doom"));
  thirdCard.add(new JButton(" Forest of Fear "));

  previousButton.setBackground(Color.yellow);
  nextButton.setBackground(Color.yellow);

  // add the buttons and the centre panel to this object
  add("West", previousButton);
  add("Center", centrePanel);
  add("East", nextButton);

  // add the cards to the centre panel
  centrePanel.add(firstCard);
  centrePanel.add(secondCard);
  centrePanel.add(thirdCard);

  // set the layout of the centre panel to a CardLayout
  centrePanel.setLayout(cardLayout);

  // add ActionListeners to the buttons
  nextButton.addActionListener(this);
  previousButton.addActionListener(this);
}
```

```
// the event handler
public void actionPerformed(ActionEvent e)
{
    if(e.getSource() == nextButton)
    {
        cardLayout.next(centrePanel); // show the next card
    }
    else if(e.getSource() == previousButton)
    {
        cardLayout.previous(centrePanel); // show the previous card
    }
}
}
```

The only things that we need to draw to your attention to here are the ones that are to do with the CardLayout class. You can see that we have created a CardLayout object as an attribute:

```
private CardLayout cardLayout = new CardLayout();
```

We have also created a panel called centrePanel that is the component to which this layout is going to be attached:

```
private JPanel centrePanel = new JPanel();
```

The three different screens that you see in figure 19.13 – in other words the "cards" – are created as JPanels:

```
private JPanel firstCard = new JPanel();
private JPanel secondCard = new JPanel();
private JPanel thirdCard = new JPanel();
```

In the constructor, various buttons and labels are added to these cards, and the centrePanel is added to the main panel along with the buttons for going back and continuing.

When all that is done we add the cards to the centre panel and then set the layout of the centre panel using the cardLayout object that we defined previously:

```
centrePanel.setLayout(cardLayout);
```

Finally we add our ActionListeners to the two control buttons.

The `actionPerformed` method then makes use of the next and previous methods of `CardLayout`:

```
public void actionPerformed(ActionEvent e)
{
   if(e.getSource() == nextButton)
   {
     cardLayout.next(centrePanel);
   }
     else if(e.getSource() == previousButton)
   {
     cardLayout.previous(centrePanel);
   }
}
```

You can see that these two methods require that the component to which the cards are attached be sent in as a parameter.

The layout managers that you have come across so far should be enough for much of the programming that you will be doing. However, those of you who will be required to produce really professional interfaces may want to have even more control over the way things look. For this purpose the `GridBagLayout` manager is an ideal layout manger. However, this is a complex layout manager, and we are not going to go into its use here – those of you who wish to know about this manager should consult a Java reference text.

19.10 *Guidelines for creating good user interfaces*

Nowadays users expect to access their programs via attractive graphical interfaces, using mice, pull-down or pop-up menus, icons and so on. A great deal has been written about the human computer interface, and there has been much research on the subject. Here we try to summarize a few of these ideas in order to furnish you with some simple guidelines to help you when you are creating user interfaces for your applications:

- The first rule is to keep it simple. Resist the temptation to show off your programming skills by making your interface too flashy or overly complex. The usual result of this is to put the user off the program.
- Don't use too many colours on one screen; the psychological effect of this can be to make the user feel bombarded by too much at one time.
- Try not to mix too many fonts. Although the idea of having a number of different fonts might sound tempting at first, the effect of this is recognized as having a negative effect on the eye.
- Think carefully about how the user might navigate through the program – don't bury menu options or different screens in large numbers of layers. Always provide a simple

route back to the main program menu or screen – and apart from that provide just one way back and one way forward.

- Think carefully about who is going to be using the program. Will it be an expert user or a novice user? What sort of language are you using, and is it appropriate for the type of user in question? For example a dialogue window that says "Sorry, but the file you have requested does not exist" is likely to be far more helpful to the average user than "File I/O error".
- Think carefully about the needs of users with disabilities. For example, a partially sighted user is likely to benefit greatly from sound prompts. However a program that actually *relied* on sound prompts would be useless to a deaf person.

Tutorial exercises

1. Distinguish between *lightweight* and *heavyweight* components.
2. Study the Swing version of the Hostel GUI in figure 19.1, and identify the various components used, and the type of border used on each component.
3. Making good use of the JOptionPane class (section 19.6), design a program that would help primary school children to test their arithmetic.

Practical work

1. Create Swing versions of some of the applications that we developed in chapters 9 and 17.
2. Look back at section 19.4 in which examples of the different border styles were presented. Experiment with other style combinations by using the various constructors and methods that you learnt about in that section.
3. Try to re-create (and perhaps improve upon) the Hostel GUI in figure 19.1; once you have had a go at this you can download our code from the website or CD-ROM and compare it.
4. (a) In practical task 4 of chapter 17 you created a graphical interface for your personal address book; convert this to a Swing GUI.
   (b) Adapt this application adding a password facility. You can use the JPasswordField class, which extends JTextField. To hide the input you should use the setEchoChar method, which takes as a parameter the character that echoes on the screen when each key is pressed (traditionally a star).
5. Implement the arithmetic program that you designed in tutorial question 3.

CASE STUDY PART 1: FROM UML TO JAVA

LEARNING OBJECTIVES

By the end of this chapter you should be able to:

➤ specify system requirements by developing a **use case model**;

➤ annotate a **composition** association on a UML diagram;

➤ implement the `Enumeration` interface;

➤ develop test cases from **behaviour specifications** found in the use case model.

20.1 Introduction

You have covered quite a few advanced topics now in this second semester. In this chapter we are going to take stock of what you have learnt by developing an application that draws upon all these topics. We will make use of Java's package notation for bundling together related classes, we will implement interfaces, we will catch and throw exceptions, we will make use of the collection classes in the `java.util` package and we will discuss the issues involved in storing objects to file. In the next chapter we will conclude the development of this application by producing an attractive interface using the Swing components we covered in the last chapter.

As with the case study we presented to you in the first semester, we will discuss the development of this application from the initial stage of requirements analysis, through to final implementation and testing stages. This will give us an opportunity to look further at the UML notation.

20.2   *System overview*

The application that we will develop will keep track of planes using a particular airport. So as not to over complicate things, we will make a few assumptions:

- there will only be four runways at the airport;
- there will be no concept of *gates* for arrival and departure, passengers will be met at a runway on arrival and sent to a runway on departure;
- planes entering airport airspace and requesting to land are either given permission to land on a free runway, or are told to join a queue of circling planes until a runway becomes available;
- no planes are housed at the airport; planes boarding and subsequently requesting take-off must therefore have previously landed at the airport;
- once a plane departs from the airport it is removed from the system;
- the detail of arrival and departure *times* will not be addressed.

20.3   *Requirements analysis and specification*

Many techniques are used to uncover system requirements. Amongst others, these include interviewing the client, sending out questionnaires to the client, reviewing any documentation if a current system already exists and observing people carrying out their work. A common way to document these requirements in UML is to develop a **use case model**. A use case model consists of **use case diagrams** and **behaviour specifications**.

A *use case diagram* is a simple way of recording the *roles* of different users within a system and the services that they require the system to deliver. The users (people or other systems) of a system are referred to as **actors** in use case diagrams and are drawn as simple stick characters. The roles these actors play in the system are used to annotate the stick character. The services they require are the so-called *use cases*. For example, in an ATM application an actor may be a customer and one of the use cases (services) required would be to withdraw cash. A very simple use case diagram for our application is given in figure 20.1.

Figure 20.1 depicts the actors in this application (air traffic controllers and information officers) and the services these actors require (registering a flight, listing arrivals and so on). Once a list of use cases has been identified, *behaviour specifications* are used to record their required functionality. A simple way of recording behaviour specifications is to give a simple textual description for each use case. Table 20.1 contains behaviour specifications for each use case given in figure 20.1. Note that the descriptions are always given from the users' point of view.

As the system develops, the use case descriptions may be modified as detailed requirements become uncovered (for example by discovering subtle error conditions or by giving more detailed HCI requirements). These descriptions will also be useful when testing the final application, as we will see later.

During the analysis stage it is also important to identify the important classes in the application and the associations between those classes. The use case descriptions can be a useful starting point for this exercise. Possible class names can be identified by scanning the use case descriptions for nouns (that is, the things being referred to) or noun-like phrases. After examining the use case descriptions in table 20.1 you may end up with the list of possible classes such as this:

> plane, airport, flight number, city of origin, plane status, runway, runway number, list of planes, airport information officer, air traffic controller.

Not all these possible classes will necessarily end up as classes in your final application. For example, some will fall outside the scope of your application. Users of the system, the airport information officer and air traffic controller are not required for this reason. Also, the system itself (the airport) is not usually considered as a useful class during the analysis stage.

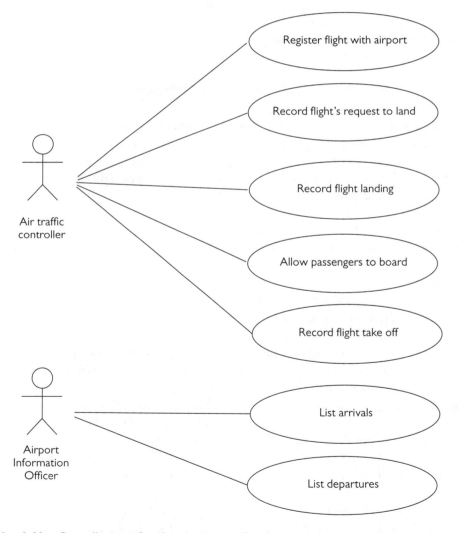

Fig 20.1   A Use Case diagram for the airport application

Table 20.1	Behaviour specifications for the airport application
Register flight with airport	An air traffic controller registers an incoming flight with the airport by submitting its unique flight number, and its city of origin. If the flight number is already registered by the airport an error is signalled.
Record flight's request to land	An air traffic controller records an incoming flight entering airport airspace, and requesting to land, by submitting its flight number. As long as the plane has previously registered with the airport, the air traffic controller is given an unoccupied runway number on which the plane will have permission to land. If all runways are occupied however, this permission is denied and the air traffic controller is informed to instruct the plane to circle the airport. If the plane has not previously registered with the airport an error is signalled.
Record flight landing	An air traffic controller records a flight landing on a runway at the airport by submitting its flight number and the runway number. If the plane was not given permission to land on that runway an error is raised.
Allow passengers to board	An air traffic controller allows passengers to board a plane, currently occupying a runway by submitting its flight number, and its destination city. If the given plane has not yet recorded landing at the airport an error is signalled.
Record flight take off	An air traffic controller records a flight taking off from the airport by submitting its flight number. If there are planes circling the airport, the first plane to have joined the circling queue is then given permission to land on that runway. If the given plane was not at the airport an error is signalled.
List arrivals	The airport information officer is given a list of planes whose status is either waiting-to-land, or landed.
List departures	The airport information officer is given a list of planes whose status is currently waiting-to-depart (taking on passengers).

Other possibilities may be too simplistic to be worth developing as a class, while some potential classes may actually be *attributes* of a class rather than a class itself. For example, *flight number* and *city of origin* would probably best be represented as attributes of a *plane*, not classes in their own right.

At the analysis stage you should be concerned with identifying the core classes. Containers for these classes are normally not required for analysis at this stage as they require design decisions. So *list of planes* will not be analysed yet but *plane* certainly should be. In fact there are two core classes, *plane* and *runway*. The important attributes and methods of these classes should be considered as well as any associations between them. Figure 20.2 gives a UML diagram depicting our initial analysis of this system. It introduces some new UML notation.

In this fairly simple analysis, we have not yet considered the types of the attributes or the interface of the methods. What we have done, however, is to capture the core classes, and the fact that these two classes are associated, and *how* they are associated. To explain the UML notation used in figure 21.2 further, we have annotated the original diagram by adding our own explanatory notes in figure 20.3.

A number on the association line indicates the **multiplicity** of the association – that is, the number of objects of the class from one end of the association line that are associated with the object of the class at the other end of the association line. This number can be a range as in this case. The triangle above the name of the association indicates in which direction the association is to be read. In this case we can see that, at most, one *plane* is "permitted to land" on, at most, one *runway*.

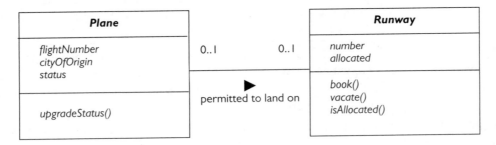

Fig 20.2   Initial analysis of the air traffic control application

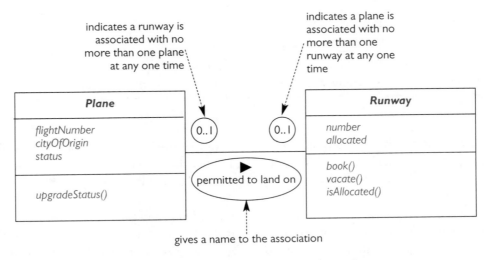

Fig 20.3   Important information can be provided on the association line

20.4   *Design*

An association from one class to another (such as "*permitted to land on*" in figure 20.3) implies that objects of the two classes will need to communicate by message passing. When designing these classes, we need to decide *in which direction* the messages should be passed. Allowing messages to pass in both directions is difficult to implement, so we have decided that Plane objects will send messages (call the methods of) Runway objects but a Runway object will not need to send messages to Plane objects. In Java, this can be achieved by adding a reference to a Runway object in the Plane class.

Figure 20.4 adds an appropriate attribute (theRunway) to the original class diagram in figure 20.1. It also adds an arrow on to the association line to indicate in which direction messages should pass, and provides Java types for the attributes and operations.

The detailed class designs are now presented in figure 20.5. We have clarified those parts of a class that should be **private** scope and those that should be **public** scope by using the UML notation of a minus sign (−) to indicate **private** scope and a plus sign (+) to indicate **public** scope. Have a look at the UML diagram and then we will discuss it.

The requirements made clear that there would be *many* planes to process in this system, so we have decided to develop a collection class, PlaneList for this purpose. It made sense to consider the collection classes in the java.util package at this point. As we record planes in the system, and process these planes, we will always be using a plane's flight number as a way of identifying an individual plane. If we used a vector (or an array for that matter), we would have to write code to search through every plane for the appropriate flight number each time we wish to process a plane. A hash table, however, takes care of this for us if we make the flight number the *key* to the hash table. The value associated with this key would then be the appropriate Plane object.

The one drawback with a hash table, however, is that it is not ordered on input. When considering which plane in a circling queue of planes to land, ordering is important as the first to join the queue should be the first to land. So we have introduced a vector to hold a queue of circling plane flight numbers.

As you can see from figure 20.5, an Airport class has been introduced to represent the functionality of the system as a whole. We are told that an airport has four runways. So an

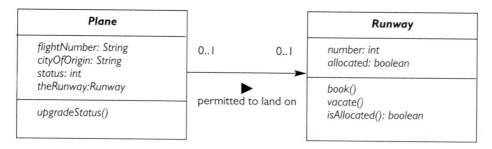

Fig 20.4   Initial design of the *Plane* and *Runway* classes

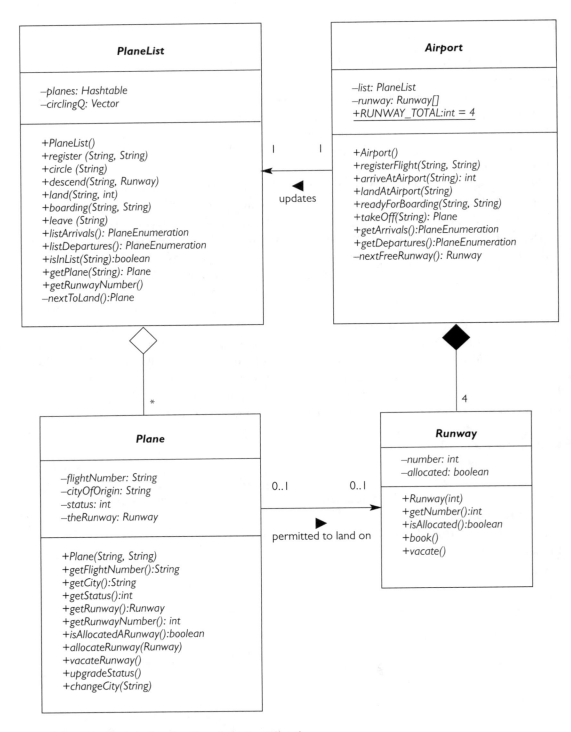

Fig 20.5   Detailed design for the airport application

instance of the `Airport` class will contain many instances (four in this case) of the `Runway` class. We use an array to hold this collection of runways.

When an object from one class contains a *fixed* number of objects from another class, this special kind of association is called a **composition**. Composition is very similar to aggregation (which we introduced in chapter 6). In both cases, objects of one class contain objects of another. The difference between the two is that with aggregation, the container class can exist regardless of whether or not it contains any contained objects. With composition the relationship is much stronger, so that when an object of the contained class is destroyed so are the contained objects themselves and vice versa — one cannot exist without the other. In this case, the `PlaneList` is an *aggregation* of planes, but an airport is *composed* of four runways. The UML notation for composition is the same as that for aggregation, except that the diamond is filled rather than hollow (see figure 20.6).

Notice that the `Airport` class contains methods that correspond closely to the use cases identified during requirements analysis and specification.

Let's now turn our attention to the implementation of these classes.

20.5 *Implementation*

Since we are developing an application involving several classes, it makes sense to bundle these classes together into a single package. We will call this package `airportSys`. This means that all our classes will begin with the following **package** statement:

```
package airportSys;
```

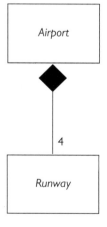

Fig 20.6   Composition is represented by a filled diamond in UML; here an airport is
**   *composed of* four runways**

This will allow our entire suite of classes to be imported into another application with the following **import** statement:

```
import airportSys.*;
```

It is a good idea to hide implementation level exceptions (such as `ArrayIndex-OutOfBoundsException`) from users of the application and, instead, always throw some general application exception. In order to be able to do this, we define our own general `AirportException` class.

THE *AirportException* **CLASS**

```
package airportSys;

public class AirportException extends Exception
{
  public AirportException ()
  {
    super("airport system violation");
  }
  public AirportException (String msg)
  {
    super(msg);
  }
}
```

Now let's consider the classes designed in figure 20.4. Most of the code for the classes follows straightforwardly from their design. For this reason, we leave their final implementation to you as a practical task at the end of this chapter (alternatively, you could download our implementation from the accompanying website or copied from the accompanying CD-ROM). We will, however, give you an outline for each class and highlight some implementation issues.

20.5.1 The *Runway* class

Here is the outline for our Runway class, take a look at it and then we will discuss it:

THE *Runway* CLASS

```java
package airportSys; // add class to package
import java.io.*; // for Serializable interface

public class Runway implements Serializable
{
    // attributes declared here

    // methods
    public Runway (int numberIn) throws AirportException
    {
        if (numberIn <1) // check if invalid runway number given
        {
            throw new AirportException ("invalid runway number " +numberIn);
        }
        number = numberIn;
        allocated = false; // runway vacant initially
    }
    // other methods implemented here
}
```

There is not much that needs to be said about this class. We have shown you the detail of the constructor so it is clear why it may throw an exception.

As we may wish to save and load objects from our system, we have to remember to indicate that this class is serializable.

```java
public class Runway implements Serializable
```

In fact, all the class in figure 20.4 need to be declared serializable. Notice that we have defined this as a **public** class so that it is accessible outside of the package. We did this as a runway is a generally useful concept in many applications; declaring this class **public** allows it to be re-used outside of the airportSys package.

20.5.2 The *Plane* class

Here is the outline code for the Plane class. Have a close look at it and then we will discuss it.

THE *Plane* CLASS

```java
package airportSys;
import java.io.*;

public class Plane implements Serializable
{
  // constants to name each plane status
  public static final int DUE = 0;
  public static final int WAITING = 1;
  public static final int LANDED = 2;
  public static final int DEPARTING = 3;

  // other attributes declared here

  // methods
  public Plane(String flightNumberIn, String cityOfOrigin)
  {
    flightNumber = flightNumberIn;
    city = cityOfOrigin;
    status = DUE; // initial plane status set to DUE
    theRunway = null; // indicates no runway allocated
  }

  public int getRunwayNumber() throws AirportException
  {
    if (theRunway == null) // check if runway allocated
    {
      throw new AirportException
        ("flight "+flightNumber+" has not been allocated a runway");
    }
    return theRunway.getNumber();
  }

  public void allocateRunway(Runway runwayIn) throws AirportException
  {
    if (runwayIn == null) // check runway has been sent
    {
      throw new AirportException ("no runway to allocate");
    }
    theRunway = runwayIn;
    theRunway.book(); // indicate the runway is now booked
  }

  // returns the String representation of the plane status
  public String getStatusName()
  {
    String statusName;
    switch(status)
```

```
    { /* each status name is set to a fixed string length to aid
        formatting */
      case DUE: statusName= "Not yet arrived ";break;
      case WAITING: statusName= "Waiting to land";break;
      case LANDED:statusName= "Landed          ";break;
      case DEPARTING: statusName= "Departing       ";break;
      default: statusName = "ERROR:NO STATUS";
    }
    return statusName;
  }

  public void upgradeStatus() throws AirportException
  {
    if (status== DEPARTING)
    {
      throw new AirportException
        ("cannot upgrade the status of a departing plane");
    }
    status++;
  }
  // other methods go here
}
```

Again, most of the points we raised with the Runway class are relevant to this Plane class. It needs to be serializable and it is declared **public**. We have also included the implementation of methods that throw exceptions so you can see why exceptions are thrown in this class (notice that in each case we throw the general AirportException).

In addition you should look at the way in which we dealt with the status attribute. During class design we declared this attribute to be an integer, so that is how it was implemented:

```
private int status;
```

A plane has a different status depending on its journey through the airport system. Initially it is *due-to-arrive*, then (when it arrives) it is *waiting-to-land*, then it will have *landed*. Sometime after landing it will be *ready-to-depart* (and so allow new passengers to board). Finally, it will *leave* the system. This final status need not be recorded as it effectively will be removed from the system at this point.

Integer values (such as 0, 1, 2 and so on) could be given to indicate a particular status. To improve readability of the code, however, it is common to declare integer value constants and then to use these constant names in the code rather than the actual numbers. This is what we have done here. The constants are declared initially:

```
// each status number is given a meaningful name
public static final int DUE = 0;
public static final int WAITING = 1;
public static final int LANDED = 2;
public static final int DEPARTING = 3;
```

They are then used in other methods rather than the actual numbers. For example, here is the code for the constructor again:

```
public Plane(String flightNumberIn, String cityOfOrigin)
{
  flightNumber = flightNumberIn;
  city = cityOfOrigin;
  status = DUE; // use constant name rather than number
  theRunway = null;
}
```

Declaring these constants as **public** allows them to be visible outside of this class. They can then be accessed within another class as follows:

```
if (status == PlaneStatus.CIRCLING)
{
  // some code here
}
```

The getStatusName method has been provided to convert the status constant to a meaningful name. Using class attributes as a means of giving meaningful names to integer values is very common. You have already used pre-defined Java classes like this many times. For example when stetting the alignment of a Label you used the class attributes, LEFT, CENTRE and RIGHT rather than the numbers 0, 1 and 2:

```
nameLabel.setAlignment (Label.RIGHT);
```

Also notice that by adding a runway attribute, theRunway, into the Plane class we can send messages to (access methods of) a Runway object, for example:

```
public void allocateRunway(Runway runwayIn)throws AirportException
{
  // some code here
  theRunway.book(); // book is a 'Runway' method
}
```

20.5.3 The *PlaneList* class

Here is our outline code for the `PlaneList` collection class. We have provided comments to help you implement the methods. Examine it closely, being sure to read the comments, and then we will discuss it.

THE *PlaneList* CLASS

```java
package airportSys;
import java.io.*;
import java.util.*; // for Hashtable and Vector

class PlaneList implements Serializable
{
  // attributes declared here

  public PlaneList ()
  {
    // initially the list is empty and no planes should circle
  }

  public void register (String flight, String cityOfOrigin)
                                         throws AirportException
  {
    /* Adds given plane details to the list. Throws exception if flight
       number already registered. */
  }

  public void circle (String flight) throws AirportException
  {
    /* Accepts a flight number and records and adds plane to the circling Q
       Throws exception if plane not previously registered, already circling
       or already at the airport.*/
  }

  public void descend (String flight, Runway runwayIn)
                                         throws AirportException
  {
    /* Accepts and records flight number and runway of a descending plane.
       Throws exception if plane not previously registered or already at the
       airport.*/
  }

  public void land (String flight, int runwayNumberIn)
                                         throws AirportException
  {
    /* Records a given flight landing on a given runway number. Throws
       an exception if the given flight is not entitled to land on this
       runway. */
  }
```

```
public void boarding (String flight, String destination)
                                            throws AirportException
{
  /* Records a given flight being prepared for boarding to a given
     destination. Throws an exception if flight is not recorded as having
     landed. */
}

public Plane leave (String flight) throws AirportException
{
  /* Accepts a given flight number and removes this flight from the list.
     Returns the next plane to land (or null if no plane). Throws an
     exception if flight is not currently recorded as being ready to
     depart. */
}

public Plane getPlane(String flight) throws AirportException
{
  /* Returns the registered plane with the given flight number. Throws
     exception of no such flight number registered. */
}

public boolean isInList(String flight)
{
  // checks if given flight is in registered list.
}

private Plane nextToLand()throws AirportException
{
  // return next plane in circling Q to land, or null if no plane.
}

// these last two methods will be discussed in detail later
public PlaneEnumeration arrivals()
{
  return new PlaneEnumeration (planes.elements(),Plane.DEPARTING,false);
}

public PlaneEnumeration departures()
{
  return new PlaneEnumeration (planes.elements(),Plane.DEPARTING, true);
}
}
```

Notice that declaring this class as serializable is sufficient to write `PlaneList` objects to file. There is no need also to declare the classes associated with the attributes `planes` and `registerQ` as being serializable. That is because these classes, `Hashtable` and `Vector`, like all Java collections classes, are already declared as serializable.

Two methods of the `PlaneList` class need elaborating – arrivals and departures. Both of these methods send back an object of type `PlaneEnumeration` (a class we defined and will discuss in a while):

```
public PlaneEnumeration arrivals()
{
   return new PlaneEnumeration (planes.elements(),Plane.DEPARTING,false);
}
public PlaneEnumeration departures()
{
  return new PlaneEnumeration (planes.elements(),Plane.DEPARTING, true);
}
```

In each case, we want to send back a list of planes that can be scanned through one at a time. One way to do this, which we discussed with you in chapter 16, is to send back an `Enumeration` object. A method exists in the `Hashtable` class to send back a list of values in the list as an enumeration; that method is called `elements`. So the following could be used to create an `Enumeration` object that contains a list of *all* planes:

```
planes.elements();
```

The problem with this enumeration is that it is not filtered to contain only those planes that are arriving, or only those planes that are departing. To achieve this we defined the `PlaneEnumeration` class that is referred to in the method headers of `arrivals` and `departures`. The `PlaneEnumeration` constructor accepts an enumeration of planes, a status type and then a `boolean` flag. The `boolean` flag determines whether or not to filter the original enumeration by looking for the given status (in which case the flag is set to **true**), or to filter by excluding the given status (in which case the flag is set to **false**).

The class implements the `Enumeration` interface so that any classes expecting an `Enumeration` object to filter through can still use this `PlaneEnumeration` object:

```java
package airportSys;

import java.util.*; // for Enumeration interface
public class PlaneEnumeration implements Enumeration
{
  // constructor accepts an enumeration, a status and a boolean flag.
  public PlaneEnumeration
            (Enumeration enumIn, int statusIn, boolean includeStatus)
  {
    // some code here
  }

  // must provide an implementation for these two methods
  public boolean hasMoreElements()
  {
  }

  public Object nextElement()
  {
  }
}
```

The technique that we will use will be to create a vector attribute to contain the required planes:

```java
private Vector items; // to hold planes after filtering
```

We will then scan through the enumeration sent into the constructor, check each plane against the given status and then add the plane into the vector if it meets the status test. We do this in the constructor:

```java
public PlaneEnumeration
              (Enumeration enumIn, int statusIn, boolean includeStatus)
{
  items = new Vector(); // initially Vector is empty
  while (enumIn.hasMoreElements()) // search through list given
  {
    Plane thisPlane = (Plane) enumIn.nextElement(); // get next plane
    if (includeStatus) // filter by status
    {
      if (thisPlane.getStatus() == statusIn)
      {
        items.add(thisPlane); // add to vector
      }
    }
}
```

```
      else // filter by excluding status
      {
        if (thisPlane.getStatus() != statusIn)
        {
          items.add(thisPlane); // add to vector
        }
      }
    }
    // one more thing to do!
}
```

As you can see in the code fragment above, we are left with one thing to do before we finish. If we want to provide methods to scan through this vector, we must provide an enumeration of the vector elements. In order to do this we need to add an Enumeration attribute.

```
private Enumeration enum; // to iterate through filtered planes
```

We can now create this Enumeration object at the end of the constructor by calling the elements method of the vector attribute items.

```
public PlaneEnumeration
                (Enumeration enumIn, int statusIn, boolean includeStatus)
{
  // as before
  enum = items.elements(); // create enumeration of filtered items
}
```

The hasMoreElements and nextElement methods of PlaneEnumeration, just correspond to the equivalent methods of the vector enumeration we just created.

```
public boolean hasMoreElements()
{
  return enum.hasMoreElements();
}
public Object nextElement()
{
  return enum.nextElement();
}
```

As an added bonus, we have provided an extra method called nextPlane. This method is identical to the nextElement method except that it type casts the next element back to a Plane object for us.

```java
public Plane nextPlane()
{
  return (Plane) enum.nextElement();
}
```

Here then is the complete code for the PlaneEnumeration class:

THE *PlaneEnumeration* CLASS

```java
package airportSys;
import java.util.*;

public class PlaneEnumeration implements Enumeration
{
  private Vector items;
  private Enumeration enum;

  public PlaneEnumeration
        (Enumeration enumIn, int statusIn, boolean includeStatus)
  {
    items = new Vector();
    while (enumIn.hasMoreElements()) // search through list given
    {
      Plane thisPlane = (Plane) enumIn.nextElement();
      if (includeStatus) // filter by status
      {
        if (thisPlane.getStatus() == statusIn)
        {
          items.add(thisPlane); // add to vector
        }
      }
      else // filter by excluding status
      {
        if (thisPlane.getStatus() != statusIn)
        {
          items.add(thisPlane); // add to vector
        }
      }
    }
    enum = items.elements(); // create enumeration of filtered items
  }

  public boolean hasMoreElements()
  {
```

```
          return enum.hasMoreElements();
      }

      public Object nextElement()
      {
          return enum.nextElement();
      }

      // an additional method
      public Plane nextPlane()
      {
          return (Plane) enum.nextElement();
      }
  }
```

Back in the `PlaneList` class this enumeration class is used to generate a collection of departing planes, by sending in all the planes in the list, setting the status type to `Plane.DEPARTING`, and the filter flag to **true**.

```
public PlaneEnumeration departures()
{
    return new PlaneEnumeration (planes.elements(),Plane.DEPARTING, true);
}
```

Likewise, the arrivals are created by setting the filter flag to **false** (in other words all those planes that are not departing are required for arrivals)

```
public PlaneEnumeration arrivals()
{
    return new PlaneEnumeration (planes.elements(),Plane.DEPARTING,false);
}
```

The final class we need to show you is the `Airport` class.

20.5.4 The *Airport* class

The `Airport` class encapsulates the functionality of the system. It does not include the interface to the application. As we have done throughout this text, the interface of an application is kept separate from its functionality. That way we can modify the way we choose to implement the functionality without needing to modify the interface, and vice versa. We provide only a very brief outline of this class, the rest of the implementation we leave as a practical task.

THE *Airport* CLASS

```
package airportSys;
import java.util.*;
import java.io.*; // for file handling routines and Serializable interface

public class Airport implements Serializable
{
  // attributes go here

  // all methods pass on AirportExceptions rather than catch them

  public Airport () throws AirportException
  {
    /* Initializes lists.
       Throws exception if number of runways invalid. */
  }

  public int arriveAtAirport (String flight)throws AirportException
  {
    /* IF runway free
         call 'descend' method of PlaneList attribute
         return runway number
       ELSE
         call 'circle' method of PlaneList attribute
         return 0
    */
  }

  private Runway nextFreeRunway()
  {
    // returns next vacant runway or null if no vacant runway
  }

  // all other methods act as wrappers for their PlaneList counterparts
}
```

With the comments that we have provided for you, the implementation of these methods should be a straightforward matter. Notice that by declaring this final class as serializable, the whole application can now be written or read to file as one object.

```
Airport myAirport = new Airport(); // create Airport object
// more code here
// write whole application to a given file as one object
FileOutputStream fileOut = new FileOutputStream("planes.dat");
objectOutputStream objOut = new ObjectOutputStream (fileOut);
objOut.writeObject(myAirport);
// more code here
// read whole application from a given file as one object
FileInputStream fileInput = new FileInputStream("planes.dat");
ObjectInputStream objInput = new ObjectInputStream (fileInput);
myAirport = (Airport) objInput.readObject();
// more code here
```

20.6 *Testing*

In chapter 8 we discussed various testing strategies. These included unit testing and integration testing. We have left unit testing to you as a practical task, but we will spend a little time here considering integration testing. A useful technique to devise test cases during integration testing is to review the behaviour specifications of use cases, derived during requirements analysis.

Remember, a use case describes some useful service that the system performs. The behaviour specifications capture this service from the point of view of the user. When testing the system you take the place of the user, and you should ensure that the behaviour specification is observed.

Often, there are several routes through a single use case. For example, when registering a plane, either the plane could be successfully registered, or an error is indicated. Different routes through a single use case are known as different **scenarios**. During integration you should take the place of the user and make sure that you test *each* scenario for *each* use case. Not surprisingly, this is often known as **scenario testing**. As an example, reconsider the "*Record flight's request to land*" use case:

> An air traffic controller records an incoming flight entering airport airspace, and requesting to land at the airport, by submitting its flight number. As long as the plane has previously registered with the airport, the air traffic controller is given an unoccupied runway number on which the plane will have permission to land. If all runways are occupied however, this permission is denied and the air traffic controller is informed to instruct the plane to circle the airport. If the plane has not previously registered with the airport an error is signalled.

From this description three scenarios can be identified:

Scenario 1

An air traffic controller records an incoming flight entering airport airspace, and requesting to land at the airport, by submitting its flight number, and is given an unoccupied runway number on which the plane will have permission to land.

Scenario 2

An air traffic controller records an incoming flight entering airport airspace, and requesting to land at the airport, by submitting its flight number. The air traffic controller is informed to instruct the plane to circle the airport as all runways are occupied.

Scenario 3

An air traffic controller records an incoming flight entering airport airspace, and requesting to land at the airport, by submitting its flight number. An error is signalled as the plane has not previously registered with the airport.

Similar scenarios can be extracted for each use case. During testing we should walk through each scenario, checking whether the outcomes are as expected. Initially a simple menu driven program, RunAirport, is developed to test system functionality.

Below is an annotated test run of this program to check the three scenarios identified above. We have separated the actual test run from the annotation by placing the test output in a box. We join the test run after several planes have already been entered and processed. Departures and arrivals are displayed so that the current state of the system is clear. First the departure list:

```
[1] Register a plane
[2] Process request to land
[3] Allow plane to land
[4] Allow passengers to board
[5] Allow plane to take off
[6] Display arrivals
[7] Display departures
[8] Quit
enter choice: [1-8] 7

DEPARTURES
FLIGHT     TO        RUNWAY
BA123      London    1
TK999      Tokyo     2
```

As you can see, two planes are currently waiting to depart. Here is the arrivals list after option [6] is selected from the menu:

```
ARRIVALS
FLIGHT    FROM      STATUS              RUNWAY
LF016     Moscow    Landed              3
SP001     Madrid    Not yet arrived
US642     Florida   Not yet arrived
```

Here, flight LF016 has landed, while the other registered flights have yet to arrive at the airport. Let's start to test the three scenarios we identified for the use case "*Record flight's request to land*". The first scenario should be the simple case of an arriving plane being told to land on a particular runway. So far, runways 1, 2, and 3 are occupied but runway 4 is unoccupied. If either flight SP001 or US642 arrives at the airport now, it should be told to land at the airport. Lets choose flight SP001. Option [2] from the menu is selected to register a flight arrival. Here is the system response:

```
Enter flight number:    SP001
Land on runway 4
```

As expected this plane is asked to come in and land on runway 4. Just to be sure that this has been recorded by the system, we can display arrivals again:

```
ARRIVALS
FLIGHT     FROM        STATUS            RUNWAY
US642      Florida     Not yet arrived
SP001      Madrid      Waiting to land   4
LF016      Moscow      Landed            3
```

Flight SP001's status has successfully changed from "*not yet arrived*" to "*waiting to land*", and the runway it has been allocated is also indicated. All runways are now occupied so we are in a position to test the second scenario of the "*Record flight's request to land*" use case.

In this scenario, the arriving flight should be told to circle the airport. Once again option [2] is chosen from the menu. Here is the system response:

```
Enter flight number:    US642
No runway available, circle the airport
```

The registered flight US642 arrives at the airport and is correctly told to circle the airport. again, to ensure this has been recorded accurately by the system we can display arrivals:

```
ARRIVALS
FLIGHT     FROM        STATUS            RUNWAY
US642      Florida     Waiting to land
SP001      Madrid      Waiting to land   4
LF016      Moscow      Landed            3
```

Flight US642 correctly has its status updated to "waiting to land", as no runway is indicated this implies the plane is circling. Finally, we will check the third scenario for the "*Record flight's request to land*" use case. In this scenario, a flight arrives at the airport without first registering; this raises an error. After choosing option [2] from the menu, the system responds as follows:

```
Enter flight number:      CK001
AirportException: this flight has not yet registered
        at PlaneList.getPlane(Compiled Code)
        at PlaneList.circle(PlaneList.java:32)
        at Airport.arriveAtAirport(Compiled Code)
        at RunAirport.option2(Compiled Code)
        at RunAirport.main(RunAirport.java:30)
```

Here, flight CK001 has not previously registered with the airport; so an error is correctly flagged. Scenarios for all other use cases could be identified and tested in a similar way.

Notice that, in the tester class we developed, we have obtained a lot of useful information from the exception object thrown. This information starts with the exception type and associated message:

```
AirportException: this flight has not yet registered
```

Following this is what is known as a **stack trace** of the exception. A stack trace lists the original method that generated the exception object (along with its associated class), then methods that received that exception object are listed. The last item in this list is the last method to receive the exception object before it was caught. As you can see, in this case, the exception was created in the getPlane method of the PlaneList class. The route that this exception object took is also made clear. Eventually it was caught in the main method.

Very often, it is useful to read this stack trace backwards. So, you can see that the main method called a private worker method option2. This is as expected since we chose option [2] from the menu. This worker method called the arriveAtAirport method of the Airport class. Again, as expected, this method determined that all runways were occupied and that the given plane should circle. This is clear because the next method that was called was the circle method of PlaneList. Finally, the exception occurred when this method tried to get the details of a flight not yet registered. This happens during the call to getPlane.

This series of events was as expected and so we can conclude the program is behaving correctly in this case. Occasionally the series of events will not be as expected. This trace can then help pinpoint errors quickly during the testing phase.

The stack trace is obtained from the exception object by calling a printStackTrace method, which we did in our RunAirport tester as follows:

```
catch (AirportException e)
{
   e.printStackTrace();
}
```

Notice there is no need to use a println statement here. The printStackTrace method automatically displays the stack trace onto the console.

Tutorial exercises

1. Develop a use case model for the Hostel application discussed in chapters 10 and 11.
2. When deciding which of the candidate classes, identified for the airport application, to keep – why were *air traffic controller, airport, runway number* and *list of planes* rejected?
3. Consider a college department that consists of 20 lecturers. Each lecturer is entitled to seven weeks' holiday a year. In any given week, however, there must be at least five lecturers at work. A system is being developed to help monitor holiday leave. Three classes, Day, Week and Lecturer have been identified. Draw a UML class diagram showing the associations among these classes by giving names to associations as well as recording multiplicity (you do not need to consider class attributes and methods).
4. In section 20.6 we developed scenarios for the use case "*Register flight arrival*". Develop scenarios for all the other use cases in table 20.1.

Practical work

1. Implement, copy from the CD-ROM (or download) all the classes identified in figure 20.5.
2. Develop tester classes for the Runway, Plane and PlaneList classes.
3. Develop your own tester program, RunAirport, and test all the scenarios you identified in tutorial question 4.

CASE STUDY PART 2: THE AIRPORT GUI

LEARNING OBJECTIVES

By the end of this chapter you should be able to:

➤ use the `JTabbedPane` Swing class to create an attractive user interface;

➤ add **tool tips** to Swing components using the `setToolTipText` method;

➤ add **short cut keys** to Swing menu items using the `setMnemonic` method.

21.1 Introduction

In this chapter we will outline the development of an attractive graphical user interface for the airport application. We will use classes from Java's Swing package to help us develop this interface. We start by considering the design of our graphical user interface.

21.2 Design of the GUI

Many Java IDE's now come with a drag and drop facility to construct user interfaces quickly and with minimal effort. We will explore this rapid approach to interface design in chapter 23. For the purposes of this chapter we will hard code our classes in the way we have always done so far. Figure 21.1 illustrates the interface design we chose for the airport application. The type of Swing components used have been labelled.

Notice that we have used a Swing label (`JLabel`) to hold a GIF image here:

```
JLabel jlblPicture = new JLabel(); // create JLabel component
jlblPicture.setIcon(new ImageIcon ("clouds.gif")); // add image
```

As you can see from figure 21.1, some of the Swing classes we use (such as JFrame) have already been introduced in chapter 19. Other Swing classes will be very similar to their AWT counterparts (JLabel, for example, is very similar to the AWT Label class). However, the JTabbedPane is a Swing class that has no AWT equivalent and has not yet been covered by us.

21.3   The JTabbedPane *class*

The JTabbedPane class is a very useful Swing component for organizing the user interface. You can think of a JTabbedPane component as a collection of overlapping tabbed "cards", on which you place other user interface components.[1] A particular card is revealed by clicking on its **tab**. This allows certain parts of the interface to be kept hidden until required, thus reducing screen clutter.

A JTabbedPane component can consist of any number of tabbed cards. Each card is actually a *single* component of your choice. If you use a container component such as a JPanel, you can effectively associate many components with a single tab (see figure 21.2).

The simplest way to construct a JTabbedPane component is to use the empty constructor as follows:

```
JTabbedPane tabs = new JTabbedPane();
```

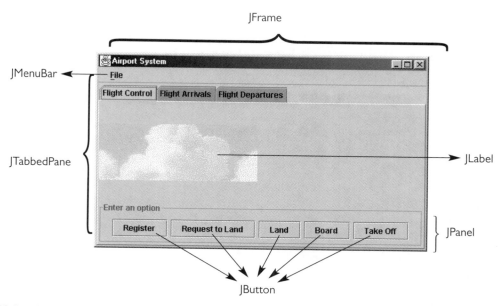

Fig 21.1   A Swing based design for the airport GUI

---

[1] A similar effect can be achieved by using the CardLayout manager discussed in chapter 19, but the JTabbedPane involves considerably less coding effort and provides a more sophisticated interface.

We can now add tabbed components to the JTabbedPane.[2] When adding a tabbed component to a JTabbedPane, you call the addTab method. The method requires two parameters – the first is the title that will appear on the tab and the second the component to add. The "Flight Control" tab can be created as follows:

```
// create a JPanel component
JPanel controlPanel = new JPanel;

// other components can be added to this panel either now or later

// add this panel to the JTabbedPane component and give the tab a title
tabs.addTab("Flight Control", controlPanel,);
```

The "Flight Arrivals" and "Flight Departures" tabs both consist of a text area for displaying plane details. Figure 21.3 shows the airport GUI after selecting the "Flight Arrivals" tab.

In this case, we do not need to associate a tab with a JPanel, as the tab will only reveal a single component. Unlike the AWT TextArea class, the Swing JTextArea class is not provided with scroll bars. We require our text area to have scroll bars, however, as the viewable area may not be sufficient.

A JTextArea component has to be used here, as it is unwise to mix heavyweight AWT components (such as TextArea) with lightweight Swing components (such as JTabbedPane). To add scroll bars to a JTextArea, the JTextArea component has to be added to a JScroll-Pane component. The JScrollPane is then added to the JTabbedPane as follows:

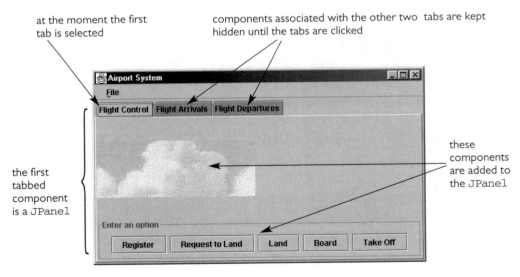

Fig 21.2 **A JTabbedPane allows parts of the interface to be revealed selectively**

---

[2] By default, the tabs you add will appear at the top of the JTabbedPane (as in figure 21.2). A version of the JTabbedPane constructor allows you to choose whether they appear at the top, the bottom, the left or the right.

```
// create text area
JTextArea jtaArrivals = new JTextArea(30,20);
// add text area to scroll pane
JScrollPane jspArrivals = new JScrollPane(jtaArrivals);
// add scroll pane to JTabbedPane component
tabs.addTab("Flight Arrivals", jspArrivals);
```

Notice that we have begun the name of swing components with a summary of the type of component, so the name of the JTextArea component begins with 'jta' and so on.

21.4   *The AirportFrame class*

The GUI for the airport application is contained within a JFrame. In previous chapters we developed GUI's by extending a Panel class, then added this Panel to a Frame in the tester class. We will take a different approach in this GUI.

If you look back at figure 21.1 you can see that the JFrame has a menu bar associated with it. This menu has options to save and load the Airport object, so the JFrame would need the Airport object to be one of its attributes. If we kept this JFrame separate from the rest of the GUI, we would have a problem as the Airport object is also required by other components on the GUI (such as the flight control buttons). So, in this case, we will not keep the JFrame separate from the rest of the GUI. Our GUI will be a class, AirportFrame, which extends JFrame rather than JPanel. The outline of this class is given below:

Fig 21.3   Both "Flight Arrivals" and "Flight Departures" consist of a text area

```
package airportSys; // add GUI to package
import java.awt.*; // for Layout managers
import java.awt.event.*; // for ActionListener interface
import javax.swing.*; // for Swing components
import javax.swing.border.*; // for Swing borders
import java.io.*; // for File Input and Output
public class AirportFrame extends JFrame implements ActionListener
{
  private Airport myAirport; // reference to Airport object
  // code to declare graphical components here

  public AirportFrame()
  {
    // code to intialise attributes to create interface here
  }

  public void actionPerformed (ActionEvent e)
  {
    // code to respond to button clicks and menu selections here
    listArrivals(); // update arrivals tab
    listDepartures(); // update departures tab
  }
  // private worker methods
  private void listArrivals()
  {
    // code to display arrivals information
  }

  private void listDepartures()
  {
    // code to display departures information
  }
}
```

As you can see, the outline of this class follows a familiar pattern. Adding the detail should be a simple matter and we leave this to you as a practical task. Our implementation can also be downloaded from the accompanying website or copied from the CD-ROM. We will just draw your attention to one or two Swing niceties that we have decided to incorporate into our implementation that will be new to you.

First, we have added **tool tips** to our buttons. A tool tip is an informative description of the purpose of a GUI component. This informative description is revealed when the user places the cursor over the component. Figure 21.4 shows the tool tip that is revealed when the cursor is placed over the "Board" button.

Adding a tool tip to a Swing component is easy; just use the setToolTipText method:

```
// create Swing component
JButton jbtnBoard = new JButton ("Board");
// add tool tip text
jbtnBoard.setToolTipText("Record a flight as ready for boarding");
```

We have also created **short cut** key access to our File menu. Ordinarily, a graphical component is selected by clicking on it with a mouse. Sometimes it is convenient to provide keyboard access to such items (this might be useful, for example, when the user does not have access to a working mouse). In the case of our GUI, the file menu can be selected with a mouse or by pressing the ALT and F keys simultaneously (ALT-F). It is clear that this is an alternative method of accessing the "File" menu by the fact that the 'F' of "File" is underlined (see figure 21.5).

Again, creating keyboard shortcuts for Swing components is straightforward, just use the setMnemonic method:

```
// create Swing component
JMenu fileMenu = new JMenu("File");
// add keyboard shortcut
fileMenu.setMnemonic('F');
```

21.5   *Airport Dialogue Boxes*

Whenever a button is selected in the "Flight Control" screen, a dialogue box is required to get and process user input. We have defined five dialogue classes for this purpose:

- RegisterDialog,
- RequestToLandDialog,
- LandingDialog,
- BoardingDialog,
- and TakeOffDialog.

The button responses are coded in the actionPerfomed method of the AirportFrame class. Here, for example, is how we generate a RegisterDialog in response to the selection of the "Register" button:

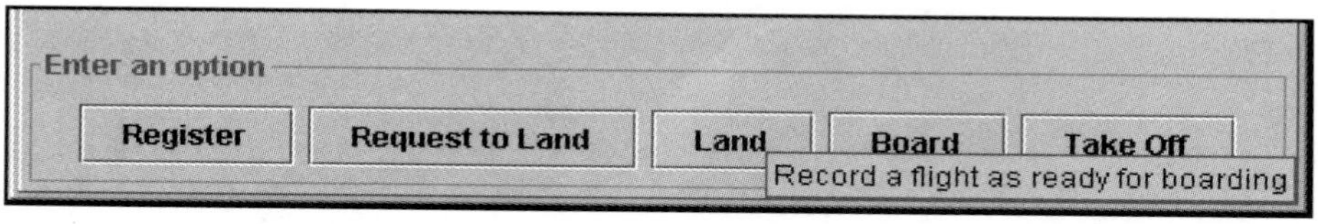

Fig 21.4   A tool tip is revealed when the mouse is placed over the "Board" button

```
public class AirportFrame extends JFrame implements ActionListener
{
  // attributes and constructor here

  // process button and menu selection here
  public void actionPerformed (ActionEvent e)
  {
    if (e.getSource()==jbtnRegister) // "Register" Button selected
    {
      // generate Register Dialogue Box
      new RegisterDialog(this,"Registration form", myAirport);
    }
    // more processing here
  }
}
```

As you can see, our dialogue constructor takes three parameters:

```
new RegisterDialog(this, "Registration form", myAirport);
```

The first is the parent frame (**this**), the second is the title of the dialogue box ("Registration form") and the final parameter is a reference to our airport object (myAirport). The last parameter is required as each dialogue box must update the airport object in some way or another.

You already know how to create dialogue classes from chapter 19. The only difference here is that you should extend the JDialog Swing class and not the Dialog AWT class. You may wish to model your dialogue boxes on ours (see figures 21.6–21.10).

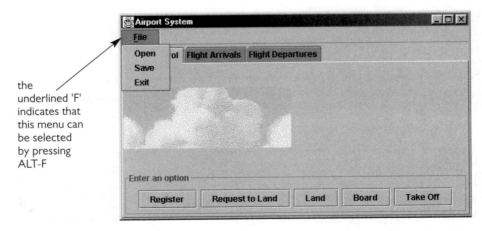

the underlined 'F' indicates that this menu can be selected by pressing ALT-F

Fig 21.5   A keyboard shortcut provides a useful alternative for accessing graphical components

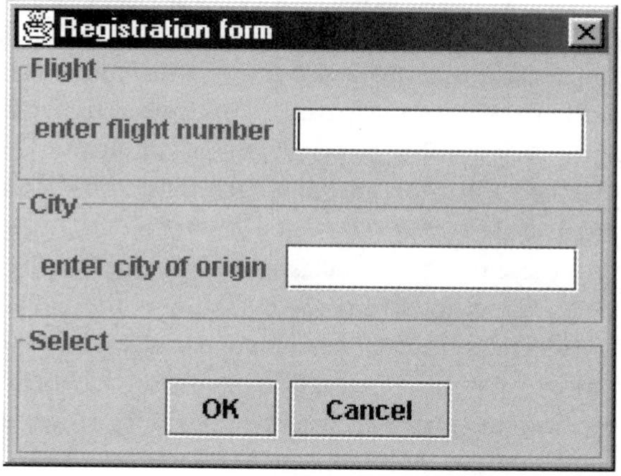

Fig 21.6   This dialogue box is created when the "Register" button is selected

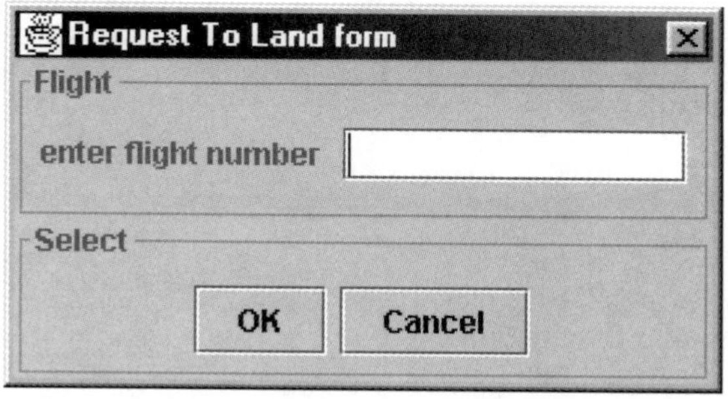

Fig 21.7   This dialogue box is created when the "Request to Land" button is selected

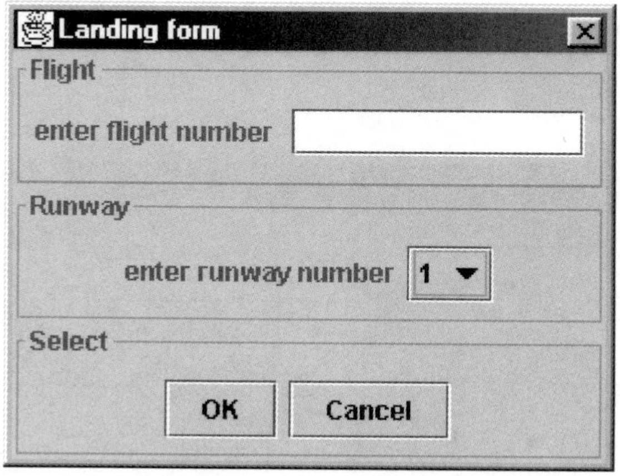

Fig 21.8   This dialogue box is created when the "Land" button is selected

21.5.1 Implementing the Airport Dialog Boxes

The `Airport` dialog boxes contain Swing components such as `JPanel`, `JLabel`, and `JTextField` rather than their AWT counterparts. If you look at figure 21.8 you can see we use a drop-down list for the runway number selection. Again, in chapter 19, you have already met the AWT component (`Choice`) for implementing such a list. We should point out to you that the equivalent Swing class is called `JComboBox` not `JChoice`.

Apart from the names of these component classes, the way in which they have been used and the names of their associated methods remain the same as their AWT counterparts. So you should be able to implement these classes on your own and we leave this to you as a practical task (you can also download our implementation from the accompanying website or from the CD-ROM). Before we do that, you may wish to consider using inheritance to reduce the coding task.

If you look back at the dialogue boxes in figures 21.6–21.10 you can see that, although no two are identical, they all share many common features. It makes sense to generalise these

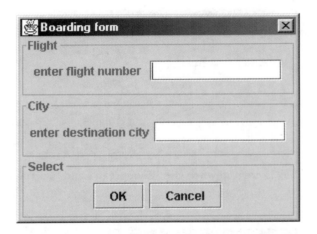

Fig 21.9   This dialogue box is created when the "Board" button is selected

Fig 21.10   This dialogue box is created when the "Take Off" button is selected

common features into a base class, AirportDialog say, and then use inheritance to develop the specialized dialogue classes (see figure 21.11).

As an example of the visual components that are common to all the Airport dialog boxes, look back at the "Request To Land" dialog box, and the "Take Off" dialog boxes. These dialog boxes contain only visual components that are common to all dialog boxes (see figure 21.12).

Here is the code for the AirportDialog base class. Take a look at it and then we will discuss it:

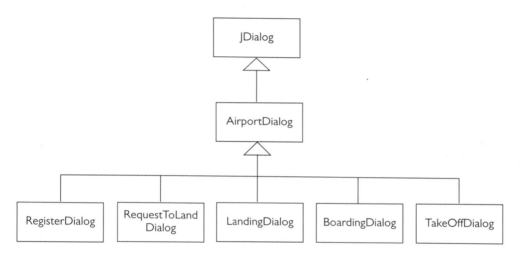

Fig 21.11   Common dialogue features are encapsulated in a base AirportDialog class

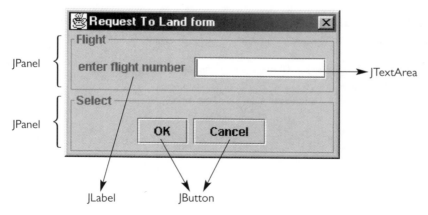

Fig 21.12   These visual components are common to all Airport dialog boxes

THE *AirportDialog* CLASS

```java
package airportSys;
import java.awt.*;
import java.awt.event.*;
import javax.swing.*;
import javax.swing.border.*;

abstract class AirportDialog extends JDialog implements ActionListener
{
  // notice we have given some attributes 'protected' access
  protected JPanel flightPanel = new JPanel();
  protected JPanel buttonPanel = new JPanel();
  private JLabel jlbFlightNumber = new JLabel ("enter flight number ");
  protected JTextField jtfFlight = new JtextField(12);
  protected JButton jbtnOk = new JButton ("OK");
  private JButton jbtnCancel = new JButton ("Cancel");

  public AirportDialog(JFrame frameIn, String titleIn)
  {
    super(frameIn, true); // associate dialog with parent frame
    // position dialog and set title
    setLocation(100,200);
    setTitle(titleIn);
    // add visual components
    flightPanel.add(jlbFlightNumber);
    flightPanel.add(jtfFlight);
    flightPanel.setBorder(new TitledBorder("Flight"));
    buttonPanel.add(jbtnOk);
    buttonPanel.add(jbtnCancel);
    buttonPanel.setBorder(new TitledBorder("Select"));
    // we will discuss the next two ActionListener lines after this code
    jbtnOk.addActionListener(this);
    jbtnCancel.addActionListener(new CancelButtonListener());

  }
  // this inner class implements the ActionListener for the 'Cancel' button
  private class CancelButtonListener implements ActionListener
  {
    public void actionPerformed(ActionEvent event)
    {
      dispose(); // destroys the dialog box
    }
  }
}
```

Most of this code should be straightforward to follow. There are just a few things we want to point out to you. First, notice that we declared some attributes as **protected** rather than **private**:

```
protected JPanel flightPanel = new JPanel();
protected JPanel buttonPanel = new JPanel();
private JLabel jlbFlightNumber = new JLabel ("enter flight number ");
protected JTextField jtfFlight = new JtextField(12);
protected JButton jbtnOk = new JButton ("OK");
private JButton jbtnCancel = new JButton ("Cancel");
```

The use of the **protected** modifier, as opposed to **public** or **private**, was explained in chapter 7. An attribute that is declared as **protected** can be accessed by a method of a subclass, or by any class within the same package.

In chapter 7 we told you that declaring attributes as **protected** has two drawbacks. First, it is not always possible to anticipate in advance that a class will be sub-classed; second, **protected** access weakens encapsulation, because access is given to all classes within the package, not just the subclasses. For these reasons we have up until now chosen not to use **protected**, but rather to plan carefully when deciding on which attributes are to have get- and set- methods. On this occasion, however, we have relaxed our rule and used **protected**, because neither of the above problems actually applies: we do know in this case that other classes will need to inherit from this class – and because these classes are not declared as **public** within our package, we do not need to worry about weakening encapsulation. The advantage of doing this is, of course, that we are able to cut out a considerable amount of additional coding.

One last thing we need to tell you about the AirportDialog class is the way we dealt with the event-handling code. There are two buttons in this class, the 'Cancel' button and the 'Ok' button, which require event-handling code.

The behaviour of the 'Ok' button will vary from dialog box to dialog box, so that will be left for each inherited class to define. The behaviour of the 'Cancel' button will be the same for all dialogue boxes, however – simply dispose of the dialog. So it is appropriate to implement the behaviour for this button in this base class. However, we have a small problem here. If we define an actionPerformed method in the base class (for the 'Cancel' button) and an actionPerformed method in an inherited class (for the 'Ok' button), the inherited class method will always override the base class method! For that reason we have defined an inner class (see section 14.6), CancelButtonListener, that contains its own actionPerformed method:

```
class AirportDialog extends JDialog
{
  // some code here

  // this actionlistener will be implemented in the inherited classes
  jbtnOk.addActionListener(this);
  /* this actionlistener will be the same for all classes so it is
     implemented once here in the base class, in an inner class below */
  jbtnCancel.addActionListener(new CancelButtonListener());

  // inner class contains actionPerformed method for the 'Cancel' button
  private class CancelButtonListener implements ActionListener
  {
    public void actionPerformed(ActionEvent event)
    {
      dispose(); // destroys the dialog box
    }
  }
}
```

Tutorial exercises

1. Identify the benefits offered by the JTabbedPane component.
2. The outline AirportFrame class of section 21.3 contained two worker methods, listArrivals and listDepartures. Write the code for both of these methods.
3. Write the code for the five dialog classes that inherit from AirportDialog.

Practical work

1. Implement all the classes required for the airport GUI as discussed in this chapter. You may wish to consider using JOptionPane dialogues to provide information and error messages (see figure 21.13).

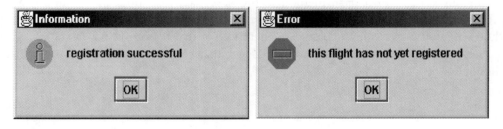

Fig 21.13   JOptionPane dialogues provide a simple way of communicating messages

MULTI-THREADED PROGRAMS

LEARNING OBJECTIVES

By the end of this chapter you should be able to:

➤ explain how concurrency is achieved by means of **time-slicing**;

➤ distinguish between **threads** and **processes**;

➤ implement threads in Java;

➤ explain the difference between **asynchronous** and **synchronized** thread execution;

➤ explain the terms **critical section** and **mutual exclusion**, and describe how Java programs can be made to implement these concepts;

➤ explain how **busy waiting** can be avoided in Java programs;

➤ provide a **state transition diagram** to illustrate the thread life-cycle;

➤ produce animated applications and applets.

22.1   Introduction

In this chapter you are going to learn how to make a program effectively perform more than one task at the same time – this is known as **multi-tasking**, and Java provides mechanisms for achieving this within a single program.

22.2   Concurrent processes

If you have been using computers for only a few years, then you will probably think nothing of the fact that your computer can appear to be doing two or more things at the same time. For example, a large file could be downloading from the Web, while you are listening to music and typing a letter into your word processor. However, those of us who were using desktop computers in the 1980s don't take this for granted! We can remember the days of having to wait for our document to be printed before we could get on with anything else – the idea of even having two applications like a spreadsheet and a database loaded at the same time on a personal computer would have been pretty exciting!

At first sight it does seem rather extraordinary that a computer with only one central processing unit (CPU) can perform more than one task at any one time. The way it achieves this is by some form of **time-slicing**; in other words it does a little bit of one task, then a little bit of the next and so on – and it does this so quickly it appears that it is all happening at the same time.

A running program is usually referred to as a **process**; two or more processes that run at the same time are called **concurrent** processes. Normally, when processes run concurrently each has its own area in memory where its program code and data are kept, and each process's memory space is protected from any other process. All this is dealt with by the operating system; modern operating systems such as Windows and Unix have a process management component whose job it is to handle all this.

22.3   *Threads*

We have just introduced the idea of a number of programs – or processes – operating concurrently. There are, however, times when we want a *single* program to perform two or more tasks at the same time. Whereas two concurrent programs are known as processes, each separate task performed by a single program is known as a **thread**. A thread is often referred to as a **lightweight process**, because it takes less of the system's resources to manage threads than it does to manage processes. The reason for this is that threads do not have completely separate areas of memory; they can share code and data areas. Managing threads, which also work on a time-slicing principle, is the job of the JVM working in conjunction with the operating system.

In all the programs we have developed so far, we have always waited for one task to complete before another one starts. So now let's develop a program where this is not the case.

What we are going to try to achieve with this program is a simple counter as shown in figure 22.1 below.[1]

The intention is that when we press the "start" button the numbers 1 to 10 will keep flashing by in the window; pressing the "stop" button should stop this process and, if we are using an EasyFrame, clicking on the crosshairs should terminate the application. In fact, our first go at this, which we have called CounterVersionOne, doesn't quite do the job. Take a look at the code:

---

[1] In this chapter we are going to be using AWT components rather than Swing because many of the examples are suitable for conversion to applets.

Fig 22.1   A simple counter

THE *CounterVersionOne* CLASS

```java
/* this class doesn't quite do what we intend!*/

import java.awt.*;
import java.awt.event.*;

class CounterVersionOne extends Panel implements ActionListener
{
  private Button startButton = new Button("Start");
  private Button stopButton = new Button("Stop");
  private TextField counterWindow = new TextField();
  private boolean go; /* it is intended that this variable should control
                         the loop */
  public CounterVersionOne()
  {
    add(startButton);
    add(stopButton);
    add(counterWindow);
    startButton.addActionListener(this);
    stopButton.addActionListener(this);
  }

  private void startCounterRunning()
  {
// continuously display the numbers 1 to 10
    int count = 1;
    while(go)
    {
      counterWindow.setText("" + count);
      count++;
      if(count > 10) // reset the counter if it has gone over 10
      {
        count=1;
      }
    }
  }
```

```
public void actionPerformed(ActionEvent e)
{
  if(e.getSource() == startButton)
  {
    go = true;
    startCounterRunning();
  }
  else if(e.getSource() == stopButton)
  /* this doesn't actually work, because the startCounterRunning method is
     still executing! */
  {
    go = false;
  }
}
```

It is quite easy to see how this program is intended to work. Pressing the "start" button sets a **boolean** attribute, go, to **true** and then calls the startCounterRunning method, which looks like this:

```
private void startCounterRunning()
{
  int count = 1;
  while(go)
  {
    counterWindow.setText("" + count);
    count++;
    if(count > 10)
    {
      count=1;
    }
  }
}
```

You can see that this method involves a **while** loop that is controlled by the value of the go attribute; while it is **true** the loop continuously displays the numbers 1 to 10 in the text window.

Pressing the "stop" button sets the value of go to false, with the intention that the loop will terminate. However, if you run this class in a frame, as in program 22.1, you will see the numbers whizzing past (you should just about be able to make them out), but pressing the "stop" button has no effect. And even if you have used an EasyFrame like we have, pressing the cross-hairs won't terminate the application!

PROGRAM 22.1

```java
import java.awt.*;

public class RunCounterVersionOne

{
   public static void main(String[] args)
   {
     EasyFrame frame = new EasyFrame();
     CounterVersionOne counter = new CounterVersionOne();
     frame.setSize(250,100);
     frame.setLocation(300,300);
     frame.add(counter);
     frame.setVisible(true);
   }
}
```

Can you see what's wrong here? The answer is that there is only one *thread of control*. The program, as always, starts with the first line of the **main** method and carries on to the end of this method; in this case this involves creating a CounterVersionOne object and setting up the frame – and then waiting for an event such as the user clicking the mouse. If the mouse is clicked on the "start" button then, as we have seen, the loop is started and the numbers start flashing by. But because there is only a single thread, this is all that can happen. The whole program is now tied up in this loop; it doesn't matter how often you click on the "stop" button, the program will never get the chance to process this event, because it is busy executing the loop.

What we need is to set up a separate thread that can busy itself with the loop, while another thread carries on with the rest of the program. Luckily Java provides us with a Thread class that allows us to do exactly that.

22.4   *The* Thread *class*

The Java Thread class provides a number of different methods that allow us to create and handle threads in our Java programs. The Thread class implements an interface called Runnable; this provides a method called run, which must be implemented. The code for this method determines the action that takes place when the thread is started.

One of the simplest ways to create a thread is to extend the Thread class. Let's do this with our previous example, and create a class called CounterThread; this is shown below. You can guess from the comment in the run method that this is okay, but could still do with a bit of improvement.

THE *CounterThread* CLASS

```java
import java.awt.*;

class CounterThread extends Thread
{
  private TextField counterWindow; /* this is the window where the numbers
                                       are displayed */
  private boolean go = true; // this variable controls the loop

  /* the text window where the numbers are displayed is sent in as a
     parameter to the constructor */
  public CounterThread(TextField windowIn)
  {
    counterWindow = windowIn;
  }

  public void run()
  {
    int count = 1;
    while(go)
    {
      counterWindow.setText(" " + count);

      /* Some additional code is going to go here later to improve our
         program */

      count++;
      if(count > 10) // reset the counter if it has gone over 10
      {
        count=1;
      }
    }
  }

  // this method will stop the numbers being displayed
  public void finish()
  {
    go = false;
  }
}
```

You can see that the business of displaying the numbers in the text window is now the responsibility of this class, and the instructions are placed within the run method. This method needs to know where to display the output, so the textField object has been passed into the constructor and assigned to an attribute of the class, making it accessible to the run method. You will see shortly that, in fact, we do not actually call this run method directly.

We have also provided a finish method that sets go back to **false**, and therefore terminates the thread.

Now we can write our new class, which we have called CounterVersionTwo:

THE *CounterVersionTwo* CLASS

```java
import java.awt.*;
import java.awt.event.*;

class CounterVersionTwo extends Panel implements ActionListener
{
  private Button startButton = new Button("Start");
  private Button stopButton = new Button("Stop");
  private TextField counterWindow = new TextField();
  private CounterThread thread;

  public CounterVersionTwo()
  {
    add(startButton);
    add(stopButton);
    add(counterWindow);

    startButton.addActionListener(this);
    stopButton.addActionListener(this);
  }

  public void actionPerformed(ActionEvent e)
  {
    if(e.getSource() == startButton)
    {
      // create a new thread
      thread = new CounterThread(counterWindow);
      // start the thread
      thread.start();
    }
    else if(e.getSource() == stopButton)
    {
      // stop the thread
      thread.finish();
    }
  }
}
```

You can see that pressing the "start" button creates a new thread and starts it running by calling the object's start method, which automatically calls the run method; as we mentioned above, the run method should not be called directly, but should always be called by invoking start. Pressing the "stop" button calls the thread's finish method.

If you run this class in, say, an EasyFrame, you will see that it now does what we wanted – but not very efficiently! Pressing "start" will, as before, cause the numbers to rush by in the display window; if you press "stop", you will see that the program does not always respond immediately, but instead continues to display the numbers for a little while before actually stopping. Moreover, if you do this a few times you will see that the time it takes between pressing the button and the thread actually stopping varies from one attempt to the next. The reason for this is explained in the section that follows, which also shows how we can get round this.

22.5   *Thread execution and scheduling*

As we explained earlier, concurrency, with a single processor, is achieved by some form of time-slicing. Each process or thread is given a little bit of time – referred to as a **quantum** – on the CPU, then the next process or thread takes its turn and so on.

Now, as you can imagine, there are some very complex issues to consider here. For example, what happens if a process that currently has the CPU cannot continue because it is waiting for some input, or perhaps is waiting for an external device like a printer to become available? When new processes come into existence, when do they get their turn? Should all processes get an equal amount of time on the CPU or should there be some way of prioritizing?

The answers to these questions are not within the domain of this book. However, it is important to understand that the responsibility for organizing all this lies with the operating system; in the case of multi-threaded Java programs this takes place in conjunction with the JVM. Different systems use different **scheduling algorithms** for deciding the order in which concurrent threads or processes are allowed CPU time. This is hidden from the user, and from the programmer. In the case of an application such as our counter program, all we can be sure about is the fact that one thread has to complete a quantum on the CPU before another thread gets its turn – we cannot, however, predict the amount of time that will be allocated to each thread, hence the rather unpredictable behaviour that we have seen.

Fortunately, however, we are not totally at the mercy of the operating system and the JVM. The Thread class provides some very useful methods, one of which is a method called sleep. This method forces a thread to give up the CPU for a specified amount of time, even if it hasn't completed its quantum. The time interval, in milliseconds, is passed in as a parameter. During this time, other threads can be given the CPU. The sleep method throws an InterruptedException and must be enclosed in a **try . . . catch** block.

So in our CounterThread example above, we could re-write our run method as shown below – the additional code is emboldened:

```
public void run()
{
  int count = 1;
  while(go)
  {
    counterWindow.setText(" " + count);
    try
    {
      sleep(1); // force the thread to sleep for 1 msec
    }
    catch(InterruptedException e)
    {
    }
    count++;
    if(count > 10)
    {
      count=1;
    }
  }
}
```

You can see that now, on every iteration of the loop, we force the thread to sleep for 1 millisecond; this gives any other thread the chance to get a turn on the CPU. So when we run this program in a frame, the "stop" button responds straight away. This is because, after each number is displayed, the thread rests for a millisecond and the main thread has a chance to get the CPU, so events like mouse-clicks can be processed. The other advantage of using the sleep method here is that the cycle can now be timed; you can try altering the sleep time to, say 500 milliseconds or 1 second, and watch the numbers being displayed accordingly. You might want to adapt this program so that the interval is passed in as a parameter.

In many programs that involve more than one thread you will find it necessary to force a thread to stop after one or more iterations to allow other events to be processed (rather than relying on the unpredictable scheduling of the operating system). If you do not want the thread to wait a specific period of time before resuming, then you can use the yield method rather than sleep; yield does not require any parameters.

22.6   *An alternative implementation*

Very often it is not possible to extend the Thread class, because the class we are writing needs to extend another class such as a Panel. The Thread class provides an alternative constructor that takes as a parameter a Runnable object where it expects to find the code for the run method.

So, the alternative approach involves creating a class that implements the Runnable interface, and then declaring a separate Thread object, either within this class or as a separate class. Study the following version of our CounterThread:

THE *AlternativeCounter* **CLASS**

```java
import java.awt.*;

class AlternativeCounter implements Runnable
{
  private TextField counterWindow;
  private boolean go = true;

  // a thread object is now created as an attribute of the class
  private Thread cThread = new Thread(this);

  public AlternativeCounter(TextField windowIn)
  {
    counterWindow = windowIn;
  }

  public void run()
  {
    int count = 1;
    while(go)
    {
      counterWindow.setText("" + count);
      count++;
      try
        {
          // the sleep method of the thread object is called
          cThread.sleep(1);
        }
      catch(InterruptedException e)
        {
        }
      if(count > 10)
      {
        count=1;
      }
    }
  }

  // a separate method is now required to start the thread
  public void begin()
  {
    cThread.start();
  }

  public void finish()
  {
    go = false;
  }
}
```

As can be seen from the comments, there are three changes that have been made.

First, a new Thread object is created as an attribute. As we explained before, the object where the run method is to be found is passed as a parameter; in the above example, it is **this** object itself that we must pass in.

Second, in the run method, we previously called the sleep method of **this** object. We can no longer do this, of course, because the AlternativeCounter class does not extend the Thread class. Instead, we call the sleep method of the thread object, cThread.

Finally, we have had to create a new method, begin, which calls the start method of cThread. Again, we have had to do this because our AlternativeCounter class is not an extension of Thread, and therefore does not have a start method of its own.

In order to make use of this new class we have had to rewrite CounterVersionTwo; we have named the new version of this class CounterVersionThree:

THE *CounterVersionThree* CLASS

```
Import java.awt.*;
import java.awt.event.*;

class CounterVersionThree extends Panel implements ActionListener
{
  private Button startButton = new Button("Start");
  private Button stopButton = new Button("Stop");
  private TextField counterWindow = new TextField();

  /* we are now using the AlternativeCounter class instead of the
     CounterThread class that we used in version two */
  private AlternativeCounter aCounter;

  public CounterVersionThree()
  {
    add(startButton);
    add(stopButton);
    add(counterWindow);

    startButton.addActionListener(this);
    stopButton.addActionListener(this);
  }

  public void actionPerformed(ActionEvent e)
  {
    if(e.getSource() == startButton)
    {
      aCounter = new AlternativeCounter(counterWindow);
      /* this time we have to use the object's begin method; it does not
         have a start method as it is not an extension of Thread */
      aCounter.begin();
    }
```

```
    else if(e.getSource() == stopButton)
    {
      aCounter.finish();
    }
  }
}
```

You can see the only real difference in this version is that we now have to call the begin method of the AlternativeCounter object, instead of the start method as we were able to do in version two.

22.7 *Synchronizing threads*

In section 22.5 we explained that under normal circumstances the behaviour of two or more threads executing concurrently is **asynchronous**; in other words their behaviour is not co-ordinated, and we are not able to predict which threads will be allocated CPU time at any given moment.

It is, however, often the case that we require two or more concurrently executing threads or processes to be co-ordinated – and if they were not, we could find we had some serious problems. There are many examples of this. One of the most common is that of a **producer–consumer** relationship, whereby one process is continually producing information that is required by another process. A very simple example of this is a program that copies a file from one place to another. One process is responsible for reading the data, another for writing the data. Since the two processes are likely to be operating at different speeds, this would normally be implemented by providing a *buffer*, that is a space in memory where the data that has been read is queued while it waits for the write process to access it and then remove it from the queue.

It should be fairly obvious that it could be pretty disastrous if the read process and the write process tried to access the buffer at the same time – both the data and the indices could easily be corrupted. In a situation like this we would need to treat the parts of the program that access the buffer as **critical sections** – that is, sections that can be accessed only by one process at a time.

Implementing critical sections is known as **mutual exclusion**, and fortunately Java provides a mechanism for the implementation of mutual exclusion in multi-threaded programs. In this book we are not going to go into any detail about how this is implemented, because the whole subject of concurrent programming is a vast one, and is best left to texts that deal with that topic. What we intend to do here is simply to explain the mechanisms that are available in Java for co-ordinating the behaviour of threads.

Java provides for the creation of a **monitor**, that is a class whose methods can be accessed by only one thread at a time. This entails the use of the modifier synchronized in the method header. For instance, a `Buffer` class in the above example might have a read method declared as:

```
public synchronized Object read()
{
   . . .
}
```

Because it is `synchronized`, as soon as some object invokes this method a **lock** is placed on it; this means that no other object can access it until it has finished executing. This can, however, cause a problem known as **busy waiting**. This means that the method that is being executed by a particular thread has to go round in a loop until some condition is met, and as a consequence the CPU time is used just to keep the thread going round and round in this loop until it times out – not very efficient! As an example of this, consider the `read` and `write` methods that we talked about in the example above. The `read` method would not be able to place any data in the buffer if the buffer were full – it would have to loop until some data was removed by the `write` method; conversely, the `write` method would not be able to obtain any data if the buffer were empty – it would have to wait for the `read` method to place some data there.

Java provides methods to help us avoid busy waiting situations. The `Object` class has a method called `wait`, which suspends the execution of a thread (taking it away from the CPU) until it receives a message from another thread telling it to wake up. The object methods `notify` and `notifyall` are used for the purpose of waking up other threads. Sensible use of these methods allow programmers to avoid busy waiting situations.

22.8   *Thread states*

A very useful way to summarize what you have learnt about threads is by means of a **state transition diagram**. Such a diagram shows the various states that an object can be in, and the allowed means of getting from one state to another – the **transitions**. The state transition diagram for a thread is shown in figure 22.2.

As we have said, much of the thread's life cycle is under the control of the operating system and the JVM; however, as you have seen, some transitions are also under the control of the programmer. In figure 22.2 the transitions that are controlled by the operating system and the JVM are italicized; those that the programmer can control are in plain font.

As you have seen, a thread is brought into existence by invoking its `start` method. At this point it goes into the **ready** state. This means it is waiting to be allocated time on the CPU; this decision is the responsibility of the operating system and JVM. Once it is **dispatched** (that is given CPU time), it is said to be in the **running** state. Once a thread is running, a number of things can happen to it:

- It can simply timeout and go back to the **ready** state; you have seen that it is possible for the programmer to force this to happen by ensuring that its `yield` method is invoked.
- The programmer can also arrange for the `sleep` method to be called, causing the thread to go into the **sleeping** state for a given period of time. When this time period has elapsed the thread wakes up and goes back to the ready state.
- The programmer can use the `wait` method to force the thread to go into the **waiting** state until a certain condition is met. Once the condition is met, the thread will be informed of this fact by a `notify` or `notifyall` method, and will return to the ready state.
- A thread can become **blocked**; this is normally because it is waiting for some input, or waiting for an output device to become available. The thread will return to the ready state when either the normal timeout period has elapsed or the input/output operation is completed.
- When the run method finishes the thread is terminated. It is actually possible to use the `stop` method of `Thread` for this purpose, but it can be very dangerous to stop a thread in the middle of its execution; it could, for example, be in the middle of writing to a file. It is far better to use a control variable instead, so that the thread terminates naturally.

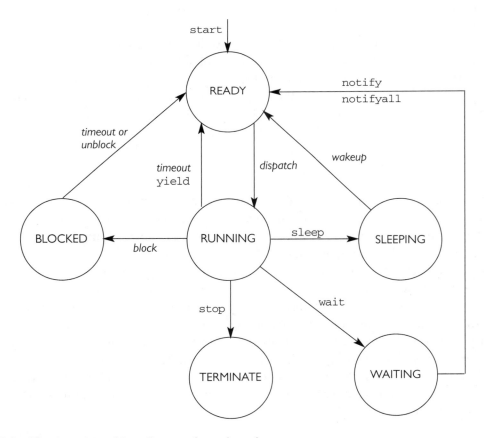

Fig 22.2 The state transition diagram for a thread

22.9   *Animations*

One of the more practical ways of utilizing threads is to produce animations. Clearly, an application that uses animated graphics is going to consist of some sort of continuous loop that displays a series of different images.

Let's start off by animating our familiar SmileyFace program. The following class, when run in a frame, produces a face that changes its expression from smile to frown once a second:

THE *AnimatedFace* CLASS

```java
import java.awt.*;
class AnimatedFace extends Canvas implements Runnable
{
  private boolean isHappy;
  // a separate thread is required to run the animation
  private Thread thread1;

  public AnimatedFace()
  {
    isHappy = true;
    // create a new thread
    thread1 = new Thread(this);
    // start the thread
    thread1.start();
  }

  public void run()
  {
    while(true) // a continuous loop
    {
      // on each iteration of the loop the mood is changed . . .
      if(isHappy == true)
      {
        isHappy = false;
      }
      else
      {
        isHappy = true;
      }
      // . . . and the face is repainted
      repaint();
      try
      {
        thread1.sleep(1000);
      }
      catch(InterruptedException e)
      {
      }
```

```
      }
   }

   public void paint(Graphics g)
   {
      g.setColor(Color.red);
      g.drawOval(85,45,75,75);
      g.setColor(Color.blue);
      g.drawOval(100,65,10,10);
      g.drawOval(135,65,10,10);
      g.drawString("Animated Face", 80,155);
      if(isHappy == true)
      {
         // draw a smiling mouth
         g.drawArc(102,85,40,25,0,-180);
      }
      else
      {
         // draw a frowning mouth
         g.drawArc(102,85,40,25,0,180);
      }
   }
}
```

As you can see, this time we have done everything in one class, the constructor of which creates and starts the thread. The run method consists of a loop that goes on forever until the thread is destroyed. On each iteration of the loop the mood is changed, the face is repainted, and the thread is forced to sleep for one second.

Program 22.2 runs the AnimatedFace class in an EasyFrame.

PROGRAM 22.2

```
import java.awt.*;

public class RunAnimatedFace
{
   public static void main(String[] args)
   {
      EasyFrame frame = new EasyFrame();
      AnimatedFace face = new AnimatedFace();
      frame.setSize(250,250);
      frame.setLocation(300,300);
      frame.setBackground(Color.yellow);
      frame.add(face);
      frame.setVisible(true);
   }
}
```

22.9.1 Reducing flicker

You will see when you run program 22.2 that there is some amount of flicker as the face changes expression – and the more you reduce the sleep interval, the worse this gets. The reason for this has to do with the `repaint` method. This method – which is a method of `Component` – does not in fact call the `paint` method directly; it actually calls a method called `update`. The default version of the `update` method clears the whole display area, repaints it in its background colour, and then calls the `paint` method. Going through this process each time is what gives rise to the flicker – especially when we are doing it so fast that we keep repainting before everything is completed.

We can reduce the flicker dramatically if we don't repaint the whole screen each time – just the bit that needs repainting. In our case this is just the mouth of the smiley face; once the rest of the face has been painted the first time, it doesn't need to be painted again. So it is an easy matter to adapt our `AnimatedFace` so as to eliminate flicker. First of all we re-write the `paint` method so that it draws everything but the mouth:

```
public void paint(Graphics g)
{
   g.setColor(Color.red);
   g.drawOval(85,45,75,75);
   g.setColor(Color.blue);
   g.drawOval(100,65,10,10);
   g.drawOval(135,65,10,10);
   g.drawString("Animated Face", 80,155);
}
```

Next, we override the update method:

```
public void update(Graphics g)
{
   // clear only the area that contains the mouth
   g.clearRect(102,85,42,27);
   // set the foreground colour
   g.setColor(Color.blue);
   if(isHappy == true)
   {
      // draw a smiling mouth
      g.drawArc(102,85,40,25,0,-180);
   }
   else
   {
      // draw a frowning mouth
      g.drawArc(102,85,40,25,0,180);
   }
}
```

You can see here that we use the `clearRect` method to clear only the area that contains the mouth (`clearRect` repaints the specified area in the background colour). Once this has been done, the appropriate mouth is then drawn. Notice we are *not* then calling paint, as would be the case with the default `update` method. The `paint` method is called once only, when the graphic first becomes visible.

22.9.2 An animated applet

The traditional way of producing animations in film has been to display a continuous series of images, which, to the eye, gives the impression of movement. In this section we are going to use that technique here to create an animated applet. The principle is, of course, the same regardless of whether we are dealing with applets or applications, but there are a number of issues to consider with applets, particularly concerning the loading of applets and images from remote sites, and the use of the four basic applet methods that you learnt about in chapter 12, namely `init`, `start`, `stop` and `destroy`.

Our animation is going to depict a record going round on a turn-table; it is not, perhaps, the most imaginative animation ever, but we have no doubt that you will be able to be far more artistic and produce some spectacular animations of your own! There are eight images involved here, as shown in figure 22.3.

The code for the applet is presented below. There are a few new techniques that are introduced here; take a quick look at the code, and then read the explanation that follows.

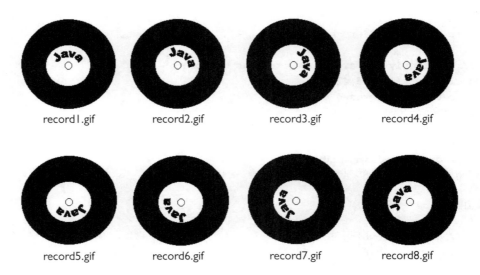

record1.gif   record2.gif   record3.gif   record4.gif

record5.gif   record6.gif   record7.gif   record8.gif

Fig 22.3   The images used with the *RecordApplet* class

THE *RecordApplet* CLASS

```java
import java.awt.*;
import java.applet.*;

public class RecordApplet extends Applet implements Runnable
{
  private final String fileName = "record";
  private final int numberOfImages = 8;
  private Image[] image;
  private int nextImage;
  private Thread animationThread;
  private boolean allLoaded;
  private boolean first;
  private boolean go;
  private int sleepTime;

  public void init() // called only once, when the applet is loaded
  {
    allLoaded = false;
    setBackground(Color.white);
    image = new Image[numberOfImages];
    sleepTime = Integer.parseInt(getParameter("sleep"));
  }

  public void start() // called each time the applet becomes visible
  {
    go = true;
    first = true;
    // create a new thread
    animationThread = new Thread(this);
    // start the thread
    animationThread.start();
  }

  public void run()
  {
    if(!allLoaded)
    // not executed once the images are loaded
    {
      MediaTracker tracker = new MediaTracker(this);
      String strImage;
      // prepare for the loading of the images
      for(int i = 0; i < numberOfImages; i++)
      {
        strImage = fileName + (i+1) + ".gif";
        image[i] = getImage(getDocumentBase(),strImage);
        tracker.addImage(image[i],i);
      }
```

```
      // load the images
      try
      {
        tracker.waitForAll();
      }
      catch(InterruptedException e)
      {
      }
      // check whether the images have loaded successfully
      allLoaded = !tracker.isErrorAny();

      if(!allLoaded) // if there was a problem loading the images
      {
        Graphics g = getGraphics();
        g.drawString("Error loading images", 115, 40);
        return;
      }

    }
    nextImage = 0;
    while(go) // continuously display the images in sequence
    {
      repaint();
      try
      {
        animationThread.sleep(sleepTime);
      }
      catch(InterruptedException e)
      {
      }
      nextImage++;
      if(nextImage == 8)
      {
        nextImage = 0;
      }
    }
  }

public void paint(Graphics g)
{
  if(!allLoaded) /* let the user know that the images are being loaded */
  {
    g.drawString("Loading images ....", 115, 20);
  }
  else
  {
```

```
          g.clearRect(115,10,150,20);
          g.setFont(new Font("Dialog",Font.BOLD,20));
          g.drawString("Java Record", 90, 20);
      }
  }

  public void update(Graphics g)
  {
    if(first) /* there is no need to repaint the whole display each time the
               next image in the sequence is displayed */
    {
      paint(g);
      first = false;
    }
    g.drawImage(image[nextImage], 65, 50, this);
  }

  public void stop() // called when another page is viewed
  {
    go = false;
  }
}
```

As you can see, we have declared a number of attributes, the purpose of which will become clear as we proceed. Let's start by exploring the `init` method.

```
public void init()
{
  allLoaded = false;
  setBackground(Color.white);
  image = new Image[numberOfImages];
  sleepTime = Integer.parseInt(getParameter("sleep"));
}
```

Now, as you will recall, this method is called only when the applet is loaded (or re-loaded). We therefore need to place here any initialization routines that should happen only at this time. So here we set the value of the **boolean** attribute, allLoaded, to **false**, indicating that the images have not yet been loaded from wherever they are stored, either locally or on a remote website; we set the background colour; we initialize an array of images; and finally we get the value of the sleep interval from the HTML file.

Next comes the `start` method:

```
public void start()
{
  go = true;
  first = true;
  animationThread = new Thread(this);
  animationThread.start();
}
```

You will remember that this method is called immediately after the init method, and is then called again every time the applet becomes visible (normally after returning from viewing another webpage). So here must be placed the code that needs to be invoked each time the applet becomes visible. Therefore the value of go, the variable that will control the main loop, is set to **true** in order to start the animation; another **boolean** attribute, first, is also set to **true** – as you will see this is necessary because certain parts of the graphic need to be painted only on the first iteration of the loop; finally a new thread is created and started.

Now we can look at the run method. You can see that this starts with a conditional set of statements that are executed only if the images have not yet been loaded. So, much of the code here is concerned with loading the images, which are likely in practice to be on a remote site. This process will inevitably take some time, and it is useful to monitor the progress so that a user of the program is not left wondering what is going on. For this purpose we can use the MediaTracker class.

The first thing we do, then, within the run method is to create a MediaTracker object; the constructor requires a parameter (an object of Component) indicating on which component the images will eventually be drawn:

```
MediaTracker tracker = new MediaTracker(this);
```

After declaring a String to hold the name of each image in turn, we then use a **for** loop to prepare for the loading of the eight images:

```
for(int i = 0; i < numberOfImages; i++)
{
  strImage = fileName + (i+1) + ".gif";
  image[i] = getImage(getDocumentBase(),strImage);
  tracker.addImage(image[i],i);
}
```

On each iteration we construct the name of the image – "record1.gif", "record2.gif" and so on – and then call a method named getImage. This is an Applet method that we are going to use in conjunction with the methods of the MediaTracker class that we mentioned earlier. This is the appropriate technique to use when we are loading images from a remote site, as opposed to using the Toolkit class that we utilized in section 17.7.

The getImage method requires two parameters; the URL (Unique Resource Locator) where the image is to be found, and the name of the image. To obtain the URL we are using another Applet method, getDocumentBase – this returns the URL of the HTML page that invoked the applet; by contrast, the getCodeBase method, which we have not used here, returns the URL of the applet itself.[2]

The getImage method does not, in itself, load the image. Rather, it forms an association between the image name and the file name. Left to its own devices the JVM will load the image at such time as it is needed, namely when it is to be displayed. A better way for this to happen is, as we have said, to use the MediaTracker class. You can see how we have done this by invoking the addImage method of the MediaTracker object that we declared earlier. This method adds the image to the list of images that are to be tracked. The relevant image is passed in as the first parameter to this method; the second parameter allows us to assign a unique integer id to this image so that we can, if we wish, refer to it later in other MediaTracker methods.

Once this process is complete for all eight images, we can then start the process of loading the images. We do this with the waitForAll method of MediaTracker, which starts the loading process, and then waits for completion. This method throws an Interrupted-Exception and so must be enclosed in a try . . . catch block:

```
try
{
   tracker.waitForAll();
}
catch(InterruptedException e)
{
}
```

Once the process is complete, we use the isErrorAny method to check that all the images have loaded successfully:

```
allLoaded = !tracker.isErrorAny();
```

If there are any errors we display an appropriate message and end the run method:

```
if(!allLoaded)
{
   Graphics g = getGraphics();
   g.drawString("Error loading images", 115, 40);
   return;
}
```

---

[2] These methods will successfully resolve local file locations to a URL.

Before moving on it is worth noting that a single image can be tracked in the same way with the `waitForID` and `isErrorID` methods, both of which take as a parameter the identity number previously assigned with the `addImage` method.

As long as everything is okay we can move on to the main body of the `run` method. Here we use the `nextImage` attribute to keep track of the image numbers as we display each one in turn – so we initialize this to zero and then start our loop:

```
while(go)
{
  repaint();
  try
  {
    animationThread.sleep(sleepTime);
  }
  catch(InterruptedException e)
  {
  }
  nextImage++;
  if(nextImage == 8)
  {
    nextImage = 0;
  }
}
```

This is quite straightforward. On each iteration, the screen is repainted and `nextImage` is incremented – if the last image is reached `nextImage` is reset to zero.

That ends the `run` method. We can now take a look at how we have organized our `paint` and `update` methods; remember that `repaint` actually calls the `update` method, not the `paint` method.

First let's look at the paint method:

```
public void paint(Graphics g)
{
  if(!allLoaded)
  {
    g.drawString("Loading images . . .", 115, 20);
  }
  else
  {
    g.clearRect(115,10,150,20);
    g.setFont(new Font("Dialog",Font.BOLD,20));
    g.drawString("Java Record", 90, 20);
  }
}
```

Bear in mind that this method is called automatically each time the object becomes visible. You can see that if the images are not yet loaded, then a message is displayed informing the user that the loading process is under way. This could take a little while, depending on the size of the images and the speed of the connection to the remote site.

After the first time, the paint method will be called again only if invoked by the update method (which is called by repaint on each iteration of the loop).

Looking at the update method below you will see that the paint method is called only on the first iteration of the loop – by this time, the images will all have been loaded and, as you can see from the coding of the paint method, a rectangle is cleared to get rid of the "loading images . . ." message, and a heading is placed on the screen.

```
public void update(Graphics g)
{
    if(first)
    {
        paint(g);
        first = false;
    }
    g.drawImage(image[nextImage], 65, 50, this);
}
```

You can see that the update method is responsible for drawing each image in the sequence.

Finally the stop method sets the loop controlling variable, go, to **false** so that the animation stops each time the browser is made to point at another page.

```
public void stop()
{
    go = false;
}
```

The following HTML code is sufficient to load and run the applet; we have given it a sleep time of 100 msecs – you can try other values:

```
<HTML>
<APPLET CODE = RecordApplet.class WIDTH = "300" HEIGHT = "300">
<PARAM NAME = "sleep" VALUE = "100">
</APPLET>
</HTML>
```

Tutorial exercises

1. Explain the difference between a *thread* and a *process*.
2. What is meant by the term *time-slicing*?
3. What is meant by the terms mutual exclusion and critical section?
4. Explain the function of the Thread methods sleep and yield.
5. Explain the function of the methods wait and notify, and why these methods are methods of the Object class and not the Thread class
6. Consider the RecordApplet of section 22.9.2. What do you think would happen if this program had been implanted as a single thread, and was then loaded into a browser?
7. Design some experiments that will help you to observe the behaviour of threads. A suggestion is to provide a Thread class with an id number that can be allocated at the time an object is created; the run method could simply print out this id a given number of times. A program could then be written to create and run a number of threads concurrently so that the output can be studied. You could vary the number of times the threads loop before terminating and see if there is any observable difference.

Practical work

1. Implement the programs from this chapter. The images that you need for the RecordApplet can be downloaded from the website. Try to design some animations of your own.
2. (a) Implement program 22.1, but use the CounterVersionTwo class from section 22.4.
   (b) Modify the CounterVersionTwo class so that the sleep interval is passed in as a parameter from the main program.
   (c) Modify program 22.1 so that two separate counters run concurrently as shown below; each counter could be made to operate with a different sleep interval.

3. Implement the classes that you designed in question 7.

JAVA IN CONTEXT

LEARNING OBJECTIVES

By the end of this chapter you should be able to:

➤ provide a brief history of the development of the Java language;

➤ identify the potential problems with **pointers**, **multiple inheritance** and **aliases**;

➤ develop `clone` methods to avoid the problem of aliases;

➤ identify **immutable objects**;

➤ explain the benefits of Java's **garbage collector**.

23.1 Introduction

Originally named *Oak*, Java was developed in 1991 by Sun Microsystems. At the time, the intention was to use it to program consumer devices such as video recorders, mobile phones and televisions. The expectation was that these devices would soon need to communicate with each other. As it turned out, however, this concept never really took off at the time. Instead, it was the growth of the Internet through the World Wide Web that was to be the real launch pad for the language.

Despite the fact that Java was never really used as a language to program consumer devices, this original motivation behind its development explains many of its characteristics. In particular, the **size** and **reliability** of the language became very important.

23.2 Language size

Generally, the processor power of a system controlling a consumer device is very small compared to that of a PC; so the language used to develop such systems should be fairly compact. Consequently, the Java language is relatively small and compact when compared to a traditional systems language like C (and its object-oriented successor C++). These two languages were very popular at the time Java was being developed, so the developers of Java decided to stick to conventional C++ syntax as much as possible. Consequently Java syntax is very similar to C++ syntax.

Just because the Java language is relatively small, however, does not mean that it is not as powerful as a language like C++. Instead, the Java developers were careful to remove certain language features that they felt led to common program errors. These include the ability for a programmer to create **pointers** and the ability for a programmer to develop **multiple inheritance** hierarchies.

23.2.1 Pointers

A pointer, in programming terms, is a variable containing an address in memory. Of course Java programmers can do something very similar to this – they can create *references*. Figure 23.1 repeats an example we showed you in chapter 4.

In figure 23.1, the variable myOblong contains a reference (address in memory) of an Oblong object. The difference between a *reference* and a *pointer* is that the *programmer* does not have control over which address in memory is used – the *system* takes care of this. Of course, internally, the system creates a pointer and controls its location. In a language like C++ the programmer can directly manipulate this pointer (move it along and back in memory). This was seen as giving the programmer greater control. However, if this ability is abused, critical areas of memory can easily be corrupted. For this reason the Java language developers did not allow users to manipulate pointers directly.

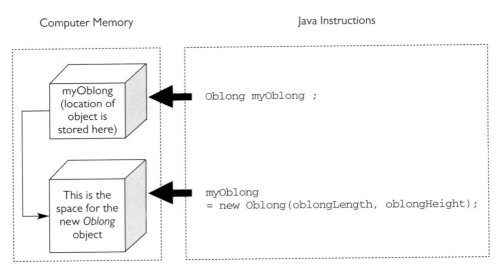

Fig 23.1   An object variable in Java contains a reference to the object data

23.2.2 Multiple inheritance

Inheritance is an important feature of object-oriented languages. Many object-oriented languages, such as C++ and Eiffel, allow an extended form of inheritance known as multiple inheritance. When programming in Java a class can only ever inherit from at most one base class. Multiple inheritance allows a class to inherit from more than one base class (see figures 23.2 and 23.3).

The Java developers decided not to allow multiple inheritance for two reasons

- it is very rarely required;
- it can lead to very complicated inheritance trees which in turn lead to programming errors.

As an example of multiple inheritance consider a football club with various employees. Figure 23.4 illustrates an inheritance structure that might be arrived at.

Here, a `Player Manager` inherits from both `Player` and `Manager`, both of which in turn inherit from `Employee`! As you can see this is starting to get a little messy. Things become even more complicated when we consider method overriding. If both `Player` and `Manager` have a method called `payBonus`, which method should be called for `Player Manager` — or should it be overridden?

Although Java disallows multiple inheritance it does offer a type of multiple inheritance — interfaces. As we have seen in previous chapters, a class can inherit from only one base class in Java but can implement many interfaces.

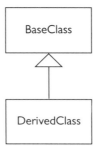

Fig 23.2   Single inheritance

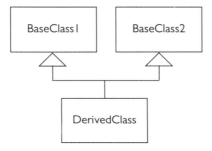

Fig 23.3   Multiple inheritance

23.3 *Language reliability*

The Java language developers placed a lot of emphasis on ensuring that programs developed in Java would be reliable. One way in which they did this, was to provide extensive exception handling techniques that we covered in chapter 14. Another way reliability was improved was to remove the ability for programmers to directly manipulate pointers as we discussed earlier in this chapter. Errors arising from pointer manipulation in other languages are very common. A related problem, however, is still prevalent in Java but can be avoided to a large extent. That is – the problem of **aliasing**.

23.3.1 Aliasing

Aliasing occurs when the *same* memory location is accessed by variables with *different* names. As an example, we could create an object, oblong1, of our Oblong class (from chapters 4 and 5) as follows:

```
Oblong oblong1 = new Oblong (10, 20);
```

We could then declare a new variable, oblong2, which could reference the same object:

```
Oblong oblong2 = oblong1;
```

Here oblong1 is simply a different name for object1 – in other words an **alias**. The effect of creating an alias is illustrated in figure 23.5.

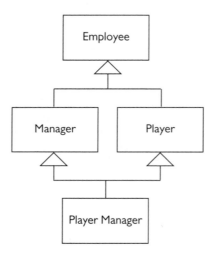

Fig 23.4   A combination of single and multiple inheritance

In practice a programmer would normally create an alias only with good reason. For example, in chapter 6, when we deleted an object from a list, we were able to make good use of aliasing by assigning an object reference to a different object with a statement like:

```
list[i] = list[i+1];
```

However, a potential problem with a language that allows aliasing is that it could lead to errors arising inadvertently. Consider for example a Customer class that keeps track of two different bank accounts. Here is the outline of that class:

```
class Customer
{
  // two private attributes to hold bank account details
  private BankAccount account1;
  private BankAccount account2;

  // more code here

  // two access methods
  public BankAccount getFirstAccount()
  {
    return account1;
  }

  public BankAccount getSecondAccount()
  {
    return account2;
  }
}
```

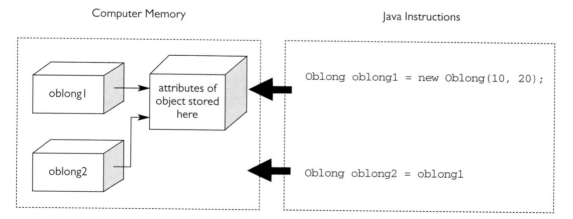

Fog 23.5   Copying an object reference creates an alias

Consider the methods getFirstAccount and getSecondAccount. In each case we have sent back a reference to a **private** attribute, which is itself an object. We did this to allow users of this class to interrogate details about the two bank accounts, with statements such as:

```
BankAccount tempAccount = someCustomer.getFirstAccount();
System.out.println("balance of first account = "+tempAccount.getBalance());
```

The problem is that this reference can also be used to manipulate the **private** attributes of the BankAccount object, with a statement like this:

```
tempAccount.withdraw(100);
```

Here, we have actually compromised the principle of encapsulation by unintentionally allowing write access to a **private** attribute when we really wanted to allow read access only.

There are a few examples in this book where we have returned references to **private** objects, but we have been careful not to take advantage of this by manipulating **private** attributes in this way. However, the important point is that they *could* be manipulated in that way. In order to make classes extra secure (for example, in the development of safety-critical systems), aliasing should be avoided.

The problem of aliases arises when a *copy* of an object is required but instead a reference to an object is returned. By sending back a reference, the original object can be manipulated, whereas a copy would not cause any harm to the original object. So, in order to provide such a copy, a class should define a method that returns an exact copy of the object rather than a reference. Such a method exists in the Object class but has to be overridden in any user defined class. The method is called clone.

23.3.2 The *clone* method

The clone method that needs to be redefined in each user-defined class has the following outline:

```
public Object clone()
{
   // code goes here
}
```

As you can see the method returns an item of type `Object`. Here is an outline of the BankAccount class with such a method provided:

```
class BankAccount
{
  // private attributes as before
  private String accountNumber;
  private String accountName;
  private double balance;

  // previous methods go here

  // now provide a clone method
  public Object clone()
  {
    // call constructor to create a new object identical to this object
    BankAccount copyOfThisAccount = new BankAccount
                            (accountNumber, accountName);
    /* after this the balance of the two bank accounts might not be the same
       so copy the balance as well */
    copyOfThisAccount.balance = balance;
    // finally, send back this copy
    return copyOfThisAccount;
  }
}
```

Notice that in order to set the balance of the copied bank account we have directly accessed the **private** balance attribute of the copy:

```
copyOfThisAccount.balance = balance;
```

This is perfectly legal as we are in a BankAccount class, so all BankAccount objects created within this class can access their **private** attributes. Now, whenever we need to copy a BankAccount object we just call the clone method. For example:

```
// create the original object
BankAccount ourAccount = new BankAccount ("98765432", "Charatan and Kans");
// now make a copy using the clone method, notice a type-cast is required
BankAccount tempAccount = (BankAccount) ourAccount.clone();
// other instructions here
```

The `clone` method sends back an exact copy of the original account not a copy of the reference (see figure 23.6).

Now, whatever we do to the copied object will leave the original object unaffected, and vice versa.

In a similar way, we can ensure that classes that contain **private** BankAccount attributes do not inadvertently send back references (and hence aliases) to these attributes:

```java
class Customer
{

  // as before here

  // next two methods now send back clones, not aliases
  public BankAccount getFirstAccount()
  {
    return (BankAccount)account1.clone();
  }

  public BankAccount getSecondAccount()
  {
    return (BankAccount)account2.clone();
  }
}
```

Now, in our earlier example, the problem is removed because of the use of the `clone` method in the Customer class, as illustrated in the fragment below:

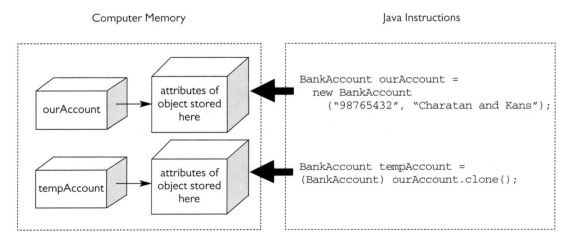

Fig 23.6   The 'clone' method creates a copy of an object

```
Customer someCustomer = new Customer();
// some code to update someCustomer here
/* now a temporary variable is created to read details of first account but
   this is not an alias it is a clone */
BankAccount tempAccount = someCustomer.getFirstaccount();
System.out.println("balance of first account = " + tempAccount.getBalance();
// assume the balance is displayed as 500

temp.withdraw(100); /* because temp is a clone the private Customer
                       attribute account1 is unaffected */
System.out.println("balance of first account = " +
                           someCustomer.getFirstAccount().getBalance());
// the balance of the customer's first account will be still be 500
```

23.3.3 Immutable Objects

We said methods that return references to **private** attributes actually create aliases and that this can be dangerous. However, these aliases are not *always* dangerous. Consider again the following highlighted features of the BankAccount class:

```
class BankAccount
{
  private String accountNumber;

  // other attributes and methods here

  public String getAccountNumber()
  {
    return accountNumber;
  }
}
```

In this case the getAccountNumber method returns a reference to a **private** String object (accountNumber). This is an alias for the **private** String attribute. However, this alias causes no harm as there are no String methods that allow a String object to be altered. So, this alias cannot be used to alter the **private** String object.

Objects which have no methods to alter their state are known as **immutable objects**. String objects are immutable objects. Objects of classes that you develop may also be immutable depending on the methods you have provided. If such objects are immutable, you do not have to worry about creating aliases of these objects and do not need to provide them with clone methods. For example, let's go back to the book store application we developed in chapter 16. Rather than show you the code, figure 23.7 shows you the UML design again.

As you can see the `BookTable` class contains a collection of `Book` objects. These `Book` objects are **private** to the `BookTable` class. However the `getBook` method returns a reference to a **private** `Book` object and so sends back an alias. This is not a problem, however, because if you look at the design of the `Book` class the only methods provided are `get` methods. That is, there are no `Book` methods that can alter the attributes of the `Book` object once the `Book` object has been created. A `Book` object is an immutable object.

23.3.4 Garbage collection

When an object is created using the **new** operator, a request is being made to grab an area of free computer memory to store the object's attributes. Because this memory is requested during the running of a program, not during compilation, the compiler cannot guarantee that enough memory exists to meet this request. Memory could become exhausted for two reasons:

- continual requests to grab memory are made when no more free memory exists,
- memory that is no longer needed is not released back to the system.

These problems are common to all programming languages and the danger of memory exhaustion is a real one for large programs, or programs running in a small memory space. Java allows both of the reasons listed above to be dealt with effectively and thus ensure that programs do not crash unexpectedly.

First, exception handling techniques can be used to monitor for memory exhaustion and code can be written to ensure the program terminates gracefully. More importantly, Java has a built in **garbage collection** facility to release unused memory. This is a facility that regularly trawls through memory looking for locations used by the program, freeing any locations that are no longer in use.

For example consider program 23.1 below.

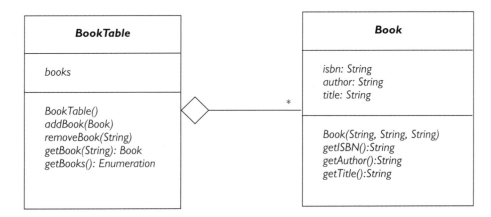

Fig 23.7   Design for the book store application

PROGRAM 23.1

```
class Tester
{
  public static void main(String[] args)
    {
      char ans;
      Oblong object; // reference to object created here
      do
      {
        System.out.print("Enter length: ");
        double length = EasyIn.getDouble();
        System.out.print("Enter height: ");
        double height = EasyIn.getDouble();
        // new object created each time we go around the loop
        object = new Oblong(length, height);
        System.out.println("area = "+ object.calculateArea());
        System.out.println("perimeter = "+ object.calculatePerimeter());
        System.out.print("Do you want another go? ");
        ans = EasyIn.getChar();
      } while (ans == 'y' || ans == 'Y');
    }
```

Here, a new object is created each time we go around the loop. The memory used for the previous object is no longer required. In a language like C++ the memory occupied by old objects would not be destroyed unless the programmer added instructions to do so. So if the programmer forgot to do this, the available memory space could easily be exhausted. The Java system, however, regularly checks for such unused objects in memory and destroys them.

Although automatic garbage collection does make extra demands on the system (slowing it down while it takes place), this extra demand is considered by many to be worthwhile by removing a heavy burden on programmers. In fact, Microsoft's new language, C# (pronounced "C Sharp"), includes a garbage collection facility.

23.4   *The role of Java*

While Java began life as a language to program consumer devices, it has now evolved into a standard application programming language and competes with other system languages such as C++.

Java retains much of the C++ syntax and this has helped its growth in popularity as C++ programmers have found it relatively easy to move over to Java. Unsafe and unsound C++ features, such as pointers and multiple inheritance, have been removed from the language. In addition, robust exception handling features have been incorporated into Java to help ensure the reliability of Java programs.

Where system efficiency is the most important criteria for a software project, languages like C++ still play an important role as the JVM model can place an overhead on the speed of the final system. Also, while Java's garbage collector certainly improves the robustness of Java programs, it can compromise program efficiency. However, with the growth of the Internet, system reliability, robustness and cross-platform capability are becoming increasingly important. Java offers all these attributes and so its future certainly looks very secure.

Tutorial exercises

1. Distinguish between a *pointer* and a *reference*.
2. What does the term multiple inheritance mean and why does Java disallow it?
3. Consider the following class

THE *Critical* CLASS

```
class CriticalClass
{
  private int value;

  public Critical (int valueIn)
  {
    value = valueIn;
  }
  public void setValue(int valueIn)
  {
    value = valueIn;
  }
  public int getValue ()
  {
    return value;
  }
}
```

   (a) Explain why Critical objects are not immutable.
   (b) Write fragments of code to create Critical objects and demonstrate the problem of aliases?
   (c) Develop a clone method in the Critical class.
   (d) Write fragments of code to demonstrate the use of this clone method.
4. Look back at the case study of chapters 10 and 11. Two collection classes exist, TenantList and PaymentList:
   (a) Which methods in these collections return aliases?
   (b) Which aliases could be dangerous?
   (c) How can these aliases be avoided?
5. What are the advantages and disadvantages of a garbage collection facility in programming a language?

Practical work

1. Implement the `Critical` class of tutorial question 3 and then write a tester program to demonstrate the problem of aliases.
2. Amend the `Critical` class by adding a `clone` method as discussed in tutorial question 3(c) and then amend the tester program you developed in the previous practical task to demonstrate the use of this `clone` method.
3. Look back at the `Hostel` case study of chapters 10 and 11, and the `Airport` case study of chapters 21 and 22. See if you can identify any ways in which the individual classes could be made more secure by eliminating any possibility of aliasing.

BEYOND THE SECOND SEMESTER

24.1 Introduction

This chapter marks the end of our Java coverage for your second semester in programming. Although you have covered a lot of material, there is still a lot of material more that you can explore. In this final chapter we give you an idea of the further potential of Java, before providing you with an extensive set of review questions to help ensure you understood the material in this book.

24.2 Rapid Application Development (RAD)

The RAD approach to program development was introduced to you in chapter 1 and is a very important, modern approach. It involves sophisticated development tools for automating or simplifying tasks that would otherwise have to be coded by the programmer. This greatly speeds up development time and so increases productivity.

Many of the programs we developed in this book have attractive graphical interfaces. As you could probably tell, these programs became very large as we started to develop more interesting interfaces. RAD programming tools help significantly in the production of such interfaces. Before we illustrate this, a word of caution: these RAD tools still generate raw Java code of the kind we have been teaching you, and you must understand this code in order to be able to tailor it to fit your exact needs. So there is no substitute for learning the Java language! The details of how to generate this code with a tool will differ from one RAD tool to another.

24.3   *The* PushMe *application revisited*

To illustrate the RAD approach we will develop the PushMe application from chapter 9, but this time use a RAD tool to help us. Figure 24.1 is the original program.

Figure 24.2 illustrates a typical screen in a RAD tool. We have added our own annotation around this screen shot. Read these annotations to get some idea of how this Tool works. The tool we have used here is JBuilder, but all RAD tools work in a similar way.

Rather than hard coding the selection and appearance of GUI components, the RAD tool allows you to pick them from a palette and modify them in much the same way as a simple drawing program. From the palette we collect, one by one, a Label, a Button and a TextField and place them onto the Frame (see figure 24.3).

As you can see, the appearance of these GUI components on the Frame does not match exactly the appearance we are after. We can do something about that. Each component's look can be modified by changing its properties in the properties list. For example, to change the text on the Label to "Enter some text and push the button", we select the Label's text property (see figure 24.4).

In a similar way, we can customize the look of the other three components to give us our desired GUI (see figure 24.5).

We have created this GUI without writing a single line of code! The RAD tool will have generated the code for us and we can inspect it and modify it if we want. The chances are that the code that has been generated will include some instructions that you did not require, you can leave them or safely delete them.

Of course, the RAD tool doesn't completely write the code for this application for us. In order for the GUI application to respond to events we still need to write the code for the event handler. We wish to write an event handler for the Button. If we double click the Button in design view, the RAD tool will automatically assign an actionListener to this Button and take us to that part of the generated code that needs completing in order for the event to be processed. In this case it will take us to an actionPerformed method:

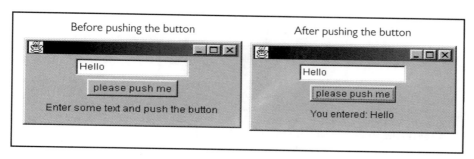

Fig 24.1   The *PushMe* **application running in a frame**

Graphical components, such as AWT Buttons and Labels are selected from a palette

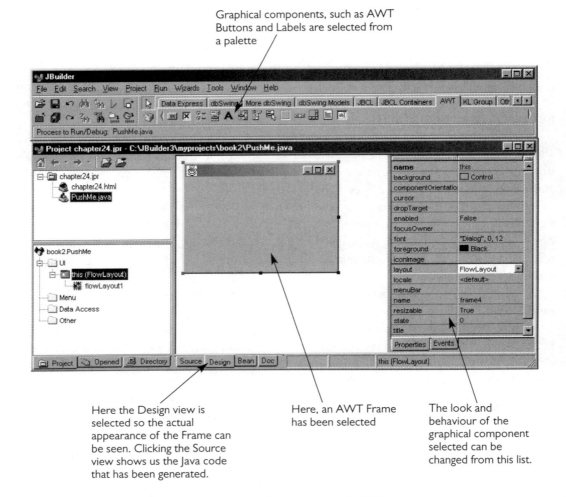

Here the Design view is selected so the actual appearance of the Frame can be seen. Clicking the Source view shows us the Java code that has been generated.

Here, an AWT Frame has been selected

The look and behaviour of the graphical component selected can be changed from this list.

Fig 24.2 A typical RAD tool provides a simple way to create GUIs

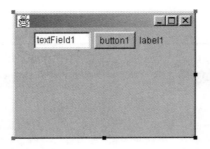

Fig 24.3 A TextField, Button and Label arranged on a Frame

```
void button1_actionPerformed(ActionEvent e)
{

}
```

The form of this `actionPerformed` button may be slightly different to the one we have been using in this book. Each RAD tool will deal with this in its own way. As you can see the method has no code inside it. We write our event handling code within these brackets. This code will be the same as that we developed in chapter 9:

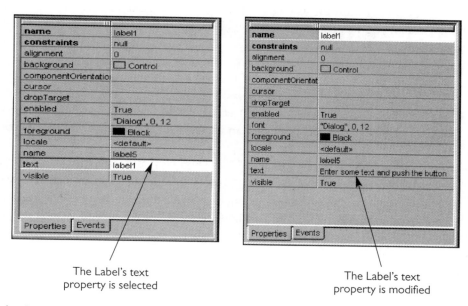

The Label's text
property is selected

The Label's text
property is modified

Fig 24.4   A graphical component's characteristics can be changed from the property list

Fig 24.5   The final *PushMe* Gui

```
void button1_actionPerformed(ActionEvent e)
{ // event handling code goes here
  String myText;
  myText = myTextField.getText();
  myLabel.setText("You entered: " + myText);
}
```

The application is now complete, with only a few lines of code needing to be completed by us. As you can see this is a very productive way to write code, but as we said before, you must understand the generated code as well as be able to write your own code in order to complete applications using RAD tools.

This is only a very brief look at the RAD approach to programming. Often this approach is referred to as Visual Programming as you are dealing with visual objects. As you find out more about this approach, you will come across a Java concept for extending the power of such RAD tools – **Java Beans**.

24.3.1 Java Beans

A **Java Bean** is a more abstract and powerful concept than a simple Java class. A Java Bean is a self contained object that can be used and tested independently of any environment restrictions.

For example, all Java GUI classes, like the AWT `Button` class and the Swing `JLabel` class are stand-alone visual objects. A stand-alone visual object is often called a **component**. Java's AWT and Swing components can be found on the palette of RAD tools to be used by programmers. They can also be found in other applications (like Microsoft Word for example) as they are self-contained units. When these components are themselves written in Java, they are referred to as Java Beans.

The great thing about Java Beans is that you can write your own Beans, add them to the component palette of your RAD tool or use them in your favourite application! For example, you might develop a graphical digital clock. This might be useful in many Java applications as well as in other applications so you may wish to make this Java class into a Java Bean.

To make a class into a Java Bean you must make sure it meets a set of Java Bean rules. We will not go into these rules here as they are beyond the scope of this book, but they include ensuring the class is declared **public** and following strict naming rules for *get* and *set* methods for **private** attributes.

If your digital clock class has a **boolean** attribute called `twentyFourHour`, for example, then you should provide a `getTwentyFourHour` method to read this property and a `setTwentyFourHour` method to set this property. Programmers can then modify this property by finding these methods in the property list in much the same way that we modified the text property of an AWT `Label`.

24.4   *Java Database Connectivity*

In this book we have developed several applications that store data to an external file and read data from that file as well as manipulate that data. Rather than writing such an application from scratch in a programming language, it would be common to use one of the many database applications available (such as Oracle, Ingress, Sybase and Access).

A common model upon which these database applications are based is the so-called **relational database model**. As this is not a database text we will not explore this model here other than to say that, conceptually, data in such a database consists of a collection of **tables**. A table in database terminology is a collection of related data organized around rows and columns.

SQL (Structured Query Language) is a common language used to retrieve and modify information within tables. Java's JDBC (Java DataBase Connectivity) API provides a set of classes for communicating with such databases with SQL statements. These classes are found in the java.sql package. The four main classes in this package are

- DriverManager: loads and sets up the software required to communicate with an external database.
- Connection: authenticates and connects the Java program to a database.
- PreparedStatement: sends SQL statements to the database for execution.
- ResultSet: allows the results of SQL statements to be analysed in the Java program.

24.5   *Networking*

The java.rmi and java.net packages provide extensive support for networking and distributed systems development. These packages include classes for simplifying the communication between objects spread over a network and include classes such as Socket, and ServerSocket.

24.6   *What next?*

Now that you appreciate the further possibilities that exist in Java you can see that there is much more you can explore. You might find out more about them in advanced units on your course. In the meantime you can get further information on the Java language at the Sun website www.java.sun.com/docs – and don't forget to check in at our website from time to time.

Now that you have completed two semesters of programming we are pretty certain that you will have come to realize what an exciting and rewarding activity it can be. So whether you are going on to a career in software engineering, or some other field in computing – or even if you are just going to enjoy programming for its own sake, we wish you the very best of luck for the future.

Revision questions

1. The following UML diagram shows the design of a class called `WordGame`:

WordGame
firstWord : String *secondWord : String*
WordGame() *WordGame(String, String)* *getFirstWord() : String* *getSecondWord() : String* *compareWords() : String*

The behaviour of the methods is described below:

WordGame ()
A constructor that assigns the value "not yet initialized" to both attributes.

WordGame (String, String)
A constructor that accepts two `String` parameters and assigns them to `firstWord` and `secondWord` respectively.

getFirstWord(): String
Returns the value of `firstWord`.

getSecondWord(): String
Returns the value of `secondWord`.

compareWords(): String
Compares the length of the two attributes, and returns one of three possible `String` values as follows:

> "The first word is longer";
> "The second word is longer";
> "The words are of equal length".

(a) Write the code for the `WordGame` class.
(b) Consider the following program, which uses the `WordGame` class. Two lines of code have been replaced by a comment (in bold):

```
public class WordTester
{
    public static void main(String[] args)
    {
        WordGame game;
        String first, second;
        System.out.print ("First word? ");
        first = EasyIn.getString();
        System.out.print ("Second word? ");
        second = EasyIn.getString();
        // two lines of code go here
        EasyIn.pause();
    }
}
```

In place of the comment, write two lines of code as follows:

- the first line creates a new WordGame object with its attributes set to the values that were entered by the user;
- the second line uses the appropriate method of WordGame, to display a message saying which, if any, of the two words is the longer.

(c) What would be the output from the following program, which uses the WordGame class?

```
public class WordTester1
{
    public static void main(String[] args)
    {
        WordGame game = new WordGame();
        System.out.println(game.getFirstWord());
        System.out.println(game.getSecondWord());
        EasyIn.pause();
    }
}
```

(d) Write the code for an additional method of WordGame, called commonLetter, which returns the position in the first word of the first occurrence of a letter that is common to both words. If there is no common letter, a value of −1 should be returned.

2. (a) Explain the meaning of the following terms:
   (i)   an abstract class;
   (ii) an abstract method.
   (b) Consider the class Vehicle below:

```
class Vehicle
{
  private String regNumber;
  double priceWhenNew;
  int yearMade;

  public Vehicle(String regIn, double priceIn, int yearIn)
  {
    regNumber = regIn;
    priceWhenNew = priceIn;
    yearMade = yearIn;
  }

  public String getRegNumber()
  {
    return regNumber;
  }

  public double getPriceWhenNew ()
  {
    return priceWhenNew;
  }

  public int getYearMade()
  {
    return yearMade;
  }

  public double calcDepreciation(int currentYear)
  {
    /* The depreciation is the amount that the vehicle has lost in value
       since it was made. It is assumed that a vehicle loses one tenth of
       its value for each year of its age */
    return priceWhenNew * (currentYear - yearMade)/10;
  }
}
```

A class called UsedVehicle is to inherit the Vehicle class and will have the following features:

- it will have an additional attribute of type **int** called yearPurchased;
- it will have a method called getYearPurchased that returns the above attribute;
- its constructor will set the above attribute in addition to the others;
- it will have a method, calcAgeWhenPurchased, that returns the age in years of the vehicle at the date of purchase;
- it will override the calcDepreciation method so that an additional £500 is added to the normal depreciation.

(i)   Write the code for the UsedVehicle class.

(ii) State the output from the following program:

```
public class VehicleTester
{
  public static void main(String[] args)
  {
    Vehicle vehicle = new Vehicle("V71 TMU", 10000, 1999);
    UsedVehicle usedVehicle
      = new UsedVehicle("M87 854", 8000, 1996, 2000);
    System.out.println(vehicle.calcDepreciation(2001));
    System.out.println(usedVehicle.calcDepreciation(2001));
    System.out.println(usedVehicle.calcAgeWhenPurchased());
    EasyIn.pause();
  }
}
```

(iii) Explain why it would not have been sensible to define the Vehicle class as abstract.

(iv) Explain the meaning of the term *polymorphism*, referring specifically to the above two classes.

3. (a) Explain what makes Java a suitable language for writing programs that run over the World Wide Web.

   (b) The code for an applet called SquareApplet appears below:

```java
import java.awt.*;
import java.applet.*;

public class SquareApplet extends Applet
{
  private int xPos;
  private int yPos;
  private int side;

  public void init()
  {
    xPos = Integer.parseInt(getParameter("x"));
    yPos = Integer.parseInt(getParameter("y"));
    side = Integer.parseInt(getParameter("dimension"));
  }

  public int getXPos()
  {
    return xPos;
  }

  public int getYPos()
  {
    return yPos;
  }

  public int getSide()
  {
    return side;
  }

  public void paint(Graphics g)
  {
    g.drawRect(xPos, yPos, side, side);
  }
}
```

   (i) Write a fragment of HTML code which will run the applet in a 350 × 300 window, and draw a square at position 30, 45, with sides 100 pixels in length.

   (ii) Consider the following class, RectangleApplet, that extends SquareApplet and draws a rectangle instead of a square. The code for the paint method has been replaced by a comment.

```
import java.awt.*;

public class RectangleApplet extends SquareApplet
{
  private int side2;

  public void init()
  {
    super.init();
    side2 = Integer.parseInt(getParameter("dimension2"));
  }

  public double getSide2()
  {
    return side2;
  }

  public void paint(Graphics g)
  {
    // code goes here
  }
}
```

Write the correct code for the paint method.

4. Consider the following UML design for a class called NameStack that represents a stack of names.

NameStack
items: String [ ] total : int
NameStack(int) push (String):boolean pop( ):String

The attributes of this class represent the following pieces of information

items: an array containing the stack of names
total: the total number of names currently in the stack

The methods of this class are described below:

NameStack(int)
Creates an empty stack, with a given maximum size.

push(String):boolean

Adds the given name onto the stack as long as the stack is not full. If the name is added successfully, this method returns **true** otherwise it returns **false**.

pop():String

Removes and returns the next appropriate name from the stack. If the stack is empty this method returns **null**.

(a) Implement the NameStack class in Java

(b) Assume a tester class, TestNameStack, is to be developed. This tester contains the following instruction:

```
NameStack names = new NameStack (10);
```

Write the fragment of code from this tester that asks the user to enter a name, adds this name onto the stack and then checks whether or not that name has been added successfully.

(c) Assume an extra method, displayAll, is required in the NameStack class to display all the names in the stack onto the screen. Write the code for this method.

(d) If a NameQueue class were to be developed, the push and pop methods would probably be called add and remove. Distinguish between a *stack* and a *queue* and discuss how these add and remove methods would compare to the push and pop methods of the NameStack class.

5. (a) You have been asked to develop a StaffList class that will be used to hold the details of the members of staff in a particular firm. Another person in the programming team has been asked to develop the Staff class. Eventually your class will form part of a larger application. Describe how you would go about testing your StaffList class.

(b) Assuming you are developing an application in Java, identify the documentation required during the following phases of software development:
- specification/design;
- implementation;
- testing;
- installation and operation.

(c) Explain why Java's garbage collection facility might make it an appropriate language for situations where it is particularly important to have very reliable and robust software.

6. Consider the following program and then answer the questions that follow:

```
class SomeClass
{
  public static void main(String[] args)
  {
    final int YEAR = 2001;
    int age = getAge();
    System.out.println ("You were born in " + (YEAR - age));
  }

  private static int getAge()
  {
    byte [] buffer = new byte[512];
    System.out.println("enter your age");
    System.in.read(buffer);
    String s = new String (buffer);
    s = s.trim();
    int num = Integer.parseInt(s);
    return num;
  }
}
```

(a) Making reference to the above program, distinguish between checked and unchecked exceptions in Java.

(b) Explain what it means for a method to claim an exception, then re-write the getAge method so that it claims any exceptions that it might throw.

(c) Explain what it means for a method to catch an exception, and then re-write the main method so that it catches any exceptions it may now throw by displaying a message on the screen indicating the exception thrown, before pausing and quitting.

(d) Re-write main so that the user is allowed to re-enter a value if an exception is caught.

INDEX